IMPROVING SCHOOLS

SAGE FOCUS EDITIONS

IMPROVING SCHOOLS

Using What We Know

Edited by
ROLF LEHMING
MICHAEL KANE

 **SAGE** PUBLICATIONS Beverly Hills London

This work was developed under a contract between the Far West Laboratory for Educational Research and Development in San Francisco and the book's authors. Funding was made available to the Laboratory by the National Institute of Education, an agency of the U.S. Department of Education. However, the contents of this book do not necessarily reflect the position or policy of the Institute or Department, and no official endorsement of these materials should be inferred.

This book was edited by Rolf Lehming and Michael Kane in their private capacity. No official support or endorsement by the National Institute of Education or the Department of Education is intended or should be inferred.

For information address:

SAGE Publications, Inc. SAGE Publications Ltd
275 South Beverly Drive 28 Banner Street
Beverly Hills, California 90212 London EC1Y 8QE, England

Printed in the United States of America

Library of Congress Cataloging in Publication Data
Main entry under title:

Improving schools.

(Sage focus editions ; 29)
Bibliography: p.
Contents: Introduction / Rolf Lehming and Michael Kane—
Three perspectives on innovation / Ernest House—Mapping the common properties of schools / Matthew B. Miles—[etc.]
    1. Public schools—United States—Addresses, essays, lectures.
2. Educational innovations—United States—Addresses, essays, lectures.
I. Kane, Michael   II. Lehming, Rolf   III. Series.
LA217.I48   371'.01'0973   81-8809
ISBN 0-8039-1623-X   AACR2
ISBN 0-8039-1624-8 (pbk.)

FIRST PRINTING

CONTENTS

IMPROVING SCHOOLS

INTRODUCTION

This book deals with studies of the incorporation of certain types of innovations—those embodying new ideas, materials, or technologies, in short, various forms of knowledge—in the daily operations of elementary and secondary schools. The work belongs in the broad research domain on knowledge utilization,[1] innovation, and organizational change (Havelock, 1969; Nelson and Winter, 1977; Radnor et al., 1978; Feller, 1979), here examined through the lens of one type of public sector organization, the contemporary American school. The authors have prepared a critical state-of-the-art review of fifteen years' research on educational change and knowledge use in education: attempts to improve the nation's schools by disseminating new knowledge, promoting its use, and (occasionally) providing assistance in its application. They have sought to state explicitly what can be learned from these studies and to provide a foundation on which future research can build in a more nearly cumulative fashion.

Schools will continue to face the need to adapt to changing educational and social circumstances. Frequently, effective action will depend on the skillful and creative use of new knowledge from outside the immediate setting, as dwindling resources make the purely local invention and trial of new approaches economically infeasible for most school districts. A multitude of dissemination and technical assistance programs—governmental, private, academic—exist (Guba and Clark, 1976; Lotto and Clark, 1978; Hood, 1979; Sharp et al., 1978; NTS, 1979); many states in fact have formal assistance organizations intermediate between the district and the state education department (Stephens, 1979). The question is: How can these various programs be most effectively designed, implemented, and managed so as to build upon local strengths, initiative, and motivation to produce educational benefits with a modicum of disruption and undesirable side effects? Disappointing experiences with past school improvement efforts (see Emrick and Peterson, 1978, for a review of five programs) suggest that some fundamental elements of successfully initiating and managing such programs have been overlooked.

The present project[2] grew out of a preliminary survey of the literature on innovation and change in schools, undertaken by the editors in developing a program of research for the National Institute of Education, a federal education research agency. The varying conceptual approaches we encountered were difficult to integrate, the methods employed frequently open to criticism, and the findings apparently contradictory and of uneven coverage. A thorough consolidation and explication of what could already be known appeared in order before undertaking further research. The scattered and unintegrated nature of the field suggested that such a review might benefit from close and critical attention by a group of scholars, working collaboratively. Accordingly, in the spring of 1979 we invited the authors to work on this task.

No attempt has been made to achieve encyclopedic exhaustiveness. Rather, the volume concentrates on those aspects of extant research that in the authors' collective judgment promise to contribute significantly to future work in this area. To limit the possible effects of individual biases and stimulate critical discourse, the authors jointly defined the overall domain of the work and the topics to be addressed by each of them, circulated working notes, and discussed each others' drafts. In this sense, the contents of this volume represent a rough consensus on the current status of research on knowledge use and school improvement and lay the groundwork for the next generation of research in this area.

The definitions presented here to orient the reader represent the consensus of the working group. The authors have used them as broad guides to their work; the text makes clear where they have been relaxed, and in what ways, to permit pursuit of a particular line of inquiry. The following draws heavily on the group's discussions and working notes.

The work's domain is the study of formal change policies in school districts: their genesis and consequences, and the factors influencing their realization and effects. Change policies that draw upon some body of knowledge are the major focus. Use of the term "policy" calls attention to the intentionality of such efforts: A policy is an announced intention that may or may not include specific programs, defined goals, or identified technologies. It may become embodied in multiple implementations (Berman and McLaughlin, 1978a, 1978b; Farrar et al., 1980) or none at all. Formal change policies are those that have been authoritatively adopted by a school district, in distinction to the variety of informal and perhaps pervasive change activities that occur continually (Huberman, 1981) or sporadically, such as coping with a sudden emergency. "Change" refers to an intended alteration in existing policy or practice or the intended introduction of a policy or practice that is new to the district.

The phrase "improving schools" appearing in the book's title requires some comment. It refers to an intention or effort to alter schools or schooling toward some state that is perceived as "better." That, of course, is the motivation behind research related to education. However, analytically the phrase is fraught with problems. The referent may be a policy, a concrete project, or a specific product or technology. One group's improvement may be seen, in the extreme case, as another's detriment: The term is imbued with valuation. Then again, specific change policies may deal with efforts that are not viewed as improvements by anyone— dealing with the consequences of declining resources, for example (Walker and Chaiken, 1981). Finally, there is the matter of motivation: A change policy may be initiated for reasons that have little in common with the stated improvement aim (Berman and McLaughlin, 1979; Herriott and Gross, 1979; Pauly, 1978). The reader should bear these ambiguities in mind when encountering the "school improvement" phrase in the text.

Change policies may vary in scope. They may aim to maintain the balance of existing system operations, produce marginal alterations in the system by adding new elements or substituting one set for another (most innovations fall into this class), or fundamentally alter core characteristics of the district or school (Herriott and Gross, 1979; Rosenblum and Louis, 1981; Miles, Sullivan, et al., 1978b). Change policies can be analyzed for two basic types of consequences: policy outcomes and consequences referring to the process of change itself. To what extent change results—let alone "improvement"—is problematical and open to empirical investigation. Policy outcomes can be classified broadly into changes in student outcomes (such as performance, attitude, ability), changes in system structure or functioning (instruction or curriculum, school or district organization, relations with the environment), and changes in the perceptions and behavior of groups and organizations outside the system toward the school or district. Process variables may conveniently be classified into extent and quality of mobilization (the initiation phase of a change policy), implementation, and the institutionalization of the operational ends and means flowing from it (Berman and McLaughlin, 1978a, 1978b; Yin et al., 1978).

Knowledge as used here is information based on evidence derived from scientific research, from practice, or from both. It is empirically or socially validated on the basis of accepted scientific or professional methods and standards, and is thought to be generalizable and worth the effort to diffuse it to potential users. Raw, uninterpreted data are excluded. Knowledge can reside in ideas, theories, explanations, advice (Sieber, 1974); or in "things," such as programs, materials, or technologies (including "soft" ones; see Yin et al., 1976). It can be generated within the school or district or reach it from outside. It may address instruction or school organization and management issues, including those dealing with change policies. It may very specifically concentrate on exigencies of a particular district or encompass broad national issues. Knowledge use, as employed in the text, refers to policies or efforts to promote the application of such knowledge in the practice setting. The term includes instrumental and conceptual uses (Caplan and Rich, 1976) and is neutral on the matter of appropriateness (Weiss, 1979; Sieber, 1974; also Sieber, this volume).

House's examination of three broad perspectives underlying federal school improvement policies characterizes the subject matter on which the other chapters are based: Research is the mirror of policy in this area. (With a suitable time lag, the examination also applies to policies emanating from state education departments and large school districts.) A perspective, as used here, is a broad orienting heuristic containing presuppositions, values, and perceptions of fact within a professional consensus of what is desirable, feasible, and important. Perspectives are world views, essentially unprovable and drawing their strength from their perceived plausibility and utility. They are the images (Firestone, 1980) that shape public debate and, in turn, are shaped by its progression. House labels them technological, political, and cultural. These perspectives are seen as developing in reaction to the shortcomings of their predecessors which they join, but never supplant. The technological perspective embodies a production image. Teaching is seen as a technique (for a discussion of the concept of technique, see Ellul, 1964) that can be analyzed by subdividing it into its components, and improved by systematically developing better teaching forms and diffusing them to schools and teachers who adopt them and put them into practice. The political perspective rejects this mechanistic view. Legitimate differences in the interests of groups involved in school change efforts are acknowledged. Conflict, bargaining, and the application of power—political, bureaucratic, economic—are recognized to exert fundamental influences on school change efforts, modifying them in major ways that are both hard to anticipate and to control. More radically, the cultural perspective abandons the basic notion of shared beliefs and values underlying the other two. It highlights discrepancies in them among different groups and traces different meanings attached to particular changes by various groups directly to such lacking commonalities. For example, under this perspective, teachers and researchers belong to different professional cultures (see Dunn, 1980), and improvement efforts are best designed and understood in terms of diffusing unfamiliar cultural forms. House advocates that more research be undertaken using models drawn from the political and cultural perspectives, to redress what he views as a strong imbalance in favor of the technological.

Miles's query addresses what we know about the school as an organization type: What are the properties that are in some sense typical, relatively stable, or commonly found in contemporary American schools? Where House has asked: "What have people thought about the nature of schools and schooling?" Miles is interested in another question: "What do we really know about schools?" The discussion is organized around nine dilemmas facing schools, along with other organizations, in conducting their affairs: whether to emphasize achieving core tasks versus (the quality of) organizational survival; diversity versus uniformity; coordination versus flexibility; dependence on environmental direction versus autonomy; openness to exchanges with the environment versus withdrawal; seeking external expertise versus self-reliance; feedback-seeking versus reliance on routine action; centralization versus sharing of influence within the organization; and emphasis on adaptation and change versus a premium on stability. Miles's chapter covers a broad compass of research in considerable depth, making an attempt to summarize its contents a hazardous enterprise. Broadly, here are his conclusions: Basic descriptive data are scarce on virtually all these dimensions; in Miles's words, data are more plentiful on variable school properties than on those that typify these organizations. Contingency analyses (see Berman, this volume) are rare. Most causal claims made for school behavior "are almost untested in any empirical sense." Several assertions appear with considerable regularity, regardless of the investigator's approach: that schools have vague goals whose achievement is difficult to ascertain, are vulnerable to their environments, have weak production functions, and have inappropriate incentives structures. All of these regularities are claimed to influence the schools' behavior towards innovation and change . . . yet few of the asserted causal links have been examined empirically. Finally, Miles points out, "innovativeness" (how schools can successfully manage to integrate new forms of structure and functioning into their daily affairs) and school effectiveness in fulfilling their multiple educational goals can usefully be examined separately, and that both kinds of studies should be undertaken.

Sieber develops a paradigm for the systematic consideration of incentives and disincentives of school personnel. These are the prospective sources of gratification and deprivation and the disposition to value or devalue particular incentive types. He employs the paradigm to examine the available literature. The analysis focuses on the individual but concludes with a discussion of the organizational incentives system of the school. The prevalent knowledge use strategies (see, for example, summaries in Zaltman et al., 1977; Havelock, 1969) are faulted for their casual attention to but a limited set of incentives and for indiscriminately lumping these together in ways which obscure their effects. Sieber asserts that the literature on educational diffusion, innovation, and change has failed to properly integrate work on organizational incentives and occupational communities. This failure is not merely a theoretical one, but has had practical consequences, reflected in the shortcomings of knowledge use policies that were based on these strategies. Sieber notes that, typically, these policies tend to emphasize a limited range of benefits without acknowledging any (noneconomic) costs they carry with them, fail to deal effectively with the competing benefits of inaction, and employ sanctions against inaction in ways that are likely to arouse resistance. Proceeding with his analysis, Sieber examines the evidence regarding incentives and disincentives for knowledge utilization inherent in: the nature of the research and development enterprise in education; the nature of the schools' environmental relations; the organizational characteristics of schools; and the occupational culture of school personnel. He suggests that the use of knowledge for personal and professional enlightenment may be both the strongest and least used lever. He offers these conclusions: Knowledge use strategies may generally have social costs that exceed their benefits (see also Knott and Wildavsky, 1980), with compensatory incentives available only under special circumstances. Problem solving provides weak incentives for knowledge utilization, because it disregards the important interplay between alternative solutions and the definition of needs. Too little is known of concrete operational incentives of school personnel to guide effective knowledge use policy. Finally, too little heed is paid the organizational incentives system that a school represents (and about which equally little is known).

Fullan examines how educators in key positions in the change process—teachers, principals, district specialists, and superintendents—utilize knowledge. He describes some major dimensions of knowledge types and use types and discusses key aspects of the school setting, then presents critical summaries of the research bearing on each group's knowledge utilization behavior and roles in school change. Not unexpectedly, overall involvement with knowledge use strategies is low (as far as can be ascertained from available evidence) as demands for maintaining and managing daily operations crowd out other activities. For teachers, inappropriateness of available knowledge resources and low peer interaction may be contributing factors. Teacher involvement in the initiation of change policies tends to lie in the areas of classroom management, curriculum, and instruction; comprehensive changes originate elsewhere. How teachers initially become mobilized for a change is not understood. Once under way, knowledge use efforts receive important sustenance from teacher interaction. There is agreement that principals are perhaps the most critical persons in knowledge utilization efforts, and that some form of active involvement on their part is essential for successful program improvement. Involvement of the typical principal tends to be low; however, principals report they would like to attend more to program improvement than they currently do. The evidence on effective strategies for principal involvement is mixed, perhaps reflecting a confounding of school types and types of knowledge use activities (that is, individualistic versus centrally derived). District specialists are important conduits for new knowledge from outside the school system but appear to be less well prepared for translating this strength into the initiation and management of school change. Organizational supports to aid them in such a task are also weakly developed, if they exist at all. About superintendents' roles, the literature is essentially silent. Available research on these four groups' knowledge use behavior and their roles in school improvement processes is on the whole poorly developed, suffers from undifferentiated conceptions of knowledge use, and pays too little attention to different levels of schooling, size of school and district, location, and populations served. Fullan comments on the implications of these shortcomings for the planning, implementation, and results of knowledge utilization efforts, and suggests research directions.

Louis synthesizes the literature on roles, functions, and efficacy of "external agents" in knowledge use policies: individuals, groups, or organizations located outside the district whom they try to assist in school improvement work. Use of such agents in education, originally inspired by the agricultural extension model, is complicated by the fact that frequently two distinct organizations are involved, the school or school district and the employing organization. Louis comments on the relative strength of the client setting in shaping agent behavior and the resulting need for boundary maintenance and avoiding cooptation. She notes that available research is devoid of theory and suffers from other limitations: an emphasis on instrumental, decision-oriented uses of knowledge, a preoccupation with research knowledge, and a data base limited mostly to studying "technology-push" approaches. The evidence on effectiveness and impact of external agents is presented as it relates to the degree of likeness between agent and client, the relative advantages of assistance from outside and inside the setting, team versus individual approaches, and personal qualities of agents. Then Louis reviews what is known about various strategy elements: degree of agent initiative, intensity of interaction, types and mixes of expertise, and scope and cost. While some evidence is available on most of these issues, only judgmental information is available on the two perhaps most critical issues: How scope, cost, and benefits of an effort are related, and what skill mixes are appropriate in given situations. This void is all the more surprising when one remembers that a large number of assistance organizations and services exist throughout the educational system. A brief research agenda that would permit filling the most critical gaps rounds out the chapter.

Berman observes that research on educational change is shifting from relatively simple views prevalent during the 1960s to more complex images of how schools change. He argues that the major significance of recent research lies not so much in its detailed findings, but rather in this emerging perception of the complexity of educational change processes. Berman sets out to make this emerging view explicit and to formulate the beginnings of a new paradigm to guide future research and action. He shows how assumptions and approaches underlying House's "technological perspective" were gradually undermined by the accumulating evidence. Berman then characterizes this emergent paradigm by three broad "meta-propositions"—ways of thinking about educational change deriving from empirical foundations. He proposes that educational change is typically implementation-dominated; that it involves complex organizational processes that are loosely, not linearly, connected; and that its outcomes are heavily time- and context-dependent. Berman then develops the implications of these meta-propositions for the conduct of research that will be substantively fruitful and relevant to policy and practice. He argues that future research must, for the time being, abandon attempts to discover universal generalizations about how schools change, in favor of exploring how specific types of school contexts condition change processes; it must incorporate time-dependent measurements and longitudinal research designs; and it must structure its analyses so that such contingent effects can be discovered instead of remaining hidden.

A few additional points might be made about the undertaking and its results. First, in a real—and expected—way, it is incomplete: It points out useful directions, but these can be explored only by future inquiry. Second, the work has raised some questions about things we thought we surely knew—what typifies schools, for example, or what the work incentives are for educators—and has pointed out conceptual and empirical problems with much existing research. Third, there are hints throughout, and more centrally addressed in Berman's chapter, that our very ways of thinking about research (and policy) on innovation in schools may have to be revised. This last point, perhaps, is the most far-reaching, raising challenges that have only begun to be met.

The authors wish to acknowledge the steady encouragement, assistance, valuable comments, and occasional criticism received from their colleagues throughout the work. The editors gladly comply with this request, for without these numerous interactions, the project could not have taken shape. The editors also wish to acknowledge the steady assistance of Paul

Hood and his staff at the Far West Laboratory for Educational Research and Development in San Francisco, who contributed to the successful completion of the enterprise. Funding for the contracts between Far West Lab and the authors was made available by the National Institute of Education, an agency of the U.S. Department of Education. Of course, no endorsement of the conclusions or opinions set forth in the work, including this introduction, should be inferred.

Rolf Lehming

Michael Kane

Washington, D.C.

NOTES

1. Knowledge utilization is intended to be broadly synonymous with knowledge transfer, knowledge use, knowledge diffusion, research utilization, technology transfer, and so on. It refers broadly to activities promoting the infusion of knowledge, technologies, and innovations into practice settings and their application therein. Note that actual practice need not change for utilization to have occurred, as conceptual uses and deliberate nonuse are included.

2. A related project to determine what lessons for public policy can be drawn from current research on knowledge utilization in education and other settings will conclude in the summer of 1981. Topics being examined include: the school governance system, its regulatory environment, declining resources, the role of the private sector, behavioral and learning processes in school change, and forms and formats of available knowledge.

1

THREE PERSPECTIVES ON INNOVATION
Technological, Political, and Cultural

Ernest R. House

THE NATURE OF A PERSPECTIVE

The central aim of this chapter "is to make explicit the status of our understanding regarding knowledge utilization processes relative to the improvement of educational practice." This analysis entails a somewhat different conception of the "status of our knowledge" than is typical. Our understanding of knowledge utilization processes is conceived not so much as a set of facts, findings, or generalizations but rather as distinct perspectives which combine facts, values, and presuppositions into a complex screen through which knowledge utilization is seen.

Whichever screen one adopts leads one to focus on certain features of knowledge utilization events, to advocate certain policies rather than others, and to conduct certain types of research and evaluation studies. Through a particular screen one sees certain events, but one may see different scenes through a different screen. Theoretically, there are no limits to the number of perspectives that may exist, but, in fact, three perspectives—the technological, the political, and the cultural—seem to account for the vast majority of studies that have been conducted.

This conception of knowledge may be put another way. Consider the vast number of studies conducted on knowledge utilization processes. These are experiences to be assimilated and understood. The usual way to assimilate these studies is to sort through them, to classify them, to draw generalizations, and thus to ascertain what they mean. This is a taxonomic and generalizing procedure, and certainly a reasonable one. This is what most reviews of research do.

Another way to assimilate the studies or points of experience is to postulate certain principles or assumptions or axioms that would "account for" the studies. That is, what axioms held by researchers would account for the studies that they have been generating? For purposes of explanation, one would want to arrive at the smallest possible number. In this case, three basic perspectives (or combinations of these) seem to account for the vast number of studies.

The approach here is similar to that of Allison (1971), who characterized three conceptual "models" through which professional analysts, as well as laymen, thought about decisions in foreign and military policy. Allison's three models were the "rational actor," the "organizational process," and the "governmental politics" models. An event such as the Cuban missile crisis could be understood in terms of each of the three models, but the interpretation of events varied depending upon the model employed.

Decisions made during the Cuban missile crisis could be seen as the result of rational choice, as the output of routinized standard operating procedures within the bureaucracy, or as the result of political forces within the government. Each decision-making model explained aspects of events not explained by the other models. Generally, Allison contended, these were the models available to analysts for interpreting all foreign affairs. The interpretation was very much shaped by the decision-making model employed.

Schon (1979) has contended that social problems are defined by underlying "deep" metaphors that account for why some aspects of a situation are considered important and others are not. These metaphors shape what people think about the problem situation. People "name" and "frame" aspects of the problem by reference to the tacit image. Certain elements in a situation are selectively portrayed.

For example, there are two quite different views of the urban slum. In one view, the slum is an unhealthy area that has become "blighted." Images of disease inform this vision. Concepts like "health," "decay," and "renewal" are employed. In the second vision, the slum is a natural community that provides important services for its residents. Concepts such as "home," "informal networks," and "dislocation" are employed.

The researcher sees the slum either as blighted or as a natural community. In seeing A as B, the evaluation in B is carried over to A. By selecting certain elements and organizing them coherently, these viewpoints explain what is wrong in a social situation and suggest transformations. The underlying image is often revealed by the language employed.

Each of the three perspectives on innovation has a different underlying image upon which it draws to interpret events in the innovation process. Underlying the technological perspective is the image of production. Concepts like input-output, flow diagrams, and specification of tasks are commonly employed. Innovation is conceived as a relatively mechanistic process. The social relationships are based on technological necessity. The concern is economic and the primary value that of efficiency.

Underlying the political perspective is the image of negotiation. Concepts such as power, authority, and competing interests are employed. Social relationships are conceived as voluntary and as resting on contractual arrangements. Individual and group interests are conceived as often in conflict. Distribution of resources in a legitimate and acceptable manner is important. The concern is political, and a primary value is the legitimacy of the authority system.

Underlying the cultural perspective is the image of community. People are bound to one another through shared meanings resting on shared values. Social relationships are traditional. Integrity of the culture is a primary value. Within a given culture, conformity to the culture's values may be important. Across cultures, tolerance of other cultures' values is critical if cultural integrity is to be maintained. From the multicultural perspective, autonomy of separate cultures is paramount. Although relationships within a culture may be binding and obligatory, relationships across cultures are relativistic.

These three perspectives act as interpretive frameworks for understanding the innovation process. By so framing the social phenomena, they serve as a guide to what is important and as a guide to action. However, people operating within the same framework do not necessarily agree with one another. Two people operating within the political perspective may agree in analyzing the innovation process in terms of competing interest groups. But one analyst may side with the interests represented by the federal government and the other with the interests represented by the local government. They agree on the relevant concepts and on what the issues are, but they take different sides on the issues. Both, however, take the political perspective.

These different frameworks define the range of possible arguments that one might advance for a course of action. In research they set limits as to what is considered useful inquiry. For example, if one adopts the political perspective, arguments for and against a policy or course of action will naturally be phrased in terms of individual or group interest. Inquiry will be directed at identifying whose interests are at stake and how they shall be served. Arguments will be conducted within this conceptual framework. Although it will be possible to take significantly different value positions on issues, there will be only a limited number of value positions available, and only certain arguments will carry any weight within the framework.

Such frameworks or perspectives may be conceived as "moral" or "action" paradigms. They "build in" valuation by restricting the range of value positions which can be adopted defensibly. In a sense, they distribute the burdens of argument in certain ways (Bernstein, 1978). The inherent valuation of the framework may be overridden only with considerable difficulty. For example, political arguments about competing interests may be overridden by other concerns, such as by moral considerations, but the overriding arguments must work against the slant of the framework.

These action perspectives result from an acceptance of normative constraints about what is rational and acceptable. They limit the very language and concepts employed in the discussions and thereby give a certain value slant. The perspectives define the limits of rational choice itself. It is through these perspectives that choices are justified and legitimized. In this sense, people are dominated by the perspectives or frameworks that they adopt. Furthermore, these perspectives operate implicitly.

These "paradigms" are not the same as those attributed by Kuhn to physical science. Kuhn (1970) saw scientific fields of endeavor as having a set of beliefs, values, and techniques that are shared within a field of scientific inquiry. Eventually the dominant paradigm is challenged by anomalous facts that cannot be explained by the old paradigm. A new paradigm emerges which can explain these new facts. However, the physical world itself remains constant.

The action perspectives, by contrast, "describe" or operate in a social and political world that is itself changing. The shift from a technological to a political to a cultural perspective on innovation must be ascribed in part to changing social and political realities and not simply to new facts unearthed by the process of inquiry. The political and cultural perspectives are made more viable by the declining belief in technology and by less social consensus on goals. The perspectives rest more upon a professional consensus of what is possible and relevant and valued rather than upon a scientific consensus as to what is true. Professional consensus, in turn, rests heavily upon current perceptions of the total social and political milieu and in particular upon the actions of the government.

In this sense, the perspective is a weaker claim to knowledge than is Kuhn's scientific paradigm. The perspective is a "way of seeing" a problem rather than a rigid set of rules and procedures. As such it is more permeable and open to change than is a paradigm. A scientific paradigm is closely defined by consensus of the relevant scientific community, whereas a professional community may hold several perspectives simultaneously. The same person may view innovation from one perspective, then from another for another purpose. The notion of a perspective better represents the status of our understanding regarding knowledge utilization processes than does the stronger notion of a scientific paradigm, and probably better represents the nature of our knowledge in the social sciences generally.

THE PERSPECTIVES

For the past decade or so, studies on innovation have been dominated by three major perspectives. These perspectives have formed the framework through which researchers, developers, and officials have understood the innovation process, and they provide the underlying framework for policy formulation. These perspectives are the technological, the political, and the cultural. (For a more complete review of the research, see House, 1979b.)

Contemporary efforts at innovation in education go back at least to the launching of Sputnik and to attacks on the schools, particularly the progressive reforms and life adjustment curricula, by university critics. Curriculum reform efforts were launched in the name of scholarship and the national defense by such federal agencies as the National Science Foundation and by private agencies like the Ford Foundation.

In the beginning these efforts proceeded from professional and scholarly authority. University scholars in mathematics and the natural sciences, and eventually in the humanities and social sciences, produced new curriculum materials that better reflected the structure of the parent discipline. So the new math included set theory, as well as attempts to teach "inductively" in accord with scientific thought processes. Professional groups like the Commission on College English tried to introduce new topics, such as semantics, linguistics, and the new literary criticism, into the high school English curriculum.

These reforms were headed by university scholars who found their authority bases in their disciplines and who developed the new training materials in an intuitive manner bred of familiarity with their subject matter. The materials were disseminated through publication and through workshops held for public school teachers. The model was that of university teaching. Teachers were simply to be given updated information on content and method. During this time period, there was a considerable degree of consensus about the purpose of the schools and the authority of scholars.

By the mid-sixties this view of curriculum and innovation based on scholastic authority gave way to a more technological view of innovation. The scholastic approach had proceeded intuitively based on tacit knowledge. The technological perspective replaced the tacit basis of innovation with a more systematized and rationalized approach. The innovation process was conceived as separated into functions based on rational analysis and empirical research.

There were important models for this rationalization of the innovation process. Both modern industry and modern agriculture were highly successful. Space technology was occupying the front pages of newspapers. Technologized processes seemed to be related to progress. Progress was achieved by introducing new techniques into an area, and the process of modernization itself could be systematized, organized, and replicated. Whereas the scholastic innovation process had proceeded by tacit knowledge, technologizing innovation based it on explicit knowledge.

Both teaching and the innovation process were conceived as technologies. Teaching could be improved by the introduction of new techniques. The new emphasis was not so much on improving a teacher as on finding particular methods of instruction and materials that would better enable the students to learn. The improvements existed more in the methods and materials than in the teacher. The teachers would adopt the new techniques. Again, explicit and replicable techniques replaced the tacit knowledge of the teacher.

The innovation process itself was also conceived as a technology. Innovation was conceived as a research, development, diffusion, adoption paradigm—the "R, D, D" model. New knowledge would be produced by research, converted into usable form in development, spread to teachers during diffusion, and, finally, put into practice by teachers during the adoption stage. More than twenty federal educational research and development laboratories and centers were established with this model in mind. These organizations became the backbone of federal innovation efforts. Some labs and centers created their own models of how they would convert knowledge into usable techniques. An early formulation of such a view was that of Clark and Guba (1965).

No sooner had the labs and centers been established than they began to have some difficulties. Although many materials were produced, many were not of high quality. Even those that were of high quality seldom demonstrated the dramatic learning results hoped for. Even worse, teachers were often reluctant to use the materials. Whereas the R, D, and D paradigm assumed a passive consumer at the end of the chain willing to adopt a new product, teachers were often unwilling or unable to do so. As it turned out, the teacher was constrained by a whole set of contextual considerations that prevented the wholesale adoption of new ideas. These contextual constraints in the school were more determinant of the teacher's behavior than were new techniques and external agencies.

In spite of such disappointments, the technological perspective remains strong today, and is by far the most dominant of the three perspectives. For example, the current competency testing movement is derived from such a perspective. Learning is conceived of as being reducible to a set of tasks. These tasks can be identified as learning objectives and measured by test items. Teaching can be focused on these particular objectives, using techniques and materials that most efficiently achieve these tasks.

The process is analogous to a task analysis of a job in industry. The efficiency engineer analyzes the job into separate tasks, then times the performance of those tasks. This is called efficiency engineering or scientific management. What is significantly different about competency testing, as compared to previous technological approaches, is that rewards and punishments are attached to successful performance of these tasks, a situation closer to that in industry.

What characterizes the technological perspective, however, is the way that formulating and addressing problems is approached. Teaching and innovation are technologies (or should be). Solutions are techniques that are replicable and transferable to other situations. Technological thinking—selecting the most efficient means to a given end—is the mode of rationality. Most innovation studies continue to explore and define issues from this perspective. A recent example is the attempt by Hall and Loucks (1977) to determine the level of implementation of an innovation. It is not likely that the technological perspective will disappear in such a technological society.

The second perspective is the political perspective. The attempts to innovate, and consequent efforts to evaluate these innovations, led to many studies of innovations. By the early seventies it seemed clear that many of the innovations were not being implemented, and it seemed reasonable to interpret the problems as principally political ones, particularly within the highly politicized social atmosphere arising from the Vietnam war. In this period conflict began to seem as natural as common purpose and consensus had seemed earlier, and political accounts of innovation began to appear (House, 1974; Berman and McLaughlin, 1975b; Greenwood et al., 1975).

From the political perspective, innovation is a matter of conflicts and compromises among factional groups. These groups may be teachers, administrators, parents, developers, governments, or individuals. For example, through the technological perspective researchers, developers, and practitioners would be seen as cooperating within a common value consensus; through the political perspective each group would be seen as having its own goals and interests, which often conflict with the purposes of the others. Cooperation on an innovation is viewed as problematic rather than automatic. Cooperation must result from negotiation and compromise.

At the individual level, the political view might be manifested in one person influencing another person. The influence might be exerted through persuasion, inducements, or coercion. Personal influence is often exerted through face-to-face contacts, and the opportunities for these tend to channel political efforts and events. At the school level, the political analyst may see the school as made up of subgroups of faculty and students. Often, in order for the innovation to succeed, an advocacy group must arise to support and promote the innovation. This, in turn, may give rise to a countergroup within the school. The progress of the innovation may be seen as factional groups competing and cooperating within the school (House, 1974).

The relationship between schools and school districts may be viewed as efforts by school district central staff to control the local schools and as efforts by the schools to resist this control in various ways. The central staff has control over hiring and budget, but the local school has grasp of everyday instructional processes. The politics of personality within this framework is the constant theme of both researchers and practitioners. Events are often explained and interpreted as power struggles among individuals (MacDonald and Walker, 1976).

Factions may align themselves along vertical divisions within the district. Here parents and community are often involved. One alignment of administrators, backed by particular parents, may push for programs for gifted children; another faction may oppose them. These fights frequently come to rest in school board politics, if they are large enough. School-community conflicts can also be interpreted easily within the political perspective.

Perhaps the most common use of the political perspective is to interpret the interaction among the local, state, and federal governments. The traditional political analysts concentrate on legislative and bureaucratic politics—the making of policy and progress of bills through legislatures. This has to do with special-interest groups and the mechanisms of legislative process. More recently, attention has been focused on the implementation of these educational programs. Accommodations between levels of government are being reexamined. Authority and power relationships are at issue (Wirt and Kirst, 1972; Burlingame, 1978).

Political analysis also is being applied to large-scale societal trends in two ways. First, the changing social trends are being assayed for their political drift and portents of the future. Is society becoming more conservative? Will much less money be available to run the schools? Will the courts continue to demand desegregation? Secondly, innovations are themselves being interpreted against the background of societal trends. Must curriculum reform be abandoned in the face of a return to basics? Or will curriculum efforts of the federal government be focused on matters essential to economic efficiency? What is the political nature of reform efforts themselves? (Cohen, 1975; Paulston, 1976.)

Finally, at the most abstract and global level, political analysts examine what role education plays in society as a whole. Does schooling reproduce the social class structure of the society? (Bourdieu and Passeron, 1977.) Does education serve to liberate or conserve? These questions have profound implications for innovation efforts. Few were asked, or can be asked, from the technological perspective.

Since the early seventies, the political perspective has become a major competitor with the technological perspective. This is evident in the number of studies conducted and the frequency with which events are interpreted from this perspective. The technological perspective is still dominant, but this is partially determined by the federal government embracing this perspective, since most studies are funded by the federal government.

The third perspective is the cultural perspective. It is not a new orientation. It is at least as old as Jules Henry's (1963: 283) analysis of the classroom ("School is an institution for drilling children in cultural orientations") and probably much older. Yet it has been undergoing a revitalization and increasing its popularity greatly among researchers as an explanation of change (Smith and Geoffrey, 1968; Sarason, 1971; Smith and Keith, 1971; Wolcott, 1973, 1977; Lortie, 1975; Hill-Burnett, 1978).

Initially, it was employed to study the effects of innovations, those effects often being diffuse and intangible. More recently it has been used to study the innovation process itself. Now it is being suggested indirectly as a model for the innovation process. That is, the different participants—teachers, developers, and so on—are seen as different cultures or subcultures. An innovation may be developed by a group of university scholars, and the innovation will reflect the norms and values of that culture. As it is disseminated to teachers, it enters a new culture with significantly different norms and values. It will be interpreted differently when used in the new culture.

Much early work in anthropology was devoted to studying the diffusion of innovations from one culture to another, for example, the "cargo-cult" study. The cultural study often employs a different methodology, such as participant observation, ethnomethodology, case study, and the like, which concentrates heavily on how people interpret events. The social and cultural particularities become exceedingly important.

Hence, on a broad scale, the innovation process is conceived as the interaction of distinct and separate cultures. Conflicts and misunderstandings are interpreted as conflicts in values. Teacher culture is often seen as distinct from the other cultures, such as researchers, parents, technocrats, or developers, who try to change it. Many of these studies show the subtle ways in which change efforts are absorbed without significant change occurring. Most studies are directed at the different "meanings" produced by the change efforts rather than at the change itself.

So far, most cultural researchers tend to be sympathetic to the recipient culture rather than to the innovators, though one may wonder whether this will remain so once the government begins sponsoring such studies. In some of these studies, formal anthropological concepts are employed. In others, more ordinary concepts and language are used. I would expect that there would be a rising concern with language, symbolic meanings, social exchange, shared values, cultural context, belief systems, and evolutionary change over the next several years.

AN EXPANSION OF THE CULTURAL PERSPECTIVE

Since the cultural perspective is less fully developed in the educational change literature than either the technological perspective or the political perspective, it is worth examining what cultural explanations of change might look like. My thesis is not that the cultural will supplant the technological and political perspectives, but that societal developments will make the cultural view more relevant as an explanation. It will compete with the other two perspectives as an explanation for events.

Within anthropology there are at least two major traditions regarding cultural change—the cultural materialism tradition and the multiculturalism tradition. In explaining cultural change the cultural materialists distinguish between relativism and evolution as explanatory modes. Cultural relativists see change within cultures as essentially divergent. Change sequences are explained by the particular tradition or history of the culture. "A distinctive pattern develops, it is said, and henceforth is the primary determinant of whether innovations are accepted" (Steward, 1955: 35). In this view the environment puts constraints on how the culture develops, and the origins of activities are pushed back in time, unexplained.

The other materialist view is the evolutionary one. In this view, change is seen as occurring in distinct stages. It is assumed that there are parallels of form and function in independent cultural traditions and that there is identical causality. Recurrent patterns are looked for. In the nineteenth century, anthropologists posited developmental stages for all independent cultures, but this view, known as "unilinear" evolution, has been discounted. "Universal" evolution conceptions try to average all the independent cultures together to arrive at common factors that characterize "culture" in general.

The third evolutionary viewpoint is that of multilinear evolution. This theory of cultural change assumes that there are limited parallels of form and function, and limited similarities of cultural sequence. A key idea is that of cultural ecology, the idea that adaptation to the environment enhances cultural change. Underlying the idea of ecology itself is the concept of community. Cultural ecology tries to account for the origin of *particular* cultural features by introducing the *local environment* as the extracultural factor (Steward, 1955).

Changes in the culture are slow and are attributable to "new adaptations required by changing technology and productive arrangements" (Steward, 1955: 38). Steward goes on to say that

> the concept of cultural ecology, however, is less concerned with the origin and diffusion of technologies than with the fact that they may be used differently and entail different social arrangements in each environment. The environment is not only permissive or prohibitive with respect to these technologies, but special local features may require social adaptations which have far-reaching consequences.

In explaining cultural change, then, cultural diffusion is of secondary importance. The culture itself is the dominant force, the culture being "learned modes of behavior that are socially transmitted from one generation to the next and from one society or individual to another" (Steward, 1955: 44). In studying such change, holistic ethnological approaches stress the normative and persistent qualities of the culture. The cultural materialist tradition of cultural change was dominant in anthropology for a few decades after the war and is now showing signs of resurgence as massive cultural shifts become apparent in response to the energy shortage. Is it relevant to education?

Some innovation theorists, such as Goodlad (1975: 205), have explicitly advocated the notion of school as an "ecological community in which both living and non-living things constitute a system and interact within it. In this conception, man is part of, not master or conqueror of, the environment. Things and sets of things, individuals and groups of people and the relationships among all these are seen as one, a unified whole. . . . All are part of the same systemic whole or ecosystem. Every person and every thing has consequences for all other persons and things." Goodlad explicitly rejects the notion of production as a metaphor for schooling in favor of the "ecosystem," the community, as metaphor.

In the Rand studies, the notion of "mutual adaptation" can be understood as either a political or a cultural concept. To the degree that one emphasizes the "mutual" agreement idea—negotiation—the idea is political in import. And mutual congruence of interests between the federal and local governments is the way the Rand studies have been interpreted. But insofar as one emphasizes the adaptation of the innovation to its environment, its local context, the notion is cultural and harbors ecological connotations.

The most straightforward evolutionary approach, however, is that of Farrar et al. (1979), who explicitly see implementation as evolution. In explaining the implementation of the Experience-Based Career Education program, they reject the center-to-periphery (technological) and bilateral process (political) models and propose an evolutionary model. "Evolution nicely characterizes this process because the metaphor stresses change. . . . Sometimes historical change will produce convergence within a district concerning a program, and sometimes it will produce the opposite" (Farrar et al., 1979: 50). The local environment is the dominant factor. "In any event, local forces are as important—usually more important—in the evolution of federal policies and programs as federal influences" (Farrar et al., 1979: 16).

Implementation, then, takes on many meanings within the local context. The loose, segmented nature of the school allows much more autonomous action on the part of teachers and administrators. The EBC program was subject to diverse influences resulting in "multilateral evolution." "The program ideas and its themes or potentialities are given new meaning as seemingly external events shift the focus of a teacher, a project, a school district, or a nation. . . . The notion of evolution captures the importance of change much better than implementation does" (Farrar et al., 1979: 50).

A second tradition of cultural change analysis is that of multiculturalism. Anthropologists have traditionally acted on the assumption that most societies are one culture. Recently, it has been proposed that the normal experience in any society is that of multiculturalism (Goodenough, 1978). Nations and societies are in fact comprised of subcultures. Increasingly, accounting for change entails recognizing the differences in these subcultures from which individuals learn their orientation. Learning a culture actually means learning a set of subcultures. To interact effectively in a subculture means developing multicultural competence, learning what to expect (Goodenough, 1978). Access to elite subcultures often becomes the focus of reform efforts.

Hill-Burnett (1978) studied the interaction of teachers and Puerto Rican students in a midwestern city by contrasting the professional teacher culture to the Puerto Rican student culture. She tried to loosen the stereotypes held by the teachers by offering them cultural explanations of puzzling student behaviors. Rudduck (1977) has analyzed the dissemination of new curricula as an encounter of cultures, an encounter between the research culture and the culture of the receiving teachers. All these analyses see society and the educational community as composed of subcultures. Multiculturalism is the way of explaining change.

For example, Wolcott (1977) constructed an ethnography of a school implementing a planning, programming, and budgeting system, and used anthropological concepts to explain events and interactions among groups. The innovators were portrayed as technocrats who belonged to a subculture that valued order and rational process. Information, rational planning, and the idea of progress were important. Exerting control, managing settings, and commanding knowledge were also highly valued by the technocrats, who were ends-oriented.

By contrast, the teachers, who were the recipients of the innovation, were means-oriented, and focused on their teaching. The teacher subculture conceived teaching as traditional and sacrosanct and teachers as autonomous but vulnerable to outside pressures. It held that only teachers really understood teaching. The fate of the innovation was determined by the interaction between these two subcultures. Wolcott conceived the two subcultures together as constituting the educator culture and as being related by "complementarity," "reciprocity," "conceptual antithesis," and "rivalry." The interaction of the two subcultures gave the school the appearance of change without anything really changing, since the plans of the technocrats were not put into effect by the teachers.

To Wolcott the anthropological analysis demonstrated the continuity and stability of the school in the face of efforts to change it—a good thing, according to Wolcott. Although the interaction of the teachers and technocrats could have been interpreted from the technological perspective as a problem of implementation or from the political perspective as a conflict of interests, Wolcott chose to ask questions such as, "What purposes, values, and ideals do all the subgroups of educators hold in common?" His inquiry was directed "not to change, itself, but to the different meanings produced by the effort to impose change." Wolcott's is a prototypical study conducted from the cultural perspective, though most do not make such extensive use of anthropological concepts.

A COMPARISON OF THE PERSPECTIVES

The technological perspective has focused on the innovation itself, on its characteristics and component parts, on how to produce and introduce it. The technique and its effects are the focal points. The political perspective has focused on the innovation in context, on the relationships between sponsors and recipients, on rewards and costs and their distribution. Power and authority relationships are the focal points. The cultural perspective has focused on the context, on how work is structured and life is lived, on how the innovation is interpreted and relationships disturbed. Meanings and values are the focal points.

So the shift has been from the innovation, to the innovation in context, to the context itself—from the technological to the political to the cultural perspective. Changes in research methodology have accompanied these shifts. The technological perspective usually conducts its investigations with psychometric instruments, such as achievement tests, attitude scales, or scaled questionnaires. The political perspective conducts its investigations primarily with semistructured questionnaires and interviews, a survey methodology. The cultural perspective lends itself to anthropological methods of investigation, such as observation, participant observation, and case study. However, the shift in perspectives precedes the shift in methodology. One uses a different methodology in order to ask different questions, and then the different answers confirm the methodology and perspective. In other words, each perspective is confirmed by its own methodology.

"Hard" data such as those produced by psychometric, sociometric, and econometric research procedures are readily aggregatable over large units in forms such as achievement test scores, social indicators, and cost benefit indices. Interview data are aggregatable and generalizable but with more difficulty. Ethnographic methods are suitable to small groups, to microcultures, but are difficult to apply to national institutions. A holistic analysis or a natural history of an entire community lends itself to smaller units (Heighton and Heighton, 1978).

The same events will be seen differently from each of the three perspectives. For example, in their review of implementation studies, Fullan and Pomfret (1977) classified these studies into three main types: fidelity studies, in which fidelity to the original innovation is at issue; mutual adaptation studies, which focus on how the innovation has been changed in the implementation; and process studies, which focus on the implementation process itself. These three types of studies conform to implementation seen from the technological, political, and cultural perspectives, respectively.

For example, from the technological perspective, *Man: A Course of Study* (MACOS) has been studied as to the degree of faithful implementation. Teachers have been tested for their knowledge of MACOS content, and students have been tested for conformity to MACOS principles (Cole, 1971). From the political perspective, MACOS has been studied as to how local personnel adapt the materials for their own uses and how local factions promote and inhibit their use. From the cultural perspective, MACOS has been studied as encounters between the social science culture that produced the materials, the disseminating group culture, and the recipient group culture. The first culture is embodied in the materials themselves, the second in the workshop settings and procedures for dissemination, and the third in the institutions and values of the traditional curriculum. The interaction of the three cultures is treated as an acculturation process in which the three cultures develop a common tradition (Rudduck, 1977).

The three perspectives also differ significantly in the degree to which there is social consensus on interests and values. The earliest version of the technological perspective assumed there was considerable consensus in both interests and values. It assumed that everyone shared a common interest in advancing innovations and that everyone operated from a common frame of values. It reflected a society which believed unabashedly in technological progress. The only problem was to find how best to achieve it. Technical reasoning (sometimes known as rational decision making) assumes that the goal is set and that the problem is to find the "best," that is, most efficient, means to that end. Federal innovation and evaluation have been directed to that pursuit, for example, planned variation approaches like Follow Through. The later technological perspective has begun to accept conflict, formerly a surprise, as the price of progress, as in competency testing.

The political perspective implies that all is not harmonious. There may be problems, conflicts of interests. Not everyone wants the same thing, or else everyone wants a greater piece of a scarce resource. Conflict is not only possible but probable. Opposing factions will have to bargain and compromise, resort to political devices. Still, the political perspective assumes that there is enough value consensus that a compromise on interests can be achieved successfully. Even though people may not be in agreement on the content of what they want, at a minimum they agree on the procedures by which they can reach a peaceful compromise and an allocation of scarce resources. In other words, the participants, however much their interests conflict, share an authority structure, a set of values.

The cultural perspective assumes a more fragmented society, more value consensus within groups and less consensus among social groups, so that separate groups must be regarded as subcultures. The groups may be professional, ethnic, regional, and so on. Separate parts of the system are seen as more different than alike. The belief system of each one is a significantly different entity. The analogy is with foreign cultures to which one does not belong. In other words, there is no agreement on values, no assumption of a shared value system. The cultural perspective is redolent of societal fragmentation. Not only do the separate groups not share values and a way of resolving conflicts, they cannot be certain what the other groups' values are. On the other hand, the cultural perspective views each particular group as having a unitary culture and value system internally.

The three perspectives also differ significantly in their ethics. From the technological perspective, it is all right to pursue innovation aggressively, since the idea of technical progress is shared by all, since the innovation proceeds from a common value framework, and since the innovation is in the common interest. In fact, the primary ethical problem is to discover the best means to the common end. The innovation, program, or policy that most efficiently leads to the common goal or maximizes the common end is the best one. There is a common, unquestioned base of authority and the ethics are authoritative (and often hierarchically institutionalized in government agencies).

From the political perspective, securing the cooperation of others is problematic. The innovation cannot be assumed to be in their interests. For example, the innovation may require a substantial increase in the teacher's workload, yet the teacher may not benefit from it. One way of proceeding is to get the other parties to agree, to come to understandings with them, to secure their assent before innovating. The ethics are contractual.

From the cultural perspective even common agreement is problematic, since two different cultures may not understand one another, and there may be no mutually accepted procedure for reaching agreement, nor common values on which to do so. The possibilities for misunderstanding and miscalculation are enormous. One must be greatly concerned about the possibility of the unanticipated effects of an innovation in an unknown culture. Action becomes difficult. One way of proceeding is to try cautiously to establish common ground between the two cultures. It is

TABLE 1.1 Summary of Three Perspectives on Innovation

	Technological	Political	Cultural
Fundamental principles and assumptions	Systematic, rational processes	Factional groups engage in conflict and compromise	Participants are seen as cultures and subcultures
	Explicit knowledge and techniques are applicable (e.g., RDD model)	Influence is exerted by persuasion, inducements, coercion	Innovation requires the interaction of separate cultures
	Passive consumer	Power struggles dominate	Effects of innovation are diffuse and intangible
	Cooperation is automatic	Cooperation is problematic	Cooperation is enigmatic
	Efficiency and accountability are issues	Legitimacy is issue	Changes have different "meanings"
	Common interests and values are assumed	There are conflicts over interests	Autonomy is issue
			There may be conflicts over values and interests

(Continued)

TABLE 1.1 Summary of Three Perspectives on Innovation (continued)

	Technological	Political	Cultural
Focal points	The innovation itself	Innovation in context	Context
	The technique and its effects	Power and authority relationships	Meanings and values
Values	Common value framework	Values are shared by all	Values are shared within small groups
	Goal is predetermined	Consensus is possible after conflict negotiation of interests	Values are different between groups and may be in conflict
	Finding the one best way to accomplish the goal		
Ethics	Ethics are authoritative	Ethics are contractual	Ethics are relativistic
	Innovation is in the common interest	Innovation is not necessarily in the best interests of individuals, groups	Innovation may have unanticipated consequences
	Technological change should be pursued aggressively	Compromise differences	Do not impose on other
Image	Production	Negotiation	Community
	Production-oriented	Conflict-oriented	Meaning-oriented

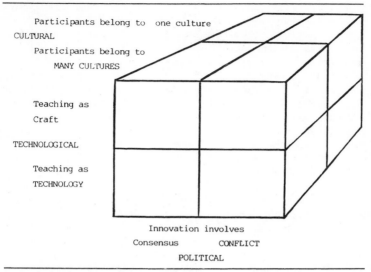

Figure 1.1 Relationships Among the Perspectives

not clear what is right and wrong, good and bad. The ethics are relativistic. (See Table 1.1 for a summary comparison of the perspectives.)

RELATIONSHIPS AMONG THE PERSPECTIVES

In Figure 1.1 the three perspectives are related to one another. The technological perspective lies along the vertical dimension and differentiates teaching as a craft from teaching as a technology. The political perspective lies along the horizontal dimension and differentiates a consensus on interests from a conflict on interests. The cultural perspective lies on the third dimension and differentiates "one culture" from "many cultures." In other words, the emergence of the technological perspective was the perception of teaching not as a craft but as a technology. The emergence of the political perspective was the perception of innovation as involving not a consensus on interests but a conflict of interests. The emergence of the cultural perspective was the perception of the innovation participants as belonging not to one culture but to many cultures. Each of these perceptions creates a new dimension.

The first distinction is whether one perceives teaching as craft or as a technology. A craft is based on experience and tacit knowledge. It is learned through apprenticeship, perhaps under the tutelage of a master craftsman. A technology, like achievement testing, is based on principles and explicit knowledge. It is learned through formal instruction. Most teachers view teaching as a craft born of long experience, even to the point of believing that only teachers can really understand teaching. Most reformers view teaching as a technology that has a specifiable content and technique, if only we can discover what it is. The technological perspective became dominant when most researchers, developers, and government officials began to view teaching as a technology subject to improvement through technical innovation. This often put them in opposition to teachers, who viewed teaching as a craft subject to improvement only through helping and improving the craftsman.

The craft approach would view change as a slow process with control located within. The technological approach would see change as faster and as coming from outside. The base of consensual authority shifts from the craftsmen to those who produce the tools and techniques. Teachers now become responsible only for implementing techniques decided upon by others.

The first shift in authority was from the craftsmen in the schools to the academics in the universities who presumably had superior subject knowledge. This was stimulated by considerations of international competition, particularly Sputnik. The early curriculum development projects were conducted by academics reforming the content of the curriculum material.

The next shift in authority came in seeing teaching as a technology. The later curriculum development projects tried to produce "teacher-proof" materials. The authority for innovation shifted to those who sponsored and developed these techniques, mostly the government and quasi-government agencies. Before, in the pre-innovation period, the content was controlled by textbook manufacturers and the teaching methods by the teachers. Now, at least hypothetically, the developers were in control. In actual fact, the teachers passively resisted many of their innovations.

By the early seventies some people operating from the technological perspective reasoned that it was not enough to develop technology; teachers would have to be induced or coerced into using it. They reasoned that the teachers' interests might be in conflict with those of developers. Accountability schemes which linked student and teacher performance to incentives became popular. Other people, still seeing teaching as a craft rather than as a technology, saw the class, racial, and factional differences in education as necessarily in conflict. They viewed the politics of innovation as negotiation, compromise, and bargaining among countervailing interests such as innovators, teachers, parents, and so on. Different groups had different career patterns, different interests. The full-scale political perspective emerged as many analysts interpreted attempts at educational innovation as conflicts over interests.

Meanwhile, the innovation establishment had tended to become centralized (Boyd, 1979c; van Geel, 1979). This exacerbated the differences between the innovators and regions and groups. Strong regional sentiments arose. Many early activities had assumed that all participants shared a common value base if not a common interest. Even where a conflict of interest existed, it was often assumed that the participants shared values. Group and regional differences suggested to some analysts that there were not only conflicts of interests but conflicts of values. Participants had different belief systems and perhaps belonged to different subcultures. The cultural perspective was adopted, which saw different cultural entities, particularly regional and local cultures and teachers, as separate subcultures. There was a resurgence of localism.

For those who saw teaching as a craft but a separate culture, strategies for innovation, such as teacher centers, allowed for evolutionary change within the teacher culture. At the same time, those who saw teaching as a technology could still pursue culturally divergent technological strategies, for example, locally developed behavioral objectives and locally based accountability schemes. Decentralized technology had long been taught in colleges of education, for example, behavioral objectives and standardized achievement testing.

The cultural perspective implicitly harbors a more conservative, traditional view of change. In anthropology change is explained by concepts such as cultural ecology, environmental adaptation, and multilinear evolution. Conflict between cultures is difficult to resolve (short of resort to power by the stronger one), and probably requires the development of a common understanding and tradition between them. Such a cultural adaptation might be expected to take a long time, and deliberate strategies for change among conflicting cultures are not yet clear. If the theories cannot explain innovation, perhaps they can explain the lack of it.

The technological perspective has held sway for the past two decades, only to be challenged within the past five years by the political perspective as an explanatory framework. The reason for this, I believe, is related to trends in the society as a whole. Similar shifts in perception are occurring in other disciplines as normally technological in orientation as economics and organizational theory (Simon, 1978; Whyte, 1978).

Yet I do not expect the emerging analytic perspectives to fully supplant the dominant technological perspective the way Newtonian physics replaced earlier physics. The disappearance of the technological perspective would presage a change in the very nature and identity of Western civilization. While significant societal change is occurring, and accounts in a real sense for the increasing salience of other perspectives, I do not expect such change to be so profound or so rapid as to extinguish the technological mentality.

What I would expect is for the technological perspective to be blended with other perspectives, such as in the ways suggested in Figure 1.1. The urge to introduce technical innovations into the school will continue but will take more cognizance of political and cultural realities it has often studiously neglected. More radical innovators will attempt purer political or culturally derived policies, but these attempts will be fewer and perceived as unusual. Mixed strategies will predominate.

This emphasizes the difference between paradigms in the physical sciences, where the physical world remains relatively constant, and the social world, where the reality itself changes. In the physical world one may test an Einsteinian conception of the world against a Newtonian one to see which better fits the facts. In the social world the facts themselves may have changed during the testing. It may make more sense to speak of the salience of various perspectives than of their ultimate truth or falsity.

THE PERSPECTIVES AND MODERNIZATION

Whatever the particular perspective, the very notion of innovation is tied to the idea of modernization. It is assumed that things should change, that innovation means progress. The process of modernization promises both better material conditions and more individual fulfillment. In particular, modernization is a shift from an unquestioned reality, which is given by tradition, to a social situation in which everything can be questioned and changed. It is a shift from "givenness" to "choice" (Berger, 1974). In the modern view, things can be chosen in industry, in agriculture, and in education.

Although all three perspectives operate within the milieu of modernity, each has a different view of the desirability and direction of the modernization process. The most favorable view of modernization, of course, is from the technological perspective. Once it is assumed that there is a consensus on values and interests, particularly on the goal of technical progress, the major problem is to find the best means to the given end, a technical problem.

Given an agreed-upon end, such as raising test scores, a researcher armed with appropriate research methodologies can determine the "best" innovation. Since both the end and the method for determining the means are agreed upon, the advocate/policy maker can proceed with considerable certainty. One is reassured that all participants benefit.

Policies originating from a technological perspective tend to be product- or goal-oriented, and evaluation conducted from such a perspective looks for success in implementation or outcome from the developer's point of view. Research tends to be "objectivistic," that is, it conceives the world as consisting of basic uninterpreted "hard" facts against which empirical claims can be legitimized.

By contrast, the cultural perspective is far more cautious about modernization. It is "meaning-oriented" rather than product-oriented. It sees individual meaning as collectively derived. Each person has a framework of meaning, and each person has the right to live in a "meaningful" world. Others must respect this private world. By transforming meanings, modernization is sometimes a threat to individuals and to cultures, according to the cultural perspective.

For both ethical and practical reasons, policies originating from the cultural perspective tend to respect the values and meanings of the people and cultures involved. "Policies that ignore indigenous definitions of a situation are prone to fail" (Berger, 1974). Evaluation derived from the cultural perspectives seeks inside information and respects indigenous definitions and values. It tries to define how people see things from within. Action originated from the cultural perspective is somewhat tentative and uncertain since one cannot always predict all the consequences of the action.

The political perspective is intermediate in its certainty of action. The primary concern is with people's interests, their capacity for getting what they want. The action must be legitimate. In democratic societies this means that everyone's interests must somehow be taken into account. Evaluation is aimed at ascertaining how people's interests are affected by the innovation process. Political research studies the manner in which various factions contend with one another. Politically oriented policies must consider the interests of the contending groups. In this perspective, modernization occurs through legitimate political institutions mediating conflicting interests.

The culture of the school itself is a very traditional one, at least compared to other sectors of society, such as industry. It is not surprising that schools would resist modernization pressures, particularly when these are originated from without. Nor is it surprising that the school, being traditional, will be slow to change without pressures. How modernization should occur, through what legitimate means, and how fast, are the issues that divide people concerned about innovation.

As I have tried to indicate, however, it is not only events in education that make the political and cultural perspectives more salient as interpretive frameworks. Our perception of trends in the larger society greatly influences how we interpret events in microcosms of society such as educational innovation. Within society as a whole, the process of modernization has been undergoing a significant transformation. Modernization processes such as economic development and mass communication, once thought to be primary forces for social integration, now seem to be leading to social fragmentation.

Contrary to expectations, in many parts of the world there has been a rising disenchantment with modernization and a reemphasis on ethnic identity leading to a "politics of disassociation" and demands for ethnic, cultural, political, and even economic sovereignty (Said and Simmons, 1976). This renewed vitality of ethnic identity has been based on primordial ties of blood, race, language, religion, and custom. Iran is the quintessential example. Intensified ethnic identification has led to sociopolitical differentiation and to demands for cultural autonomy. Conflicts among groups abound. Under these circumstances, appeals to the national interest carry little weight.

Generally, the rise in ethnicity is attributed to mass communications that permit ethnic groups to become visible and differentiate themselves from other groups. Modernization scholars, imbued with a notion of rational and linear progress, have usually treated ethnicity as a transitional stage in which individuals will come eventually to identify with the higher national group (Said and Simmons, 1976). This thesis looks more dubious today. Even a cursory examination of educational innovation in the United States and other countries reveals that the origin and fate of innovations are significantly shaped by ethnic forces.

Parallel to the persistence of ethnicity as a social force is a "neoethnic" response to the depersonalization and rationalization of postindustrial society. This is a transition from an acquired national consciousness to communal forms of identity, to a search for community in modern society. The quest for community is a search for cultural purpose, membership, status, and continuity.

While ethnic identity is rooted in presumptions of common origins based on ascriptive characteristics, neoethnic behavior is rooted in the quest for identity to replace earlier ethnic forms. This results in subcultures based on work, occupations, common functions, and alternative forms of community. Social conflict arises when there is competition among these ethnic and neoethnic groups for socially available rewards. One could, for example, interpret the great conflict over school decentralization between New York City teachers and blacks in this fashion, or the yet-to-come conflict over bilingual-bicultural programs.

All of these trends weaken the power of the state and the idea of modernization on which the modern state is based. Group identity is strengthened at the expense of national unity. State action in the name of technological progress becomes much more problematic. At the same time, ethnic and neoethnic groups mobilize to press their demands on the government, which is expected somehow to meet demands from all groups. Groups are politically mobilized by entrepreneurs who lead the groups through self-awareness and identity, to awareness of group needs, to an articulation of group demands (Mowlana and Robinson, 1976). Under such circumstances the political and cultural perspectives become much more salient as explanatory frameworks for innovation in education, as well as for a host of other social phenomena.

IMPLICATIONS FOR RESEARCH AND POLICY

A common view of social research is that its purpose is to clarify goals and to provide evidence for choosing alternative means to given ends. It is assumed that there is broad agreement on the goals of social policy and a separation of the determination of ends from the determination of means (Cohen and Garet, 1975). But this conception of research and policy analysis is derived from a technological perspective.

Cohen and Garet (1975) contend that social policy is a system of knowledge and belief. "A policy, then, might be described as a grand story; a large and loose set of ideas about how the society works, why it goes wrong and how it can be set right." Social research influences broad assumptions and beliefs, "the policy climate," rather than particular decisions about programs. The social research itself is held together by larger ideas and assumptions not empirical in nature. It is a thesis of this chapter that a significant part of the underlying beliefs and assumptions are the fundamental perspectives. The perspectives provide explanations in terms of regular and predictable conceptual categories, suggest what evidence is considered relevant, and what factors determine events. They provide answers to the questions of "What happened? Why did it happen? What will happen?" (Allison, 1971). Different perspectives produce different explanations and different policies.

Yet the relationship among research, policy, and the analytic perspectives is not a determinant one. The perspectives suggest explanations and factors for review rather than totally determine them. Many different policies and research studies can be drawn from the same perspective. Nor is the influence all one way. The research conducted and the policies implemented affect the perspectives one holds, both in the detailed nature of one's explanation and especially in the number of people interpreting an event from a particular framework.

It follows from this that research is extremely important in setting the policy climate generally, and in influencing how people view events connected with innovation. If research studies are all conducted from the technological perspective, as they were for years, then most people will harbor such a view of innovation, thereby disregarding the factors implicit in the political and cultural perspectives. One might expect innovation policy to be similarly technological in concept, in spite of failures.

One might also expect somewhat different action strategies to be derived from the three perspectives. A technological strategy might concentrate on the development of an innovation and its proper employment in the school. An effective innovation and proper skills to implement it might be the focus. A political strategy might focus on the interests of the participating groups, anticipating that the ultimate success of the innovation would reside in how motivated people are to employ it. A cultural strategy might take cognizance of the values of the teachers and consider how congruent the innovation is with the school culture. Factors identified by the analysts would become matters of concern for the strategist. A truly comprehensive strategy would view the situation from all three perspectives.

A technological strategy might spend large sums of money on developing an innovation so technologically sound that it would be far better than current approaches. A political strategy might focus on negotiating a mutual agreement with the participants as to who would do what and how the costs and rewards would be distributed. A cultural strategy might find long-term ways of changing the teacher culture, such as by training the teachers to do research on their own classrooms. As examples of the technological strategy one might cite the development of "teacher-proof" materials and competency testing. As an example of the political strategy, one might cite mandated parent participation in government programs. As an example of a cultural strategy, one might cite teacher centers. But one cannot adopt a particular strategy unless the professional community and government leaders understand matters from the appropriate perspective.

The companion reviews of the literature in this volume indicate the character of past research. Miles's review of the generic properties of the school is fundamentally technological in approach. Sieber's review of incentives and disincentives for knowledge utilization uses research generated from all three perspectives, but again the mass of the literature is technological in origin. This is even more true of Louis's review of external change agents. Almost all the studies reviewed have been conceived within a center-periphery notion of change. Fullan's review of internal human agents contains more literature generated from the other perspectives. Some political and cultural work has been done on the internal workings of the district. Finally, Berman's chapter reflects the shift away from the adoption-technological concept of innovation toward the implementation--political/cultural viewpoints. However, the great mass of research literature remains so overwhelmingly technological in orientation that any review of it must reflect that weight. Our research is shaped by our fundamental perspective, and our perspective is limited by our research.

The three perspectives are pure types into which no individual researcher, theorist, or policy maker fits perfectly. As indicated in Figure 1.1, the three perspectives can be represented as different dimensions in three-dimensional space. A particular position could be located anywhere within the three-dimensional space, the three dimensions being independent but not exclusive of one another. For example, an evaluation study might simultaneously try to ascertain how the interests of various groups are affected by an innovation (a political position) and expend an equal effort in defining the indigenous values and meanings of the participating groups (a cultural position). However, it would seem that most studies are recognizable as predominantly based on one perspective or another.

Why these perspectives rather than others? The answer is not altogether clear. One might say that the technological perspective represents the interests of those who sponsor innovation; the cultural perspective, the interests of those who are "being innovated"; and the political perspective, the negotiation of those interests. But that analysis itself is conducted from a political perspective. It is significant that the three perspectives reflect the viewpoints of dominant societal institutions. These viewpoints have already been institutionalized within the academic disciplines such as economics, engineering (technological), political science and sociology (political), and anthropology (cultural). There is seldom represented the viewpoint of the weaker societal institutions, such as religion.

Can one of these perspectives be "proved correct" the way a scientific theory can? It would not seem so. Each perspective focuses on different aspects of reality, and, in fact, values the same aspects differently. There is widespread belief now that the exclusively technological perspective employed in the last decade in the form of the research, development, diffusion paradigm of innovation was not very workable, but that seems to be a matter of professional consensus and belief. In other times and other places, such as in agriculture in the 1940s and 1950s, the R, D, and D paradigm seemed to "work." In education the technological perspective has become less relevant and less workable, rather than incorrect. A critical difference between physical phenomena and social phenomena is that the latter change with time and do not provide a permanent base against which to test a theory or a perspective. Hence, perspectives are inherently less stable and change with social conditions. The more that teachers or the

Third World countries resist modernization, the more the political or cultural perspectives provide interpretations of ongoing changing events.

What can government funders do, given that perspectives cannot be proved to be correct or incorrect? In a pluralistic society it seems sensible to fund all legitimate points of view. The government can sponsor studies that examine knowledge utilization from the technological, political, and cultural perspectives. In the past, government funding has gone overwhelmingly into studies and projects conducted from the technological perspective. Somewhat better balance in funding is called for. To a considerable degree government-funded studies can affect how people view knowledge utilization.

Researchers seem to lend themselves to one perspective or the other. Perhaps an awareness that there are other legitimate perspectives is all that is required, an acknowledgment that there are other ways of viewing a situation. It might also be useful for researchers to think about knowledge utilization from the other perspectives, just as a thought experiment, to suggest other possibilities to themselves. Some research is already conducted from a combination of perspectives.

The problem for policy makers is somewhat more difficult. Policy decisions must often be made which conflict with the other two perspectives. Perhaps the best that can be hoped for is that the policy makers inform themselves about the decision situation by analyses drawn from different perspectives. It would seem that the worst policy decisions are made without regard for other points of view, the policy maker being falsely assured by the security of a unitary point of view that he or she has captured the significant aspects of social reality.

2

MAPPING THE COMMON
PROPERTIES OF SCHOOLS

Matthew B. Miles

INTRODUCTION

"If you want to alter a social system, you'll get much further if you have a good map of it." Who could argue with such a dictum? It has that hollow, trite ring of truth that usually leads us to place our attention elsewhere. But the fact is that maps are important, not only for planning a trip, but for guiding the journey, helping one out of confusion, and reviewing the whole experience afterward.

This chapter invites those who try to understand, support, or manage processes labeled "school improvement" to reflect on the maps they are using. Just what sort of an enterprise is a school?

The chapter focuses on the common properties shared by elementary and secondary schools in the American context. There are several senses, not mutually exclusive, in which such properties can be seen as "common": (1) that they are present in all schools, are "universals"—or are at least "typical," or "standard"; (2) that they are relatively stable and vary only slowly (or not at all) over time; or (3)—more inferentially—that they are somehow inherent, focal, or central to the very idea of a school as we know it in America today.

Illustrative Common Properties of Schools

To exemplify what various writers have meant by "common property," here are some samples adapted from Fullan et al. (1978):

Goal diffuseness: The organization's mission is usually abstractly stated, with output measurement a difficult matter (Miles, 1967;

Miles and Schmuck, 1971), partly because of the long time line involved.

Suboptimal technical capability: The knowledge base underlying educational practice is relatively weak, and/or not well diffused to practitioners (Sieber, 1968).

Coordination problems: Schools and school districts tend to be low-interdependent, "loosely coupled" systems (Bidwell, 1965; Weick, 1976) where goals do not connect well with means, and where accountability is low and autonomy high.

Boundary management problems: From the inside,, the skin of the organization seems unbearably thin, overpermeable to dissatisfied stakeholders; from the outside, the barriers to citizen influence seem tough and elastic.

Domestication: Schools are owned by their environments and are noncompetitive with other schools for resources (Carlson, 1965a). Survival is guaranteed, more or less, and the incentives for innovation are feeble (Pincus, 1974).

Location in a constrained, decentralized suprasystem: Though each of 16,000 U.S. school districts and 89,000 buildings is nominally autonomous, there are many national constraints exerted by standardized testing, a national textbook market, various accreditation and certification requirements, and a variety of legislation (Miles, 1978).

While these common properties have been asserted by a range of writers, there is no very clear way to assess their plausibility or truth value. This chapter summarizes and examines the evidence available, to weigh the various claims being made.

Importance of the Topic

There are several theoretical and practical reasons for attending to schools' common properties. First, anyone researching or managing a deliberate change process in schools who wants to avoid superficiality and wrongheadedness is well advised to be clear about what might be called their "deep structure"—to note that the common features of schools point to a series of meta-issues underlying the day-to-day events and processes of "school as usual."

Second, a focus on common properties can help one see how such properties constrain and limit change efforts, as well as how they provide active driving and restraining forces. Primary "leverage points" for change efforts may be identifiable.

Third, common properties are certainly not all-determinative. Schools show a very wide range of *variable* properties (ranging from dollar expenditure to the principal's leadership style and classroom climate). A focus on common properties may help one see which *variable* properties are more important and why—and how much range of variation to expect.

APPROACHES TO UNDERSTANDING
COMMON PROPERTIES

There are several possible avenues of inquiry on common properties of schools: "naive observation," stipulative/speculative analysis, comparative analysis, typological classification, and empirical research.

"Naive Observation"

Sarason (1971) suggests a thought experiment: One should imagine oneself as a being from outer space, by chance hovering over a bounded place which Americans label a "school."

> At some times of the day, and some times of week and year, the "school" is filled with people, and at other times it is empty. There are few large people, and many small people. The large people are rarely found talking with other large people. Larger people speak much more frequently than smaller people.

This sort of analysis is useful in locating programmatic and behavioral regularities, detached from the associated justificatory value positions. But such analysis has its limits. Most acutely, it is short on *meanings*. As Deutsch (1979) suggests:

> If these outsiders are not also insiders enough to understand the culture, they will select irrelevant variables, or will not be able to identify the quality or nature of the relationships between variables.

The main value of the exercise lies in providing detachment, encouraging the fish to contemplate the water in which it swims, and, as Sarason suggests, to derive significance from the unspecified, missing "universe of alternatives" (what if schools were open 24 hours a day? What if the average student spoke as much as the average teacher?). The "naive observer" mode, in fact, almost immediately conveys the thinker into a stipulative/speculative mode.

Stipulative/Speculative Analysis

The most frequently used approach to understanding schools' common properties postulates generic or typical properties of schools, and speculates about their antecedents, interrelations, and consequences, with little reference to empirical data. Many such analyses have appeared. Here are a couple, displayed in schematic format to show the nature of the interrelations proposed in the authors' verbal expositions.

Willower (1970), a long-time researcher in educational administration, for example, proposes the following set of basic properties (Figure 2.1): vulnerability, goal vagueness, weak technology, and compulsory attendance. Other variables follow from these, leading to certain dependent variables: Schools are seen as adopting "ornamental" innovations, as

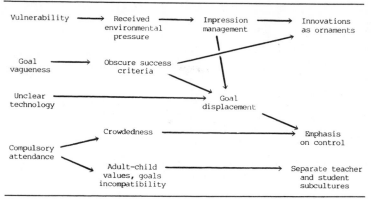

Figure 2.1 Common Properties of Schools, as Inferred from Willower (1970)

having a strong control orientation, and as composed of separate teacher and student subcultures.

As a second exhibit, we might examine the work of Meyer and Rowan (1977), organizational theorists with a "loose coupling" bent. They suggest a general scheme for organization-environment relations, and apply it (Meyer and Rowan 1978) to the special case of schools. The relationships suggested in their verbal analysis appear in Figure 2.2.

The authors conceive the school as essentially a sorting mechanism for society, and claim that the aspects of schools which bear on this function are rigidly maintained, resulting in satisfaction of external constituencies. However, both the decentralized structure of American education and the need to avoid conflict and uncertainty are seen as promoting the decoupling of actual instruction from administrative and curricular aspects of schools. In this view, only the "ritual classification" aspects of schools are rigid, and there is plenty of room for adaptive change at the instructional level, so long as it does not disrupt external relations.

Space does not permit the display of additional stipulative networks; an earlier version of this chapter included the schemata proposed by Elboim-Dror (1970) using a policy-sciences perspective, by Sieber in the present book (a structural-fuctional approach), and by Boyd (1978), stressing the history and politics of education.

A review suggests certain characteristics of the stipulative/speculative approach:

(1) The choice of start, intervening, and dependent variables seems quite arbitrary, depending essentially on theoretical predilection, personal observation/recollection, and only rarely on empirical data.
(2) The networks are generally quite incommensurable, and may lead to conflicting conclusions (example: Willower and Meyer and Rowan on how control-oriented schools are).
(3) Claims of "inherent" or "historically universal" status are made for a wide range of school properties, on a sheerly stipulative basis.

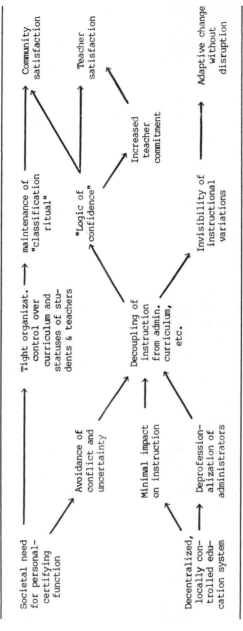

Figure 2.2 Common Properties of Schools, as Inferred from Meyer and Rowan (1978)

It is hard not to concur with Giacquinta's (1973: 197) comments:

> Various authors have pointed to the possible effects of properties of schools on speed and degree of change. Some of these properties are special features of schools, and others are common characteristics of all complex organizations. All have received minimal empirical support and have been mainly speculative. Furthermore, since on logical grounds different predictions for many of these conditions appear possible, little can be said in the way of their effects on change in schools.

Comparative Analysis

A third possible approach to understanding common properties of schools involves systematic comparison. Schools in America should be compared to other types of organizations in America (universities, mental health centers, factories, prisons), and schools in America should be compared to schools in other countries (Canada, the Netherlands, Upper Volta). That way it should be possible to separate out just what is school-specific for this particular culture. But it is fair to say that little of the first type of comparison has been done, and that most of the second type (comparative educational research) has focused on macro-level issues, with little attention to common properties as they are played out in specific school buildings (see Noah and Eckstein, 1969; King, 1979).[1]

Typological Classification

A fourth possible approach to locating common properties of any sort of organization involves asking what "type" of organization is being examined, in comparison to other types. Silverman (1971) summarizes efforts in this direction, pointing out that some typologies rest on issues of *environmental input* (for example, unstable, threatening environments induce an "organic" organizational type; see Burns and Stalker, 1961); mass-production market requirements induce a bureaucratic structure, while small-batch or process technologies induce an "expert"-dominated organization (Woodward, 1958). Other typologies derive from *output to the environment:* Parsons's (1965) AGIL formulation; Katz and Kahn's (1966) classification of organizations by the productive, maintenance, adaptive, or managerial-political functions they play for their surroundings; Blau and Scott's (1962) focus on "who benefits?" resulting in mutual-benefit, business, service and "commonweal" types; and Weber's (1964) traditional, charismatic, and rational-legal bases for authority. Finally, organizations can be classified according to *internal* characteristics: Etzioni's (1961) view of member involvement and compliance methods as divisible into coercive-alienative, remunerative-calculative, and normative-moral; Clark and Wilson's (1961) typology based on incentives (utilitarian, solidarity, and purposive); and Goffman's (1961) view of organizations as "total" or "non-total."

This listing shows us two things. First, classifying an organization on one dimension (such as its authority base, market requirements, or benefiting audience) obscures many other important dimensions, as Firestone (1980) thoughtfully acknowledges. Are schools, for example, "rational bureaucracies"? Yes, in many respects. But, Firestone argues, they can also fruitfully be viewed as "sects" with a central ideology, as political systems shot through with conflict and bargaining, as "hospitals" run by the expertise of professionals, aided by administrators, and as loosely coupled anarchies where individuals pursue their interests without serious conflict.

Second, in any case, assignment of organizations to types, as noted above, is not a straightforward matter. Are schools essentially normative organizations, or basically coercive in nature? Are they defined as mass-production (hence bureaucratic) systems, or as small-batch enterprises, with experts (teachers) playing a prominent role? Empirical data are sparse enough, and alternative views diverse enough, that type classification is problematic.

Empirical Research

Empirical studies examining common properties of educational systems in America, particularly with an eye to relating these to matters of knowledge utilization and school improvement, are relatively rare. Most empirical efforts somehow go into studying the *variable* properties of schools. This chapter has relied most frequently on the following empirical studies: Hood et al.'s (1976) survey of educational practitioners' use of information (N = 628); Abramowitz and Tenenbaum's (1978) national survey of high school principals' views of their organizations (N = 1448); Packard et al.'s (1978) study of team teaching in 29 elementary schools; Meyer et al.'s (1978) research on the organizational functioning of 188 elementary schools; Havelock et al.'s (1973) national survey of school superintendents' views of innovations in their districts (N = 353); the NEA's Nationwide Teacher Opinion Poll (N = 1777; Teacher Education Reports, 1979); Giacquinta and Kazlow's (1979) nationally stratified sample of school districts asked about their uses of open education (N = 300); and Daft and Becker's (1978) study of innovation adoption in 13 high school districts.

Concluding Comments

This review of alternative approaches to the understanding of schools' common properties has noted certain themes: the dominance of stipulative/speculative analyses and weakness of empirical support; the limited value of "naive observation" and of typological approaches; and the rarity of relevant comparative analyses. Two other themes have been implicitly present.

Wide assumptive range. The intellectual frameworks brought to bear on this topic are relatively diverse; this in itself provides a quasi-comparative advantage. Bureaucratic theory (for example, see Bidwell, 1965; Spence et al., 1978), variations of structural/functional thinking (Corwin, 1971; Sieber, 1968), systems theory (Miles, 1965), approaches from the policy sciences (Elboim-Dror, 1970, 1973), educational administration theory

(Willower, 1971), variants of "loose coupling" theory (Weick, 1976; Cohen et al., 1972; Meyer and Rowan, 1977, 1978), and concepts from anthropology (Gallaher, 1965) have all been applied. We are not suffering from a "received" view of the issues in this area, and there is a moderate amount of disputation going on.

Stabilization bias. Most analyses of common properties seem to view them as promoting noninnovation, resistance, and business as usual. A good example is Morrish (1976), who, in a chapter explicitly entitled "Why Schools Change So Slowly," lists properties ranging from overcentralization to absence of change agents, underdeveloped scientific base, confused goals, uniformity, monopoly and noncompetition, passivity, "separation of members and units" and "hierarchy and status." All are asserted to be barriers to change, though a case can easily be made that some (loose coupling or hierarchy, to take two diverse examples) could as well aid change.

This "pessimistic" bias, which Sieber's chapter (this volume) discusses as typical of the literature on educational change, is probably empirically unjustified. The bias is probably generated by the fact that most analysts are positioned *outside* the schools, with a set toward change and reform. As part of the "innovation establishment" (Fullan's term), or as "reform professionals" (Boyd, 1978), they have a vested interest in claiming that the object of change efforts is resistant (hence needs to be studied, intervened in, and so on, through the medium of funds directed toward the analyst).

The remainder of this chapter, in turn, (1) proposes a general conceptualization of the area; (2) outlines what is "known" about common properties of schools (whether stipulatively or empirically); and (3) draws general implications for the study, support, and management of educational change efforts.

The reader who would like a substantive overview of the material covered can refer forward to Table 2.1.

CONCEPTUALIZATION OF THE AREA

Common Properties

The literature reviewed here contains assertions by many different analysts that one or another property of schools is common, "generic," basic, essential, typical, focal, inherent, and so on. Such properties may be sorted into two categories.

Inherent/intrinsic. Some properties seem to be derivable from core features of the educational enterprise as such (for example, the idea that education involves "people processing").

Historical. Other properties labeled "common" seem to have been historically derived: particular events (such as the passage of legislation on compulsory education), social processes (such as the emphasis on "effi-

(text continues on page 54)

TABLE 2.1 Regularities, Claimed Antecedents, and Knowledge Gaps, by Dilemmas

Dilemma	Noted Regularities*	Claimed Antecedents	Knowledge Gaps
1. Core task accomplishment vs. survival	Goal conflict?	Goal measurement difficulty	Causal claims assessment
	Goal displacement?	Value-laden goals	Extent of practical goal consensus
	Input focus	Compulsory attendance	Comparative studies of vulnerability
	Symbolic/ceremonial success criteria	Vulnerability	
2. Diversity vs. uniformity	Structural supports for uniform treatment	Output measurement difficulty	Description of actual instructional modes
	Minimal use of learner-responsive technologies	Large numbers of clients?	Relation of diversity/ uniformity to innovativeness
	Preoccupation with control over students	Vested interests of employees	Relation of diversity/ uniformity to effectiveness
		Immaturity of clients	
	Increase in bureaucratization?	Client motivation weak	

50

3. Coordination vs. flexibility	Influence discontinuities	Legitimacy maintenance	Organizational model fitting
	Low interdependence	Custodial function of schools	Relation of coordination/flexibility to knowledge use and innovation
	Low surveillance	Domain conflict	Nature of teacher autonomy
	Low control?		Meaning of teacher isolation
4. Environmental dependence vs. autonomy	Domestication?	Education as a state/local function	Local "latitude" for action
	Quasi-monopolistic position	Compulsory education	Correlates of school pro-activeness
	Popular support	Normal children as clients	Cognitive mapping of environment
	Decentralized constraint	Development of the educational establishment	
	Increased regulation		
5. Environmental contact vs. withdrawal	Vulnerability	Avoidance of disruption	Parents' influence at the "micro" level
	Buffering	Weak production function	Models of "constructive" involvement

(Continued)

TABLE 2.1 Regularities, Claimed Antecedents, and Knowledge Gaps, by Dilemmas (continued)

Dilemma	Noted Regularities*	Claimed Antecedents	Knowledge Gaps
6. Seeking external expertise vs. self-reliance	Weak parent and citizen participation	Self-defeating federal policies	
		Vested interests of educators	
	Infrequent use of formal external channels	Weak knowledge base	Knowledge utilization base rates
	Presence of non-instrumental incentives	Structural aspects of teaching	Correlates of utilization
	Quasi-professionalism	Modernity	
7. Feedback-seeking vs. intuitive/routine action	Labor-intensiveness	Input variability	"Alignment" among outcomes, instruction, assessment
	Immediate client response as data	Goal vagueness	Educational production function
	Lack of output control	Complex operations	Barriers and aids to the diffusion of self-study technology
	Weak self-monitoring capability	Weak production function	

		Disconnection of operations and outcomes from rewards	
8. Centralized vs. shared influence	Low student influence	Compulsory attendence	Contingency analysis of "participation"
	"Zoning" of decisions	Managerial professionalization	Processes and effects of shared-influence structures
	"Local" centralization	Domain conflict	
	Increasing teacher power	Democratic ideology	
	Shared influence as a support for innovation?		
9. Change vs. stability	"Non-rationality" toward innovations	Outcome vagueness	Base rates of innovation
	Local adaptation	Weak incentive structure	Limits to "technology transfer"
	"Low" innovation rates?	Weak production function	Nature of internal change
		Vulnerability	

* Claimed regularities whose status remains in doubt are marked by a question mark.

ciency" in educational management in the 1920s and 1930s), or general "historical drifts" (the growth of collective bargaining by teachers) variously seem to have created features common to all schools.

Neither historically nor inherently derived properties are directly observable, but one can discern particular regularities in schools and make the inference that they are derived from the "source" property. For example, the goal displacement (preoccupation with educational *means*) noted by some observers may be traceable back to an "inherent/intrinsic" property, the fact that a "people-processing" system necessarily has diffuse, hard-to-measure goals.

Or the supposed vulnerability of schools to influence from their communities can be seen as a natural consequence of the historically generated constitutional allocation of education to the states, and the de facto assumption of that function by local communities. Still other widely observed regularities in schools (such as the fact that schools tend to have an aggregated, "cellular" structure, with low observability of role performance) may have no very clear or plausible antecedents, yet have "core-like" status.

The Role of Common Properties in Change

How might common properties of schools play a part in efforts to alter schools? Figure 2.3 suggests a general schema.

Schools as social systems have certain *primary tasks* (such as managing their goals, carrying out internal operations, relating to their environments). The demands of these tasks, along with the *inherently and historically derived properties* of schools in this particular culture, lead to certain *observed regularities* and some *dilemmas* (for example, whether schools and school systems should be centralized and tightly managed, or decentralized, with much local authority for decision making).

Each local district, building, and classroom also has many *variable* properties stemming from the uniqueness of *local conditions* (a state-mandated program, a weak superintendent, cosmopolitan teachers, rural suspicion of "Washington" programs, influx of lower-SES students, and so on). These local conditions, in concert with the regularities and dilemmas seen as common properties, generate *operational and change-relevant behavior* (by teachers, administrators, boards, change agents) which can be seen as patterned resolution of dilemmas. Such patterns do not wholly flow from rational "decisions," plans, or even coherently acted-on intentions; they often "just happen." Nevertheless, they do seem to follow from the regularities and dilemmas *common* to all schools, and the *uniqueness* of local, variable conditions.

The label "behavior" is used to remind the reader that "tasks," "properties," "conditions," "dilemmas," and similarly abstract entities cannot really be reified. Ultimately, they can only be inferred from what people do or say. ("Shall we apply for the Title IV-C grant?" "Tell Sandra's mother I'll call her back." "You're suspended." "Not *that* text-book again.") Aggregated over time, dozens and hundreds of such behaviors constitute organizational processes of operation and change.

Furthermore, "school improvement" programs represent only a portion of the dilemma-resolution pie: these efforts to change schools which are relatively deliberate, bounded, and named. And as we shall see below, "knowledge utilization" is only one of nine basic dilemmas being posited. Many, many other things go on in schools.

The editors' introduction to this book reviews types of change in schools. Here we should note that most discussions of schools' common properties devote most attention to *marginal,* part-innovative change, somewhat less attention to *core* change (as in discussions of "self-renewal"), and least to common properties' effects on *maintenance*-level change.

Given this imbalance, clean empirical connections can probably not be made between common properties of schools and operational and change-relevant behaviors in them. Furthermore, local variability affects dilemma resolution as much as do observed school regularities (see Figure 2.3). Thus, monolithic assertions about any "common property's" effect on "innovativeness" of schools are dubious. Figure 2.3 leaves open the possibility that *some* common properties are so essential, so basic, that they transcend any possible local variation in determining amounts and types of change in schools. But the empirical fact of wide variation in schools' changefulness (or indeed more specifically, their utilization of knowledge) makes that extremely doubtful.

Primary Tasks of Schools

We need not dwell at length on the primary tasks schools face as social systems embedded in an environment.[2] In brief, schools must work on the following issues:

- *core task accomplishment* (delivery of educational and associated services)
- *integration* (linking, connection of parts)
- *relation with immediate environment* (transactions with local community)
- *relation with distal environment* (vendors, universities, intermediate units, legislatures, and the like)
- *goal setting* (relevant to any of the four preceding tasks)
- *management* (steering of work on all other tasks)
- *adaptation* (altering self and relevant parts of the environment in a reciprocal way)

Dilemmas of Operation and Change

As schools and their districts cope with the seven tasks outlined above, in the context of their common properties, they typically encounter

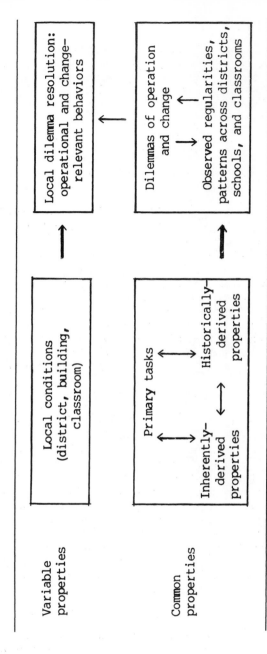

Figure 2.3 Variable and Common Properties of Schools

dilemmas. For purposes of this discussion a "dilemma" represents a choice[3] between two goods, which are defined as mutually exclusive.

The remainder of the chapter is organized around nine major dilemmas:
Internal:

(1) Core task focus versus "survival" emphasis.
(2) Diversity versus uniformity.
(3) Coordination versus flexibility.
(4) Environmental dependence versus autonomy.
(5) Environmental contact versus withdrawal.
(6) Environmental expertise seeking versus self-reliance.

Management of internal-external functioning:

(7) Feedback seeking versus intuitive/routine action.
(8) Centralized versus shared influence.
(9) Change versus stability.

These nine dilemmas are created by the interaction of schools' common properties and their primary tasks; they are suggested as recurrent, pervasive ones with which any organization, and schools in particular, must cope. The dilemmas appear at the individual (student, teacher, administrator) level, at the subsystem (team, grade, department) level, at the school organization level, and at the district level. Just how the dilemmas are resolved in the form of specific operational and change-relevant behavior depends on the vicissitudes of local conditions, including the behavior of local and external managers and change agents.

REGULARITIES IN SCHOOLS AND THEIR ANTECEDENTS

This section of the chapter summarizes the range of empirical data, claims, and assertions made about what is typical, stable, or somehow "inherent" in American schools. It is organized according to the nine dilemmas, although where a particular property is fitted is sometimes arbitrary.

Each dilemma is explained. Then the discussion reviews the *regularities* various analysts have observed or asserted, with an effort to assess the confidence with which we can say that X is in fact a "regularity." Then *causal questions* are addressed: What inherent or historical properties (and associated primary tasks) have been claimed as antecedents by various analysts? The discussion for each dilemma concludes with a listing of *gaps:* issues where more empirical data are needed.

Dilemma 1:
Core Task Accomplishment versus Survival

Schools are always faced with multiple goals. A school may choose to place primary energy on its core task—delivery of educational services. But then crucial bureaucratic and political goals may go unachieved (key teachers are transferred out, the board refuses to fund a promising program and so on). Schools, as we shall see, usually survive, even though the *quality* of their survival can be appalling if bureaucratic and political issues are ignored. But—as with all our dilemmas—an exclusive emphasis on one horn forecloses the other. A school where most decisions are bureaucratic/political typically treats its core task as peripheral: It matters little what goes on in the classroom so long as the parents and the central office are not complaining.

This dilemma can also be reconstrued: How central are *professional* concerns? Teachers are labeled "professionals" who are to apply their expertise to the instruction of learners placed in their care. But they are not free-standing professionals like doctors in private practice; they must function in an organization, in a political context. So their continued ability to "do what is best for children" depends in part on how well they play the bureaucratic/political game.

REGULARITIES NOTED

1. Goal conflict. Several analysts suggest that schools typically are saddled with multiple, often inconsistent goals. Boyd (1979a: 13), for example, suggests:

> New goals are acquired even while the established goals are retained. Expectations for the role of the schools seem to expand continuously. The school is asked to be an engine for progress and reform, but at the same time is always expected to maintain society. Thus, by a process of accretion, goals proliferate and increasingly compete with one another for scarce resources.

Elboim-Dror (1970: 240) also notes a lack of priorities: There is no

> hierarchy of goals, subgoals and intermediate goals . . . means-end chains or even a sequence of subgoals. Without such chains no systematic or logical order of goal priorities is possible.

She suggests that this occurs, in part, because

> while in other organizations people are concerned more about the outcomes of policy formation than the premises on which decisions are made, in education their main concern is with whose values, preferences and subjective experiences will prevail. The intrinsic quality of the goals, rather than their utility, becomes the issue. Because of the need for consensus, the education policy formation system, through the process of bargaining, adopts different and conflicting goals [Elboim-Dror, 1970: 239].

As Elboim-Dror notes, goal conflict is in part muted, blurred, and accommodated through the convenient device of goal diffuseness and ambiguity. But such blurring, like goal conflict itself, makes it more likely that schools will not focus squarely on the core-task horn of the dilemma.

2. Goal displacement. Many observers have noted that goal ambiguity leads to preoccupation with other issues. Willower (1970), for example, says that internal controls fashioned to constrain and channel student behavior are a prime feature of school organization. Routines and rules abound and assume a preeminent place in the life of the school. Control goals readily become ends in themselves rather than means.... Goal displacement is facilitated by the difficulty of showing goal achievement.

Hawley (1975: 192) also proposes that difficulties in output assessment lead organizational members to

[define] the processes that are intuitively related to output and measure the effectiveness of workers in terms of their deviances from these processes ... [and to] emphasize those activities that appear to be most readily measured, whether or not those activities are central to the function of the enterprise.

Niedermeyer (1979: 20) also notes school emphasis on

the "programs," "approaches," "materials" or "innovations" [schools] are currently implementing and using. ... The universal assumption seems to be that activity means learning, yet rarely is the amount of actual learning ever assessed and determined. It simply is assumed.

The most thorough discussion of goal displacement is by Elboim-Dror (1970), who suggests with some documentation that schools tend to shift their energies from intangible, hard-to-measure goals toward goals that are (1) action-oriented, procedural; (2) measurable (for example, cognitive rather than affective); and (3) instrumental. But she notes that the most widespread form of goal displacement is toward organizational maintenance and growth.

3. Input focus. Weisbord (1978), in doing some comparative organizational analysis from the standpoint of a professional change agent, suggests that systems with hard-to-measure goals (such as universities) divert their attention away from output toward inputs, particularly admission of staff.

We might predict that schools would also pay more attention to their inputs in the form of students (and their associated parents), than to core tasks. There are some data suggesting this clearly. The recent national study of high schools by Abramowitz and Tenenbaum (1978) asked principals about the seriousness of various problems. The most frequently mentioned problems checked (by from 30 to 90 percent) were "parents' lack of involvement in school matters," "student apathy," "parents' lack of interest in school matters," "student absenteeism," "students' cutting classes," and "student disruption."[4] Items such as "teacher incompetence" (5 percent), "inadequate instructional materials" (10 percent), and even "teacher lack of commitment" (15 percent) lagged far behind. In other words, students (and their parents), not the school itself, are the main difficulty. Similarly, the 1979 national teacher opinion poll conducted by the NEA (Teacher Education Reports, 1979), found that the changes in schools favored by the majority of teachers were:

Reducing class size.

Educating parents in how to help with their children's education.

Enforcing stricter discipline.

Devoting more attention to the "basics."

Enforcing stricter attendance requirements.

Requiring higher standards for student performance.

Of these, only two ("basics," and "higher standards") refer directly to the performance of core tasks: the remainder are input matters. Furthermore, a majority of teachers did *not* favor such changes as:

Wider range and variety of courses.

Added extracurricular activities.

So emphasis on inputs rather than on core task accomplishment has some empirical support.

4. Symbolic/ceremonial success criteria. Some analysts suggest that schools continue to flourish in their environments through emphasis on what Boyd (1979b) calls the "symbolic politics of efficiency," by presenting a well-managed impression of a "quality school." Meyer and Rowan (1978) go further: They propose that schools have successfully defined themselves as presiding over the "ceremonial enactment of the rituals of schooling," which involve, essentially, the classification of students, subject matter, teachers, and schools. "Education is a certified teacher teaching a standardized curricular topic to a registered student in an accredited school" (Meyer and Rowan, 1978: 94). In this view, schools gain their legitimacy and support not by efforts to achieve core educative goals, or even by cutting costs, but by becoming isomorphic with the legal and normative rules of society, and (in effect) substituting clear success criteria for cloudy ones: goal displacement at a grand level. Thus stated, the argument is hard to disprove. But one cannot escape some questions: If symbolic/ceremonial success criteria are so central, how does it happen that so much energy goes into "the evaluation industry," various "accountability" schemes, development of behavioral objectives, and indeed the widespread use of achievement testing itself? One can dismiss these phenomena as themselves symbolic, but that is a tautological escape: one can also claim that they are "decoupled" from actual school operations (an issue to which we will return below). In any case, the presence of symbolic and ceremonially driven *judgments* about the achievement of core tasks (as contrasted with actual energy placed on *achieving* core tasks) is undeniable in general terms.

CLAIMED ANTECEDENTS

What might plausibly cause such regularities (assuming for the moment that they may be present in many or most schools)? Here we are on tenuous ground, because most causal claims are (a) asserted, not shown empirically, and (b) embedded (as we have already seen) in a complex network of variables largely unique to the particular analyst at hand. The discussion will only list various causal claims, labeled as "inherent" or "historically derived" properties of schools.

1. Goal measurement difficulty. Because schools are officially aimed at bringing about change in people, it is often noted (Miles, 1965, 1967; Sieber, 1968; Hawley, 1975) that their goals are inherently diffuse, vague, nontangible, and therefore hard to measure. The "inherentness" of this property can be questioned, as Meyer and Rowan (1978: 88) noted:

> The view that education . . . lacks output measures is misdirected. Schools use elaborate tests to evaluate pupils and to shape the course of their present and future lives. But the same data are almost never aggregated and used to evaluate the performance of teachers, schools or school systems.

But even if one takes the view that measurability exists, or that "output measurement difficulty . . . seems to be a form of organizational defense or protection against criticism" (Miles, 1965), there is still plenty of room for goal indeterminacy in the mission of schools,[5] and it is reasonable to conclude (as do many of the authors just cited) that it causes goal displacement, input focus, and symbolic evaluation.

2. Value-laden character of goals. Because schools are people-changing systems, their goals cannot be articulated on narrowly technical, pragmatic, or obvious grounds, but involve normative and ideological choices. Is more emphasis to be put on "the basics" or other matters? How important are affective outcomes? How about scientific literacy? Good citizenship? At a more general level, it is often asserted that schools' goals are basically those of sorting or allocating students to the various levels of society (Meyer and Rowan, 1977) and providing minimum necessary socialization (achievement motivation, punctuality, and so on), or simply serving an essentially custodial function (Spence et al., 1978), meanwhile keeping older children conveniently out of the labor market. In sum, the goals of schools, manifest and latent, represent a sort of multilevel value tangle, and goal conflict is thereby claimed as inevitable.

3. Compulsory attendance. The core task of schools must, since the advent of laws in the late nineteenth century requiring school attendance, be carried out with all children up to a particular age. The primary clients of schools must present themselves for processing, whether or not they want to (Willower, forthcoming). Furthermore, from the school's standpoint, no selection of clients is possible. There is, thus, a two-way compulsion, in which students (except for wealthy ones) cannot exercise the "exit option" (Hawley, 1976) and the school cannot slough off students who are reluctant, intractable, stupid, or disruptive.[6]

This historical feature of schools seems like a plausible cause of the "input focus" noted earlier, as well as of goal displacement: With unselected, unwilling clients, as Willower (1970) suggests, attention shifts away from "education" to matters of behavioral control, tracking, batch processing—themselves, Meyer and Rowan (1978) propose, aimed as much at image management for the school's external audience as at managing learners.

4. Vulnerability. American schools were constitutionally defined as to be managed by the states; the states in turn have traditionally given de facto power to local communities. The "vulnerability" theme will be discussed more fully later; here we should only note that schools in this country, to a far greater extent than (say) in most Western European countries, are influenceable by local citizen pressure. As Willower (forthcoming) notes:

> In the most general terms, the school is seen as vulnerable to external environmental pressures, and to internal strains generated by the number and variety of clients to be served and the reluctance of some of them concerning the service. In consequence, a wide range of adaptive structures protect the organization and its adult members. . . . Such structures channel variety and threat . . . uncertainty is reduced.

It does seem reasonable to conclude that phenomena such as goal displacement, goal conflict, and symbolic evaluation of school efforts cannot be derived wholly from goal measurement difficulty or the presence of compulsory clients, but are in part a result of school vulnerability; schools well-buffered from citizen control would presumably need to devote less attention to political issues and image management, and could put more emphasis on delivering educational services. However, the argument is not wholly compelling: Most observers would agree that urban schools have far less vigorous parent participation than suburban ones, but the energy devoted to bureaucratic and political matters remains substantial.

KNOWLEDGE GAPS

The discussion in this section has summarized claims that schools, in the domain covered by the "core task versus survival" dilemma, lean toward the survival horn; they tend to show goal conflict and goal displacement, are more preoccupied with their inputs than their outputs, and manage their environments via "ceremonial/ritual" presentations. These phenomena, say some analysts, are generated by the difficult-to-measure, value-laden character of schools' goals, as well as by the historically given facts of compulsory attendance and local control.

1. Assessment of causal claims. Firmer empirical data on all these regularities (except, perhaps, for input focus) would be welcome. The causal claims, in particular, should be assessed for their validity. For example, in states where goal measurement difficulty has been (somewhat) reduced through accountability and minimum competency mandates, is there any evidence of reduced displacement of goals away from core task accomplishment?

2. Extent of practical goal consensus. Most education systems are careful to have a set of publicly stated goals. But what working de facto (or surrogate) goals really guide day-to-day effort—not only in the accomplishment of core tasks, but in system integration and relation to the immediate and distal environments?

3. Comparative studies of vulnerability. We know little about vulnerability and its consequences for core task focus. Partly, the concept itself is woolly; it seems to refer variously to how far the school can be influenced by its environment; to whether that influence is predictable or uncertain; and to the insecurity of specific role inhabitants. Once the concept is unpacked, comparative studies would be useful: states with vigorously versus weakly enforced mandates for various changes; states with strong local influence structures (such as California) versus others; districts of comparable wealth which have had sustained, predictable community support versus those where capriciousness has reigned. In all such comparisons, what relative balance between core task emphasis and bureaucratic/political emphasis seems to be present?

Dilemma 2:
Diversity versus Uniformity

At the classroom level, people in schools must decide how far to try to meet the individual, diverse needs of students, using the diverse, individual skills of teachers—as opposed to an equitable, efficient, uniform approach that meets expected standards of quality. The socialization of children in part demands "universalistic," impersonal treatment of learners (who have to learn that the world does not revolve around their infant wishes, and that their teachers are not their fathers and mothers), and in part demands the evocation of children's uniqueness, the development of particular potential, and an affective bond between teacher and student. At the organization level, there is a similar tension: Should each teacher be free to use any text, or should there be schoolwide concurrence? The conflict is between "Let a hundred flowers bloom" and "If I do it for you, I'll have to do it for everyone."

REGULARITIES NOTED

1. Structural supports for uniform treatment. Certain aspects of American schools are so "obvious" that their role in supporting uniform treatment of students often escapes notice. For example, students are age-graded, though the range of intellectual and social competence in almost any group of 10-year olds may include students who think and act like 7-year olds and 15-year olds. Nominal efforts to deal with such diversity through the medium of ability grouping and vocational tracking (Packard, 1977) are nearly universal, but as Carlson (1964) points out, they often result in "segregation" of different classes of learners (for instance, vocational programs are used as "dumping grounds") and in preferential treatment (more favoring of middle-class students). Most observers of schools would agree that the majority of instruction takes place in a "batch processing" mode rather than in small groups, one-to-one tutoring, or individual work.[7] (However, it should be noted that firm data on this are rarely cited.)

Other structural supports favoring the uniformity horn of the dilemma appear closer to the school's core technology: instruction. As Packard asserts (1977: 25) in his fascinating analysis of the school as a "work organization" (in contrast with the school viewed as a client-serving organization or a bureaucracy):

One of the most striking features about the school work place is that the students are usually assigned to groups which may remain intact for various periods depending on the manner of sub-batching. Work is assigned *en masse* and in parallel. Members of a pupil batch receive the same instructions on task completion at the same time. Each member of the group is usually assigned the same task, which each is expected to complete individually.

Packard notes, however, that because of "loose coupling" this standardization of assignments to batch members does not apply to the adjacent work role, that of teachers.

What has constantly surprised classroom observers are the differences in classroom management, particularly how teachers develop different tasks for themselves and their students and how they distribute time among them [Packard, 1977: 32].

Packard quotes Meyer and Cohen (1971) as wryly noting that "the student is the only class of employee for whom the school can be regarded as a bureaucracy." The image is thus one of a diverse set of subsystems (classrooms) within each of which a good deal of uniformity and standardization exists for students.

Finally, schools are environments closely regulated by time schedules: As Jackson (1968) notes, "School is the place where things often happen not because students want them to happen, but because it is time for them to occur"; and as Spence et al. (1978) emphasize, "Where a teacher or a student should be at any given time of the school day is unambiguously prescribed." Abramowitz and Tenenbaum's (1978) national study of high schools found that 93 percent used traditional 35- to 60-minute periods; only 1 to 2 percent used more diversity-responsive methods such as modular, flexible, or demand scheduling, or use of large time blocks.

2. Minimal use of learner-responsive technologies. It is often suggested that schools do not use instructional methods which are aimed at "individualization," respecting the diversity of student attributes. For example, Sarason (1971) reports a study finding that elementary teachers asked 45-150 questions of students (usually with a "fact" answer expected) in a typical half-hour, while students (in the *aggregate*) asked only 2 questions. Havelock et al. (1973), in their national survey of innovations, found that only 15 percent of superintendents reported use of "individualization and team teaching." Giacquinta and Kazlow (1979) found that 61 percent of school systems in a national sample had never tried "open education" (including such features as "diverse materials and activities," "pupil progression at their own pace," and "children free to move about the school"), and another 22 percent had reduced or discontinued their first efforts in this direction. Only 13 percent had a stable first effort, and 5 percent showed an increase.

Data from Abramowitz and Tenenbaum's (1978) study of high schools at first glance look somewhat more supportive of diversity: They found that 87 percent of schools offered the individual need-meeting feature of remedial instruction, 65 percent offered early graduation, and 37 percent had alternative programs. However, if individualization is defined more crisply, we note that only 23 percent used "individually paced learning" and 11 percent "diagnostic prescriptive education." And although nearly all schools had students working off campus (work experience, volunteer work, study projects, and so on), such potentially individualized experiences were only available for a few students (9 percent of eleventh graders, and 16 percent of twelfth graders).

3. Preoccupation with student control. Many observers have focused on this as a central feature of schools. Willower (1970), who has written widely on pupil control as a central feature of schools, suggests:

> Internal controls fashioned to constrain and channel student behavior are a prime feature of school organization. Routines and rules abound and assume a preeminent place in the life of the school. Control goals readily become ends in themselves, rather than means.

Lortie (1977b: 27) notes that compulsion begins with required attendance; this along with financing based on "average daily attendance" leads to:

> an elaborate apparatus of registers, hall passes, medical excuses, and attendance officers. Teachers and school administrators take on, willy-nilly, some of the functions of prison guards, finding that much time is spent on non-instructional activities.

Packard (1977: 33) suggests:

> Control of student behavior is a dominant school theme. Supervision is tight in the classroom and often in other areas of the school as well. Principals and teachers are sometimes stationed in hallways while students are changing rooms. Close scrutiny is often given in the lunch room and in the auditorium. Even after-school events require supervision.

And in the classroom (especially in grades 5 and upward), Packard (1977) says:

> students, irrespective of their group assignment, are treated as low-level workers. They are assigned work and closely supervised. They have little or no autonomy over task selection, work pace, work locus, acceptable levels of production and work quality. They have little freedom of movement. They are expected to adhere to a fixed schedule of school and classroom activities [p. 12].

> Students are told not only what they are to do, but often are also instructed in the manner in which they are to complete the work, including when, where, and at what level of proficiency [p. 15].

Lest it be thought that control of students is restricted to rambunctious adolescents, we should note that Giacquinta and Kazlow (1979) found in their national study of elementary-level open education that only 24 percent of respondents thought their school systems accepted the idea that "pupils should make key decisions about learning," 22 percent accepted "pupil self-grouping according to interests," and 9 percent accepted "pupil-determined activities with no fixed timetables."

The NEA's 1979 nationwide teacher opinion poll found almost unanimous agreement that "enforcing stricter discipline" was a needed change in schools, and gave "discipline" top priority as a research topic.

The empirical data from Abramowitz and Tenenbaum (1978) are instructive: Only 7 percent of high school principals say that "student disruptiveness" is a serious problem. A possible reason for this can be seen in the fact that control through rules is very typical. For example, 73 percent formally require hall passes, 58 percent require students to stay on campus at lunch time, 82 percent make students responsible for property damage, and 69 percent have formal rules requiring teachers to handle discipline problems within their classes (another 24 percent said this was informally the case). For contrast, we might note that only 7 percent of principals said there were formal rules controlling the amount of homework given students, and 31 percent mentioned rules governing student dress, a matter which once exercised administrators and teachers mightily.

Even though assertions about student control are often polemical and deploring in tone, there are enough empirical data to support the generalization that student behavior is rather closely regulated most of the time in schools, with student choice over immediate activities generally minimized.[8]

4. Increase in bureaucratization. Many analysts have suggested that schools in America became bureaucracies in the late nineteenth century, and have become more "bureaucratic" over the last hundred years. The label usually alludes to features such as increased division of labor and complexity, a more substantial managerial role, and increased routinization, formalization, and objectification of rules and policies guiding decisions.

Revisionist critics such as Katz (1975) have suggested that the bureaucratization of American schools was a process engaged in by administrators in order to serve elite interests and maintain the existing inequities of the social structure. Bureaucracy is seen as a "crystallization of bourgeois social values." These views have been sharply countered by Michaelson (1977), who points out that large changes in bureaucratization occurred primarily as a result of compulsory education legislation advocated by teachers and administrators (up to then paid by individual parent billing) to establish their financial security. Schooling by the mid-nineteenth century was in fact nearly universal, though not free or compulsory.

> Full tax and compulsion firmly established the power of common school administrators and, in a different way, teachers over parents and children. Indeed, they created the essential conditions for insulating school management from citizens generally; namely, the assurance of a budget independent of satisfied consumers [Michaelson, 1977: 236].

Michaelson (1977: 239) continues, noting that

> we may assume that bureaucrats, including schoolmen, seek . . . to survive, to enlarge the scope of their activities, to gain prestige, to avoid conflict, to control the organization and content of their daily round as much as possible. . . . By accepting this theory of motivation, we do not rule out altruism. Administrators and teachers, like entrepreneurs, take pride in their work and strive for excellence. . . . Each bureaucrat, then, will seek in good faith to maximize the activities over which he has control.

So, although explanations differ rather substantially, both authors are agreed that bureaucratization (that is, the emergence of modern organizations) has occurred in schools.

Has it in fact advanced? The answer is undoubtedly positive, even without extensive retrieval of empirical data. Features such as the steady consolidation of school districts; the increased size of schools and school districts; the professionalization of administrators; the application of "scientific management" procedures from business after World War I (and of management-systems thinking currently as well); the emergence of a wide range of administrative roles unheard of even twenty years ago (from federal projects officer to director of organization development); the growth of civil service examinations for administrative and teaching positions; and the detailed formulation of policies and operating rules are familiar indicators.

But do schools actually operate like traditional bureaucracies, or should they be construed in other terms? The issue here is perhaps less empirical and more a matter of what frames are most fruitful and explanatory. Hanson (1978), for example, suggests that traditional bureaucratic theory needs modification: Presence of professionals means that the organization should be seen as including two authority structures—with a balance of power between teachers and administrators—each with its sphere of influence. The growth of collective bargaining has, if anything, eroded administrative power, he claims. Analyses offered by Bidwell (1965) and Corwin (1971) also stress the conflict between professional and bureaucratic modes of operation.

The Abramowitz and Tenenbaum (1978) study found a good deal of evidence that high schools' structure and coordination mechanisms were not like those of traditional bureaucracies. Staffing patterns were relatively noncomplex (for example: 60 percent had only one assistant principal; 45 percent had only one specialist or counselor; 40 percent had fewer than 9 subject matter departments). Principals claimed that their own roles were not narrowly conceived in authoritative terms, that there was widespread participation by teachers and specialists in decision making (a topic we shall return to), and that they considered their collegial role very important (83 percent mentioned work with teachers on instruction), along with their "ambassadorial" role (74 percent mentioned "relating personally with parents and community"), and their strictly managerial role (76 percent mentioned "enforcing school rules and policies").

Furthermore, principals spent very little time actually observing teachers: 55 percent said they were in classrooms once a month or less (since the average school in the study had 47 teachers, any given teacher was probably seen no more frequently than the once-a-year evaluation required in most schools.) These data lead the authors to propose a "loose coupling" model as more appropriate than a bureaucratic one.

As we have seen, Spence et al. (1978: 15) offer a strong critique of loose coupling formulations, arguing that teachers' classroom behavior is narrowly prescribed and highly institutionalized. They cite direct and indirect controls which regulate the behavior of the teacher in the classroom—scheduling, record keeping, resource allocation, hiring and firing, and certification.

They doubt that "teachers have more than an ordinary range of bureaucratic discretion in carrying out their duties." Using Weber's image of the "iron cage," they point out that

> a person can be in a cage without being constantly under observation or supervision. Indeed, the point of the cage is to make such actions unnecessary. . . . The cage does the regulation of the person continuously, impersonally, unobtrusively until it becomes to its occupant a part of the facts of life [Spence et al., 1978: 21-22].

They suggest that "the cage" consists of the teacher's required order-maintaining presence at specific times and places, along with records, lesson plans, and so on, and conclude that schools are indeed bureaucracies, though they have been "radically changed" from service organizations carrying out teaching to custodial processing systems. Once again we should note that empirical data to support these claims are thin.[9]

CLAIMED ANTECEDENTS

Generally speaking, we have noted that, when the diversity versus uniformity dilemma is considered, schools are seen to contain many structural supports for uniform treatment of students (and teachers); that technology supportive of particularistic attention to learners tends to be under-used; that much emphasis is placed on control of students; and that schools (with some qualifications) exhibit many of the features of bureaucracies. What historical or "inherent" properties of schools are claimed to cause these regularities?

1. Output measurement difficulty. As with the earlier discussion, it is claimed that features such as routinization and standardization can be traced to the presence of "hard-to-measure" goals (Hawley, 1975). The claim is not a very strong one, however, since (for example) profit-making organizations do not show perceptibly less routinization than schools.

2. Large numbers of clients. It is more plausibly claimed that the sheer presence of many learners generates both uniform treatment and a strong control orientation (Sieber, this volume; Willower, 1970; Carlson, 1964.) The presence of many learners is said to stem from the passage of compulsory education laws. Yet we note with Michaelson (1977) that prior to the passage of compulsory education legislation, schools were, for practical purposes, universal (90 percent of students attending) *and* less bureaucratized than they shortly became.

3. Vested interests of employees. Michaelson's (1977: 240-241) view is that routinization and uniformity were (and are) essentially driven by the security needs of teachers and administrators, in conjunction with the presence of numbers of students:

> A process of bargaining between the teachers and their principals and between the principals and the central administration leads to

reasonably acceptable arrangements for all concerned. The needs of teachers and principals for control over their jobs most often take precedence over the needs of individual children and their families. . . . This bargain, insuring to the district's employees significant independent influence over the internal agenda, is the central feature of the school bureaucracy. . . . The easiest way for a teacher to manage 20 or more students, given the bargain just described— which precludes, among other things, material rewards for superior performance—is to treat them all alike when, of course, they are often quite different from each other.

4. Immaturity of clients. Still other observers suggest that uniformity and control orientation occur because students, after all, are less than adult. Lortie (1977b: 27) notes that

children and adolescents . . . are not yet mature. In some respects teachers are trying to get regular work from irregular workers while teaching those who are still trying to learn. In other words, we can think of school professionals as making up the "deficit" in self-control, work motivation, learning skills, etc., among their students. . . . Because students are normally in groups, the particular immaturities of some children may force procedures on all that prove alienating; for example, to maintain order, teachers may be forced to become more austere than they wish to be.

And just as elementary schoolchildren supposedly need to be controlled and managed uniformly because they are "too young," we can note that adolescents deserve the same treatment because they are not quite so young; their *ressentiment* and mobilization against the teacher subculture (Willower, 1971) must be warded off.

More generally, if the social function of schools is essentially custodial, as Spence et al. (1978) propose, and as Meyer and Rowan (1977, 1978) also suggest, then uniform treatment is much more likely than if instruction is the core social purpose.

5. Client motivation problems. Sieber's chapter (this volume) proposes that the involuntary presence of clients requires arrangements (such as tracking) to cope with the fact that not all students want to learn. More generally, Packard (1977: 7) notes that though

work motivations may vary considerably from individual to individual . . . the inflow of student motivation is decidedly uneven from time to time and across individual students. . . . Students may also "spend" their motivation on other commodities available in society and so reduce the supply available for school work. Otherwise, students may simply withhold this resource. Student work motivation represents the most obvious resource for which schools must compete with other, sometimes unknown rivals. As schools have little or no jurisdiction over their competitors or parents the supply of student motivation is a problematic issue.

Packard suggests that schools, because of the delayed rewards society offers for student productivity (college admission, jobs), cope through the creation of standardized grading systems (which are, however, counter-productive, since low grades are usually awarded to the least motivated students, reducing their motivation still further).

KNOWLEDGE GAPS

In the general domain covered by what we have labeled the diversity-uniformity dilemma, what are the main uncertainties and empty spaces?

1. Actual instructional modes. We do not know, in any systematic way, what instructional modes are occurring, on a day-to-day basis, across a well-drawn sample of American schools. How much time is actually given to large group instruction? To small group work? To one-on-one tutoring? To individual effort? And one step finer: In, for example, the case of individual effort, what proportion of students is engaging in a mass-assigned task, as opposed to one tailored to individual needs? There is a great deal of rhetoric about "individualization" in schools, but we do not have good baseline data on what is actually occurring. Such analyses should of course be broken by school level, or perhaps by the "phases" Packard (1977) suggests: "nurturant" (grades 1 to 4 or so), "basic work" (grades 4 to 8 or so), and "pre-occupational" (grades 9 to 12).

2. Relations to innovativeness. We also need studies of whether, and how, the uniformity/diversity dimension is related to school innovative-ness. Corwin (1975), for example, found that *less* standardized (rule-oriented, uniform procedure-using) schools in his sample of 131 were more likely to be innovative. But Kelly (1977), looking at 30 urban high schools, found that *more* formalized, more standardized schools were more likely to be innovative. The difference may come from the fact that Kelly asked specifically for *curriculum*-relevant organizational formaliza-tion. Or it may come from the fact that Kelly's sample members also reported high correlations between formalization and their degree of *participation* in curriculum change efforts. Kelly's view is that the presence of clear working structures, when accompanied by participative effort, "decreases role ambiguity and conflict and lead[s] to higher rates of curriculum innovation." Perhaps the most parsimonious hypothesis is that routinization and uniformity in schools can be used as a platform for innovation, or to block change efforts, depending on the ideology and commitments of the staff.

3. Relation to effectiveness. Finally, we need to know how routiniza-tion and diversity are associated with school *effectiveness* (an issue, in spite of shortcut assumptions to the contrary, that can be examined independently of the innovativeness question). Here there is some evidence that a coherent, somewhat formalized organizational structure makes for better school output. Miskel (1979), in a study of 125 schools, found that more effective schools (as identified by teachers) had more formalized general rules, more complexity (high professional activity), along with more participative, less centralized power structures (a finding reminiscent of Kelly's).

Rutter et al.'s (1979) longitudinal study of urban London high schools found that more effective schools (as measured by exam passing, better student behavior, and less delinquency) had many features that added up to organizational coherence (routinization): There were high expectations for students, homework was regularly assigned and read, students had "quasi-supervisory" positions, punishment was fair and consistent, teachers knew that heads would check on homework assigned, and teachers engaged in joint planning.

The message may simply be that a "better organized" system is more likely to deliver the goods. Still, much remains ambiguous: As with innovativeness, we do not really know which sorts of choices toward the routine horn of the dilemma support and encourage school productivity, and which sorts bring about the standardizing, dulling effects of schooling decried by generations of reformers.

Dilemma 3:
Coordination versus Flexibility

Should the various parts of a school (and the parts of a district called schools) be coherently, carefully, and rationally knitted together, or does it make more sense to allow autonomy and flexibility to the parts? Tightly coupled coordination means knowing what and how things are happening in a system, and enables quick coping when things go awry. But loose coupling takes less energy, permits more innovation, and is less vulnerable to incompetence (for example, one poor teacher in a self-contained classroom doesn't damage the whole school) and environmental threat. The coordination/flexibility dilemma poses the questions of how much autonomy and latitude individuals and units should have, how much surveillance and control should be present in the system, and how much intervention should occur from "outside" when people are implementing a new program or policy.[10]

REGULARITIES NOTED

1. Influence discontinuities. Several analysts have noted that the operation of schools seems best explained by the idea that there are separate "spheres of influence." Hanson (1975), for example, describes the existence of "two authority structures," in the hands of administrators and teachers, respectively. In a case study of four schools in one district, Hanson (1978) extended the idea to that of "interacting spheres" of influence: Principals wanted to preserve schoolwide decisions dealing with attendance, budget, facilities use, mandated curriculum, and the like; teachers wished to keep power over issues such as department spending, department-head hiring, in-class discipline, course content, and instructional methods. In the "contested" area between the overlapping spheres, teachers and administrators struggled over such issues as schedule preparation, large-scale innovations, and performance of tenured teachers. Own spheres were defined through a variety of informal means (such as the "pocket veto" through inaction, and the use of temporary coalitions). Hanson noted tighter "coupling" between spheres under conditions of crisis, environmental threat, or time pressure.

Deal and Nutt (1979), in their analysis of rural school systems, invoke the "zones" idea, suggesting that schools operate through the overlapping/ interacting contact among "administrative," "instructional," "local" (parents, residents, associations), and "remote" (county, state, and federal governments, universities, and so on) zones. Meyer et al. (1978) pointed to the ways in which teachers and principals are separated by jurisdictional boundaries. In a substudy of 16 elementary schools, focusing on how the teaching of reading was organized, they found fairly close teacher/ principal agreement on such matters as budget details and the materials being used, but very little agreement on such matters as how discipline was handled, pupil assignment, and evaluation. Meyer et al. (1978: 252-253) suggest:

> They agree in general on their roles, but they seem to have little agreement on specifics within each school. They also apparently agreed that what each one does within his or her own jurisdiction is by and large not the other's business. And they apparently agree that their jurisdictions do not overlap very much.

Firestone and Herriott (1980) found, in a study of 13 elementary, junior high, and high schools, that control over organizational decisions was "zoned," with teachers having almost complete say over daily lesson plans and activities, but limited or no influence over decisions such as hiring new teachers, setting salary schedules, or assigning extra duties.

These views of "zones," "spheres," and "jurisdictions"[11] all tend to share a conception of the school as a negotiated order among conflicting interests, most typically those of administrators and teachers; the general problem is how "professionals" with larger loyalties can function effectively in a "bureaucratic" organization (see Corwin, 1965, 1971; Bidwell, 1965). As we shall see, the view is not incongruent with more radically phrased "loose coupling" formulations, but there is a real difference between a conflict/struggle model and a decoupled, anarchic model. Which is a better fit to "the facts" is an open question.

2. Low interdependence. Many analysts have noted that schools' parts do not seem to need or influence each other. Meyer et al. (1978: 235), for example, assert:

> Schools as districts are not made up of specialized, functionally interdependent components but of relatively distinct and functional[ly] similar ones.

They supply data from 188 elementary schools, in 34 districts. Essentially there are very low rates of agreement in descriptions of policy and practice regarding the teaching of reading between principals and superintendents, among principals in the same district, between teachers and principals in the same school, and among teachers in the same school.[12] For example, though teachers' and principals' answers on number of teacher aides in the school correlated .93, the figure was only .09 when the issue was how often reading group membership changed over time.

And even though Lortie (1975) claims that district central offices provide limits and boundaries for school functioning, Meyer et al. (1978) found only weak agreement between superintendents and principals, even on such specific matters as how frequently schools are evaluated by the district office ($r = .45$, accounting for only 20 percent of the variance).

Packard (1977) suggests that teachers operate according to a "basic rule . . . only one teacher will supervise a given student in a designated subject area at a time," and cites data from Charters and Jones (1975) that suggest that this holds true even for teaching teams which are nominally interdependent.

Low interdependence does not seem to lead to anarchy (Meyer and Rowan, 1977; Willower, 1979), and it is dubious that the "garbage can" model of Cohen et al. (1972; fluid participation of decision makers, "solutions looking for problems," and so on) applies to schools in the way it may to universities. As Meyer et al. (1978) suggest, the institutionalized aspects of schools supply some stability and predictability. But, on balance, the operations of teachers, departments, grade levels, and schools within a district do not seem to share a common fate: When a role occupant fails to do something, or succeeds in doing something, the implications for others are minimal. As a clincher, we might note that Abramowitz and Tenenbaum (1978) found that in larger, more complexly structured high schools, interdependent structures (such as rules, meetings, personnel evaluation, or collaborative arrangements) were *not* found more frequently than in smaller, simpler schools.

It can be variously argued that low interdependence in schools is a good thing (it permits innovation and protects the organization against the spread of failure in a particular part); that the "undifferentiated cellular structure" (Lortie, 1977a) permits, somehow, a "federation of effort"; or that it retards knowledge utilization (Fullan, this volume). These claims are more difficult to assess than the basic one of low interdependence itself.

3. Low surveillance and control. Many assertions and some evidence support the idea that the core technology of schools is not scrutinized by anyone with power to alter its operations. (Students see teaching all the time, but their right to supply feedback or counterinfluence is very much in doubt.) As we have noted, Meyer and Rowan (1977) suggest that "inspection, evaluation, and control of activities are minimized" as institutionalized organizations such as schools seek to "protect their formal structures from evaluation." Hawley (1975) makes a similar claim. Packard (1977: 24) notes:

> Administrators have been associated with responsibility for supervising teachers. This broadly shared misconception is held by administrators, students, and others. The fact of the matter is that elementary administrators rarely supervise teachers. . . . Secondary administrators probably do not display any greater proclivity to supervise teachers.

Packard does cite supporting data for these conclusions, and also quotes a number of studies, concluding:

> Administrators rarely intercede in classroom affairs, especially in ways that serve to alter and standardize teacher behavior. While we

lack evidence on the subject, one would guess that . . . school principals are rarely, if ever, supervised by their organizational superiors,
and that they may vary as much in their behaviors and attitudes as
teachers do in their separate classrooms [p. 32].

We can also note the previously cited finding (Abramowitz and Tenenbaum, 1978) that 55 percent of high school principals studied said they
were in classrooms once a month or less. Department heads, who might be
expected to observe teachers more closely, actually participated in teacher
evaluation in only about 25 percent of schools.

So teachers, freed from inspection, supposedly have a good deal of
discretionary power over what happens in the classroom. The question of
whether they *actually* do (or are indeed hedged in with strong cultural/
institutional expectations, and/or rule-bound specifications of what they
must do, when, where, and with whom) is, as we have seen, somewhat
ambiguous.

It should be said in passing that the presence of low surveillance and
control need not at all imply administrative indifference or irrationality.
Meyer and Rowan (1977) stress the presence of a "logic of confidence and
good faith" as an essential feature of an unmonitored enterprise. And
Lortie (1977a), following Thompson (1967), suggests that schools, like
most organizations, need to buffer their core technologies from close
external inspection. Administrators who seek to protect teachers from
parental criticism and pressure are, in a real sense, in a better position to
do so if they themselves know little of what is actually going on in the
classroom.

4. Teacher isolation. The natural concomitant of low surveillance
(whether or not it is accompanied by low control) is isolation. Teaching, as
Charters and Packard (1979) point out, has classically been a solitary
undertaking. Lortie (1977a) has argued that the "egg-crate" architecture
of the school and its one-teacher-one-class deployment pattern has led to a
situation in which teachers are "time and place bound—during working
hours, they have very little physical mobility and few occasions for joint
undertakings." Lortie also speaks of the "privatizing" that such isolation
engenders, the idea that teaching becomes more and more a performance
shaped by the unique aspects of particular teachers. Lieberman (1977) and
Lieberman and Miller (1979) also make a case for the idea that teaching
becomes, over time, a more and more personalistic, idiosyncratic (and
therefore variable) matter.

Packard (1977: 32), citing Meyer and Cohen (1971) and Pellegrin
(1976), suggests that teaching is essentially "idiosyncratic specialization":

> The similarities that exist in the behavior and attitudes of teachers
> even in the same school seem to be more a result of local, informal
> socialization processes and common professional training experi-
> ences. What has consistently surprised classroom observers are the
> differences in classroom management, particularly how teachers
> develop different tasks for themselves and their students, and how
> they distribute time among them.

Paul (1977: 48), in his review of studies of change, reached a similar conclusion:

> Teacher autonomy, lack of interdependence among teachers, vague educational goals, and satisfaction based on student rather than adult contact act together to promote a classroom-centered orientation.

Packard et al. (1978), in their longitudinal study of 450 teachers in 29 elementary schools, 16 of which were implementing the IGE version of the multiunit plan (involving team teaching and collegial decision making), found that prior to implementation of the IGE approach only about 6 percent of decisions about instructional processes were made collegially; most were reserved for individual discretion. That can be seen as a measure of teacher autonomy, but its correlate might well be isolation.

In summary, the available evidence suggests that schools have discontinuities of influence among various participants, relatively low amounts of required interdependence, rare occasions of direct viewing (or control) of work performance by superiors (or peers), and a fair degree of isolation from adult contact. So the evidence is strongly weighted toward the "flexibility," not the "coordination" horn of the dilemma.

CLAIMED ANTECEDENTS

What might presumably generate such phenomena? They do appear, in fact, to be relatively durable. Packard et al. (1978) found that the IGE program—an innovation essentially aimed at increasing teacher interdependence—did, over a two-year period, increase the proportion of collegially made instructional decisions from about 9 percent to 18 percent, and the proportion of teacher-deployment decisions from 30 percent to 43 percent.[13] Yet 62 percent of instructional decisions were *still* made by teachers at their discretion, and 36 percent of deployment decisions were still made by the principal alone. Packard et al. also remark that the response to the IGE innovation "seemed to hinge upon immutable characteristics of the schools" (such as low interdependence, uncodified, decentralized control, and cultural definitions of "teacher work") more than upon the change strategies employed. They also noted that "within-school participation in instructional interdependence seemed to be highly spontaneous and voluntaristic," with "little stability in the work relationships among teachers."[14]

This finding is also echoed by Deal and Celotti (1977: 11), reporting on the Stanford studies of open-space elementary schools:

> Teacher collaboration is highly unstable over time. Teams form, dissolve and reform with variations in membership over even a two-year period. . . . Teacher teaming constitutes a very fragile set of relationships, particularly where teams are large, or where team members are highly interdependent in the sense that they engage in the joint teaching of classes or assume joint responsibility for students.

So, closely coordinative relationships tend to be precarious, as if more flexible solutions to the dilemma we are considering are somehow more "natural" or "inherent." What explanations might be offered?

1. Legitimacy maintenance. Meyer and Rowan (1978) argue that schooling, "the bureaucratic standardization of ritual classifications," needs to maintain its legitimacy in the larger society it serves, and thus decouples its work structures from its actual activities and outcomes. The decoupling is helpful because: (1) it increases commitment (avoidance of inspection implies trust and the "logic of confidence"); (2) it permits judging education "ceremonially," by how much is spent for it rather than what it does; (3) it softens the impact of "uncertainties arising in the technical core"; and (4) it permits adaptation to internal conflict among conflicting programs and roles. Basically, they claim, legitimacy is purchased by assurance that "ritual classifications" (definitions of what a teacher, a student, a course, or a school is) are being maintained effectively.

2. Custodial function of schools. Spence et al. (1978) offer a sharply countering explanation. First, they argue that so-called loose coupling phenomena are merely "administrative inattention to differences that don't make a difference, which are to be found in any regulatory system." Increased alienation in organizations (such as inability to tell whether an action is useful or meaningful, or personal detachment from work) induces a situation in which

> the willingness and ability of teachers to teach and even the time allotted to teaching activities becomes attenuated until custodial processing becomes the primary concern and activity of schools. Under these circumstances teaching activities appear to be abstractly "free" or independent of administrative surveillance [Spence et al., 1978: 24].

Spence et al. propose the "opposite" of the Meyer and Rowan formulation, suggesting that

> schooling is justified to the community by the myth of providing the service of teaching while custodial activities are actually pursued under conditions of systemic deception [p. 24].

From this standpoint, low coordination of instructional activities is simply a natural spinoff from the idea that custodial control is what matters, and is what schools are held accountable for by their environments.

3. Domain conflict. Following Kouzes and Mico (1979), we might speculate that weak coordination is a way for public human service organizations to cope with the fact that they must combine the claims of three different domains: the political, resource-allocating one; the managerial one; and the professionalized, service-delivery one. Tight interdependence would only exacerbate conflict, and since educational goals are ambiguous and the production function uncertain, it makes most sense to settle for a world in which appearances are accepted, the pain and energy costs of confrontation avoided, and the best judgment of the professional closest to the problem honored.

On the face of it, there do not appear to be historical explanations for weak coordination in schools; there are no abrupt discontinuities where self-contained classrooms were mandated, or evaluation of teaching forbidden. In fact, one might say that the early "scientific management" movement toward "efficiency" in education could be seen as a vain effort to move against something "inherent" in educational systems—though it did succeed, as we have seen, in entrenching the role of administrators.

KNOWLEDGE GAPS

What puzzles, uncertainties, gaps are there here?

1. Model fitting. It remains quite unclear what sorts of organizational models are the best "fit" to schools as they are: If standard bureaucracy is not the best bet (as seems likely), what is better—conflicting role and interest groups? Various versions of decoupled "anarchies"? The "sect" with a charismatic leader? The professionalized, highly autonomous "hospital"? Praise is due Firestone and Herriott (1980), to Meyer et al. (1978), and to Abramowitz and Tenenbaum (1978) for their efforts in this direction; many more such studies are needed.

2. Implications for knowledge utilization and innovation. Highly flexible and low-coordinative systems should, in principle, permit safer, more vigorous (faddist?) but *localized* use of expert knowledge, experiments by those most interested, and so on. They should also, in principle, be more resistant to internal diffusion and institutionalization of improvements. Miles, Fullan, et al. (1978a) found that school systems successfully using organization development (OD), an interdependence-increasing strategy, were more likely to adopt specific instructional innovations. But we need more studies relating interdependence to utilization of knowledge, and to innovation more generally.

3. Teacher "autonomy." Analysts vary widely as to whether teachers are possessed of much autonomy or little. There is little doubt that surveillance is minimal, but do teachers have real *control* over aspects of their lives that matter in school improvement? The inquiries will not be simple: The issue of the unattended "cage" teachers supposedly find themselves in must be examined. As in the IGE studies by Packard et al. (1978), we can probably gain a good deal by examining situations in which deliberate efforts have been made to increase teacher control/autonomy.[15]

4. The meaning of isolation. Much is made of the fact that teachers see few other adults during the working day, and that this "privatizes" teachers, heightens idiosyncrasy, and perhaps makes them more childlike to boot. Little is known about this, or about the degree to which children serve to ward off the teacher's psychological isolation, act as surrogates for peers, or serve as agents for socialization/resocialization.

Dilemma 4:
Environmental Dependence versus Autonomy

All organizations are dependent on their environments (for raw materials, personnel, information, money). But all organizations are also to some degree autonomous, exercising choice over the courses of action they will pursue. The dilemma here for schools rests in how far to define themselves as dependent (subject to the controlling whims of local voters and public opinion, or the prisoner of state and federal legislation) or as autonomous (oriented to cosmopolitan, professional values, and seeking to pursue their own goals around, through, and in spite of local opinion and the official rules). Dependency is useful: It increases predictability (if one has good data on one's surroundings), and, if well-managed, assures a flow of resources. Autonomy is also useful: You are more likely to get what you want. But both dependency and autonomy have risks and pains. And organizations, like people, cannot have it both ways.

REGULARITIES NOTED

What conclusions have typically been drawn here? As we have noted earlier, schools have both immediate (local community) and distal (state, regional, federal, professional, commercial, and legal) environments. The discussion here begins with the local setting.

1. Domestication. That schools are "tame," owned by their environments, is perhaps as much a high-level, stipulatively driven inference as an empirical observation. Carlson (1964, 1965a) suggested the concept, deriving it from the idea that public schools cannot choose their clients, and its clients cannot choose not to participate. Put another way, a steady flow of unselected clients, and of funds, is assured, with the supply of neither depending closely on system performance. So schools are environmentally dependent—but since for most consumers they are "the only wheel in town," they can afford a certain amount of autonomy. Thus the picture is ambiguous. As Sieber points out in his chapter (this volume), though schools' survival is for practical purposes guaranteed, they must compete to some extent for students (whose parents may or may not move into the community, may or may not decide to pay for private schooling) and for faculty.

On balance, however, most analysts lean toward a "domestication" view. Gallaher (1965) speaks of the "surrender to clients," suggesting that school functionaries are not really legitimated to specify goals for schooling, and must accept lay control. Lortie (1977b) says, "Schools are 'bound in' to their publics in a particularly intense way," since they must seek financial support directly from their clients, and get trapped in "foreshortened planning" because of short-run budgeting in local communities. Herriott (1979) notes further that local cultural climates constrain school innovation efforts, and suggests less range of tolerance for change in rural settings.

2. Quasi-monopolistic position. But as noted above, the real practical constraints on student (or parent) exit make for a certain independence on the school's part. Furthermore, as Meyer and Rowan (1977) note, alternative and private schools must conform quite closely to regulations that constrain what a "school" must be like, and may thus offer no more than marginal advantages to a consumer thinking of shopping around. So schools may have more room for autonomy than they characteristically choose to exercise. Bale (1977), for example, studied 7500 elementary schools adopting *The Electric Company,* a children's TV show, for regular viewing in school. Local environmental characteristics (such as disposition to innovate, suburban location, turbulent environment) contributed almost *no* variance to measures of various stages in organizational change, from problem diagnosis through adoption. Perhaps this particular innovation was nondisruptive to community expectations (parents had doubtless seen it at home), but even so, the idea that there is room for autonomy remains worth entertaining.

3. Popular support. Domestication notwithstanding, the typical superintendent spends a good deal of energy in placating the board which represents the district's interface with the surrounding community, coopting it if possible (Kerr, 1964). Though actual survival is never at issue (note that even in the direst of fiscal crises in New York, Cleveland, and Chicago, the idea that *school itself* would cease to be was never really entertained, even by the most apocalyptic commentators), the quality of survival (especially in an environment of declining resources) can be problematic. Struggles for resource maintenance and acquisition, however, obscure what Meyer and Rowan (1978: 89) have pointed out—that schools are

> a network of organizations that has grown rapidly for many decades, that obtains huge economic resources in a stable way year after year, that is protected from failure by laws that make its use compulsory, that is constantly shown by surveys to have the confidence and support of its constituency, and that is known to have high levels of job satisfaction among its participants.

So here too it seems worthwhile to question the conventional wisdom that schools are embattled, without friends, and necessarily in a dependent position toward their immediate environments. It is correct, as Paul (1977) points out in his review of change studies, to conclude that serious community opposition to specific *innovations* can easily block those specific changes. But the idea of school, of schooling, is never seriously questioned, Illich to the contrary.

Schools also have complicated, not-well-understood distal environments. Two regularities can be noted here.

4. Decentralized constraint. As Wayland (1964) has pointed out, American schools are embedded in a large and complicated quasi-system that is nominally decentralized, but exerts clear constraints on local action. Many ancillary structures, outside the legislative, judicial, and political system, affect schools: They include materials vendors, professional associations, test producers, accrediting and certifying bodies, private colleges and universities, and R&D producers. Though in many countries such structures are part of the official establishment, in this country they operate apart from it. For example, though there is no American ministry approving textbooks, there is indeed a narrowly constrained national textbook market, which is driven by (and encourages) the fact that 20 percent of Americans change their places of residence each year.[16]

Corwin and Edelfelt (1978: 25-33) detail the importance of interaction among the large array of organizations in the educational arena, and note that

> at best, local communities must *share* the governance of their schools with many groups at all levels of government and in the private sector [p. 32].

They suggest that the bases of authority in play vary considerably (traditional, expert, legal, and charismatic): "thus, it seems, that almost anyone can claim some formal 'right' to control education." Such control is never really unilateral (even in the case of "veto" groups, influence is exercised to prevent action, not to initiate it). Corwin and Edelfelt suggest that the multilateral nature of environmental influence in fact provides *more* autonomy (increased options) for alert, assertive local actors.

Though, as Halperin (1980) points out, federal and state decision making on educational policy is a highly fragmented, factionalized, decontrolled, multilevel, multiparticipant process without any central direction, it would be a mistake to assume it is only a "mess" or a disordered interorganizational field. His analysis implies underlying coherence, and suggests the diversity-protecting functions of messiness, which may need only marginal "tidying."

5. Increased regulation. A number of analysts agree that local schools have become more fully regulated by federal and state legislation over the past two or three decades. Federally mandated changes (such as PL 94-142 on handicapped children, Title IX on sex discrimination, Title I of ESEA, and a wide range of desegregation rulings) are accompanied by state-level initiatives on accountability and competency based testing. As Kirst (1980) notes, about half of all state monies (currently boosted by inflation) are spent on education, and most state departments of education, partly through federal support, have increased their staff and analytical resources dramatically. Halperin (1980), too, points to a substantially increased regulatory role for the federal government, abetted by what he calls "legislative and judicial activism."[17] Boyd (1978: 579) notes a "remarkable recent growth of the influence and authority of state and national (both federal and nongovernmental) agencies over the curriculum."

These formal regulatory activities (Kirst, 1980) are also stimulated by national informal networks (for example, those persons and organizations interested in the competency-based testing movement, or school finance reform). Kirst suggests that local boards and superintendents are experiencing a "decreasing zone of discretion," squeezed as they are between federal and state mandates and the demands of staff bargaining organizations. More harshly, Wise (1977) considers that the country is heading toward an "unplanned, de facto" national system of education, built along narrowly rationalistic lines.

Against this view we should naturally juxtapose that of Berman (1978a), who points out the intensely long and vulnerable chain of processes that intervene between federal policy formulation and the implementation of change in local schools. So from the federal end, influencing schools seems difficult, even hopeless; from the local end, there are clear threats to autonomy.

Some of the local sense of "loss of control" is real, and some probably ideologically driven, since schools are "supposed" to be locally controlled. As Lieberman (1977) notes, schools are still undoubtedly the most influenceable American institution as far as citizens are concerned; Dalin and Rust (1979) have similar views, when comparisons with European educational systems are drawn.

To summarize: The evidence presented here, much of it rather general and impressionistic, suggests that schools facing the environmental dependence/autonomy dilemma lean toward the sense of being "domesticated," perhaps underutilizing the resources for autonomy which their quasi-monopolistic position and general public support offer. Against this must be placed the fact of local schools' existence in a constraining, complex suprasystem that is only imperfectly understood, and from which emanate increasing amounts of regulation and control—much of which can doubtless be evaded or redirected.

CLAIMED ANTECEDENTS

What might explain these regularities?

1. Education as a state/local function. The American Constitution classically reserves education to the states, which in turn have delegated their power to local communities. Thus the idea that schools "belong" to their local communities, which used to (and in most states still do) supply the major portion of revenues. But states can take back informally delegated powers, a natural response when they are supplying more and more of the money for schools.

2. Compulsory education. We have reviewed the genesis of legislation requiring school attendance earlier, and discussed its *internal* consequences for the school (batching, control orientation, and so on). As Carlson (1964, 1965a) suggests, a community that mandates something called "education" for all children naturally needs a "tame" institution to handle the job—and there is no point in making its survival problematic.

3. Normal children as clients. The fact that schools have temporary possession of valued, immature persons is probably a strong force for local control, and environmental dependence, on the part of the school. Furthermore, these persons return home each afternoon with more or less explicit news of how they have been treated. Note that prisons, correctional homes, mental hospitals, and hospitals—all people-processing institutions—do not face similar problems, and can operate more like "total institutions" (Goffman, 1961).

Lortie (1977b) comments as well that schools actually have multiple clients, sometimes with conflicting demands: Students and parents are the most obvious, but employers, colleges, the military, and other governmental agencies also have client-like claims to make, reducing schools' autonomy further.

4. Development of the establishment. Boyd (1978) believes that the historical centralization, consolidation, and rationalization of the educational macrostructure which began in the 1900s has, paradoxically, increased local autonomy, via "loose coupling" across levels, so that almost any change advocated from outside the school can in fact be vetoed, explicitly or implicitly. The autonomy is thus of the "power to say no" variety, rather than that of pursuing one's own objectives.

KNOWLEDGE GAPS

What do we need to know in this domain?

1. Local "latitude" for action. This discussion has suggested that schools may not be exercising as much choice toward their local environments as they in fact have space for. Any decision situation can, of course, be seen to contain broader options than those taken, but studies of unnecessarily self-limiting behavior by schools might be instructive.

2. Correlates of proactiveness. School districts vary rather widely in how they resolve the dependence/autonomy dilemma. Some, for example, make up as much as a third of their budgets from federal and state "soft money," rather than passively complaining about "loss of control." What determines such behavior? An entrepreneurial superintendent? The presence of a grants officer? And what are its consequences? Would Berman and McLaughlin's (1978b) finding regarding the dubious aftermath of "opportunistic" grant seeking be replicated?

3. Cognitive mapping of the environment. Superintendents and other district officers must act toward their immediate and distal environments with some more or less explicit image of what is "out there." We have little or no information on how the larger educationally relevant world is seen, how differentiated such views are, and in what respects they correspond to the actual "territory."

More generally, it is not at all clear just how the environments of schools can best be characterized. Are they, for example, a mixture of "placid" and "turbulent" types (Emery and Trist, 1965; Berman, 1978a)? What general descriptors of environments (see Jurkovich, 1974) are most relevant for schools?

Dilemma 5:
Environmental Contact versus Withdrawal

This dilemma centers around boundary management. One choice involves making the boundary permeable, for both insiders and outsiders; it is easy in some schools for parents to enter, offer criticism, influence, or praise, and for their part school people reach out proactively to locate resources, lobby, and fight when necessary. The other choice means tightening the boundary: The school is buffered, protected from outside influence, well defended; school people occupy themselves with keeping school, focusing on internal issues. Withdrawal and buffering are often essential when an innovation must be protected in its early phases, but they may be fatal if the issue is obtaining resources and endorsement from the environment. Proactive outward contact and open access from the community may solve political problems, but divert energy from crucial core task accomplishment.[18]

Note that this dilemma and the preceding one are orthogonal: There can be dependent-withdrawing or dependent-contacting choices, along with autonomous-withdrawing or autonomous-contacting ones.

REGULARITIES NOTED

Analysts have pointed to several features in this domain.

1. Vulnerability. As we have noted, the concept of vulnerability is a loose one; various writers seem to mean (1) the presence of effective external influence (thus a "thin skin" for the organization), (2) the predictability of that influence, and (3) the insecurity of role inhabitants presented with influence attempts. Freeman (1979: 121) seems tacitly to adopt the "thin skin" definition:

> School districts are vulnerable to outside criticism because it is difficult for them to demonstrate their effectiveness and because there are almost infinite alternatives which can be advocated by various interest groups. On the other hand, the critics cannot affect change easily because they cannot make a strong enough case. The anarchical tendencies of educational organizations can be used to thwart them. But school districts, being public organizations, are particularly vulnerable when they must request support from outside agencies, as they frequently do in seeking tax increases through the electoral process.

Both Sieber (1968) and Miles (1967) mention vulnerability as a prominent characteristic, but leave the term loosely defined as effective environmental influence. Tumin (1977: 50-51) speaks of public visibility and control:

> The public school is perhaps more publicly controlled and financed than any other major social institution, and its actions are often more highly visible and subject to public scrutiny. That means that one is literally living in a fishbowl part of the time when one is teaching.

Most generally, the term is usually taken to refer not just to any external influence, but to influence which is somehow disruptive or damaging. As Pauly (1978) points out, most school administrators are especially eager to avoid situations of conflict and disruption, since their career advancement depends on others' recognition that they have maintained smooth, effective relationships with their immediate environments. Lortie (1977b) points out that the superintendent's short-term contract makes the occupant of that role especially personally vulnerable, and cites supporting research.

2. Buffering. An obvious solution when disruption threatens is that of strengthening the boundary between school and local community. Hawley

(1975) suggests that this is often accomplished through the "myth of professionalism," and the invocation of technical authority. Boyd (1978) conceptualizes buffering as the creation of a "zone of tolerance" around the school's operations, into which there is reasonable consensus that the public will not penetrate. Packard (1977: 23-24) speaks even more concretely:

> Administrators also have the responsibility to control the access of outsiders to the classroom and the school, and generally to see that uncertainties do not arise in the work process. More specifically, administrators are expected to monitor the entry, passage and exit of parents and other non-members of the school . . . [entry check-in, guards, locks]. Parent access is also controlled by encouraging their entrance only at "down times" or under conditions of high preparedness [special theatrical, musical, and athletic events, parent conferences, and so on] . . . attention is directed away from class activities.

Lortie (1977a: 11) suggests that

> educators, and particular classroom teachers are ambivalent about such public participation. . . . Most teachers seem to want parents . . . to be "distant assistants" who help outside the school setting. . . . There are, moreover, identifiable conflicts between the minor themes of professionalization and citizen participation: if those who do not work in schools are not "laymen," how can teachers, they wonder, be "professionals"?

And he details the need for buffering core processes:

> Public involvement can, under certain circumstances, prove disruptive to classroom performance. Teachers . . . need to create a jural order with children from different families, to set up a rule system which is universalistic and outside kinship membership. Unless parental claims are held in check, they have the potential to tear apart that carefully-constructed small society; special consideration for some can threaten the whole. Nor can teachers work well if constantly challenged by persons with special outlooks; imagine teaching social studies . . . while a student tape records one's words for the John Birch Society or a militant member of a minority group paces back and forth across the room [p. 129].

Miles, Sullivan, et al. (1978b), in a longitudinal study of the creation of two open-space elementary schools, found that the principal's ability to defuse protest and buffer the innovative teaching processes being tried was critical to success; in contrast, a principal of another open-space school who permitted easy community access (Gold and Miles, 1978) encountered severe conflict and lost his job.

3. Weak parent and citizen participation. As Berman notes in his chapter (this volume), even in programs where citizen involvement is federally mandated, the "evidence is overwhelming that parents and community members are seldom involved in innovative efforts." Similar findings have been noted for the case of curriculum development by Schaffarzick (1975). In the Abramowitz and Tenenbaum (1978) study of high schools, parent and community groups were mentioned by principals as being "usually involved" in a range of decisions from adding courses to formulating school goals *less* frequently in some cases than were elected or appointed groups of students (on the issue of adding courses, the figures are 23 percent for students and 18 percent for parents; for adopting student behavior rules, 49 percent and 30 percent). On "bigger" issues the figures are reversed, but not strikingly so (on formulating school goals, students 33 percent, parents 38 percent; developing a budget for the school buildings, 3 percent and 5 percent). Across seven issues, parents are mentioned at a 17 percent level and student groups at 19 percent.

Michaelson (1977: 242), looking at the large picture back of data such as these, says flatly:

> As a general solution, community control [of schools] will not be able to overcome the structure of incentives inherent in the bureau-cratic form of school organization under representative government.

And in speaking of "accountability" schemes that might involve rewarding teachers according to achievement of goals by students, Michaelson (1977: 243) asks, "Is there any hope for such a plan?" He answers:

> I think not. Consider that administrators will have the power and indeed the responsibility to make the judgments the accountability schemes require. Clients can enter the process only to the extent that administrators and teachers permit them to do so. . . . In California, the recently enacted teacher evaluation law . . . provides teachers with the right to participate in and bargain for the standards that are to apply in each individual case. As a consequence, the law has left the basic bargain between administrators and teachers undis-turbed. Personal observation reveals no significant change in teaching performance attributable to the law.

As a further exhibit, we might examine the case of voucher plans, originally proposed as a counter to schools' quasi-monopolistic "guaran-teed survival" (hence nonresponsiveness to parents/citizens). To date the only implementation of a voucher plan has occurred in Alum Rock, California; it was limited by the California legislature to alternative schools within the district (thus leaving local funding untouched). Analysis by Bass (1978) and Thomas (1978) suggests that even this emasculated version succeeded not because of citizen pressure, but because principals saw a chance for increased power and autonomy.

Furthermore, a recent campaign to place a voucher plan on the ballot, amending the California constitution, failed. Professional education groups charged that the idea would lead to chaos, was unconstitutional, and would be expensive and impossible to administer; its proponents were dismissed as "well-meaning fools" (New York *Times*, August 4, 1979). An analysis by Burcham and Cohn (1979) claimed that the idea would increase racial segregation, and would in any case not enlarge parental influence vis-à-vis the usual coalition of superintendent, central office staff, and board. On balance, it appears that this opportunity to redress the power balance did not succeed, in part because of the very weakness the proposal was designed to correct.

Finally, we should note the thoroughgoing research on citizen participation carried out by Gittell et al. (1979). According to a summary from the Institute for Responsive Education, the sponsoring agency:

> The authors found . . . that low-income community organizations have changed: advocacy has become service as broad-based movements have become narrowly defined organizations. They have had to forsake the strategies which build power. After more than a decade of government initiatives and mandated organizations, the authors comment, "the nature of citizen participation has changed," and that change has not always been for the better:

> . . . In fact, advocates of citizen participation have more reasons to despair now than they did ten years ago. Citizen organizations have little influence over the educational decision making process.

Similarly, Huguenin et al. (1979: 3), writing as part of the IRE inquiry, cite eight different studies, concluding that

> the one thing these numerous parent and community organizations have not been successful in doing . . . is to exert influence on the decision making process of schools.

The general picture here is one of cooptation. The shift away from advocacy could also be explained by the large amounts of energy (and financial support) required to maintain a strong voluntary citizen organization, and the resistance of educators who said that "they were already receiving the necessary input" from federally mandated advisory committees, which the study found "had the most direct access but the least influence on school policy."

Coming as they do from an organization (IRE) deeply committed to citizen participation, these conclusions about weak citizen/parent influence gain added validity.

CLAIMED ANTECEDENTS

What might explain the observed regularities we have outlined: vulnerability of schools, extensive buffering, and weak parent and citizen participation? Why, in short, might schools so frequently resolve the boundary dilemma by making it less permeable?

We may, of course, invoke the same explanations just offered for the dependence/autonomy dilemma, particularly those of the tradition of local control and compulsory education. There are several other possibilities as well.

1. Avoidance of disruption. Perhaps all organizations do seek to buffer their core processes, have them occur backstage, so to speak. The presence of influence from persons external to the system, who do not understand its technology, is unlikely to contribute to organizational efficiency (see Lortie, 1977a).

2. Weak production function. Freeman (1979: 120-121) suggests a causal chain. The technology of learning is poorly understood, so districts and schools

> rely upon teacher professionalism and essentially decouple levels in the hierarchy. This makes educational organizations particularly subject to outside criticism so that principals, superintendents, and school boards are much involved in public relations in which procedural rationality is stressed because substantive rationality is impossible.

The idea here is that vulnerability (and hence buffering) is heightened because of technical uncertainty; educators are unable to ward off critical attacks with confident and unquestioned expertise.

3. Self-defeating federal policies. The prescriptions for improvement of citizen participation by Huguenin et al. (1979) of IRE contain an explanation couched in terms of the unintended effects of federal policies mandating citizen participation. They note proliferation and competition among mandated "advisory committees," emphasis on funds and numbers of participants rather than organizational structure, and inattention to the local community context. Such factors, affecting lower-class groups most, hindered still further their ineffective influence as compared to independent middle-class advocacy groups. However, the authors also acknowledge that the internal structure and operations of local school systems are also crucial:

> Unless concurrent changes are made in the way schools are set up, especially in points of access, official lines of communication, and places where decisions are made, community organizations have no hope of exerting influence [Huguenin et al., 1979].

4. Vested interests of educators. More pointedly, it seems likely that school people's protection of their own financial and professional interests is a primary driving force, as noted in the California voucher initiative failure. We might also quote Michaelson (1977: 242), who here is considering what might happen if schools were really "community-controlled":

> Community-controlled schools will, like other public schools, receive their budgets as direct institutional grants from a legislative body . . . administrators and teachers will enjoy superior access to the processes of this body and would be able to retain their present secure position.

More basically, Michaelson (1977: 236), as we saw earlier, sees the creation of compulsory education as the basic means by which educators protected their interests (and now maintain them):

> Full tax support and compulsion firmly established the power of common school administrators and, in a different way, teachers over parents and children. Indeed, they created the essential conditions for insulating school management from citizens generally; namely, the assurance of a budget independent of satisfied consumers.

KNOWLEDGE GAPS

What inquiries would be useful here?

1. Parents' influence at the "micro" level. It is possible that parental influence over school operations, rather than appearing through political, citizen-like channels, occurs more subtly—either through expectations addressed to the child, who behaves in such a way (when aggregated with many other children) that school personnel accommodate, or through support or criticism which is teacher-specific, addressed to particular behaviors (and, if luck has it, the general policies and procedures bearing on such behaviors). Inquiry here would help.

2. Models of "constructive" involvement. We concur with Lortie (1977a) that parent participation and "professionalism" need not be mutually exclusive, and that situations where they have proved mutually furthering or supportive of school improvement should be examined. Emphasis should be as much on norms, climate, negotiated relationships, and the chronology of participative efforts as on the structural arrangements, judging from Huguenin et al.'s (1979) critique of "mandated" structures.

Dilemma 6:
External Expertise Seeking versus Self-Reliance

A third environmentally focused dilemma, of special concern in this chapter, deals with knowledge defined as "technical," "expert," or "specialized." Such knowledge is generalizable, validated, based on accepted evidence; it may appear in the form of accepted professional practice (craft, lore), programs, products, scientific or technical reports, and may be on paper or carried by a person (advice, consultation, training). People in schools regularly face a choice: Should we seek (and utilize) outside expert information as an aid in dealing with some instructional, organizational, or community problem[19]—or can we rely on our own resources? External knowledge is likely to be technically good; one can "stand on the shoulders of giants," people who have specialized skills and have thought the problem through. But people inside the system know what its special quirks, needs, problems, and issues are; they know what will work, and who will stand still for it. Insiders' knowledge carries commitment and belief with it; using insiders' energies increases their commitment to the effective use of their knowledge.

REGULARITIES NOTED

As Sieber's review (this volume) shows, how schools solve this dilemma represents a very complex set of issues. The reader is also referred to the thorough discussions by Fullan and Louis. In general, we can very briefly note the following:

1. Infrequent use of formal external channels. Sieber quotes Paul Hood (1979a): "Generally, the local, easily accessible, and typically personal sources are used in preference to more distant, inaccessible or formal sources" of expert knowledge. Base-rate data on knowledge-seeking behavior are very hard to come by, if only because of the bewildering variety of external resources to which school personnel could (in principle) turn at almost any point during the school day (or when anticipating the next one).[20]

Aoki, quoted in Fullan's chapter (this volume) found that teachers rated other teachers highest as sources of help and information. District staff were seen as moderately useful. But external sources of knowledge (department of education, unions, and university consultants) received low ratings.

Havelock et al. (1973) asked a national sample of superintendents about locally implemented innovations. In describing a "showcase" innovation (the most significant one during the preceding year in the district), 55-67 percent of superintendents (depending on district size) mentioned that teachers had been involved in adoption/implementation; the figures for principals were 26-49 percent. By contrast, outside actors were rarely involved (outside companies, 2-6 percent; universities, 3-9 percent). When asked about "resources" that had been utilized, respondents mainly mentioned internal resources (such as teacher discussions, 48 percent; curriculum supervisor, 35 percent; research and evaluation office and staff, 34 percent). Some mentions of external resources were close to this level (state educational agency, 32 percent; university, 28 percent; various federal programs, 11-20 percent), but others were substantially less frequently mentioned (ERIC, 11 percent; regional laboratories, 6 percent—both resources charged with active knowledge utilization).

Hood et al. (1976), in a survey of 1328 information users, including 628 building-level practitioners, found that 60 percent of teachers said they would go (as first, second, or third sources) to teachers in their own district; 47 percent said principals; and 28 percent mentioned other local personnel. "Colleagues in other organizations" were mentioned by 16 percent, and experts or authorities fared little better (19 percent), along with information service personnel (22 percent). Other external services (external libraries, professional organizations, state or federal agencies, ERIC) typically ranged from 3 to 15 percent. Interestingly, local *school* libraries were mentioned by 37 percent.

Such patterns can in part be explained by the top-ranking reasons offered for preferring certain sources:

Is likely to have the information I want.

Is near at hand or easily accessible.

Is responsive to my particular problem or question.

Is easy to use.

Is usually available when I need it.

Thus reliance on local resources is "rational," not necessarily driven by "resistance" to external expertise. But we should note that criteria such as "objective, impartial, not biased" appeared at the bottom of the list, and "is authoritative, accurate, reliable" ranked only ninth among fifteen items.

Sheer "frequency of use" date (very highly correlated with received "usefulness") showed that the highest-ranking sources of information for school practitioners in connection with their "most important" work activities, were "face-to-face discussion or conferences with people in my own organization," "notes and files in my own office," "personal library," and other local items. But we should also note that fairly high rankings were given to "educational journals," "curriculum materials," and "textbooks, reference books"; these along with the "personal library" and "notes and files" items suggest active retrieval of expert information, but *locally stored* and available. Still scoring at the bottom of the array were "technical reports, government publications," "other libraries, resource centers, or information services," and "abstracts, indexes, bibliographies." "Conventions and professional association meetings," and "face-to-face discussion or conferences with people in other organizations" fared only slightly better. Again, it appears that distance and "externality" are inhibiting factors.

Paul (1977: 40), in his review of change studies, concludes, at a "firm" level of confidence, that

> teachers work best with and rely most on fellow teachers in information sharing and collaboration for change . . . fellow teachers have more credibility and are able to elicit greater trust and reduce discomfort.

Furthermore, he concludes, with somewhat less confidence:

> Teachers will tend to rely on their own experience for curriculum ideas rather than use curriculum guides prepared by central administrative staff, ideas from principals, or ideas from university courses [p. 41].

As to explanations, Paul speaks not only of teacher resistance, but of the need for overload protection, and for warding off "difficult, esoteric, or unworthy techniques."

2. Presence of "noninstrumental" incentives. Sieber's chapter (this volume) concludes, with extensive documentation, that a very wide range of knowledge-seeking incentives (and *dis*incentives) exists beyond the narrowly instrumental (such as "solving educational problems"). He mentions, for example, general "enlightenment": internal forces such as district career advancement, esteem, legitimation, overload avoidance, and relief from boredom; and external forces such as coercive power, money, and the need to be responsive to the local community in exchange for support. Similarly, Deal (1979) comments on purposes for knowledge seeking and utilization other than use in change or reform, including successful relabeling of old practices, excitement, myth creation, and the marshalling of community support through the presentation of "appearances." Perhaps it is stretching a point to call such listings a "regularity"; the general point, however, is that many political and personal features affect the resolution of the dilemma we are considering, and that "expert knowledge" is not necessarily sought (or rejected) for its own sake alone.

3. Quasi-professionalism. Professionals are usually defined as persons working from a well-formulated knowledge base, with defined competence standards and a set of ethical guidelines; entry to a profession is restricted, and depends on completion of specified training.

A number of analysts consider that teachers do not meet the definition above. Sieber (1968) terms them "quasi-professionals," pointing out that they work from a very weak knowledge base; Lortie (1975, 1977b) uses the label "truncated professional" and notes that though teachers have high discretion and job security (features often associated with professionals in other organizations), they exercise little collegial power, and "the individual teacher has limited ability to shape his or her own daily work." Hanson (1975) speaks of "semi-professionals," and concludes that a "hospital" model of organization (clear-cut delineation of administrative and care-delivery functions) did not apply in the detailed case study he conducted of five schools ih one district.

Teachers, of course, bristle at such labels, claim a strong knowledge base (in spite of a great deal of ambiguity about the consequences of alternative teaching methods) and argue (in spite of evidence that teaching attracts the lower-performing portion of college cohorts, typically requires no competency test for certification, and provides few rewards for good performance) that they deserve full legitimation as a profession.

But note a recent controversy (New York *Times,* July 13 and 31, 1979) over whether teachers should be licensed as professionals in New York State. For any given field, a state Professional Practices Board, composed of experienced practitioners and public members, sets entry requirements, specifies credentials and competencies, and defines a code of professional ethics. "Professionals" range from doctors to landscape architects and providers of massage. ("Actually," said a state regent, "what we have is about a dozen professions and 18 occupations with good lawyers.") But though the state commissioner and the New York State United Teachers were pressing strongly for the formal move to license teachers as professionals, supported by the regents ("if such changes can be tied to the quality of teaching"), there was, in fact, organized resistance from teachers to (a) the continuing education requirement that is associated with relicensing in many professions, and (b) the idea of a code of ethics, on the grounds that teachers are (or should be) well supervised. ("If there is an incompetent teacher, that means that the supervisor is not doing his job.") As the regents' representative noted, "They've got to realize that when they assume the benefits of profession, they have to meet all the requirements as well."

This case is perhaps not fully representative; for example, several states and a number of universities are developing or using competency-based entrance requirements for teachers. But, on balance, it seems likely that the "quasi-professional" label is not inaccurate.

CLAIMED ANTECEDENTS

What might account for the regularities listed above?

1. Weak knowledge base. As Sieber (1968), Miles (1967), and others have noted, reliance on own resources (and operation as a quasi-professional) may well be driven by the fact that knowledge on teaching processes and their consequences is lacking. Such weakness may be intrinsic (few means/ends connections have been established, as Stephens, 1967, and Averch et al., 1972, document), or it may be that the knowledge is poorly synthesized and assembled.[21] Or knowledge may be inadequately transformed into teacher-usable form (whether it is derived from scientific inquiry, or from a distillation of "craft"; Cohen, 1977). Knowledge-base weaknesses are probably exacerbated by the complexity and nonroutineness of the task of "social control combined with socialization," as Sieber points out. Presumably a massage provider or even a landscape architect could get away with an objectively "weaker" base, given simpler tasks.

2. Structural aspects of teaching. It is claimed that "quasi-professionalism" is at least in part caused by the "non-staged" character of teaching (Lortie, 1975; Sieber, this volume): Neither upward mobility nor increased financial reward is present, so commitment to the "profession" is low.

It is also argued (Lortie, 1975) that teaching itself, because of its isolation and steady exposure to children, induces traits of "individuation, presentism, and conservatism," none likely to encourage use of external expert knowledge. More generally, it is sometimes claimed that since teaching is an extremely familiar process to all adults (who have experienced it on the receiving end for 10,000 to 15,000 hours), it is a "demystified" process with little expertise attached. It is difficult to assess the merit of these claims, in part because one can note the comparatively higher status of teachers in most Western European countries, though the conditions and extensity of teaching are quite similar.[22]

3. Modernity. Finally, there is a perverse sense in which educational and social development itself discourages the use of expert knowledge from outside local systems. This comes clearest when one notes that Havelock and Huberman (1978), reviewing the experience of educational innovation in developing countries, stress that there is widespread use of external assistance (largely as a consequence of awareness of lagging educational practice, and a lack of prior experience with innovations and innovative process management). When innovations are a dime a dozen, and offer only the probability of a marginal advantage (rather than the putative benefits of nation building), ho-hum reactions might be predicted.

KNOWLEDGE GAPS

In the general area of incentives for knowledge utilization, Sieber (this volume) has offered such an extensive and differentiated list of topics for inquiry that adding others seems hardly necessary or even advisable. But in the domain we are concerned with (common properties), the following might be suggested.

1. Utilization base rate studies. It does seem that we need better information on actual seeking/utilization of externally available knowledge by people in schools (as contrasted with retrospectively reported questionnaire responses). Such studies should certainly examine "utilization" in "enlightenment" and "noninstrumental" terms, as well as in terms of "school improvement," "problem solving," and "capacity building."

2. Correlates of utilization. As the reader has doubtless noted, many if not most of the "regularities" we have noted are not fully "common" in any sort of generic or inherent sense. Not all teachers are isolated, some schools have strong parent participation, some outputs can be measured quite well, and so on. Rates of use of externally available knowledge (or its rejection in favor of local resources) should, for example, be examined for more and less "professionalized" teachers; for fields where good knowledge syntheses are available or lacking; for districts which have "master" or "lead teacher" roles and those which do not.[23]

Dilemma 7:
Feedback Seeking versus Intuitive/Routine Action

Choice making in schools, as in other organizations, is a function of the information available to choice makers. The dilemma, once again, is a choice between goods. Should one collect thorough, systematic data on the results of one's efforts (such as student discussions on how the class is going, teacher morale, figures on parents' encouragement of homework) to guide subsequent planning and action? Or should one proceed intuitively and directly, on the assumption that things are all right, and that existing routines (lesson plans, regular faculty meetings, teacher/parent conferences) are the best guides to action? Collecting data is a risky, time-consuming, and potentially threatening process. *Not* collecting data can make for unpleasant surprises, not to mention failure in a course of action.

REGULARITIES NOTED

Certain themes recur in this domain.

1. Labor intensiveness. It is often noted that the bulk (usually 80 percent or more) of any school district's budget goes to salaries. Buildings, equipment, materials, and machines form a minor portion of expenditures. It follows that the technology of learning is, as House (1976) points out, "people-vulnerable" and very much dependent on their characteristics and skills. Similar comments are made by Berman (1978a) and Elboim-Dror (1970).

2. Immediate client response as data. Since the delivery of teaching/learning "technology" (the quotes connote its "soft" character) occurs, as Berman (1978a) suggests, in a "bilateral" setting, the information teachers use to guide action is typically short-run characteristics of interaction, such as level of student interest, obedience, or smooth classroom functioning (see Lieberman, 1977). Data on the *outcomes* of teaching strategies (see below) are less available and tend to be used less frequently for steering purposes. Spuck (1974) believes, with some empirical support, that so-called intrinsic rewards, such as social interaction with students, pride in workmanship, and teachers' agreement with school goals and policies, carry more weight than do supposedly instrumental rewards (the fact that students have learned).

3. Lack of output control. Meyer and Rowan (1978: 82) suggest that

> a striking fact about American education at all levels is that student achievement data are rarely used to evaluate the performance of teachers or schools.

They cite the finding that only 1 of 34 superintendents surveyed reported using standardized achievement data to evaluate schools in his district. But we should also note that the NEA's national teacher opinion poll (Teacher Education Reports, 1979) found that 80 percent of teachers said they had used group standardized test scores within the past three years. Still, only half of the respondents thought that the tests helped their teaching, diagnosis of individual learning needs, and so on, and said that "most of the really important aspects of student progress are not measured by tests."

Is the issue only a technical one? The proceedings of a recent work conference on research on testing (Tyler and White, 1979) take that view, suggesting that existing measures are too narrow, culturally biased, insufficiently criterion-referenced, and so on. Niedermeyer (1979), too, argues that the problem is one of mismatch or nonalignment between expected outcomes, actual instruction, and assessment information. He reports research showing substantial learner gains when a laboratory-developed reading program with good "alignment" among these three components was implemented, and asserts that

> school districts in all types of locations will be able to document impressive instructional accomplishment, regardless of the backgrounds or social characteristics of their pupils [Niedermeyer, 1979: 5].

But that claim cuts both ways: School districts will also presumably be able to document resounding failures—or, as is more typical, little difference in comparison to ordinary practice.

The Meyer and Rowan claim that output control is nearly absent seems extreme, in view of the fact that some cities (New York, Chicago) require an annual public report of reading test scores by schools, and that a number of states are instituting minimum competency tests as a graduation requirement. But even so, the likelihood of close output control seems minimal. As Boyd (1978: 605) comments:

> The trouble begins when the illusion breaks down that this can be simply a *technical* process. To manage and be accountable for educational outcomes requires that the goals and objectives of education be specified. In the absence of a widespread consensus on these goals, this raises the politically sensitive question of who will set them. And even if a set of goals can be agreed to comfortably, in the absence of a highly developed science of education, the selection

of the best means to achieve these goals remains highly debatable. Because even the best known means (instructional or curricular) are far from successful with all students, teachers and administrators understandably are reluctant to be held accountable for educational outcomes. Thus they are inclined to resist accountability schemes and to seek to protect the degree of professional autonomy they traditionally have enjoyed.

4. Weak self-monitoring capability. As Wheeler (1966: 104) notes:

The fact is that most socializing organizations must operate and act in the absence of data that bear in a patent way on the effectiveness of their programs.

The qualifier "must" suggests Wheeler's view that the problem is an "inherent" one. In any case, he notes the tendency to use "any convenient variable" to assess performance, and to resolve differences over the merit of alternative treatment strategies via power struggles rather than through examination of documented information on consequences. Other analysts (Hawley, 1976; Boyd, 1978) similarly point to lack of reflexive mechanisms for classroom (or indeed building or district) use. Though most larger districts have offices for research and evaluation, it appears relatively rare for their resources to be devoted to self-study in any sense that will seriously affect ongoing operations. Deal et al. (1975) suggest, more generally, that evaluation is rarely used directly for performance improvement or local decision making (though it is typically required as a condition for refunding of special programs). Even when supposedly feedback-seeking programs such as "diagnostic prescriptive instruction" are employed, the picture changes little. Intili and Deal (1977) found that only 26 percent of teachers using such programs utilized students' skills and interests in planning instruction on at least a weekly basis. Furthermore, the programs themselves, which are designed to be revised on the basis of feedback, are only infrequently improved by teachers; 31 percent do not revise at all, and the majority do it on a two-year cycle.

Various technologies for school- and district-level self-study and improvement exist: as early as the mid-1960s, it was shown that "survey feedback" could be used productively with schools (Miles et al., 1969); Deal et al. (1975) make the same case. But such self-study methods have not diffused widely in schools: Miles, Fullan, et al. (1978b) concluded that organization development programs (of which survey feedback is a special case) had spread to only about 1 percent of American and Canadian school districts, though their current users were very much satisfied with the results. The prospects for diffusion of other school- or district-level self-study schemes, such as Scriven's School Evaluation Profile (Hood, 1979b) do not seem substantially more promising.

CLAIMED ANTECEDENTS

Various explanations have been offered for the regularities noted above (which add up to the general view that schools, as a labor-intensive enterprise, rely largely on what might be termed informally collected process data, rather than outcome information, and lack capability[24] either at the level of individual practitioners or systems, for self-study and improvement).

1. Input variability. Wheeler (1966) claims that inputs (students and teachers in our case) are so variable for all socializing organizations that it is nearly impossible to assess outcomes and tie them with any certainty to treatment processes. School people hold this view too, as we have seen in the discussion under Dilemma 1; they attribute poor performance, however, mainly to student variability rather than to their own.

2. Goal vagueness. As we noted earlier, there is a reasonable case to be made for the idea that educational goals are inherently diffuse and hard to measure. Thus, developing feedback systems becomes in turn very difficult.

3. Complex operations. Lortie (1977b), following Thompson (1967), suggests that schools employ a combination of "mediating" technology (that is, operations which bring together persons to meet their diverse needs) and "long-linked" technology (operations requiring a certain degree of sequencing over time), and less often "intensive" technology (focus on idiosyncratic processing of individual cases). It can be argued that such a blend is unusually hard to track and steer in any systematic sense. Sieber, too, emphasizes the complex, demanding nature of the combined socialization and social-control task that faces teachers confronted with large numbers of compelled clients.

Furthermore, there is at least some evidence (Rutter et al., 1979) that school outputs are as much a function of complex organizational processes (such as norms supporting high expectations by teachers) as they are of what specific teaching strategies are followed.

4. Weak production function. A number of authors (Berman, 1978a; Boyd, 1978; Freeman, 1979), as we have seen, claim that the basic cause of weak self-monitoring, lack of output control, and the like is that no reliable information exists on how teaching strategies are associated with outcomes. The claim seems to rest on syntheses such as those by Stephens (1967) and Averch et al. (1972), but probably deserves more detailed examination. It is probably "inherently" true that the known causal links between, say, physical or chemical operations and outcomes are stronger than those for the person-transforming domain, even if we allow for the fact that the physical sciences have been in business longer.

5. Disconnection of operations and outcomes from rewards. As we have noted, at the individual practitioner level good performance by teachers (and, it should be said, administrators) does not seem to be tied to financial rewards, or to career advancement. This is partly due to the "non-staged" nature of teaching (Sieber, this volume) and partly to reliance on substitute indicators of performance (such as avoidance of nonsmooth system operation, for administrators).

We should also note, as does Packard (1977: 6), that the same decoupling occurs at the school district level:

> Schools do not exchange their products for economic or other raw materials. Stated differently, the money that schools receive is not contingent upon the acceptability of their product.

KNOWLEDGE GAPS

What are some nominations for inquiry in this area?

1. "Alignment" among outcomes, instruction, and assessment. The findings at SWRL reported by Niedermeyer (1979) deserve careful replication. The issue, however, is not just whether such close coupling will lead to improved student performance (regardless of level of student input, as Niedermeyer claims), but whether such a *system* (a) remains institutionalized in user schools, and (b) can easily diffuse to other schools.

2. Studies of the educational production function. The widely made claim that we do not know with much certainty what educational interventions lead to what outcomes deserves careful attention. Meta-analyses of the very large body of "methods" research studies would be an economical start.

3. Barriers and aids to the diffusion of self-study technology. A number of studies are currently under way on how local school districts use evaluation information. These might be amplified by examination of what has retarded and aided the diffusion of survey feedback (or OD more generally)—technologies which go beyond sheer reporting of data to utilization through corrective action.

Innovations which have carefully defined classroom-management systems attached to them (as do many of the basic skills programs available through the National Diffusion Network) might also be examined rather closely to see whether (and how) they alter teacher decision making about instructional strategies. And do such innovations diffuse more slowly or more rapidly than those with weaker self-monitoring capability?

Dilemma 8:
Centralized versus Shared Influence

Where, how, and by whom should decisions be made in a school? The dilemma appears at the classroom level (should students and teachers share influence over assignments, scheduling, subgrouping, or should the teacher's authority be primary?); at the school building level (will a new program be mandated by the principal, or agreed on with full participation of teachers?); and at the district level (do principals have a say in district-wide budgeting decisions?). This is *not* the same as the coordination-flexibility dilemma, with which it is widely confused. Many highly centralized systems, as we shall see, are quite loosely coupled (that is, orders come from one place, but are not followed up and may be diversely responded to); and a tightly coupled system can be very vigorously participative.

The dilemma of influence distribution is an old one, and has been much discussed in the last twenty years: see McGregor's (1960) delineation of "Theory X" (traditional, dominative, mistrustful mapping of organizations) and "Theory Y" (modern, collaborative, trustful ideas). The ideological flavor of much that has been written on the topic, in and out of schools, is pronounced, and the sprawling literature cannot possibly be encompassed in this brief synthesis effort. Our focus must be on the common properties (if any) which schools have in this general domain.

One additional note: Social systems, from small groups[25] to societies, are hierarchically organized; the distribution of power (and associated benefits) is lopsided. "To them that hath shall be given" stands as a universal description of social life, though reformers of every age have decried it. The question, in short, is not whether influence is centralized in social systems—it *always* is—but *how* centralized it is.

REGULARITIES NOTED

What generalizations can be drawn about common properties in this domain?

1. Low influence by students. We have already reviewed evidence bearing on this under Dilemma 1, under the heading of goal displacement and "control orientation." We might add here some data from the Abramowitz and Tenenbaum (1978) study of high schools. When principals were asked which of a number of roles and groups were "involved in making decisions" relating to a range of school issues, students as individuals were usually lowest on the totem pole. For example, for the issue "determining course objectives," 80 percent of principals said that they themselves were involved; the figures for other roles were teachers as individuals, 83 percent; department heads, 59 percent; assistant administrators, 34 percent; guidance counselors, 22 percent; student groups, 10 percent; and students as individuals, 9 percent. (Parents were also mentioned 9 percent of the time.) Even on an issue where students might be expected to have shared influence—adopting rules for student behavior—the figures were: principal, 96 percent; school board, 74 percent; superintendent, 70 percent; teachers as individuals, 55 percent; assistant administrators, 51 percent; student groups, 49 percent; and students as individuals, 24 percent (parents, 30 percent on this issue).

2. Zoning of decisions. We have already alluded (under Dilemma 3) to the idea of "influence discontinuities," the presence of partially overlapping zones, spheres, or domains of influence where decision rights tend to be arrogated to particular roles. In terms of our present discussion, one can note that the degree of centralization in schools is not monolithic, but depends very much on the issue at hand (see Downs and Mohr, 1976).

For example, in Packard et al.'s (1978) study of 29 elementary schools, "teachers as individuals" made nearly two-thirds of all "instructional" decisions (those on teaching methods, materials, scheduling, and the like). In the sample's *non*-IGE schools, traditionally organized, over half of decisions on "deployment" issues (pupil assignment to classes, teaching assignments) were made by principals; such decisions were more likely to be made collegially/jointly in IGE schools. And about half of "systemic" decisions (such as curricular areas, textbook adoptions, and methods of reporting to parents) were made outside the school (typically, in the central office); the figure for IGE schools was about 40 percent.

Similarly, Daft and Becker (1978), examining the initiation of innovations, found that teachers in their sample of 13 suburban high schools initiated 70 percent of *instructional* innovations, principals 8 percent, superintendents 9 percent. Shared initiation (collaborations) occurred 12 percent of the time. By contrast, when *administrative* innovations (student scheduling, school structure, program budgeting) were considered, superintendents initiated 45 percent, principals 22 percent, and teachers only 13 percent; collaborations accounted for 13 percent. (Students started only 1 percent and 4 percent, respectively, of each innovation type.)

3. "Local" centralization. The Abramowitz and Tenenbaum (1978) data are instructive in pointing out another feature: that the chain of hierarchy, when a range of seven key issues in schools are considered, does not necessarily go monotonically up through the central office. The involvement of students as individuals averages 13 percent; student groups, 19 percent; department heads, 45 percent; individual teachers, 53 percent; and principals, 90 percent. But involvement of central office administrators hovers around 33 percent; superintendents, 63 percent; and school boards, 50 percent. Of course, the figures for principals are undoubtedly inflated by the fact that principals were filling out the questionnaires, and the idea of "involvement" does not specify who has what scale of decision power.

Another set of items in the same study, however, shows that 77 percent of principals have "complete" or "considerable" authority to allocate budget among departments; 65 percent enjoy similar authority when the issue is allocating money to aides versus teachers; 43 percent do so for deciding on budget allocations to their own schools; and 56 percent say they can choose to fill teacher vacancies, with usual endorsement by the central office. The picture is one of centralization of power at the principal, not the central office level, along with some principal-central office sharing.

In passing, traditional decision structures seem typical in the 1428 high schools studied: "School policy or planning groups" were mentioned as being involved only 20 percent of the time, across issues.

We might speculate, as researchers have for other sorts of organizations, that "mirroring" occurs at varying levels of school organization: Just as principals exert little direct control over what teachers actually do in their classrooms from day to day, so superintendents have relatively little day to day influence over what principals (often identified by school people as "kings," or as being in charge of "fiefdoms") do. As Lortie (1977a: 4) remarks:

> The formal powers of the central office are such that there can be no doubt as to where responsibility lies. . . . No matter how remote the

central office may seem to teachers and students . . . it possesses powers [hiring, firing, promotion, rules, funds, curriculum] which encompass teaching and learning.

But, he goes on:

Such dependency and constraint does not mean that the central office is able to enforce its desires at will in classrooms under its jurisdiction, for it is one matter to prevent or constrain action and quite another to give it specific shape [p. 5].

In any case, if mirroring does occur, it seems to stop abruptly when we move to the student level; the teachers who have much latitude within their classrooms (at least as judged by the sort of data just noted) do not seem to grant similar latitude to students.

4. Increasing teacher power. Some observers suggest that the growth of teacher unionization and use of collective bargaining have reduced the central power of principals and other administrators. That may be so, especially since contractual specifications serve as a constraint on administrator action. But we should note that the principals in the Abramowitz and Tenenbaum (1978) study mentioned teacher unions and organizations as being involved, on the average, only about 6 percent of the time, across decision issues. That may represent a veridical view that unions do not concern themselves with "professional" issues, but such an interpretation does not fit with the figures of 12 percent given for union involvement in "formulating school goals" versus 1 percent for "teacher selection" and 3 percent for "developing a budget for your school."

Elsewhere in the Abramowitz data we note that 62 percent of high school principals say that "the number of persons involved in school decision making" has increased in the past five years; only 2 percent mention a decrease. In addition, 52 percent mention an increase in "joint planning among teachers" (4 percent see a decrease). Interdependence among departments is seen as increasing by only 17 percent, however, so the issue is not so much better organizational knitting, but apparently more teacher collegiality (and perhaps mobilization).

5. Shared influence as a support for innovation. "Participation" is a sort of shibboleth in the folklore of school improvement. Giacquinta (1973: 189), however, claims that

on the basis of the empirical work to date, little can be said about the effects of participation strategies as compared to strategies where administrators introduce change without prior rank and file involvement in the decisions. Furthermore, why participation is important has not been made clear. There are cogent reasons for believing that strategies involving subordinate participation can lead to conflicting demands, exacerbation of differences among members, greater reluctance to try change, and thus less effectiveness.

Giacquinta's skepticism can be lauded, but we should note that the "empirical work" he cites has few if any examples of innovation/introduction in educational settings as such.

Paul's (1977) review of change studies cites six reports (five of them in education) that lead to this conclusion:

> Involvement and participation in the decision-making process by those affected by a change program will be beneficial [p. 44].

Paul treats this as a "firm" conclusion, but notes that the issue is not monolithic: Participation in early stages of a change effort will enable commitment, and increased need-responsiveness of the program. But participation (and the usually associated decentralization) may "inhibit coordination and control which are necessary for the implementation of new programs" (Paul, 1977: 44).

Fullan and Pomfret (1977), examining studies of curriculum implementation, provide further differentiation. They, like Giacquinta, feel that available research "tells us very little about [participation]. . . . Questions about the nature, timing and scope of participation are left unanswered." But they go on to note that a generalized view of "participation" should be recast into "managerial" and "user" perspectives; the former taking a fidelity-oriented, user-resocializing approach, and the latter aimed at adaptation and active decision making. They conclude:

> There is no evidence that leads us to select one approach over the other, but the following observations seem in order. First, if one is interested in standardizing the implementation of an innovation that has a high degree of *a priori* explicitness, it can be argued that a managerial/retraining approach is more effective. Second, our assessment of the trend in most recent curriculum reforms is that *a priori* explicitness is difficult if not impossible, and undesirable, because they usually require a high degree of user input (i.e., inquiry and self-directed learning). This favors the user perspective as the most effective for high degrees of implementation [Fullan and Pomfret, 1977: 381].

Berman's chapter (this volume) draws a similar conclusion, suggesting that participation is most important for less structured innovations, where high complexity and uncertainty are typical; he also suggests that local agreement on the "change policy" (in effect, commitment to the innovation) and the local administrative structure will condition the effects of participation.

Two additional studies that "unpack" the participation issue can be cited. Rosenblum and Louis (1981), in their study of comprehensive, districtwide change efforts in rural schools, found (a) that the more successful efforts were associated with superintendent dominance over both planning and decision making, *and* (b) that efforts could succeed with high principal and teacher influence *if* the superintendent's power was low, *but* (c) teacher and principal influence was *negatively* associated with success when the superintendent had high power (suggesting a district/building-level competition). Once again, we are led to the possibility that who "should" participate in a change effort if it is to be successful depends on what the change effort is and/or in whose zone or domain it falls.

Daft and Becker (1978: 106) have some illuminating findings in this respect. They conclude that

> the districts where teachers propose the largest percentage of educational [instructional] innovations also adopt a greater absolute number of educational innovations. . . . And the districts where administrators propose the largest percentage of administrative ideas also tend to adopt a greater number of administrative innovations. School districts appear only to adopt a large number of innovations of either type when individuals in the relevant task domain initiate them.

But these processes vary according to the level of teacher professionalism (measured, it will be recalled, by the proportion having Master's degrees). High-professional districts tended to work from the bottom up (93 percent of initiations of educational innovations came from teachers) and shared initiation of administrative innovations with administrators (47 percent each). But in low-professional districts, teachers only suggested 53 percent of educational innovations, and *no* administrative innovations, which came 97 percent of the time from administrators. Top-down initiation, under those circumstances, appeared perfectly workable.

Daft and Becker also append one interesting note: The frequency of "collaborative" initiations of educational innovations was *least* (7 percent) in high-innovative districts, and *most* in low-innovative districts (32 percent). In the high-innovative districts, they reasoned, "there is little need for administrators to collaborate with teachers," who are taking initiative already. The so-called collaborations in the low-innovative districts appeared to be (cooptive?) accompaniments of greater administrative initiative in a low-professional setting.

The Daft and Becker findings, even though they may be restricted in generalizability from their suburban high school setting and by the fact that the sample was of *implemented* innovations,[26] are useful in reminding us of the contingencies among innovation domain, level of professionalism, and the direction of innovative pushes.

We might note one further recurrent finding in the "shared influence" realm. One of the best documented (or at least most widely acclaimed) generalizations about change efficacy centers on the question of "support" from superiors (see Sieber's chapter, this volume, for a summary and analysis). Fullan also reviews these findings and suggests the importance of "active" support (not just "naive endorsement" and not "direct imposition"). The label "support," surprisingly enough, has usually remained undefined. However, its affective overtones, and the usual connotation that assistance or help is involved, serve to obscure something important: A principal who is "supporting" is probably accepting a good deal of influence from teachers in the process—she/he is attending to their goals, accepting them as worthwhile, and construing their needs for assistance as legitimate. The force of this argument can be assessed by looking at its converse: It is quite unlikely that a principal who is mandating a change or using coercive power will be seen as "supportive." *Mutatis mutandis,* the same applies to the superintendent, who is equivalently seen in the literature as needing to provide support at the district level.

In summary, this review suggests, with somewhat less certainty than for preceding dilemmas, that "centralization" in the tried and true sense familiar to students of organization does not quite apply in schools. Students (and parents) have low influence, teachers have much more (and their influence may be increasing), and principals may have most of all, with the central office making background and constraining decisions. In any case, decisions seem to be very much "zoned," with teachers, principals, central office personnel (and presumably boards) specializing in particular areas. In this sense, many decisions are not "shared" in the collaborative sense, but in effect farmed out to (and/or negotiated among) different parts of the system. Finally, though shared collaborative influence may be associated with implementation of change, that relationship too is conditioned by innovation type, by stage of the process, by decision zoning, and by teacher professionalism. (The length of this summary, indeed, suggests the lumpiness of our conclusions.)

CLAIMED ANTECEDENTS

Once again, it is not at all clear that we can be very crisp in identifying explanations, perhaps because the "regularities" identified above have in fact appeared more "variable" than regular. However:

1. Compulsory attendance. We have already outlined the view (Willower, 1970) that the presence of large numbers of immature, perhaps unwilling, students leads to a strong control orientation.

2. Managerial professionalization. The growth of specialized administrative roles, particularly those of superintendent and principal, was, as Michaelson (1977) notes, supported as much by the creation of compulsory attendance laws as by the infusion of the "efficiency" movement in school administration.

3. Domain conflict. Again following Kouzes and Mico (1979), we might speculate that the inherently conflicting demands of a publicly controlled policy-making sector, a bureaucratically oriented managerial sector, and an instructionally oriented service delivery sector make for the sorts of "vertical decoupling" noted above. Note that the historical feature of local control probably sharpens such conflict over its "natural" levels in a centralized macrostructure such as those in most European countries.

4. Democratic ideology. The importance of participation in change may be partially driven by the idea that the governed ought to have the right of consent. One is reminded of the early and successful experiments in "overcoming resistance to change" (Coch and French, 1948) through group discussion and decision, which failed of replication in a Norwegian factory where it happened that workers did not regard their participation in managerial matters as legitimate.

KNOWLEDGE GAPS

What might be studied more fully in this domain?

1. Contingency analysis of "participation." We need to know more about the conditions under which participative approaches are essential or unnecessary in change efforts, connecting them with innovation type, stages of the change process, professionalism, and possibly community context (note that the Rosenblum and Louis, 1981, findings may well be limited to rural settings).

2. *Processes and effects of shared influence structures.* It is clear from the Packard et al. (1978) studies that the multiunit IGE structure, in part a method for increasing shared influence, does not have striking effects in that direction, though some shifts over a two-year period are evident. Similarly, "policy and planning groups" are only rarely mentioned by principals in the Abramowitz and Tenenbaum (1978) study. There is the possibility (the case for the conservative) that such structures are in effect "countergeneric," working against what is somehow "natural" for schools. It would be very useful to understand more about their genesis in particular schools, their process vicissitudes, their consequences, and their survival over time.

Dilemma 9:
Change versus Stability

Our last dilemma is perhaps the first and most basic, from the point of view of knowledge utilization and school improvement. Should people in schools choose new, different, "modern" means for accomplishing goals, or stay with the tried, coherent, and familiar? Should, indeed, any efforts at "improvement," whether marginal or fundamental, take place? Perhaps most effort should be going into stabilization of what is known to be working well. At the macro level, schools face the dilemma in terms of social functions: Should they be performing a critical or a conservative function for society? The dilemma of change versus stability—reform versus consolidation, liberal versus conservative, yin versus yang—is one of the oldest in human affairs, and it cuts across, underlies, the eight preceding dilemmas.

Once again: This review cannot possibly encompass the large and rambling literature in and out of education devoted to innovation, planned (and unplanned) change, utilization of new knowledge, diffusion, dissemination, technology transfer, and similar topics. We will aim to focus on what might be "common" in this domain when the local school is examined in its context.

REGULARITIES NOTED

What generalizations, possibly related to schools' common properties, have been made in this domain?

1. *"Nonrationality" toward innovation.* Some analysts suggest (having in mind such issues as goal diffuseness and measurement difficulty) that there are no real incentives for schools to adopt supposedly efficacious innovations available in the environment. Pincus (1974) suggests that financially costly innovations may well be adopted to promote the appearance of modernity, efficacy, and so on; financially costly innovations rejected are likely to be those involving high *bureaucratic* costs (disruptions, energy). Sieber (1977), though he criticizes Pincus for ignoring

current economic pressures, has noted a study showing that innovations rated by judges as "less effective" *and* more difficult to implement (such as TV and programmed instruction) were frequently adopted, perhaps for symbolic reasons ("up-to-dateness"). De Arman (1975), studying the adoption and abandonment of 33 innovations by 3271 high schools, found an adoption average of 9.7, and an abandonment average of only .76 (suggesting either very rational adoption processes or symbolic ones). Complex, expensive, and administratively difficult innovations were abandoned more frequently. Both teacher resistance and poor student outcomes were cited as reasons for abandonment.

   2. Local adaptation. Much has been made of the idea, advanced by Berman and McLaughlin (1974), that innovations and school organizations engage in a sort of mutually influencing interaction: The school bends, revises, selects from, and adds to the innovation so that it can be effectively fitted to the local situation, and in turn supposedly alters itself (if only by the addition of the innovation).

   But the Rand studies themselves make it clear that "mutual adaptation" is actually quite rare, and that what the authors called "cooptation" is much more frequent; the school changes minimally, and the innovation substantially. Mann (1978: 12), speaking of the federal "change agent" programs at work in schools, says:

> All projects [Vol. III, Rand studies] displayed a clear and similar pattern of adaptation. With the passage of time they: (a) become less ambitious about the system-wide efforts they sought; (b) simplified their treatments; (c) slowed the pace of their activities; (d) decreased the amount of changed behavior expected from any individual; and (e) decreased their expectations about how many people in a site could be changed.

Berman, who originally labeled the phenomen "mutation," says in this volume, with thorough documentation:

> The interaction of an educational innovation with its setting (that is, its implementation) generally results in changes in the initially conceived innovation.

   In a more extreme version of this view, Farrar et al. (1980), considering the use of Experience-Based Career Education, a complex work experience program, propose that any given innovation can potentially meet so many diverse needs of so many diverse internal and external audiences, that the process of "adaptation" is multilateral and evolutionary. The image suggested is that of people attending a garden party: All parties to the enterprise try to understand what they want, and to get it, and the diverse meanings and nature of the innovation change over time. Innovations, in this view, are not much more than a sort of vehicle (or even projective screen) for the transactions of people in and around the school.

   Not surprisingly, such findings have led to a good deal of pessimism as to whether educational "technology" (instructional or administrative innovations) can in fact be "transferred" (House, 1976; Mann, 1978). Against this we should place what appears to be the relative success of the National Diffusion Network (Emrick et al., 1977), and the R&D Utilization Project (Louis, 1980), both efforts to bring new technology to schools via change-agent-supported efforts at stimulating awareness, adoption, training, and implementation.

Both these studies suggest that something like technology transfer is indeed possible. For example, Louis (1980) notes that in the R&DU sample of over 300 schools, 80 percent of teachers eligible to use the product installed with linking agent help were doing so, and that 64 percent of principals said it had been incorporated into school curriculum plans; 62 percent predicted extensive future use. Furthermore, characteristics of the product itself (its validation, its complexity, and its pupil-affecting nature) were especially strong predictors of institutionalization and organizational change in a subsample of 55 schools.

The *NDN Reporter* for November 1978 claims that 5800 to 7000 "deep-rooted adoptions" of over 200 different educational programs have occurred since the founding of the NDN in 1974.

The mismatch between empirical results and claims like these on the one hand, and pessimism about local change in schools on the other may have several causes: (1) the Rand and Farrar et al. studies emphasized more complex, less "thing-y" innovations than most of those in the NDN and RDU pools; (2) the NDN adoptions, at least, are not in fact "deep-rooted," and would show up weakly on what Downs and Mohr (1976) call "extent of adoption" (commitment, institutionalization, internal diffusion, and so on; (3) NDN adoptions may have included a large amount of local adaptation (or as in the case of the RDU projects, choice and/or redesign of nonvalidated products). Continuing analysis of the RDU data, and the new data being collected by the Study of Dissemination Efforts Supporting School Improvement (Crandall, 1980) should shed some light on these competing explanations.

3. "Slow" innovation rates. The tacit corollary of "local adaptation" is the view that schools, as such, are changing only slowly, if at all. A number of observers have suggested that schools are notable for their resistance to change. We have already noted Morrish's (1976) lengthy diatribe headed "Why Schools Change So Slowly." To this we might add Elboim-Dror's (1970) view that educational decision making is characteristically "tradition-bound, slow and incremental," and Hawley's (1975) view that all the common properties of schools lean them inexorably toward "rigidity." Most recently, there is Blumberg's (1980) confidently titled chapter "School Organizations: A Case of Generic Resistance to Change," in which he claims that a "siege mentality" and "ontological insecurity" induce a strong "commitment to smoothness" in schools. The result, he asserts, is acceptance of "first-order" changes (part-innovation, in effect), and rejection of "second-order" (system-changing) intervention. It is difficult to assess the merit of these claims without empirical data.

If the tone of the preceding paragraph communicates skepticism, then it is being understood. Sieber's chapter (this volume) makes a case against the "myth of a stagnant educational system," suggesting that change rates in elementary and secondary education have been substantial, especially when compared with other types of systems. He lists the wide range of innovations that have been adopted, from desegregation through language labs to teacher centers, and cites (without providing detail) several "national surveys" (such as Havelock et al., 1973); Abramowitz and Tenenbaum, 1978; Nelson and Sieber, 1976). The problem, however, is that (a) such data are noncomparative—we do not know whether schools are any more or less likely than other sorts of organizations to welcome change; (b) they are ahistorical—we do not know whether change rates have accelerated or decreased since Paul Mort's famous "50-year lag" dictum, pronounced in the 1940s.[27] Furthermore, cross-study comparisons are not easy: When Havelock et al. (1973) note that superintendents reported something over 9 innovations, on the average, for the 1970-1971 school year, is that commensurable with Brickell's (1964) finding that New York State districts he surveyed in 1961 had adopted (and kept), on the average, 4.2 innovations since 1953?

So, on balance, the verdict on "slow" innovation rates must remain "not proven."

4. *"Weak" internal change capability.* Schools supposedly lack internal change-supportive roles or mechanisms in place as part of routine operations. For example, the development of internal cadres of organizational improvement consultants (Schmuck et al., 1977) is quite rare; in-service training is widely conceded to be superficial, unhelpful (Rubin, 1971), and infrequent. Abramowitz and Tenenbaum's (1978) principals reported an average of only 4.8 days a year (about 3 percent of working time) devoted to in-service training. Most assistant superintendents for personnel do not think of their role as being that of "human resource developer," as they might in an industrial setting; and research and evaluation departments in large city systems seem rarely to carry out the research and development function, in the sense of creating new products and practices.

Against these claims we must place the finding (Miles, Fullan, et al., 1978a, 1978b) that organizational development programs in school districts were predominantly carried out by line managers (principals and central office personnel), rather successfully, even though they had little formal training for the job; that district office consultants (Fullan's chapter this volume), though often ineffective, can be crucial to the success of change efforts; and the familiar and fairly well-documented view that the support of principals and superintendents is the *sine qua non* of school improvement. So, as with the preceding "regularity," we need to know a good deal more.

5. *Expanding external change resources.* Here we are on somewhat more solid ground. It is quite clear that the last decade has seen a very substantial increase in all sorts of externally generated programs and practices, including categorical grants for innovation (Title III); mandated changes (desegregation, bilingual education, mainstreaming); specific educational programs (on basic skills, career education, early childhood devel-

opment, environmental education, the arts); extended information storage and retrieval systems (ERIC, Lockheed); the creation of new delivery systems (National Diffusion Network, R&D Utilization Program) using "linkers" (professionalized change agents) to help in assessing promising innovations from pools of available practices, deciding on adoption, and proceeding through implementation; and the availability of funds for local invention and lateral dissemination to other districts (Title IV-C). Partly as a result of these initiatives, there has also grown up a very substantial "evaluation industry" (Bank et al., 1979) with promise for the improvement of school self-study capability, and collaboration with linkers.

The increase in funds and change-relevant staff for state departments of education has already been alluded to; we should also note the increased state dissemination capability supported by federal initiatives (Madey et al., 1979), the historical shift of more than a few state departments from a "regulatory" to a "facilitative" role, and the growth of regional or intermediate service units aimed at supporting school improvement (see Cates et al., 1979, for a review).

Thus the educational macrostructure, as complex, poorly coordinated, and constraining as it is, has clearly shifted in the direction of supportiveness toward the "change" horn of the dilemma we are considering.

CLAIMED ANTECEDENTS

To summarize, the regularities noted in the change versus stability domain have included the idea that schools have a "nonrational" stance toward innovation, and that an extensive amount of local adaptation in externally arising innovations is typical, along with minimal alteration in the schools' structures and processes. The question of whether schools are "slower," more "rigid," more resistant to change than other sorts of organizations (and the question of whether school change rates have altered over the last few decades) is ambiguous, though more claims are made on the pessimistic side. Finally, though it is unclear whether schools lack internal change capabilities, the evidence is strong that external resources for change have increased substantially over the past twenty years. What explanations have been offered?

1. Outcome vagueness. Many different authors have invoked the idea that educational goals are intangible and hard to measure (Elboim-Dror, 1970; Hawley, 1975), not least because of the long time perspective involved between educational intervention and ultimate results.

2. Weak incentive structure. Both slower innovation rates and resistance to structural alteration have been claimed to follow from faulty incentive structures, at the level of individual practitioners (see Sieber's comments on the "unstaged" nature of the teaching career), and at the level of the local school district (Pincus, 1974; Packard, 1977). At neither level are financial rewards connected to outcome achievement; thus the argument goes that there is little reason to consider new, possibly more efficacious procedures.

3. Weak production function. As noted earlier, the idea that little is supposedly known about the reliable consequences of educational interventions is another claimed antecedent for movement toward the "stability" horn of the dilemma.

We might summarize here an analysis by Boyd (1979b), who notes that retrenchment pressures do not seem to have led (contrary to what some organizational theory would predict) to innovativeness in schools, but to simple "reduction in scale," "less of the same" strategies. He concludes that "the lack of a well-understood production function" contributes to emphasis on "maintaining educational quality" rather than improving educational *productivity,* a stance he characterizes as "the symbolic politics of efficiency."

4. Vulnerability. The view that schools are open to damaging inputs from their environments, and that this induces caution and conservatism, appears in a number of versions: Blumberg's (1980) "ontological insecurity"; Elboim-Dror's (1970) claim that vulnerability leads to local power struggles and submissiveness, hence reliance on routine; Willower's (1970) argument that vulnerability and received pressure on schools generate the need for "impression management" and the tendency to invoke innovations as "ornaments"; and Meyer and Rowan's (1978) view that locally controlled systems which are charged with formal "certifying" functions tend to decouple instruction from administration and curriculum, and carry out local adaptations without disrupting what really matters to their constituencies (the *appearance* of a stable school).

5. The professionalization of reform. Boyd (1978) has noted the growth of a sort of establishment aimed at educational reform (in foundations, the federal government, and universities); we should add to this the substantial increase in stored (and reasonably synthesized) knowledge about knowledge utilization itself, and the development of a "dissemination community." As Boyd points out, the very development of these vested interests and the increased complexity of the educational macrostructure may indeed be making change—at least center-to-periphery change—more cumbersome, more difficult, and more unlikely. That claim, however, deserves assessment, as opposed to the competing claim that since schools now have substantially more resources—both in terms of new educational "products" and facilitative "process" assistance—to draw on, the likelihood of movement toward the change horn of the dilemma is enhanced.

KNOWLEDGE GAPS

What does it seem that we need to know here?

1. Base rates of innovation. As suggested here and earlier (Miles, 1974), there is a real need to know, on a regular, recurrent basis, what schools are doing in the way of innovation, knowledge utilization, and school improvement. National sample surveys like those carried out by Havelock et al. (1973) would provide substantial help, especially if they were differentiated enough to examine questions such as: (1) the prevalence of "first-level" versus "second-level" (system-altering) changes (and more generally, a breakdown of "innovations" according to the attributes of change

efforts outlined by Berman in this volume); (2) extensity of local exposure
to innovations (number of students, teachers, administrators involved); (3)
as per Berman, the distribution of changes by various contingent conditions (elementary/secondary, stable versus turbulent environments,
urban/rural/suburban settings); (4) the nature and extent of local adaptation; and (5) "depth of adoption" variables, such as institutionalization
and internal diffusion.

2. *The limits to "technology transfer."* According to the general perspective (see House's chapter, this volume) one brings to questions of
school improvement, the promise of knowledge-utilization structures such
as the National Diffusion Network and the R&D Utilization Program is
either very great or quite limited. We need studies of actual amounts of
local adaptation; of the character of "deep-rooted" adoptions; and of
whether there are classes of innovation, in interaction with local contextual properties, which are especially well or poorly suited to a technology
transfer model. Such studies should, of course, be built on the findings
from the R&D Utilization evaluation, and the Study of Dissemination
Efforts Supporting School Improvement. They should also not be trapped
in a narrowly technological view of the process. As Downs and Mohr
(1978) point out, it is unprofitable to consider "properties of the innovation" (or indeed of the organization) in isolation; the proper unit of
analysis is the innovation-organization pair.

3. *Nature of internal change supports.* There seems to be a good deal of
ambiguity about mechanisms and processes internal to local schools that
support movement toward the "change" horn of the dilemma. We will not
try to duplicate Fullan's suggestions here, but merely note that studies of
such domains as in-service training, internal cadres, the role of principals
and central office staff, linkage between insiders and external assisters, and
the role of teachers as change initiators are all in order.

CONCLUSIONS:
A SUGGESTED RESEARCH AGENDA

The basic mission of this chapter has been to summarize what seems to
be known about the common properties of schools, on an empirical basis,
to do some assessment of the explanations offered for the presence of such
properties, and to outline an agenda for future research, both to provide
more descriptive data and to test competing explanations.

Table 2.1 summarizes the main "regularities" noted or claimed for
schools, sorted by the nine basic dilemmas of school operation and change,
along with explanatory antecedents. It also lists the recommendations for
research made for each dilemma. Question marks are appended where
doubt or ambiguity seems present.

This table shows us several things. First, it seems clear that much more
directly descriptive data are needed on matters of the most straightforward
sort: the actual instructional modes being used by teachers; their auton-

omy to make decisions affecting their work; the main types of knowledge people seek inside and outside their local organizations, and from whom/ what they seek it; the degree to which such knowledge is actually "utilized" in work; what people in schools use as their practical definitions of goals; how parent influence is exercised; the decisions of administrators and boards, and how far they are constrained by the local community. In most cases we do not have reliable, carefully sampled studies that would tell us, simply, what is really going on.

A second comment, echoing that made by Berman, is that we need many more *contingent analyses,* showing, for example, under what contextual conditions active teacher involvement in planning change will be productive; for what sorts of innovations, in what sorts of organizational and community contexts, a "technology transfer" approach will work well or poorly; what aspects of routinization and uniformity in schools are associated with innovativeness; or the differential consequences of externally mandated change in stable and turbulent environments.

Third, it seems quite clear that most of the *causal claims* asserted (the supposed antecedents of the regularities noted) are almost untested in any empirical sense. If they are to do more than survive as folklore or dubious wisdom, direct inquiry is needed. Two approaches seem workable: *comparative analysis,* where naturally occurring variation in supposedly critical antecedent variables can be mapped; and *intervention evaluation,* where such variables are altered experimentally (as in the case of voucher plans, shifts to team teaching, and so on).

Though the review above was carried out in an essentially exploratory, inductive way, there are several antecedent variables that do seem to recur, that may generate regularities in several domains. These include goal vagueness/measurement difficulty, vulnerability, weak production function, inappropriate incentive structures, and compulsory attendance. Furthermore, with the exception of compulsory attendance, all these variables are claimed to be causal for the change versus stability dilemma. And, again with the exception of compulsory attendance (which will probably never be undone), all these variables are presumably amenable to empirical study, and even to experimental manipulation. They might well take priority over other inquiry.

Fourth, though Table 2.1 only suggests it here and there, it would undoubtedly be useful to treat both *innovativeness* (read "implementation," "deep-rooted adoption," "school improvement," "institutionalization," and so on) and school *effectiveness* as dependent variables for many or all of the noted regularities specified under each dilemma. To take a single example: There are many polemics decrying the well-established fact that students have little power in schools. But can any causal linkages be established between student influence and the change-relevant capabilities of the school, or its production of learning?

This review has been, in effect, a sort of map-making journey. As in most explorations, there has been much of interest along the way, a certain amount of cognitive overload, and the discovery of new uncertainties. The test of any map is perhaps not so much its micro-level accuracy as its practical usefulness in helping you get where you want to go. So the question is how far the rough mapping offered here, and the reflection it may have stimulated in the reader, can advance our understanding of what is underlying, durable, typical, stable, "essential" in American schools—and thus in our efforts to support them, operate them, study them, and improve them. That, too, is an empirical question.

NOTES

1. There is, of course, another comparative possibility: comparing American schools of today with those of earlier times. For example, rereading Waller's (1932) vivid accounts and analyses of what life in schools was like during the late twenties in small-town America shows us how radically the status and legitimacy of the teaching profession has shifted, and that a then unconceived-of "knowledge utilization" infrastructure has grown up. But most historians of education have not focused on the isolation of "common properties."

2. Any such listing is arbitrary in some sense; this draws on Berman and McLaughlin (1979), Miles (1978), Miles, Sullivan et al. (1978a), and Schmuck et al. (1977).

3. The "choice" implied in a particular dilemma may not be particularly apparent to any particular actor. A particular event or behavior (say, hiring a complaining parent as an aide) may often be seen as the "only" or the "natural" thing to do, with other alternatives only dimly considered (Miles, Sullivan, et al., 1978a). Yet to an observer, one horn of the dilemma has clearly been honored over the other.

4. Federal and state "paperwork" were also mentioned by 42 percent and 36 percent of principals, respectively, but the topic may well be a prompted artifact. After all, the questionnaire itself was "paperwork."

5. Hard-to-measure goals are not necessarily disadvantageous. Elboim-Dror (1970), for example, points out that intangible goals provide more latitude and flexibility, aid compromise, inspire support and commitment, and intensify the socializing power of the institution.

6. Except tacitly, through making it easy for older students to become dropouts or implicitly condoning very high absence rates, as in some urban high schools (New York City's absence rate runs about 30 percent).

7. Batch processing should not be seen as deliberate, repressive, inhumane, or the like, but as a natural response to the presence of numbers of learners in one place. Herskovitz (1963) notes the existence of batched "bush schools" in preliterate societies, for example.

8. We should note in passing, as do Spence et al. (1978), that the energy spent in student control has (as in all influence situations) back effects: Teachers and administrators are themselves constrained and controlled by the need to control students. Enforcing rules, living by bell schedules, and turning in students caught smoking in the restroom, all reduce choice and autonomy for those nominally more powerful than students. As Lortie (1977a: 26) notes, teachers, more than almost any other profession, are "time and place-bound—during working hours, they have very little physical mobility and few occasions for joint undertakings."

9. One recent study does suggest that, if a "cage" does exist, there is still room for movement within it on issues that matter. Rutter et al. (1979), in their 7-year study of 12 secondary schools in London, found that the amount of time spent during classes on noninstructional matters (time off task, in effect) ranged from 15 percent to 35 percent. We should also note Cusick's (1973) finding that some teachers spend less than half as much time actually teaching as others.

10. The general question here, of course, is whether a "loose coupling" model is a good fit to the case of schools. Weick (1980, 1976), who has done most to encourage

use of the concept, has pointed out that the term is full (probably desirably) of surplus meaning, and is in fact itself "loosely coupled." The term has also been variously attacked as "old wine in new bottles" (Spence et al., 1978), as merely another term for the old concept of "functional autonomy" (Sieber, this volume), or as equivalent to the prior concept of "structural looseness" (Bidwell, 1965). "Loose coupling" has been used to refer to disconnection between goals and technology, to low surveillance and control, to lack of consensus among role occupants, and indeed to almost any organizational phenomenon that doesn't look like something expected in a proper bureaucracy. For these reasons, this section will bypass the term, and focus primarily on aspects of the coordination/flexibility dilemma that seem to be most salient.

11. See Kouzes and Mico (1979), who suggest that not just schools but all human-service organizations exhibit different "domains" (specifically, those of policy, management, and direct service delivery). Each domain "operates by different and contrasting principles, success measures, structural arrangements and work modes, and . . . the interactions between these create conditions of disjunction and discordance" (Kouzes and Mico, 1979: 449).

12. The weaknesses of agreement among teachers do appear to be genuine: Meyer et al. (1978) found that teachers who were working as members of teams had higher agreement on such matters as cross-grouping for reading, use of materials, and the principal's degree of influence.

13. Drawn from graphic displays (Packard et al., 1978: 180-181). Note that schools which were about to adopt IGE had a 9 percent rate of collegial decisions, while "control" schools had only 3 percent (thus the 6 percent figure noted).

14. Charters and Packard (1979: 26) conclude:

> We found only four instances throughout all of the schools that approximated the highly intensive collaboration indicative of genuine team teaching . . . [IGE] was . . . a diffuse encouragement for teachers to seek out collaborative relationships—an encouragement to which some teachers acceded and some did not.

Levels of collaboration in their data were lower than those found in the Stanford studies (because, they speculate, the Stanford collegial arrangements "evolved" rather than being installed as part of an externally generated program).

15. Charters and Packard (1979: 30) suggest from analysis of their IGE data that teacher autonomy is

> the resultant of countervailing forces—an autonomy-enhancing force emanating from the ability of teacher groups to influence educational affairs of the school and a strong, autonomy-depressing force from the principal's control of the teacher's classroom performance.

They tie this finding to Meyer and Cohen's (1971) conclusion that sheer freedom from interference must be accompanied by ability to control resources if autonomy is to be experienced.

16. Textbook content is also disproportionately influenced by the fact that several large states (Texas, for example) make statewide adoption decisions; publishers' natural conservative response to this fact illustrates well the interaction between ancillary and formal structures.

17. Halperin (1980) also notes that federal and state agencies also influence local schools in many nonregulatory ways: stimulation through categorical aid; research and development; service and technical assistance; general financial aid (support of operating costs); and "moral leadership"—emphasis on priorities and goals. In many respects, such functions may have even more impact than direct regulation on local districts. See, for example, Herriott (1979).

18. Or worse. Gold and Miles (1978) studied an open-space elementary school which invited parents to work as aides, hoping to coopt their opposition to the faculty's team-teaching methods. Many parents volunteered—then used the experience as ammunition to denounce the faculty for incompetence. The faculty had to abandon their methods.

19. Under some circumstances, expert knowledge on the very process of knowledge seeking and utilization itself may also be relevant.

20. Note that the issue addressed here is *not* whether educational practitioners seek knowledge or are resistant to doing so. As Hood and Blackwell (1976a) show, 50 percent of teachers, in any given year, seek information about new methods, and 40 percent do so for instructional materials. Rather, the question is one of the relative *balance* between external and internal resources.

21. This claim is made plausible by Glass and Smith's (1979) recent "meta-analysis" techniques. Class size research has produced a literature supposedly full of no-difference findings. But meta-analysis discovered some meaningful regularities, such as the fact that (for well-controlled studies in particular) there was a clear relation between class size and achievement, with steadily greater achievement for class sizes under 20.

22. A more reasonable claim, made by Fullan (this volume), is that teacher isolation simply makes access to external information sources more infrequent and difficult. He also points out that Sieber et al. (1972) and Emrick et al. (1977) both found increased rates of external knowledge utilization when external change agents were available to the school.

23. Such studies will also have to face the question of *what* expert knowledge is being utilized. Daft and Becker (1978), in their study of innovation adoptions in 13 suburban high schools, found that professionalism (as measured by proportion with Master's degrees) was positively correlated (r of .65) with the adoption of innovations for college-bound students, but insignificantly with adoption of innovations for terminal students. Even so, they found that more professionalized teachers were more likely than less professionalized ones to initiate both types of innovations. For highly professionalized teachers, the probability of initiation by them (rather than by administrators or a teacher-administrator coalition) was over .9; for less professionalized teachers, the figure dropped to less than .6.

24. Or lack the *will*? The author is reminded of the case (Miles, 1978) of a principal in a new elementary school, who, when offered the chance to discuss systematic survey data with his faculty for purposes of stock-taking and self-improvement, said, "That would be like going into a patch of poison ivy and lifting up each leaf to see what was under it."

25. For the classic review, which shows how informal groups (which might on the face of it seem to be the best bet for a collaborative, shared-influence model) develop hierarchies of participation and influence quickly, see Riecken and Homans (1954).

26. Daft and Becker (1978) note with some interest and amazement that though the school personnel interviewed identified 414 different adoptions of 68 different innovations, there were "only half a dozen instances . . . where the innovation was proposed but not adopted." The alternatives of forgetting, selective proposing of likely-to-succeed innovations, and low rejection rates for *any* innovation are mentioned, but not clearly evaluated by the authors.

27. One can make crude inferences: for example, in the Abramowitz and Tenenbaum (1978) study, we can note that 36 percent of high schools receive funds from Title IV-C to support innovative programs; or that 27 percent include courses on environmental or ocean studies (typically not present 10 years ago, one assumes); or (alternatively) that 93 percent use traditional methods of scheduling, and 84 percent A-B-C-D-F grading systems. But such inferences remain not much more than guess-work, in the absence of comparative and historical data.

3

KNOWLEDGE UTILIZATION
IN PUBLIC EDUCATION

Incentives and Disincentives

Sam D. Sieber

The purpose of this chapter is threefold: to suggest a paradigm for studying knowledge utilization (KU) that obliges us to take fully into account the perspectives, sensibilities, and aspirations of school personnel in various settings; to explore the utility of the paradigm by applying it to a broad spectrum of research; and to indicate areas in which further inquiry is needed.

The failure of social engineering approaches that have stemmed from the preconceptions of experts who were unwilling or unable to identify with educational personnel, or at least to consider their everyday frames of reference in objective fashion, has made a more phenomenological approach to KU a necessary step. Thus, I shall be interested mainly in the *meanings* to educational personnel of KU efforts in terms of the perceived rewards and costs of action.

It is true that the literature on educational change abounds in appeals to "incentives for change" and the importance of understanding "incentive systems," but these admonitions are rarely accompanied by an effort to identify types of incentives, their sources, the conditions under which they operate, or the way they should be combined to enhance motivation. On those rare occasions when a particular inducement, such as career advancement, problem solving, or enlightenment, is given full attention, there is a tendency to raise it to a status of omnipotence that underplays the

AUTHOR'S NOTE: This chapter is a condensed version of a study commissioned by the National Institute of Education, which is referred to in the text as Sieber (1979).

existence of a host of alternative inducements. Nor is reference made to incentives that work at cross-purposes, or to the unanticipated consequences of rewards that turn out not to be incentives at all, but may actually operate as disincentives. Indeed, it is often taken for granted that everyone knows what an incentive is, in spite of the paucity of definitions and the conflict among them. In light of this cavalier treatment of the subject, it seems that references to incentives have been more in the nature of rhetorical gestures than serious conceptual guideposts.

Recent trends in the study of planned educational change have made a systematic understanding of incentives for KU an urgent task. They have also made it possible to approach the task with greater confidence than in the past owing to the results of a number of major research studies. First, we have witnessed a growing appreciation of the non-task-oriented, or "extrinsic" rewards, that come into play in the process of innovation. In particular, recognition of an "opportunistic" motivation for adoption of federal projects and demonstration of its negative influence on implementation (Berman and McLaughlin, 1974) have focused attention on a fact that seems to have been stubbornly ignored by educational policy makers: a strong tendency for the target system to exploit the resources of an intervention for non-project purposes.

A second development that has sensitized us to the ubiquitous role of incentives has been growing recognition of the importance of understanding implementation as distinct from the adoption of innovations (Giacquinta, 1973; Fullan and Pomfret, 1975).[1] This shift in emphasis has prompted the realization that different rewards accompany different *stages* of the change process (see, for example, Pincus, 1974: 133.) Further, the formulation of a concerns-based adoption model (Hall, 1974) has drawn attention to a succession of concerns.

A third trend has been recognition of the failure of certain putative incentives to have the expected result, and of the success of certain presumed disincentives to motivate KU. The idea that participation in decision making will provide a sense of ownership and personal recognition that are needed for engagement in change projects has yielded mixed results, for example. Conversely, we have learned that under certain conditions the sheer threat of sanctions may effect change, reminding us of the role of "negative" incentives. (Later I will clearly differentiate between negative incentives and disincentives.)

A fourth trend, which likewise reflects the importance of variable local conditions, is mounting evidence that school personnel do not turn to formal, external sources of knowledge. Hood (1979a) has summarized this familiar observation: "Generally, the local, easily accessible, and typically personal sources are used in preference to more distant, inaccessible or formal sources." This tendency is commonly attributed either to sheer convenience of local resources or to ignorance of external ones. Equally or more important, however, might be the function of reaffirming social bonds within the local work group, and in particular the norms of autonomy and self-sufficiency. Thus, even when offered exogenous expertise in the planning and implementation of new, innovative schools, school personnel still tend to prefer local sources of information and assistance (Miles, Sullivan, et al., 1978c: 15-17). It is also probable that referral of a professional problem to an external agency is an admission of failure to nonpracticing experts, who invariably occupy higher status in the profession (see, for example, Zaltman et al., 1973: 87.) Thus, the offer of external resources and expertise might pose a *disincentive* for KU.

Finally, there is an emerging body of research on the types of rewards that are endorsed by teachers in general and their influence on KU behavior. One can cite Lortie's (1975) research on the "psychic" rewards of teaching. Of a more quantitative cast are the studies by Spuck (1974) and Stephens (1974). Spuck found that a perception of "intrinsic" rewards by high school staff was related to the school's ease of recruitment, low absenteeism, and retention. In contrast, a perception of "extrinsic" rewards was not related to any of these measures of staff commitment. Stephens reports that teachers in innovative schools are more likely than teachers in traditional schools to perceive that quality of work and creativity are rewarded, while the reverse is true of perceptions of seniority and good relations with the administration as bases of reward. More important, perhaps, Stephens found that performance rewards were endorsed much more often than others, and virtually to the same extent, in both kinds of setting. Such findings as these lend strong support to the idea that teachers are not simply endowed with a "civil service mentality," as some observers have put it (Derr, 1976), but that many are located in settings that do not provide incentives for commitment in general and for KU in particular. Thus, one needs to consider incentive *systems* as well as individual incentives for KU.

These five developments or emergent themes in the study of educational KU invite a fresh assessment of incentives and disincentives at both the individual and the organizational levels.

By focusing on incentives for KU, I do not wish to imply that the educational system is stagnant and requires massive infusion of inducements for change. Many of the disincentives reside not in the schools, but in their external environments, including the very agencies that are responsible for the delivery and implementation of new ideas and practices. Conversely, many incentives for KU can be found *within* the schools. I do not concur, therefore, with the widespread notion that the public schools are the main source of disincentives for KU and are therefore sluggish in their pursuit of enlightened reform. Emrick and Peterson (1978: 66) reflect this conventional viewpoint when they assert, "Their modus operandi is 'status quo' unless externally imposed incentives and resources impinge on them."

If one is reluctant to believe the national surveys of innovation adoption (Havelock et al., 1973; Nelson and Sieber, 1976; Abramowitz and Tenenbaum, 1978; Rosenblum and Louis, 1978), all of which show substantial activity, then one may ponder the fact that in any given year about 50 percent of teachers make some "special effort" to find information about new methods and 40 percent do so with regard to selecting instructional materials (Hood and Blackwell, 1976b). As Gross et al. (1971: 204) correctly point out: "In many organizations the empirical reality is that a number of their members are exposed to irritating problems and needless strain, and consequently would welcome innovations that appear to offer solutions to their difficulties."

The remainder of this chapter is organized into four major sections. I will first try to stake out the territory by clarification of some key terms, and then present a taxonomy of incentives that incorporates these terms as well as a number of individual inducements for KU. I will then argue that this *molecular* approach is superior to the many strategies and models that one encounters in the educational literature on change.

In the second major section I will pull together some research that bears on *external* sources of incentives and disincentives for KU, including the RDD&E system and the local school environment. I will then turn to *internal* sources in a third section, and pay particular attention to problem solving and enlightenment as putative incentives. A number of other locally available incentives and disincentives will be examined also, however.

Finally, in a fourth section, I will offer some tentative observations about local incentives systems, thus moving from an individual level of analysis to a more contextual perspective.

CONCEPTUAL GUIDELINES

If we are to move beyond the current unruly state of thinking about incentives for KU, we must formulate a framework that will permit us to identify and sort out the many types of incentives found in education. But first it is important to understand that the terms "incentive" and "disincentive" are here conceived quite broadly as any prospective source of gratification or deprivation, respectively. They therefore include such rewards as money, professional esteem, job security, and the solution of a felt problem, and such penalties as performance failure, work overload, status threats, and negative reactions of the community. Positive and negative reinforcers are near synonyms, but the behavioristic connotations of these terms, evoking as they do images of white mice, Pavlovian dogs, and Skinnerian lumps of clay, render them undesirable for my purposes. In particular, the idea of incentives implies not only external stimuli, but a certain susceptibility or predisposition to notice, value, or embrace a particular stimulus. Thus, it is inadequate to define an incentive as a "gratification," as Wilson (1966) does, for this obscures the role of predispositions as well as the existence of external sources of gratification.

As commonsensical as the idea of predispositions seems to be, it is often overlooked in the manipulation of rewards. Many school personnel, for example, are simply not favorably disposed to the prospect of rational problem solving, quality of new practices, participation in decision making, pay for training, and so forth, and yet such putative incentives continue to be offered to all and sundry.

The significance of disincentives is not only that they are quite common and often overlooked, and even fostered by RDD&E (research, development, dissemination, and evaluation) personnel, but also that incentives will not induce action unless they outweigh disincentives, that is, unless imputed benefits exceed imputed costs. This is not to say, however, that school personnel engage in a careful calculation of costs and benefits as businessmen are purported to do. As Barnard (1938: 140) noted some years ago: "Only occasionally as to most persons and perhaps as to all persons is the determination of satisfactions and dissatisfactions a matter of logical thought."

A common distinction among incentives is that of "intrinsic" versus "extrinsic." This distinction may be used to imply several things: a source of gratification that is self-contained versus a resource that is useful for purchase of gratification elsewhere (Zald and Jacobs, 1978: 411); a predisposition toward ideal goals versus self-interested goals (Neal, 1965); a role emphasis on individual performance versus an emphasis on incumbency as conditions for acquiring rewards (Katz and Kahn, 1966; Fraser, 1969); and intangible versus tangible benefits (Clark and Wilson, 1961). Because of the ambiguities and hidden dimensions of the intrinsic-extrinsic dichotomy, I will refer instead to "performance related" and "material" *incentives,* and also to client-oriented versus self-interested *motivations.* Further, the dimension of being rewarded for either individual performance or sheer incumbency will be dealt with later as an aspect of incentive *systems.*

Another major distinction is less commonly recognized than those already mentioned: the positive or negative nature of the sanction involved. A person may be rewarded (positive sanction) or penalized (negative sanction) for either compliance or noncompliance with expectations. Thus, one may speak of positive or negative incentives in which a reward is offered for KU or a penalty is offered for non-KU, respectively. And one may speak of either positive or negative disincentives in which a reward is offered for non-KU or a penalty for KU, respectively. An example of a positive disincentive would be a deliberate emphasis on classroom regimentation and discipline owing to the rewards of custodialism as opposed to child-centered educational efforts. An example of a negative disincentive would be peer group rejection for trying to be innovative. Table 3.1 shows the relationship between these two dimensions and the four possibilities that are generated.

Because the positive-negative dimension has rarely been made explicit in research on KU behavior, it will seldom be referred to in my later discussion. This does not mean that the dimension is irrelevant to an understanding of the role of incentives in educational change, but only that it has been ignored by researchers. Clearly, it is time to realize that there are carrots and sticks for non-KU as well as for KU.

Theoretically, then, the strongest combination in favor of KU would be a subtle blend of positive and negative incentives that would appeal to

TABLE 3.1   Incentives by Sanctions

	Incentive	Disincentive
Positive sanction	Reward for KU	Reward for non-KU
Negative sanction	Penalty for non-KU	Penalty for KU

both self-interested and idealistic (or client-oriented) personnel, together with some effort to anticipate and to cope with positive and negative disincentives, including those disincentives that are imposed by the delivery system itself. But it seems that this configuration is a rare ideal. Policies that are aimed at promoting innovation or other forms of Ku almost never entail efforts to bring this configuration about and, consequently, tend to be self-defeating. Thus, the two positive incentives that are typically offered are the prospective outcomes of the new practice and funds; negative disincentives (penalties for KU), especially those that are introduced by the delivery system itself, are not diagnosed; little or no effort is made to overcome positive disincentives (benefits claimed for non-KU); and negative incentives (penalties for non-KU) are not combined with positive incentives (rewards for KU) in a fashion that counteracts disincentives without provoking resistance. Moreover, predispositions to either value or disprize particular rewards or penalties are seldom given consideration. But perhaps it is unjust to berate policy makers for overlooking certain complexities of incentive systems that have been only dimly perceived by researchers themselves.

Another dimension that emerges from the literature concerns the features of KU efforts themselves that might serve as incentives/disincentives. This issue is suggested in particular by Doyle and Ponder's (1977-1978) emphasis on the procedural clarity and feasibility of innovations as being of paramount concern to teachers, and Pincus's (1974) notion of the "bureaucratic safety" factor. But not only new practices or ideas afford incentives for effort—the interpersonal rewards of engagement in KU might also be inducements. This suggests that the very process of initiating, evaluating, implementing, and so forth, may generate rewards and penalties quite apart from the ends that are envisioned. As Berman and McLaughlin (1977: 83) conclude from their data: "Mobilization strategies can generate staff commitment, and should therefore be a prime consideration in project planning." Such incentives/disincentives might be called *operational* as contrasted with *consummatory* ones.

Although seldom mentioned in the literature on incentives (see, for example, Lortie's "ancillary" rewards), a final dimension needs to be acknowledged: formal versus informal incentives/disincentives. Formal ones are enunciated and applied as a result of explicit policy, while informal ones arise from sources over which organizational policy has little or no control, such as peer relationships, supervisory attitudes, community values, and so forth. And just as informal norms may conflict with and even override formal norms (for example, restrictive work norms of industrial workers versus production norms of management), informal and formal incentives may also conflict.[2]

Thus far I have directed attention to the *individual* level of analysis, but it should also be borne in mind that incentive systems exist at the *organizational* level. The array of incentives/disincentives, their distribution and methods of allocation, and the motivational modes that determine the value loadings of incentives/disincentives may be regarded as the incentive system of a school. These systems range from being highly coherent and resistant to change to being quite disorderly and dynamic, and even internally contradictory. Since I wish to focus attention on the simpler level of individual incentives in this chapter, I will postpone discussion of incentive systems until a final section.

A large number of individual rewards and penalties for organizational action have been identified in the behavioral science literature. It is important to take this literature into account before seeking to identify KU incentives in particular for two reasons. First, it is possible that KU efforts will pose a threat to any typical reward or to the way in which it is customarily allocated. For example, in a discussion of "status risk taking," Giacquinta (1975) has interpreted the findings of Gross et al. (1971) in the following terms: "In short, as threats to certain perquisites (professional esteem among colleagues, job security, work satisfaction and professional satisfaction with children) accruing to them as teachers became clearer, they became less receptive to the idea of the open classroom and more resistant to its implementation." All of the rewards cited by Giacquinta are typical organizational rewards which are vulnerable to interdiction by KU efforts. In the second place, KU might serve as a means of increasing any customary reward offered by the organization. Thus, if an opportunity to improve one's role performance, to gain a position of power, or to enjoy collegial relationships is a customary incentive, KU might be viewed by the actor as an instrumentality for enhancing these rewards.

In sum, we need to know what organizational members value before trying to engage their interest in new knowledge of various kinds. As Schultz (1969) has put it: "Incentives for more effective and efficient performance of public programs cannot be considered apart from the structure of motivations, rewards, and penalties which determine the attitudes and actions of the bureaucracy."

For these reasons, social theory (Weber, 1925; Thomas, 1918), industrial and occupational research (Blauner, 1960), social psychological theory of organizational behavior (Collins and Guetzkow, 1964; Clark and Wilson, 1961; Barnard, 1938; Katz and Kahn, 1966; Neal, 1965), research on the motivations and rewards of educational personnel (Lortie, 1975; Spuck, 1974; Ashley et al., 1970; Kester and Hull, 1973), and research on KU in particular (Havelock, 1969; Weiss, 1979; Caplan, 1979), and especially with reference to education (Pincus, 1974; Sieber, 1974; Greenwood et al., 1975; Giacquinta, 1975; Stephens, 1974), have been drawn upon for developing the taxonomy of incentives/disincentives for KU displayed in

Table 3.2.[3] This taxonomy incorporates the dimensions that we have discussed as well as a number of discrete rewards and penalties. A few refinements have been made to reflect the special nature of KU in education, especially in the realm of "performance-related" incentives. Thus, the incentive of "role efficiency" was suggested by the frequent observation that KU efforts are often resisted because they impose disruption and overload, which implies that role efficiency (or economy of effort) is an important, taken-for-granted source of gratification. The plurality of performance-related incentives, moreover, demonstrates that the term "intrinsic" covers several distinct types of rewards.

All but a very few of the incentives listed will be examined in relation to educational KU in later portions of this chapter. But before undertaking that analysis, it is instructive to compare an *incentive* approach to the understanding of KU behavior with the traditional *strategies* approach.

Change Strategies and Incentives: Alternative Models

One of the chief merits of a taxonomy of incentives is that it provides us with the basic building blocks that constitute the many "strategies of change" found in the literature. These typologies have been exhaustively reviewed by Zaltman et al. (1977: 73-82), and I have no intention of repeating their efforts. If we briefly reexamine the three condensed types proposed by these reviewers (power, manipulative, and rational) in terms of my taxonomy, however, it can be seen that these types are implicitly based on selected aspects of that taxonomy. Thus, by juxtaposing these two lines of theory, we might be able to integrate two bodies of thought that have developed quite independently of one another.

The bridge between these two traditions becomes obvious when one realizes that the strategies pursued by different change agents are ultimately derived from certain assumptions about the sensibilities, motives, and rewards that are salient to school personnel (see, for example, Chin and Benne, 1961; Sieber, 1972). By making these assumptions explicit, we are able to focus on the building blocks rather than on the idiosyncratic constructions of the strategy theorists. In particular, an incentive perspective promises greater flexibility because it suggests that new approaches can be designed by rearranging the essential elements that motivate or discourage KU. Table 3.3 shows the "incentive bases" for each of the Zaltman et al. strategies, which incorporate a number of others mentioned in the literature.

The table reveals two things about current conceptualizations of change strategies: (1) They are implicitly based on selected aspects of an incentive taxonomy, and (2) they are sorely inadequate to the task of reflecting or elaborating fully the numerous types of incentives/disincentives that have been identified in the organizational and educational literature, for they combine incentives indiscriminately and they fail to acknowledge the presence of others.

**TABLE 3.2   A Taxonomy of Incentives/Disincentives for
                      Knowledge Utilization**

I.   Types of incentives (external sources of gratification ⟩
      A. Positive
           1. Performance-related
                     Task/role autonomy (freedom to control tasks and conditions)
                     Opportunity for value expression or for compliance with inter-
                     nalized norms
                     Opportunity to apply or to improve professional skills
                     Opportunity to satisfy professional curiosity; enlarge effective
                     scope; enlightenment
                     Performance-environment feedback (goal achievement, problem
                     solving)
                     Role efficiency (economy of effort)
                     Attributes of knowledge (merit, simplicity, relevance, and so on)
                     Legitimation of practices or ideas
           2. Material
                     Money
                     Security (personal or organizational)
                     Time off (vacations, leisure time)
                     Fringes (health benefits, etc.)
           3. Authoritative
                     Opportunity to comply with legitimate orders
                     Power or authority over others
           4. Affiliative
                     Esteem, prestige—appreciation of:
                           Organizational personnel (peers, sub- and superordinates)
                           Others (clients, friends, strangers)
                     Amiability, pleasantness of relationships, acceptance
           5. Physical environment
                     Control over physical environment
                     Pleasantness of physical environment
           6. Career advancement
           7. Novelty, new experience
      B. Negative (threatened deprivation of any of above rewards on behalf of
           KU)

II.   Types of disincentives
      A. Positive (prospective rewards for non-KU)
      B. Negative (threatened deprivation of any of above rewards for KU)

III. Schedule of conferral of rewards (immediacy)
      A. Operational (immediate, part of process of change)
      B. Consummatory (deferred, outcome of change)

                                                                      (Continued)

TABLE 3.2   A Taxonomy of Incentives/Disincentives for
Knowledge Utilization (continued)

IV.   Sources*

    A. Internal-external

    B. Formal-informal

V.   Transferability of rewards

    A. Low or limited ("intrinsic")

    B. High ("extrinsic")

* This dimension will also be included in the taxonomy of incentive systems presented in Table 3.4.

For example, the "power" strategy, as described by Zaltman et al. is
said to be unique in its involvement of rewards and punishments, while in
fact these enter into *all* types of change efforts and strategies. (Is one not
punished by the stress of implementing a complex innovation that disrupts
role relationships, or by an innovation that simply does not work?)
Moreover, it lumps together the exercise of coercion (a threatened deprivation in my taxonomy) and the granting of rewards, such as prestige or
money. The "persuasive" strategy as described by these authors ignores
the issue of dealing with negative or positive *dis*incentives (for example,
overcoming role anxieties, and persuading *against* current policies or practices as well as persuading *for* new ones). And while it focuses on the
benefits that will flow from change (performance related rewards in my
taxonomy), it obscures some critical distinctions among these rewards,
such as problem solving, role efficiency, legitimation of practices, and
task/role autonomy. Similarly, the "facilitative" strategy is focused on a
narrow range of operational incentives/disincentives located within the
school. Thus, no mention is made of positive or negative attributes of
imported practices or of external change agents. It also seems to exclude
performance-related rewards, which are also of value in "facilitation."

Their "rational" strategy is concerned with getting the user to believe
that "change is in his own best interest," thereby lumping together a wide
array of tangible and intangible benefits, including performance-environmental feedback, status, power, and money. It is not clear how the
provision of these benefits is different from the "power" strategy
described above. (Surely it is in one's "own best interest" to avoid
punishment or to acquire prestige.) It is also said to depend upon a certain
kind of predisposition that may need to be fostered, a condition that is
ignored with reference to the other strategies.

Finally, and perhaps most telling, the strategy perspective does not
seem to countenance the idea that strategies can inadvertently pose *dis*incentives for KU, that is, can work against themselves through the unanticipated consequences of KU efforts of various kinds. This is most
obvious with regard to the power strategy in its use of coercion, but

TABLE 3.3 Change Strategies and Their Incentive Bases

Change Strategies of Zaltman et al. (1977)	Specific Incentive	Incentive Bases	Type of Incentive
Power (also "authority strategy")	Promised rewards and threatened deprivations		Positive and negative incentives
Manipulative			
Persuasive ("urges acceptance of change")			
Utilitarian	Material incentives		Positive, consummatory incentives
Normative	Performance-related incentives		Positive, consummatory incentives
Facilitative (also "didactic strategy," easing of implementation	(Unspecified)		Operational incentives
Rational or reason (also KU is "in own best interest," "product development strategy")	Performance-related incentives		Positive consummatory incentives
	Material, power, etc. incentives (?)		Positive consummatory incentives
"Reeducative"	[Predispositional change (resocialization)]		[Change in type of orientation]

equally true of the others, as we shall see when we examine the incentives and disincentives that flow from the RDD&E system itself.

The three models of change that were identified by Havelock (1969)—RD&D, Social Interaction, and Problem Solving—might be subjected to the same type of critique. Briefly, the merit of new knowledge, interpersonal relationships, and problem solving, respectively, are the core incentives assumed to govern behavior. Quite obviously, a number of incentives for KU are overlooked, and hence tend to be missing from Havelock's "linkage" model, which seeks to integrate the three classical perspectives. An example is the incentive of career advancement, which some writers regard as among the most powerful incentives for innovation (Giacquinta, 1975; Pauly, 1978).

In sum, it would seem that the molecular terminology of incentives/disincentives is preferable to the global language of strategy builders for delving into the complex social psychological world of school personnel and formulating policies that promote KU.

Now let us turn to a discussion of the array of incentives/disincentives that flow from external and internal sources.

EXTERNAL SOURCES

External sources of incentives/disincentives for educational KU are divided into: the RDD&E system, including attributes of knowledge itself (innovations, information, and model change approaches); and the local community context.

The RDD&E System

In this section I will examine that conglomeration of agencies and roles external to the school that have a stake in educational change based on systematic research, dissemination, development, and evaluation.[4] It includes the following activities: management (funding, administration), evaluation, capacity building (organization development and promoting readiness for KU), socialization (training, human development), technical assistance (consultation, process helping), resource building, needs assessment of local districts and schools, dissemination, and persuasion (advocacy, demonstration, marketing).

While one would assume that the RDD&E system would offer a number of inducements to local educators for KU, it seems that the complex issue of incentives has been either overlooked or grossly mishandled. This has probably resulted from an early assumption that school personnel were able and willing to try out or adopt any practice that would demonstrably improve performance. Consequently, a great deal of emphasis was placed on enhancing the *merit* of substantive resources (up-to-date, field tested, and so on), their *availability* through dissemination systems, and the *financial means* of implementing them. And here we have the three classical, putative incentives for KU that have been endorsed by most segments of the delivery system: demonstrated effectiveness, access, and money. The emphasis on these putative incentives has yielded a techno-logical-pecuniary strategy that rests on a number of implicit assumptions about the target system of local districts and schools, assumptions that have been increasingly challenged by research. (See House's chapter in this volume.) In effect, we have too long entertained the Rational Poor Man image of educators, which holds that they are not only information processors but problem-solving addicts, and need only the wherewithal to gratify their habit.

The incentives/disincentives to be considered stem from: features of external knowledge, financial support, government coercion, academic agencies, consultants and resource linkers, and resource agencies.

Features of external knowledge. I will first examine the attributes of information and of innovations (practices and products), and then turn to change agent approaches that have been externally developed and tried out in schools.

As suggested above, a Rational Man image of practitioners is based on an assumption that information deemed to be of high quality by experts will be adopted and used as intended. Evidence of the *low* priority of the inherent quality of external information to school personnel is supplied by Hood and Blackwell (1976b: VI-13). They found that up-to-dateness, authoritativeness, impartiality, and lack of bias of information were all virtually at the bottom of the hierarchy of preferred characteristics of information sources among teachers and principals. Characteristics that were most important were relevance ("is likely to have the information I want"), accessibility, and ease of use. Only principals gave high priority to "provides for new ideas or different viewpoints." Also, local, interpersonal sources of information are preferred and utilized much more often than formal or more remote sources (Hood and Blackwell, 1976b: V-3-9). The emphasis on interactive information gathering from local sources no doubt reflects the importance of convenience, nonthreatening peer relationships, and the desire for autonomy (self-sufficiency). Here we discern the signifi-cance of *operational* incentives for KU.

With regard to innovative practices, Nelson and Sieber (1976: 224) found a moderate relationship between the judged "educational worth" of 14 innovations and their frequency of adoption in urban high schools. (The rank order correlation was .34.) As they note: "Perhaps it is not inappropriate to observe that within a perfectly functioning system of research, development, and dissemination, this correlation would approach unity. Thus, it appears that we are still far from realizing this ideal goal."

Although Yin et al. (1976: 72-75) did not restrict their analysis to educational settings, it is of considerable interest they failed to find a relationship between the "previously demonstrated merit" of techno-logical innovations and their incorporation. Indeed, a *negative* relationship was found between demonstrated merit over existing practices and success. In short, it seems that the quality of an innovation (as deemed by experts) is not a predictor of ultimate use. Berman and McLaughlin (1978b: 161) reached the same conclusion on the basis of their study of some 300 educational innovations.

An emphasis on the objective merit of externally developed practices might even present a disincentive for adoption or implementation, for implied in this emphasis are two things: (1) What practitioners have been doing all along is inferior, and (2) the innovation should be adopted without alteration. These implications attack one's positive self-appraisal and violate task/role autonomy, thereby encouraging token adoption at best.

While the consummatory incentive of informational merit seems to be of minor importance, another incentive related to ultimate use seems to be quite influential, namely, *relevance*. In fact, relevance might be regarded as the basic prerequisite for ultimate use of information. Hood and Blackwell (1976b: VI-13) found that the item "is likely to have the information I want" was the most important feature of the information sources that were preferred by educational practitioners. The guarantee of relevance might be one reason that educators tend to seek information from local colleagues rather than from the available external sources. Sieber et al. (1972: 570-572) found that "not relevant to my problem or need" was one of the most frequently voiced complaints of personnel in two of the three states they investigated, with almost a third citing this problem in these two states. (Computerized searches were more often responsible for this complaint than manual searches.)

The concept of relevance, it should be noted, is a multifaceted one. A person who seeks relevance in new knowledge could be concerned with: applicability to a particular self-defined need or problem; suitability to one's clientele; feasibility of implementation or acceptance under local conditions; congruence with personal goals, values, and beliefs, especially with "common" knowledge as distinguished from technical knowledge;[5] or appropriateness to one's level of concern (for example, practice improvement versus enlightenment), or to one's stage in a change process. A finding of nonrelevance, then, is only the beginning of understanding. However, to my knowledge, no one has probed the diverse meanings of this attribute.

Many attributes of innovations have been identified in the theoretical literature (Rogers and Shoemaker, 1971; Miles, 1964), but it seems that research has lagged far behind in measuring the impact of these attributes and combinations thereof. When Zaltman et al. (1977) turned their attention to attributes of innovation, they cited only a single study. Fullan and Pomfret (1975) cite several case studies of schools, but discuss only two attributes of innovations: complexity and explicitness. Despite the assumption that innovation attributes are influential factors in adoption and implementation, the data base is surprisingly thin. The one systematic study of which I am aware failed to confirm the relationships reported by reviewers of noneducational innovations. In a study of the effects of relative advantage, compatibility, complexity, trialability, and observability on adoption, Allan and Wolf (1978) found that only perceived complexity yielded the expected relationship. (Two subattributes of rela-tive advantage were also predictive of adoption, however: "money saved" and "popularity increased.") In short, we seem to be far from having resolved all the questions about the influence of innovation attributes on adoption, much less on implementation and continuation, within the sphere of public education.

The one secure generalization that we can make concerns the role of complexity as a disincentive for KU, as suggested by Allan and Wolf (1978). This has been confirmed by Paul (1977), Giacquinta (1973), Fullan and Pomfret (1975), and Charters and Pellegrin (1972). If complex innovations that have been externally conceived are pursued with any persistence, they are in effect redesigned locally. This was clearly revealed by Charters and Pellegrin (1972) and by Greenwood et al. (1975: 29). Ironically, then, the more ambitious and organizationally complicated an innovation invented outside the school, the greater the number of altera-tions made to suit local interests and constraints.[6]

Thus far we have looked at some attributes of "information" and "innovations" that serve as incentives/disincentives. But there is a third kind of externally generated knowledge that has become increasingly prominent in public education: approaches or strategies that are intended to facilitate planned change. While the data base for the assessment of these approaches in terms of incentives is severely limited, it is possible to offer a few generalizations.

In the first place, it seems that the sheer *merit* of such approaches (their rationality, sequencing, importance of objectives, and so on) is no more likely to influence adoption and use than is the case with information and innovations. An evaluation of Program Information Packages, for example, which were developed under USOE sponsorship as a set of autonomous management guidelines for local districts engaged in planned change, recommended that "the concept of self-contained, stand-alone packages be given serious reconsideration." These packages were least effective with new practices that entailed organizational or behavioral change as con-trasted with the use of simple "pullout" programs. Also, it was found that an intermediary was needed for dissemination, and that other kinds of technical support were needed for installation of new programs (Emrick and Peterson, 1978: 27). The Rand studies (Berman and McLaughlin, 1978b: 27) reached similar conclusions about packaged approaches to planned change, noting in addition that "they seem to pose a severe problem for continuation, depriving the staff of a necessary sense of ownership of the materials." This unanticipated consequence points to the deprivation of *task/role autonomy* as a disincentive.

A more traditional means of facilitating KU is training in the implemen-tation and use of new practices. Berman and Pauly (1975: 60-61) found that staff training in new practices was related to teacher change, but that it "did not significantly increase perceived success and tended toward decreasing success [of implementation] in elementary schools." This dis-crepancy between impact on teachers and influence on implementation was explained in terms of the frequent *irrelevance* of training to applications of the new methods in the classroom—an interpretation that was reinforced by the finding that if staff meetings are held in conjunction with training, both perceived success and fidelity of implementation are increased. In short, it appears that relevance to classroom applications is enhanced by being linked to regular and frequent meetings of the project staff. This suggests that the operational incentives of perceived *relevance* and *ownership* of training through participatory planning and feedback sessions play a decisive role. (And since *payment* for undertaking training was found to be unrelated to perceived goal achievement and to teacher change, it seems clear that performance-related incentives were more important than material incentives.)

It should be borne in mind that training, like any other form of participation in implementation or change, can cause teachers to fall behind in their regular work and interfere with ordinary performance satisfaction. In addition, it strongly implies that staff members are lacking in professional know-how. Moreover, the solution of offering opportunities for participation in decision making and clear relevance to classroom problems is deceptively simple; effective in-service education requires a great deal of planning, coordination, organizational support, follow-up assistance, and personal commitment by the participants (see Fullan, 1979: 6).

Another change approach that has recently been subjected to systematic research is the problem-solving sequence. At least four steps are involved: problem identification (including, perhaps, a systematic needs assessment); a search for a solution from an array of possibilities; selection of a solution according to explicit criteria; and implementation, including some training and monitoring. Each of these steps entails collaborative decision making by a problem-solving team. Preliminary data from a study of schools across the nation that tried out the approach under NIE auspices in the late seventies (Louis et al., 1979; Sieber, 1978) suggest several conclusions. As Louis et al. (1979) report:

> A great majority of the schools participating in the program are implementing projects that are relevant to locally defined problems in the [mandated] area of basic skills and career education.
>
> Schools participating in the program are engaging in more systematic needs assessments than they did prior to involvement in the program and hope to apply this process to other problem areas in their schools.
>
> Individual teachers actively involved in the program report personal development in leadership skills, awareness of R&D products, problem-solving skills, and teaching techniques.
>
> Services of educational linking agents are valued by schools involved in the program. Linkers are perceived primarily as facilitators of school decision making rather than as decision makers.

The major incentives for commitment and participation seemed to be (in the terms of my taxonomy): task/role autonomy (freedom to control tasks and conditions); opportunity for value expression or for compliance with internalized norms; performance-environmental feedback (goal achievement, problem solving); and the affiliative rewards of appreciation by others and amiability in interaction. The main disincentives were: interference with role efficiency (because of time demands); and threat to task/role autonomy (because of the stipulation that only externally validated solutions be considered for adoption). This latter disincentive was revealed by Sieber's (1978) analysis of preliminary case studies which found that, despite problem identification and a search procedure that involved external retrieval agents, the selection was often made without reference to validated products or practices. School personnel preferred to select their solutions from familiar, interpersonal sources: a teacher in a neighboring district, a professor of education who had taught local personnel, a state agency consultant who happened to drop by the school, and so on. In effect, the task/role autonomy that was fostered by the opportunity to engage in collaborative decision making was extended to the domain of product selection in a fashion that undermined one of the program's objectives, namely, to encourage the use of validated practices.

The importance of task/role autonomy, or "ownership" as it is sometimes called with respect to particular practices or products, is revealed once again in an evaluative review of Organization Development (OD) techniques by Fullan et al. (1978). And here we shift our attention to an approach that is more concerned with capacity building than with implementation of particular practices. To summarize their findings: Once again it seems that practical *relevance* to the problems of the system and to the daily interests of school staff is highly important; also, some sense of *control* over the OD process, as suggested by the value of participative modes of intervention and internal change agents, seems to be a decisive incentive. On the other hand, it seems that OD tends to pose the disincentive of conceptual or philosophical implicitness, or *lack of communicability.* As Fullan et al. put it: "Many activities which are called OD are not really OD at all. . . . Many of the definitions of OD were general and tended to mask the complexities, specific components and dilemmas involved in its use." Another possible disincentive is the length of time (at least a year) that is supposed to be invested in an OD effort, posing a threat to *role efficiency.* These disincentives are reflected in Fullan et al.'s observation that successful OD requires an unusually high degree of commitment.[7]

I have referred to collaborative decision making at several points in my discussion of change approaches. Since this practice is intended primarily as an appeal to the desire for classroom and organizational control, and since it is often introduced by administrators without external intervention, I will defer discussion of it until the section on internal sources of incentives/disincentives.

Money and its costs. An inducement that has been assumed to have universal appeal is financial resources for the planning, implementation, or continuation of new practices, including the change approaches discussed

above. This incentive is offered on the twofold assumption that "organizational slack" (Cyert and March, 1963) is necessary for engagement in
practices that go beyond maintenance of the organization, and that money
is a provider of such slack. What this theory overlooks is the fact that the
"maintenance" needs of organizations (and perhaps especially client-
serving agencies like schools) are extremely elastic. After achieving a
certain minimal level of survival, such needs are *socially* defined by each
organization in terms of the aspirations of its members. Research by
Janowitz (1971), for example, indicates that increased funds for urban
school systems in the sixties were used to reduce class size rather than to
introduce needed innovation in practices. And the diversion of federal
funds for innovation to activities that are explicitly disallowed is well
known. (Judging from experience with some schools, swimming pools are
regarded as a maintenance need.) In short, new funds will always be used
to enhance "maintenance" instead of KU if there are activities that have
higher priority than KU and can be legitimized as "maintenance." And
that covers almost every activity of schools. Indeed, one study (Daft and
Becker, 1978) found a *negative* relationship between organizational slack
and the adoption of innovations. It is possible, then, that the concept of
organizational slack is itself rather slack.

The persistent priority of non-KU activities is reflected in Greenwood
et al.'s (1975: 19) finding that exogenous funding not only attracts those
who wish to solve a local educational problem, but those for whom "the
dominant stimulant in local initiation of innovative projects is simply the
availability of outside dollars." A desire to receive funds, moreover, was
found to be no guarantee of KU, for the amount of federal funds received
by the projects was unrelated to project outcomes. Likewise, Rosenblum
and Louis (1978: 266) found that the level of funding for implementation
among rural districts in the Experimental School Program was unrelated to
the districts' scope of implementation. And Berman and McLaughlin
(1977: 74) discovered a *negative* relationship with continuation of project
materials. This latter finding might have been due to the prohibitive
expense of continuing a project after federal funds had been phased out.
But it might also have been due to a tendency for material incentives to
undermine performance motivation. Here one would do well to borrow a
lesson from educational psychology. As Glaser (1978: 36) points out in a
recent review of behavioral modification theory: "Results obtained from
research . . . indicate that giving a reward can have an effect counter to
that desired; giving points, tokens, M&Ms, etc., to a child for learning a
lesson can decrease the intrinsic satisfaction of the lesson."

With respect to change approaches, Fullan et al. (1978: 34-40) found
that the amount of federal funds for OD was moderately related to
impact, but slightly negatively related to institutionalization in those cases
where the measurement of institutionalization was particularly clear-cut.

It is interesting to observe that these findings are not restricted to the
field of education, according to Yin et al. (1976: 139). They found that
the receipt of grants and contracts from federal sources was not related to
successful outcomes of technological innovations in many kinds of service

organizations, and that a negative relationship existed between overall federal support and incorporation. In sum, it appears that opportunism at the adoption stage, the undermining of intrinsic satisfactions of KU at the implementation stage, and the inability to pick up the tab at the incorporation stage (when external funding ends) might ensure failure and abandonment of KU efforts.

The converse of this conclusion is that local investment *is* related to conscientious adoption and successful implementation (see, for example, Mahan, 1972: 148), but this relationship seems to be somewhat spurious. Local money is not so much a cause of innovation as a symptom of genuine commitment, a commitment that is perhaps reinforced over time by awareness of past local investment.

External funds have also been used to encourage school personnel to undertake special training. Mann (1976: 327) found, however, that extra pay was not a significant incentive to begin training, but that it could be a useful reinforcement to continue if institutionalized in pay schedules. Unhappily, however, receiving extra pay for training was not related to the following outcome measures: reports that a high percentage of goals were achieved, a change in classroom practices, improved student performance, and continuation of project methods or materials; and in some cases there were slight negative relationships.

Money should not be thought of as a self-contained, independent inducement, for almost invariably its provision entails a number of obligations—for clerical monitoring, for standardization of procedures and goals, for supplementation from local sources, for cooperation with external evaluators, and for continuation on local funds when external support is withdrawn. Thus, the acceptance of external funds costs a good deal to local recipients. And any of these "strings" can serve as a disincentive, either at the inception stage or later on. This is especially likely to be the case if a local district has minimal capacities for meeting federal standards that govern local expenditures. Red tape in particular can make inordinate demands on limited administrative capacities, demands that sap enthusiasm for the high hopes of a program. Thus, when asked to signify how serious each of 19 problems was in their schools, high school principals in a recent nationwide survey responded with greatest dissatisfaction to the item: "too much paperwork in complying with federal requirements" (Abramowitz and Tenenbaum, 1978).

Evaluation of projects can also pose serious problems for local personnel. As Fullan and Pomfret (1975: 119) observe: "This very process of carrying out exhaustive research may interfere with the effectiveness of implementation by overburdening users, by creating feelings of being under a microscope, and so on." It appears to be very difficult for researchers and evaluators to empathize with these concerns for role efficiency on the part of educational personnel.

Added to the burdens and anxieties imposed on local personnel by demands for monitoring and evaluation of KU efforts are the unavoidable dysfunctions of federal bureaucracy, such as lack of flexibility in understanding or dealing with individual client systems, delays in responding to

needs and questions, turnover of key personnel, shifts in goals and operational patterns without adequate warning or explanation to grant recipients, and commitment to procedures regardless of goals. (For an analysis
of how these problems severely undermined the commitment of local
districts to the Experimental Schools program, see Kirst, 1978.) Many of
these problems are fostered by the context in which federal offices are
embedded, including political demands and constraints. The typical grant
recipient is unaware of these forces, and consequently tends to view
federal vagaries of policy and behavior as a demonic conspiracy to undermine progress.

   Governmental coercion. Employment of the negative incentive of
coercion has yielded mixed results, depending to a large extent upon the
source of coercion. Federal power, exercised indirectly through demands
for equal educational opportunity or more directly on KU efforts of
particular kinds, has a dismal record of accomplishment. With respect to
the first type of indirect influence on KU, there seems to be a negative
relationship between the decision to innovate and being under court order
to desegregate (Pauly, 1978: 282). Presumably, the destabilization that
occurs in the first stages of imposed desegregation discourages innovative
action that threatens to add fuel to the controversy. Or perhaps the
energies that are absorbed by segregation are withdrawn from other
activities. With respect to direct influence on KU, the ideology of local and
state control of education impedes the exercise of even relatively mild
forms of federal authority. In general, for example, the policy of the
Kennedy administration of attempting to bypass and wrest control from
state departments of education, teachers' organizations, school administrators, and college professors led to widespread conflict and defensiveness
(see, for instance, Corwin's account of the Teachers Corps, 1973: 315).

   While federal policy can buy limited compliance with guidelines, it
cannot influence the design of methods that are based on local priorities
and initiative (Berman and Pauly, 1975: 38-39). Nor does it appear that
the federal bureaucrat is especially eager to lay down the law to local or
state agencies. Lacking the political muscle to enforce compliance with
federal expectations, pressed by Congress to distribute funds as widely and
as quickly as possible, and dependent on local officials, many of whom are
former colleagues, for his own record of accomplishment, the federal
bureaucrat is often deterred from using what little power he has at his
command.

   The federal government is not the only possible source of coercive
power over local educational reform, of course, but its role is the most
visible, the most studied, and the most criticized. State authority presents
a complex picture, not only because of historical variation among states,
but also because of the many legal and quasi-legal relationships between
local districts and state agencies. Even here, however, power has definite
limits. The highly centralized legal authority over the curriculum found in
a state such as Arizona, for example, is described by two researchers as "a

powerful but a relatively *blunt* instrument. The state legislature, the board, or the Department can squelch many local plans and policies, but it cannot effectively carry out its own policies without persuading local officials and educators of their value" (Block and van Geel, 1975, cited by Boyd, 1978: 604).

It cannot be denied, however, that the mandating of textbooks is a rather sharp instrument at times. In fact, the economic power that a few large states, such as California or Texas, can exert over changes in textbooks determines the curriculum of other states as well (Black, 1967). Further, it appears that "state involvement in determining the school program has increased substantially in all states" (Boyd, 1978: 610). In addition to the increased regulatory authority of the states (with the assistance of state assessment and accountability schemes), the courts and teachers' organizations have also exerted greater control over local education, including curriculum.

The report of the NIE Task Force on curriculum development (National Institute of Education, 1976) discloses a strong antifederal establishment movement, as well as a great deal of competition among public and private organizations for a piece of the curriculum development pie. Unless the federal government is able to support curriculum development at the local level on a less contentious scale than at present, it is probable that agencies and associations in the middle range (between federal and local levels) will preempt curriculum decisions in a political free-for-all that will be a credit to the American penchant for special interest conflict. A sophisticated study of the emerging distribution of power over curriculum development in the nation, and the conditions under which political pressure and legal coercion are effective means for enhancing KU, would seem to be a worthwhile endeavor.

Higher education. Turning from government as a source of incentives/disincentives, let us briefly examine the role of higher education. A number of years ago, Brickell (1961: 19) made an observation that has been attested to by more recent commentators:

> College faculty members explained again and again during the survey interviews that they had experienced utter futility in equipping teachers with skills which were not needed or not wanted in the elementary and secondary schools in which those teachers subsequently went to work. Local community traditions, the accustomed ways of the existing staff, the attitude of the administrators—all converge upon the beginning teacher and shear off any college-taught skills which do not fit local patterns.

From the point of view of the teachers themselves, courses in local colleges and universities are "irrelevant." Sarason (1971: 166) observes that although the teachers he had studied were intellectually stimulated by courses, "they did not, or could not, see the relevance of these courses to their daily work in the classroom.... As a group teachers have long been living with the knowledge that their college experiences were for the most part irrelevant to their work." These observations indicate that use of specific skills or information about teaching and learning is not influenced by the incentives traditionally supplied by higher education, namely, grades and degrees.

As for in-service training, a review by Erickson and Rose (1976: 247) asserts that "relatively few universities have accepted their responsibilities to develop programs of in-service training." Some programs, such as the University of Oregon's externship in educational administration, do award academic credit for dealing with specific day-to-day educational problems in association with consultants and peers, however, which suggests that academic incentives *can* be used to promote knowledge utilization. But this seems to be a rare happenstance.

A special feature of the academic community is the research and service (or R&D) agency affiliated with graduate schools and departments of education. These agencies originated with the school efficiency movement of the early decades of the century, the main goal being to provide a service, such as testing or school surveys, geared to improving the efficiency of schooling (Sieber and Lazarsfeld, 1966). But not until the USOE's Cooperative Research Program of the late fifties, together with the founding of R&D Centers in a few universities in the sixties, was the research function of these agencies placed on a more secure footing. In the process, the pendulum swung from instant service to long-term research and development, and the dissemination and implementation functions of these agencies was shoved into the background. Further, since their work was no longer dictated by school efficiency needs, but by federal mandates and decisions of the agencies themselves, these new agencies held little inherent appeal for local administrators. Indeed, they seemed to provide more disincentives than incentives for KU by schools.

According to studies by Baldridge et al. (1974), the major stumbling blocks were: the centers' violation of the status-norms of school personnel by their efforts to monopolize expertise; their duplication of effort in the field owing to lack of coordination among researchers; their lack of adequate feedback to R&D sites in return for the privilege of access to local subjects; and the sense of anxiety and apprehension generated by evaluation projects. In short, the R&D Centers threatened to deprive school personnel of *profession-standing, continuity and efficiency* of school operations, a *sense of accomplishment,* and status *security*—and all this without offering compensatory assistance or usable feedback. (For several possible solutions to these problems, some of which have been successfully tried out, see Baldridge et al., 1974.)

It is the ad hoc consultative arrangement, however, which is the most frequent type of linkage with higher education today (Guba and Clark, 1976: III-59). But the ad hoc consultant has received a mixed press from students of KU. The most frequent complaints focus on the academic's difficulty in grasping the special conditions of the local setting and communicating practical advice rather than abstract knowledge. More fundamentally, the academic expert poses a disincentive for KU insofar as his or her very presence implies that school personnel are an inferior breed despite their grappling daily with the problems of teaching and learning. Thus, resistance or skepticism may be automatically triggered. In addition, there is the implicit threat to *task/role autonomy* insofar as the client is not permitted to participate in the design of the proposed practice or training session.

Havelock et al.'s (1973: 116) national survey of innovation casts considerable doubt on the impact of higher education consultants. Only 2 percent of the districts mentioned university personnel as key participants in their "showcase" innovations. This amount of key participation was somewhat lower than that of parents (10 percent) and the school board (7 percent), and much lower than that of teachers (38 percent) and administrators (37 percent). Overall, university personnel participated in or were informed about the showcase innovation in only 8 percent of the national sample of districts.

Consultants and linkers in general. What has been said about higher education personnel is probably applicable to other types of external consultants, since school personnel make little distinction among the institutional bases of outside experts. As Berman and McLaughlin (1978b: 27) write with regard to implementation of federal projects: "Project staff typically saw the assistance offered by outside consultants as too general, untimely, and irrelevant to the problems of their classrooms." Consequently, external consultants had only a marginal influence on the projects. With regard to reading innovations, Berman and McLaughlin (1975b: 28-30) found that technical assistance was not useful because it was too academic, too remote ("never around when projects need them"), offered conflicting advice when there was more than one technical assistant, and entailed personality clashes with the project staff. Since it was the "opportunistic" projects in the Rand studies that tended to rely more on outside developers and consultants (Greenwood et al. 1975: 22), the chief incentive for using such assistance might be to give perfunctory *legitimation* to efforts that do not enjoy high priority in the district. On the whole, however, disincentives posed by external consultants seem to outweigh the incentives.

A special type of outside consultant is the OD (organization development) expert who is mainly concerned with improving the school's group capacities for change. In their exhaustive review of these programs, Miles, Fullan, et al. (1978a: 33-34) found that the number of consultants was the single best predictor of "impact," but that it was negatively related to institutionalization of OD. This latter finding is explained by the researchers as follows: "Excessive reliance on outside consultants seems to reduce ownership, hence institutionalization." The insider, it appears, is more important for institutionalization of OD. "In fact, given the more important role of *insiders*," they conclude, "the role of external change agents should be directed at providing support and transferring knowledge, materials, skills, etc., to key insiders." In this way, it is hoped, a sense of *task/role autonomy* will not be jeopardized and internal capacities will be fully developed.

Still another type of outsider is known as a linker, or, more traditionally, an "extension agent." Seemingly a very effective mechanism for the stimulation of KU in local schools, the external resource linker offers a personal, nonthreatening bridge between a wide range of educational resources, on the one hand, and practitioners located at all levels of the district on the other. The disincentives posed by substantive consultants of status threat, lack of human relations and diagnostic skills, narrow specialization, ignorance of local practices and norms, threat to sense of ownership, and lack of timely availability are overcome by many linkers. These linkers do not pose as experts, and they employ human relations techniques in gaining access and working with clients. Also, they utilize the broad knowledge base of retrieval systems and are familiar with local practices because of their location in the field. Finally, they are not identified as "owners" of the practices they bring to the attention of school personnel. Thus, they pose a number of operational incentives for KU. (See Sieber et al., 1972; Louis and Sieber, 1979; Emrick and Peterson, 1978).

There are two major features of external resource linkers that pose disincentives, however: *low communicability* of the linker's role and *cost* of supporting full-time personnel. The first feature is a function of the unique location of the role. A permanent boundary-spanning role that serves as a bridge for the interchange of external resources and local needs is difficult for many school personnel to comprehend. Also, the key feature of *adaptiveness* to client needs and settings means that any verbal definition of the role is inadequate and perhaps even misleading. With respect to cost, linkage personnel require salary, travel, and retrieval expenses that impose burdens on state and district budgets in the absence of federal support. None of the Pilot State projects (Sieber et al., 1972), for example, continued to support generalists in the field after termination of federal funds. Since linkers are literally a marginal feature of the states' marginal dissemination programs, their fate is virtually sealed in times of austerity.[8]

Resource agencies. The external resource linker is only one feature, albeit conceivably the most important, of the knowledge delivery system that has emerged in recent years. Resource agencies are also critical. As mentioned earlier, Hood and Blackwell (1976b: VI-13) found that perceived relevance and convenience are the paramount features of information sources that are most preferred by teachers and principals. District level personnel are somewhat less concerned about convenience and somewhat more so about quality ("authoritative, accurate, reliable"), which is no doubt due to the fact that use of external knowledge is more common among such personnel.

A resource agency that has received a good deal of attention in recent years is the Teacher Center, which is loosely defined by Miles (1975: 163) as an arrangement for "providing local opportunities for teachers to exchange ideas, acquire new skills and further their development." Despite great variation, *in principle* these agencies offer a host of incentives for KU that are found wanting in other components of the RDD&E system. Unlike the R&D emphasis on quality and teacher-proofness of resources, the centers supposedly encourage adaptation of resources, and development and sharing of indigenous practices. Unlike preservice and most in-service training, they offer peer teaching by practitioners, emphasize the day-to-day needs of school personnel, give teachers the opportunity to display their own ideas and practices, do not threaten to impose negative incentives (such as poor grades in education courses), and in general operate independently of the career interests of college faculty and the institutional constraints of higher education. Unlike consultation, there is egalitarian interaction among peers around practical issues of mutual concern, emphasis on internalization of knowledge and "ownership" of materials, and timely access to a range of human and material resources. And unlike various federal "thrusts," there is sufficient time to learn and to implement, an absence of close, formal supervision, an emphasis on adaptations of external practices to one's setting, an absence of sporadic efforts at remote control by agencies with shifting or diffuse goals, and an absence of extrinsic incentives like money that invite exploitation by the administration for "maintenance." In general, then, the *ideal* teacher center (largely inherited from the British, incidentally) offers self-management, peer support, resources of relevance, and personal recognition in the eyes of significant others for exemplary task performance.

These inducements are all powerful incentives. As Miles (1975: 205) notes, "The attractiveness—and possibly the future viability of the teacher center concept—rests on its ability to tap into relatively deep personal motivational streams. Three can be singled out: need power, need achievement, and need affiliation." But as Miles is careful to point out, "there are no systematic, empirical data available on the actual person-changing processes or outcomes of teacher centers anywhere." Further, to change persons, even by ministering to an array of robust needs, is not to change the organization in which they are perforce embedded.

Finally, we arrive at an external source of knowledge that resides in the school itself—as neighbor, formal demonstration site, co-member of school study council or other consortium, or member of a diffuse, national reference group. Glowing claims of success have been put forth by advocates of school study councils, but actual impact data are lacking (see, for example, Kohl, 1973). Less formalized networks are even more poorly understood. And yet, it cannot be doubted that practices in neighboring districts and schools play a substantial role in creating awareness of new practices and competitive pressure for adoption.

The most elaborate, formal mechanism for demonstrating locally generated practices is, of course, the National Diffusion Network (NDN). An evaluation of NDN concludes that "LEA visits to demonstration sites, which provide visible models and referents for the adopting LEA," was one of the significant determinants of effectiveness (Emrick and Peterson, 1978: 35). The precise incentives that are posed by demonstrations are not clear, however. Research by the Center for New Schools suggests that some major incentives are the craft-oriented nature of practices (an appeal to task/role autonomy, one suspects), the opportunity for peer interaction centered on professional problems, and credibility of the practices as a result of actually seeing them in use.[9] Thus, demonstrations seem to afford technical information, collective inspiration, a sense of operational feasibility, and referent power legitimation. In addition, there might be incentives for site visits that are tangential to KU, such as the desire to escape from the classroom and to take a trip with all expenses paid, that is, the incentive of "new experience." On the other hand, demonstrations can also pose disincentives, as suggested by their frequent failure to influence change elsewhere (Turnbull et al., 1975: 11-12). As Greenwood et al. (1975: 56) observe: "Visitors to a demonstration site seemed to feel threatened. They often saw the accomplishments of the project as 'overwhelming.' For example, visitors remarked that they couldn't imagine how the project could be carried out in their own district." Accordingly, these researchers recommend the "traveling circus" approach, which they say worked much better in the schools which they studied. Mann (1976: 338) suggests that since a visitation is an acknowledgment of one's inferiority, more distant school systems might pose less of a status threat to local personnel.

SUMMARY

We have seen ample evidence that the RDD&E system poses disincentives as well as incentives for KU, with the former perhaps preponderating the farther one moves from the local school or district (with the possible exception of demonstration sites in other schools). In large measure, this situation is due to preoccupation with only a few putative rewards, such as the merit of new practices or products, money, accessibility to information, and the prospect of rational problem solving. In general, imposed disincentives are not diagnosed, positive incentives are limited in scope, negative incentives are not managed in a way that precludes resistance or rebellion, predispositions to embrace or to reject certain putative rewards are not taken into account, and the reasons that certain incentives often *do* work (for example, relevance) and others have only a middling track record (for example, demonstrations) are not well understood. If the RDD&E system devoted as much attention to measuring and controlling the *unintended* consequences of its activities as it gives to measuring and controlling the compliance of educators with its *intended* consequences, it might stand a chance of salvaging the liberal interventionist dream. (For a theory of the nature, causes, and possible cures of "regressive intervention," and guidelines for measuring unintended consequences, see Sieber, 1981.)

Another signal failure of the RDD&E system is neglect of the inducements and constraints on KU that emanate from the local system of education and its context. But before taking up the issue of internally generated concerns, let us examine the local context of education, which itself affords a cornucopia of incentives/disincentives for KU. Analyses of educational systems that exclude community influences are superficial at best and dangerously misleading to policy makers at worst.

The Local Contest of Education

The market structure and competition. An overarching feature of schools' relationships with their environment that has often been remarked upon is the market structure of education. It is this situation that underlies what Carlson (1965a) calls the "domestication" of public schools: "They do not compete with other organizations for clients; in fact, a steady flow of clients is assured. There is no struggle for survival for this type of organization—existence is guaranteed." The implication of this circumstance is that the prod of competition for customers is weak or nonexistent, and so the need to satisfy customers with new practices or improved performance is concomitantly lessened.

It is possible that this economic explanation for lack of change in schools has been overstated. As Corwin (1967) has pointed out: "The parents of public school students do have something to say about where their children will attend school, as they can move, pay tuition to another district, or attend private schools. . . . Moreover, schools do compete for favored students, as well as faculty; do struggle to perpetuate a favorable reputation." The trouble with the present form of competition is that it discriminates against minority and lower income students. Those parents who are able to move or to assess the offerings of different schools are more able to benefit. And the schools that attract these parents enjoy a buyer's market for faculty (especially in times of declining enrollment) that reinforces the inequality of educational programs.

Pincus (1974) has gone beyond the notion that the educational market structure discourages KU by pointing out that it discourages only certain kinds of KU. In his view, the educational market structure prompts a susceptibility to costly, faddist innovations that do not alter basic institutional structures, and a rejection of innovations that would increase competition. With regard to cost, however, Pincus gives too little heed to the economic pressures on schools to keep innovative costs down, especially under today's conditions of rising teacher militancy and stagflation in society. To say that schools are more likely than competitive firms to adopt cost-raising innovations, therefore, is not saying very much. With regard to the adoption of nondisruptive fads, this tendency is what constantly occurs in private industry under the label of marginal differentiation of product. And the extent to which it occurs in education can be better accounted for by *political* rather than economic factors.

As an alternative to the economic market model and its implied disincentives for KU, then, one needs to consider the value of a political model.

Local political relationships. School systems in America are subject to an inherently ambivalent relationship with their environment. In exchange for a monopoly on the functions of socialization and training, they have undertaken to remain responsive to social trends, basic values, and educational needs. But responsiveness has been placed at the local level, which means that professional norms of autonomy and universalism, and organizational norms of internal control over goals and activities, are threatened by community and parental norms of particularism and democratic participation. The formal monopoly, in other words, becomes highly vulnerable to a host of external demands, many of which conflict because of the segmentation of the community along socioeconomic and racial lines. Nor is it true that the community is uninterested in the planned changes of its local school system. Havelock et al.'s (1973: 116) national survey of educational innovation found that the community was cited as a key participant in the districts' "showcase" innovations in 18 percent of the cases, and that parents were cited in another 6 percent.

The prevention of school-community conflict rests to a large degree on a number of implicit bargains that are struck over the educational program, the treatment of children, the allocation of funds, the authority of teachers, and so forth. These implicit bargains establish consensus between school and community on zones of legitimate authority; the need to protect these bargains from degenerating into open conflict is the source of many incentives and disincentives for innovation. Thus, it has long been suspected that the tacit threat of community criticism serves as a negative disincentive (threatened penalties) for adoption of innovations that run counter to the values or lifestyles of the community, such as year-round schooling, open education, the teaching of evolution, or realistic civics education. Educators do not go to bat for such innovations in many locales because they are not worth the public furor. By the same token, practices that fall within the community's zone of tolerance are adopted faster.

On occasion, of course, the community violates the tacit consensus on boundaries of authority and exerts direct pressure for or against particular reforms. The adoption, abandonment, or compromise of innovations is often the result. *Implementation* as well as adoption is subject to community influence. When Berman and Pauly (1975: 40-43) asked teachers to identify problems that arose in the course of implementation from a list of 12 items, only 8 percent selected "parental or community opposition." But in spite of its being infrequently mentioned, this factor was considered *most decisive* in teachers' perceptions of project difficulties. Thus, parental or community opposition yielded the highest correlation with perceptions of difficulty of any of the 12 items on the list, which included planning deficiencies and troublesome attributes of the innovation.

Berman and McLaughlin (1977: 154, 165) also found that hostile community reaction to poor test scores was positively related to *continuation* of projects. The authors add: "The most interesting aspect of this finding, however, is that many of these continued projects were not perceived as particularly successful. We wonder if district officials felt under pressure to demonstrate they were 'doing something' about problems."

There are probably certain attributes of innovations apart from their value congruence with the local culture that cause the community to be more or less favorably disposed toward them. These probably include communicability (for example, everyone knows what educational TV is, but few know what IPI is), relevance to local problems (career education in a low employment area is especially popular), and sheer popularity among various segments of the population. Rosenblum and Louis (1978: 317) found that such features of change programs as school carpeting and student field trips "won over many community residents who were skeptical of 'experiments' that might affect their children, or who suspected that strings might be attached to all that federal money." Highly visible programs with such appealing features as those mentioned were much more likely to be continued, according to the researchers. It is also possible that the scope and anticipated impact of an innovation influence community opinion. Miles (1978) notes that planners and implementers of new schools try to avoid risks by postponing contact with the local environment, a strategy that can backfire as demonstrated by one of Miles's case studies.

Another way in which schools are affected by community sentiment is through lip service to its demands. The effect of such action is to reduce future innovation by providing the community with a false sense of security about the school's responsiveness. Smith and Keith (1971) conclude that schools create a "facade" based on outstanding instances of innovation and continual espousal of high hopes that serves to obscure the embarrassing gap between doctrine and reality. In short, community demands often foster *symbolic adoption* without implementation.

A final manner in which the community influences KU is by obliging the school district to adduce research or expertise that will *legitimize* what it is already doing or what it plans to do. Herriot and Gross (1979) observed in the Experimental Schools Project that "consultants rapidly became the buffer between the superintendent and his many publics. Consultants were used to explain the ES project to the community, to the teaching staff, and occasionally to the feds. In this role, their words were to be taken as dictum." And they add: "Too frequently, consultants are hired for political purposes—to persuade skeptical publics or to sway opinions among those impressed with a consultant's status."

A final incentive for KU supplied by the community is political advancement for key participants. A striking case is that of a superintendent in Herriott and Gross's (1979: 123) study: "Securing federal funds and thus creating new jobs ... served a political function for Hinton [the superintendent] .... By making judicious use of his authority to recommend individuals for employment, the superintendent would either repay past support from key families and friends, or otherwise maintain and extend the base of support for himself as well as his professional ideas and activities." Subsequently, the superintendent withdrew from direct involvement in the project, delegating authority to principals. The latter were overburdened, which put the entire responsibility for management of comprehensive change on the project coordinator.

SUMMARY

The local context supplies both incentives and disincentives for KU that seem to be predominantly nonperformance-oriented and negative, that is, pressures for or against KU with threats of penalties. This situation arises from the school's resistance to lay influence, which in turn is prompted by the tenuous claims of professional autonomy. Schools seek to protect themselves by insulative mechanisms such as cooptation, symbolic adoption of innovations, and the legitimative use of expertise. In the terms of our incentive taxonomy, the disincentives for genuine KU of threats to *task/role autonomy, role efficiency,* and individual or organizational *security* tend to exceed the incentives of improved performance as educators.[10]

INTERNAL SOURCES

Several sources of internal reward have already been alluded to, such as task/role autonomy, role efficiency, and problem solving. But there are several other possible incentives for KU. In this section I will discuss the following: problem solving, enlightenment, role efficiency, superordinates' leadership or power, students as source of psychic rewards, peer relationships, task/role autonomy, career advancement, and legitimation.

Problem Solving

Havelock (1969: ch. 10, p. 29) has characterized the problem-solving perspective as follows: "[An individual or group] initiates the process of change by identifying an area of concern or by sensing a need for change. Once the problem area is identified, the receiver undertakes to alter the situation either through his own efforts, or by recruiting suitable outside assistance." This notion is firmly rooted in the organizational literature. As March and Simon (1958: 173-174) assert: "[An] organization does not search for or consider alternatives to the present course of action unless that present course is in some sense 'unsatisfactory.' " Similarly, Abbott (1969: 170) claims that "dissatisfaction with existing procedures or arrangements will occur when there exists a perceived disparity between performance and aspirations." And Zaltman et al. (1973: 55) embrace Downs's (1966: 191) viewpoint that innovations are triggered by a "performance gap," which is simply an operational definition of a problem that requires solution. Now, what does research have to say about this widely shared theory?

I have already cited the finding of the Rand studies that most federally funded projects in education were initiated for "opportunistic" rather than "problem-solving" reasons.[11] Mann (1976: 324), a member of the Rand research team, goes even further with reference to staff development:

> The literature on planned change stresses the importance of a high level of felt need for change. . . . *None* of these projects was initiated

in response to a significantly felt need to change among school staff. . . . Most projects came into being because of a small cell of persons who operated independently of or in opposition to the wishes of district superordinates and the trainee group as well.

Most school districts store their needs in a bottomless pit. When outside money appears, the district fishes around the pit until it finds a need that matches the announced purposes of the soft money. That need is then elevated to the status of a priority in order to demonstrate the district's commitment, and not incidentally in order to capture the bucks. . . . The process invalidates the central tenet of a district-based goal-seeking model of change.

Conceivably, the small cell of persons may sometimes be motivated by a salient performance gap; but this was not the case with the majority of those who participated in the decision to adopt these federal projects. The major incentive, it seems, was money, with the consequence of limited implementation.

Further, if problem solving were a major motivation for seeking outside resources, then the demonstrated effectiveness of new resources would be a matter of uppermost concern. As Yin et al. (1976: 13-14) point out, "The problem-solver approach . . . makes the key assumptions that most if not all organizational changes stem from the existence of a problem and that the service-improving innovation will be fully implemented by the organization once the service improvement has been initially demonstrated." But it will be recalled from our earlier discussion that demonstrated merit has *not* been found to be significantly associated with adoption, implementation, or outcomes. The only aspects of "relative advantage" that Allan and Wolfe (1978) found to be related to adoption were increased popularity and money saved.

With regard to a number of service agencies, Yin et al. (1976: 98, 121) failed to find a relationship between their measure of a performance gap (need to meet service demands or to reduce cost) among local and state service agencies and either successful innovation efforts or service improvement. "Some innovations may occur independently of any problem," they conclude, "and there may be conditions other than service improvement . . . which can lead to the implementation of an innovation."

Similarly, among rural schools in the Experimental Schools project, Rosenblum and Louis (1978) did not find a correlation between a perceived discrepancy between goals and achievement, on the one hand, and implementation, on the other. They did find a moderate correlation between the staff's perception of problems within the school and implementation, but one that was much lower than the correlation with staff morale. Such findings do not bode well for the performance gap theory of KU.

The belief that innovation is preeminently inspired by identification of an overarching problem or need will undoubtedly persist, however, because it serves a definite function for practitioners and R&D experts alike. In a word, it legitimizes action by reference to widely shared rationalistic values. In spite of the weak role of problem solving as an incentive, therefore, it receives a good deal of emphasis in the rhetoric of local school personnel.

The idea also serves to justify the R&D enterprise. For the purported importance of a performance gap in fostering KU is the school-level version of the technological bias found at the R&D level. Although change theorists often view the R&D perspective and the problem-solving perspective as alternative "models" of KU (Havelock, 1969), in fact the latter developed as a corollary of the former, at least in the field of education. R&D products or practices were never intended to be imposed upon schools by fiat, as in the military or business firm. The central assumption was that R&D provided the technical resources, while the schools would provide the rationally recognized need for these resources. The technological perspective, which is in the business of dispensing definitive *solutions,* requires schools with definitive *problems* to justify its existence. Sadly for those who have invested so much, not even the engineering of local problem-solving processes guarantees the salability of R&D resources, and in fact might insure their rejection (as noted earlier in the case of the problem-solving approach at local levels).

Now let us turn our attention to some incentives that are more closely related to the occupational and organizational structures of education.

Enlightenment

The many complex demands that are made on teaching and administration, together with the decentralized structure of American education, foster an incentive for KU that seems to be more important than problem solving: the opportunity to acquire knowledge that enlarges one's sense of participation in a common professional enterprise, provides guidelines at a conceptual level, and offers alternative goals and alternative ways of interpreting one's needs. This incentive is represented by the enlightenment function of KU.

Holzner (1974: 25) has pointed out that " 'problems'—practical or otherwise—are never simple givens, [are] always symbolically constructed and defined (in W. I. Thomas' sense of the definition of the situation), and . . . the mode of the problem definition is embedded in a social and cultural context which limits the range of possible approaches." Thus, Holzner notes that problems come into existence only in terms of certain "structures of relevance." In some fields the structure of relevance is fairly clear, as in engineering, medical practice, or law. Public school teachers seek knowledge for teaching, but their role is far more complex than that of many other fields because of organizational demands, the age, diversity, and resistance of pupils, the necessity of combining "symbolic" and "instrumental" leadership in the classroom, and the lack of a strong reference group that defines the major issues of the field. Consequently, their structure of relevance is *diffuse* and may even shift with the demands of different role partners (pupils, parents, administrators, and peers). This diffuseness prevents a few needs from becoming focused and preempting the field, that is, from coalescing into one or a few special "problems." To transform a welter of diffuse needs into focused problems, educators require the stimulus of new alternatives, new frames of reference, or even new jargon so that their structure of relevance gains greater clarity and coherence. Thus, it might be impossible to diagnose needs within a mental environment that is purged of specific options of thought and action, which seems to be what the "needs assessment" model of rational problem solving strives to do. If there is little input in the way of new and stimulating alternatives, then the needs that are identified will tend to be conventionally dictated—by administrators, funding agencies, parents, and so forth—on the basis of tradition, prejudice, and "common sense." In short, a definition of "need" may be little more than a ritualistic response to pressures for "problem solving." What this suggests is that some form of enlightenment should *precede* the problem-solving process, including the provision of concrete alternative practices to stimulate thinking about local requirements and feasibilities.

The enlightenment function might be particularly germane to education because of the highly decentralized character of this social sector. Weiss (1979: 441-442) notes that the logistical problems of influencing policy making in decentralized sectors are formidable because of the many independent centers of authority that need to be convinced. Accordingly, "a social science idea or analysis may have impact across dispersed policy makers, but seldom through an accumulation of individual social engineering efforts. . . . It tends to be conceptual use of social science that spreads ideas and information through a decentralized sector." Creating a climate of informed opinion, then, might be the best way to reach into the far corners of the educational world, as has been demonstrated time and again by the rapid diffusion of "fads."

In addition to preparing the way for genuine problem solving, enlightenment has social functions that make it appealing to school personnel. It supports and affirms the professional role by helping them to understand and articulate diffuse needs, problems, and aspirations with reference to external values and beliefs. In other words, it fosters self-actualization by means of professional identification. Also, being up-to-date has a status conferral value locally. And since concrete decisions and actions with their attendant risks of failure are not involved in simply becoming better informed, it is a low-risk endeavor. In sum, enlightenment promises to satisfy the need for cognitive, affective, and social *meaning* in one's occupational role, a role beset with technical difficulties, self-doubt, isolation, and low status.

Still another source of the desire for enlightenment apart from problem solving might be what W. I. Thomas called the "wish for new experience." Sarason (1971: 161-169) has emphasized the effects of boredom and routine on teachers, including withdrawal from the profession. And as he points out, "if teaching becomes neither terribly interesting nor exciting to many teachers, can one expect them to make learning interesting or exciting to children?" Attendance at universities in the summer, conventions, demonstrations, travel—all are important means of expanding horizons for those practitioners who can afford such breaks in their routine.

Perhaps our image of school personnel as civil service drudges who are content to teach the same thing in the same way year after year has prevented us from appreciating the blandishments of novelty, of experimentation, of radical departure from the quotidian as rewarding in themselves. It is curious that research is silent about the "wish for new experience" as a vital incentive for KU; but research does tell us something about the salience of enlightenment as an incentive.

Hood and Blackwell (1976b: VII-3) found that the purpose for seeking information that was most frequently cited by local educational personnel at all levels (from a list of nine purposes) was "to help keep me aware of developments and activities in education." And the second and third most often mentioned purposes were "to identify new educational programs, materials, or procedures," and "to identify new sources of assistance." Only then do we come to the purposes of "developing alternative approaches to solving problems" and "to find answers to specific questions arising in relation to my work." In sum, the three most common purposes of information seeking pertain to enlightenment. Similarly, Sieber et al. (1972: 521) found that the clients of the Pilot State Dissemination project checked "I learned something new" as a specific benefit of the information they had received more often than any other in a list of 14 benefits (56 percent so indicating).

If enlightenment were merely a matter of subjective satisfaction without any bearing on behavior, it would be of limited interest. But there are reasons to believe that more up-to-date, informed, "tuned in" individuals take more initiative in educational change. The cosmopolitanism of school personnel has often been found to foster innovation. Rosenblum and Louis (1978: 187-189) report that school personnel's educational level, modernity (technological level of state where they were previously employed), and amount of professional reading were all highly related to implementation of comprehensive change in the Rural Experimental Schools program. These measures of cosmopolitanism remind us that the concept of professionalism includes enlightenment as a core ingredient, for professionalism denotes a reference to *extra*organizational standards of conduct, a tendency to look beyond the boundaries of the work environment for models of thought and behavior. A number of studies have found that "the higher the proportion of professionals on an agency's staff, the more receptive to innovative efforts the agency will be" (Yin et al., 1976: 88).

More directly related to implementation of new practices is the procedure of looking over a range of concrete alternatives as an aid to sharpening one's focus on needs and constraints as well as on possible solutions. A case study by Halpern (1978), for example, reports a teacher as noting that "for her and for the other teachers, the products were most useful as generators of ideas, to be used as brainstorming devices." Sifting through an array of options and judging their local appropriateness forces one to stipulate one's needs and constraints with ever greater precision.

It is true that the procedure of perusing options and selecting bits and pieces can occur without significant change in practice or teacher behavior, an outcome that Berman and McLaughlin (1978b: 16) call "cooptation." If monitored adequately, however, it might promote genuine change, especially if *conceptual* enlightenment has preceded the picking and choosing process and is then integrated with it. In short, solutions can be midwives to structures of relevance. This emphasis on knowledge as catalyst is part of the classical diffusion approach that seems to have been displaced by the problem-solving strategy of educational engineers, and is therefore in some danger of being ignored.

The enlightenment function might be divided into three subfunctions: (1) the inducement of an informed, cosmopolitan climate of opinion; (2) the infusion of new concepts that underlie particular change efforts; and (3) the provision of options and of specific bits of advice, products, and practices for creative adaptation to local settings. And perhaps the success of the second subfunction is dependent upon the first, and the third upon the second.

Despite its potency, the enlightenment incentive has been very neglected by researchers. One problem is the difficulty of *measuring* the process of enlightenment and its effects. Another barrier seems to be preoccupation with the problem-solving model in which definitive needs are assumed to *precede* the search for solutions. This assumption, in fact, might interfere with the development of the appropriate means for measuring enlightenment. Thus, Crandall and Harris (1978: 4) stipulate that "effective assessment of *use* ... requires knowing *first* how the information was intended to be used." This approach completely rules out the gradual accretion of knowledge and its impact on use as topics of study. The same view is enunciated by Hensley and Nelson (1979: 17): "Information needs are especially important in the evaluation of various dissemination systems since pre-stated needs provide a ready criterion for evaluation." These strictures are reminiscent of looking under a street light for something that was lost in a back alley.

Here, then, is a whole domain of research awaiting cultivation, one that presents both methodological and substantive challenges of a high order. Some particular questions are: How is knowledge from various sources sifted, integrated, and assimilated into the frames of reference of personnel, and how are these frames of reference altered? Does enlightenment contribute to improved teaching and learning; and if so, how? Is there a desirable sequence of the three subfunctions mentioned earlier for genuine change to occur? Does enlightenment contribute to noninstrumental aspects of educational roles, such as pride of craft, prestige, or morale? What types of personnel are most susceptible to this incentive? What group processes can be designed to stimulate and direct the enlightenment function locally? What are the barriers and disincentives to enlightenment locally? Questions of this ilk are often asked about the problem-solving function of KU, an incentive that we have found to be of only moderate importance. Moreover, it is possible that without enlightenment, problem-solving efforts will be unsuccessful.

In sum, it is time that we turned our attention to one of the most significant incentives for KU, even if it is bothersome to measure and not legitimized by the technological obsession with the matching of definitive solutions to definitive problems.

Role Efficiency

Teachers and administrators are extremely busy with their tasks of processing and controlling students, managing the organization, and coping with the environment. Thus it is that efforts to promote KU often entail threats of overload or conflict with regular classroom and schoolwide responsibilities. "From the standpoint of teachers the complexity of their task reflects in large measure the fact that a classroom of twenty-five children or so is a lot of children for any one person to handle," observes Sarason (1971: 152). "In addition, the children vary enormously. . . . Reduced class size is a teacher's ultimate reward in comparison to which inadequate salaries pale in significance." The additional work that is imposed by adoption and implementation of new practices might therefore serve as a major disincentive for KU, *unless* the practice is geared to relieving overload.

Role overload created by innovative efforts was found to be one of the paramount barriers to implementation by Gross et al. (1971) and by Charters et al. (1973). When Berman and Pauly (1975: 40-43) asked teachers to indicate their problems in implementing a project from a list of 11 items, the item "teachers already overloaded" was third place in frequency of mention, 27 percent so responding. Only lack of familiarity with the innovation and inadequate resources were mentioned more often. Moreover, the correlation between teachers' perceptions of implementation difficulty and overload was *higher* than that found with more frequently expressed problems. In fact, only "parental or community opposition" yielded a correlation with perceptions of difficulty that was stronger than the correlation with perceived overload, and this problem occurred far less frequently than overload.

If a particular form of KU is devoted to relieving work load or enhancing efficiency of effort, then role efficiency might well serve as an incentive for KU. As one researcher has put it: "Since teachers feel over-burdened with restrictions and inroads on their time, one category of rewards is related to the removal of some of the unpalatable chores" (Hancock, 1974: 274). One means of relieving workload in the process of a KU effort might be to lift many constraints in the school simultaneously. This might provide more flexibility and adaptability: The innovation will not compete or conflict with other obligations because these are alleviated. This effect might account for the finding of Greenwood et al. (1975: 43) that *comprehensive* change efforts entailed less conflict with other innovative activities. In particular, workload may be relieved by generous allocations of funds for released time. As one of the case studies in the RDU project (Smith and Granville, 1978: 34) observed: "In a rural district release time can be a powerful incentive to teachers, and figures centrally in a school's system of reward and punishment."

In any case, it is clear that greater attention needs to be given to the design of KU efforts so that role efficiency is maintained or, if possible, enhanced. Presently there is a tendency to shift the burden for dealing with overload problems to local managers, as if the creators and sponsors of new knowledge had little responsibility for the difficulties they impose, and as if more local planning to prevent burdens did not itself impose overload problems. The way to achieve KU is not to impose a disincentive and then demand that local managers overcome it.

Superordinate Support, Leadership, and Power

Another major source of incentives/disincentives that resides in the complex nature of the educational enterprise is that of the attitudes and behavior of administrators. Many observers have noted the key role in KU that is played by administrators (Fullan and Pomfret, 1975: 102; Greenwood et al., 1975: 40-42; Smith and Keith, 1971: 123; Emrick and Peterson, 1978: 70; Gross, 1978). While teachers enjoy a good deal of freedom from control in the classrooms, and principals enjoy a good deal of leeway vis à vis district-level staff, when it comes to implementation of new practices the attitudes and performances of superordinates are often decisive. To be sure, implementation can occur in situations where superordinates are passive, but it rarely occurs when they are opposed (Emrick and Peterson, 1978: 71).

Several factors might account for this situation: Superordinates can make resources available, provide training in new skills, and make organizational allowances for implementation; compliance with expectations of superordinates can be traded for support or autonomy in other domains (such as protection from parents, or student discipline); respect for the professional leadership of, and desire for recognition from, administrators can engender trust and compliance with their proposals for change; a sense of professionalism is released by the responsibilities for reform that might be delegated to teachers, especially if self-determination is encouraged; one's career is influenced by superordinates' ratings for KU participation via teacher assessment reports; certain individuals are picked by the administrator to carry out a change program.

These alternative explanations reflect different theories of administrative influence, theories that might be labeled as follows: instrumental support, negotiation, symbolic leadership, liberation, power-coercion, and selective recruitment of individuals predisposed to KU. The first, which views the administrator's influence almost solely in *instrumental* terms, is the basis of Gross's Leadership Obstacle Course (LOC) theory of change (Gross, 1978). This theory holds that administrators are responsible for creating five conditions necessary for the implementation and incorporation of practices: clear understanding of the proposed innovation, skills and capabilities for carrying it out, materials and equipment, compatible organizational arrangements, and motivation of participants. If administrators fail to provide these predominantly *operational* incentives, personnel will be discouraged or thwarted in their KU efforts, especially in the implementation phase.

Gross's enunciation of this theory, it should be carefully noted, is mainly *normative* rather than predictive. That is, he stipulates what someone *ought* to do rather than the circumstances under which he is inclined to do it. Thus the key influence is shifted to another level of the system, but this influence itself remains unexplained. This is curious inasmuch as Gross prefaced his discussion of the LOC theory with complaints about the "atheoretical" nature of the literature on educational change processes, and concurred with Giacquinta's (1973: 197) criticisms that the primary concern of organizational change efforts has been with "precipitating change rather than studying it" and that the literature fails to explain "how organizations like the schools vary in the degree of speed with which they change." Presumably Gross would answer that such variation is determined by the extent to which administrators play an instrumental leadership role. This surely is an oversimplification. Further, he fails to say what determines instrumental leadership, and therefore fails to explain the speed even of change that is owing to this factor. But most important, he fails to weigh the *alternative* theories of administrative influence mentioned above.

Principals are not the only administrators who supply incentives and disincentives for KU, of course. In smaller systems that are engaged in districtwide change in particular, district-level personnel might be equally or more influential. In their study of comprehensive change in rural schools, Rosenblum and Louis (1978: 222-223) report that, when the effects of other actors over planning are analytically removed, only the superintendent's influence is positively correlated with implementation. Principals' influence is negatively correlated, and teachers' influence is negligible. But here again we need to know what accounts for the relationship between dominance and change.

It is sometimes inadequate to examine the role of a particular administrative actor without taking into account the influence of other actors in the setting. What needs to be examined is the total structure of influence. Rosenblum and Louis (1978) demonstrate the value of this global approach in their analysis of the differential power exerted by teachers, principals, and superintendents in the same setting. What emerges from their analysis is quite interesting because it suggests that the influence of the superintendent will be subverted by principals and teachers when the latter also have power. Further, it seems that principals and teachers will use their influence to promote implementation if the superintendent's power is constrained. As the researchers report: "When the superintendents' influence on planning is high, both principal and teacher planning influence are negatively associated with implementation. But, under conditions of low superintendent influence, both teacher and principal influence are positively associated with change" (Rosenblum and Louis, 1978: 225-226). This is not the case with the relationship between teachers and principals, however: Implementation is slightly more likely to occur when *both* are influential. What seems to be operating, then, is a "competitive tension" between school and district levels with "major implications for the process of initiating and implementing planned change on a district-wide level."

This pattern of findings gives us an important clue to the circumstances that determine whether the exertion of power is an incentive or a disincentive for KU by subordinates. Part of the answer seems to reside in the power held by other actors: If they have little influence, then top down directives will tend to be complied with; if they have considerable influence of their own, then such directives will serve as a disincentive because they will threaten concentrations of power at lower levels. Under the first circumstance, power is a negative incentive; under the second, it is a negative disincentive, because one's autonomy is threatened. In the latter situation, one stands to be penalized for KU by loss of autonomy, a penalty that exceeds any other penalties for noncompliance with directives.

It is probable that in larger, nonrural districts this pattern also prevails between principals and teachers. The intimacy between them in small isolated schools probably invites a closing of ranks vis à vis the district level, while the greater social distance in larger schools might involve them in the same kind of "competitive tension" as occurs between school and district level. Thus, in addition to the distribution of power among statuses, the social distance between levels probably also determines whether power will be a disincentive or an incentive for KU that entails substantial change.

These observations cast some doubt on the prevalent assumption that the sheer exercise of power by administrators is often self-defeating in professional organizations such as schools. (This assumption serves as the foundation of the human relations approach to planned change and its emphasis on participatory decision making.) Here is a concrete case provided by Greenwood et al. (1975: III-13): "The [elementary] director himself admits that he more or less bullied project teachers into sticking with the project as mutiny threatened in the first and second years. . . . The project director . . . explicitly called herself a 'negative change agent' and sees her project as representing a 'negative model of change' or change by imposition of goals and treatments." Lortie (1975: 199) detects a tendency toward ready compliance with principals' requests and rules among elementary teachers. And while some teachers make a sharp distinction between compliance on schoolwide versus classroom matters, Lortie reports that others "move toward a general conception of compliance, preferring the principal's support over personal autonomy." This suggests that those who feel most vulnerable to parents, troublesome students, and uncooperative colleagues are most inclined to reach this sort of feudal bargain with their lords (a metaphor used by Lortie). Also, a tendency to subservience might simply be prescribed by the local culture. The issue is unsettled, but at least it puts us on notice that authoritative commands (negative incentives) can and do foster KU independently of participation in decision making.

Further, while some instrumental assistance from the administrator might be important, it seems that sheer tightness of the organization can promote compliance with KU demands. Rosenblum and Louis (1978: 236-239) found that "formalization" of structure was conducive to KU in the rural experimental schools. (This finding has significant implications for so-called loose coupling theory that need to be explored.)

Much of the influence of principals on teachers might also be due to their qualities of symbolic leadership, as suggested by Lortie (1975: 199). When teachers were asked to discuss their obligations to the principal, "a large proportion (63 percent) said that they owe the principal the fulfillment of their role obligations, the assurance of work fully and conscientiously done. It is as if the teachers are making the principal the personification of their work conscience—they project their sense of duty onto him." Katz and Kahn (1966: 344) refer to "the gratification a person may find in the praise of a powerful and respected figure. Such a person wants to do things which will insure continued approbation from his superior, even without the implication of upgrading and higher pay." This type of orientation, which is remote from the instrumental incentives prescribed by Gross, would seem to favor automatic compliance with KU efforts introduced by the principal as symbolic leader.

Whatever the reason for the strategic importance of superordinates, their pervasive influence raises the question of the incentives/disincentives for KU that operate on educational managers themselves. Earlier we looked at some external influences; here we will examine some influences that are generated within the local system.

One of the main reasons that principals are reluctant to assume responsibility for the outcomes of a KU effort (apart from personal or professional shortcomings) is probably insecurity in relation to any of their several significant role partners, including parents, district administrators, teachers, other principals (Smith and Keith, 1971: 23), and students. This inventory underscores the extent to which principals are people-in-the-middle, a position that ordinarily does not stimulate radical change efforts. This picture of structurally induced caution is perhaps more applicable to administrators who are content with their current jobs or positions. Those who strive for higher positions are probably more likely to embrace KU as a means of gaining recognition and promotion (see Pauly, 1978, on careerism.) But this incentive can pose a hindrance to sustained KU efforts if the individual loses interest once he has attained his goal of self-advertisement.

Another structurally induced source of KU on the part of administrators seems to be their succession to a new position in another school or district. The well-known relationship between innovativeness and succession by outsiders (Carlson, 1965a; Nelson, 1975: 279) indicates that administrators who gain new positions elsewhere either need to prove themselves, do not feel restrained by old loyalties, or have more cosmopolitan resources to draw upon. This early flair for innovation does not endure, however, since the longer an administrator holds office, the less innovative he or she becomes (Nelson, 1975: 271; Pauly, 1978: 282). In fact, greatest innovativeness among principals is found among those who are *both* young and new to the position (Nelson, 1975: 274). Whether this attrition of interest is due to having finally gained tenure, to mounting organizational restraints, to disappointment with past KU efforts undertaken in a spirit of naive idealism, or to some other factor is not known.

Since sheer power, or decision-making authority, is responsible for some amount of successful implementation, the question arises as to the source of such authority. One obvious source is the degree of decentralization in the system as a whole. Nelson (1975: 287) found that principals in decentralized city systems have higher innovation rates than those in centralized city systems. That this relationship is mainly confined to cities with a high proportion of Black students, however, suggests that autonomy fosters KU only when there is an environmental crisis. (Nelson's data were collected in the late 1960s in the heyday of Black militance.) Thus, a negative incentive stemming from the local context might be necessary to activate the principal's autonomy in behalf of KU, which reminds us of the critical role of the environment discussed earlier.

Clearly, shifting the primary responsibility for KU to the school manager and leaving it there does not begin to probe the political, organizational, and other social pressures that cause administrators to promote KU. The available research is not much help in this respect either.

Students as Source of Psychic Rewards

Lortie (1975: 106) claims that teachers are primarily attuned to task-related feedback from students as a source of daily reward. All other sources "pale in comparison with teachers' exchanges with students and feeling that students have learned." This generalization has been widely cited in the literature and therefore its affect on KU deserves careful scrutiny.

In the first place, it seems that Lortie's conclusions apply chiefly to experienced elementary teachers. A review of research by Fuller (1969) reveals that beginning teachers are much more concerned with self (security, control, and so on) than with pupils' learning. And Mann (1976: 329) points out that pupil feedback is of lesser concern to secondary teachers because of their segmental interaction with pupils.

Moreover, Lortie's research, and the research by NEA that he cites, omitted an array of material, interpersonal, and performance rewards from their precoded lists that are couched in attractive (or euphemistic) terms. The data do not tell us whether teachers are *actually* rewarded by student learning, but only that this source of rewards is of great concern to them. If students are *not* meeting their teachers' expectations, then other, compensatory sources of reward might loom significantly large.

Silver (1973) sheds some light on this question. Drawing her data from Black elementary teachers in Washington, D.C., she found that relationships with peers, relationships with administrators, and participation in running the school were each more highly related to job satisfaction than satisfaction with the quality of students' work. These findings point to aspects of teachers' reward structure that are tangential to the classroom, casting doubt on Lortie's conclusion that all rewards other than feedback from students "pale in comparison." Still another source of gratification to teachers, according to Silver's (1973: 102, 120) data, is a perception of classroom autonomy, a relationship that is no less strong than that between satisfaction with quality of students' work and job satisfaction.

Silver explains the strong relationship between job satisfaction and peer relations in terms of a "defensive subculture." She notes that "even though peer relations are less likely to be good in low- than in high-SES schools, their influence on adaptations in the schools is greater in low-than in high-SES schools. . . . The effects of the teachers' subculture are stronger in low-SES schools, where threats to professional status are greater" (Silver, 1973: 200).

Even if performance feedback from students were as vital to teachers as Lortie claims, a resort to KU as a means of improving one's performance is by no means inevitable; teachers might tend to minimize or rationalize student failure precisely because of its psychic impact on them, and therefore reject the implication that new approaches are needed. As Lortie (1975) remarks at one point, "We suspect that teachers sometimes define the desirable outcomes of their work in ways which simplify self-assessment and make it possible to enjoy the gratification of getting results." This tendency is probably most marked in the elementary grades where teachers identify personally with "my class" (McPherson, 1973). It is perhaps not surprising, then, that when Silver (1973: 100-101) asked the Washington, D.C. teachers how satisfied they were with the quality of their students' work, a remarkably high 60 percent claimed to be "very" or "somewhat" satisfied; and when asked how much students liked school, 70 percent responded "very much" or "quite a bit." As Silver remarks, "Teachers' evaluation of students' achievement may reflect indirect evaluation of their own ability to teach successfully."

Now let us turn to a source of incentives that was found above to be at least as critical as students' performance: interpersonal relationships among peers.

Peer Relationships

While the influence of the work group on individual behavior and attitudes has been one of the main topics of occupational research for years, it has been sorely neglected by educational researchers, many of whom stress instead the "isolation" of the teacher without noting his/her embeddedness in a system of peer norms and pressures. Lortie devotes only a few pages to the topic, but provides evidence of the pressure exerted by teachers to be "a good colleague" (Lortie, 1975: 194). Have-lock (1969) devotes a chapter to "interpersonal linkage" but cites few empirical studies in education. The general conclusion from Silver's (1973: 199) research is therefore worth recording here:

> That peer relations in the school are neither linked with the working process nor organized specifically to provide better services to stu-

dents leads to [the conclusion that its function is] mainly to preserve teachers' own security. Indeed, support from peers is essential to teachers' coping with problems in the schools.

The functional potency of teachers' subculture is here underscored because it is very likely that group norms, rewards, and activities are key mediators between new knowledge and individual participation. This influence may operate *directly* through the formal or informal sharing of ideas and practices, or *indirectly* through the climate of values supported by the staff.

The extent of direct, deliberate interpersonal influence that takes place is often underrated. Despite the common image of teachers as being *incommunicado* from one another and shunning the discussion of problems, there is a good deal of information sharing. Lin et al. (1966) found that three-quarters of the high school personnel they studied said that they had first heard about a particular innovation in their schools through interpersonal sources. Hotvedt (1973) and Wolf (1973) found a great deal of overlap between teachers' closest friends, closest associates, and information sources. Hood and Blackwell (1976b: IX-14) reveal that other teachers and other principals are by far the most frequently used sources of information or advice (40 percent of the teachers cited peers and 35 percent of the principals did so). Sieber et al. (1972: 526-527) found that about three-quarters of the clients of the three state dissemination services discussed the information with others. And when asked to indicate the specific benefits that were derived from the information, half of the clients mentioned "it gave me new resources for helping other staff members," a benefit that ranked second in frequency in a list of 14 possible benefits (Sieber et al., 1972: 521).

The indirect influence of the peer climate on KU is also strong. In a study of nine elementary and secondary schools, Chesler et al. (1963) divided the schools into four types, according to whether support for new teaching practices was perceived from both principal and teachers, from the principal only, from teachers only, or from neither. They found that perceived support solely from teachers was related to innovative classroom behavior to the same degree as perceived support solely from principals, and that either type prompted greater innovativeness than occurred in their absence. (Support from both sources simultaneously yielded only slightly higher scores.) These findings are a sobering reminder that the peer group is as important a source of pressure for implementation of new practices as administrators.

However, whether participation in major change efforts serves mainly to integrate the staff rather than to effect change is an important question. Rosenblum and Louis (1978: 210) found that "collegiality" was more highly related to scope of change (number of students and teachers involved) than to qualitative difference made by the change in the Rural Experimental Schools project. This suggests that a strong social network contributes mainly to participation rather than to effectiveness—or, put slightly differently, a healthy social climate ensures breadth of implementation more than it ensures impact. Similarly, Berman and Pauly (1975:

56) found that perceived staff morale was related to ease and fidelity of implementation, but not to actual change in teacher behavior. These findings suggest a certain amount of goal displacement from innovative effectiveness to social integration.

The peer culture of a school is not homogeneous, of course, but divisible into subgroups and into informal leaders and followers. This social differentiation makes prediction of KU behavior in a particular school on the basis of global assessments of attitudes quite difficult. Differentiation permits the emergence of cliques that advocate KU or reform in general, and raises the spectre of intergroup conflict and resistance to KU advocates among peers. We have already noted that a small cell of enthusiasts is mainly responsible for initiation and follow-through of KU efforts in schools (Mann, 1976: 324; Havelock et al., 1973: 186; Miles, Fullan, et al., 1978a: 52). And Havelock (1969: 7-13) points out that innovators are not necessarily opinion leaders, and indeed are often viewed as troublesome mavericks. While the strategic role of opinion leaders in KU would seem to offer a critical leverage point for KU advocates, this opportunity seems to be exploited rarely in the field of educational dissemination. (See also Turnbull et al., 1975: 10, on the utility of "market segmentation.")

Another means of tapping the reservoir of internal linkage motivation is to increase the opportunity for visibility of performance combined with team meetings to discuss pupil and curriculum problems. Cohen (1973) found that the more teachers wished to help young teachers, lead workshops, share their styles and techniques with others, and engage in supervisory evaluations of other teachers, the lower their job satisfaction in *traditional* schools but the higher their satisfaction in *open-space* schools that provide for increased visibility of performance and team discussion. Clearly, there are ways of restructuring schools that make it possible for internal linkers to operate more effectively. (For further discussion of the role of internal linkers, see the chapter by Fullan in this volume.)

Thus far I have been concerned only with relationships *on the job*. What about the role of an occupational community based on off-the-job socializing? Blauner (1960) asserts that there are three essential features of occupational communities: (1) Workers in their off-hours spend more time with each other than with a cross section of occupational types; (2) the participants talk shop during their off-hours intercourse; and (3) they form reference groups that set standards of behavior and a system of status and rank that guide conduct. The consequences are greater satisfaction with social relationships on the job, greater devotion to one's line of work, greater insulation from the public's image of low status, and greater influence of one's skill and expertise on one's status and prestige. Conceivably, such rewards of an occupational community among educators could override the many disincentives for professional effort and commitment found within schools. It seems, however, that teachers' occupation communities are rather weak, especially in urban areas where their residences are dispersed. Although seemingly remote from our interest in KU, the fostering of strong, local occupational communities among school personnel might have greater impact on professional initiative than many of the strategies currently being pursued so diligently within the school by external KU sponsors. (See also my remarks on Teachers' Centers.)

Task/Role Autonomy

It has been noted at several points that KU efforts that threaten to deprive school personnel of task/role autonomy usually fail. By the same token, those that tend to enhance autonomy (such as local adaptation or development of materials, internal linkers, or genuine participation in decision making) or which at least acquiesce to existing structures of autonomy, are more likely to succeed. Now it is necessary to look more closely at this important incentive.

Task/role autonomy does not denote a libertarian disengagement from affairs, but a desire to control one's activities and working conditions. Because teachers are engaged in a complex, nonroutine technology, they require classroom autonomy to make instantaneous decisions based on subtle feedback cues, to develop routines that seem most suitable to themselves and their clients, and to shield themselves from close supervision while performing a diffuse role that entails high risk. The achievement of task/role autonomy, however, lowers the visibility of good teaching, and retards the accumulation of a technical culture among peers. Even if the reward system were geared more to individual performance, therefore, it would be difficult to implement because of the low visibility of performance. Further, the absence of feedback to administrators regarding teachers' "productivity" prevents them from identifying weaknesses in the system. And finally, as noted earlier, prefabricated practices and expert consultants are often resisted or substantially modified because of the need for "ownership."

Under these circumstances, it is not surprising that degree of classroom autonomy was found by Rosenblum and Louis (1978: 220) to be negatively related to implementation of an externally introduced change project. However, this negative relationship was found to occur only under conditions of high collegiality (Rosenblum and Louis, 1978: 214-215). This suggests that only when teachers have support from peers do they feel sufficiently secure to use their autonomy to resist external intervention.

Turning attention to control over decisions that affect the setting beyond an individual's classroom, we are brought to consider the role of participatory decision making. Few issues in the study of KU have ignited more interest and debate, and few have been confronted with less clarity, conceptually and empirically. The value of participation to teachers' occupational satisfaction is revealed by Silver's data (1973: 123, 126). In fact, it appears that such participation accounts to a large extent for the relationship between sense of classroom autonomy and job satisfaction. This strongly suggests that enjoyment of classroom autonomy does not stem simply from retreating into the classroom and closing the door, but from a larger sense of being able to influence decisions by others with regard to one's teaching conditions and activities. This interpretation is consistent with findings by Meyer and Cohen (1971: ch. 7) in their research on open schools. "The sense of autonomy appears to grow out of the increased overall authority of the teacher *group*," they write. "It seems that a worker who is simply left on his own to make decisions, without delegation of power to make those decisions, does not necessarily feel autonomous; he may simply feel neglected."

The contribution of participatory decision making to KU is by no means clear-cut, however. A few years ago Giacquinta (1973: 188) concluded with respect to the general organizational literature: "On the basis of the empirical work to date, little can be said about the effects of participation strategies as compared to strategies where administrators introduce change without prior rank-and-file involvement in the decisions." Participation in *implementation,* however, may be another matter. Berman and Pauly (1975: 61) report that if "teachers felt they did not participate in day-to-day decisions as the project was implemented, implementation was more difficult, and the chances of success, of fidelity to the project design, and of teacher change was reduced." On occasion, as Fullan and Pomfret (1975: 98) conclude, "having the right to decide may lead to confusion, frustration, role overload, and eventually rejection of the innovation." And Corwin (1973: 265) found that when a project was actually imposed by administrators, teachers' participation in local decisions about the Teachers Corps simply gave them a welcome opportunity to sabotage the project.

One of the reasons for the ambiguous status of participation is its complexity as a source of incentives/disincentives. On the one hand, it offers several performance-related rewards, such as control, opportunity for value expression, opportunity to expand horizons, and actual problem solving; it also offers interpersonal rewards, a certain amount of new power, and material perquisites (special resources, time off, and so on). It might even contribute to career advancement. On the other hand, it offers the disincentives of interpersonal conflict, overload, risk of failure as a decision maker, and possibly reduced power or role autonomy because of manipulative leaders.

My own review of the research (Zaltman et al., 1973: 85; Wilson, 1966: 212; Fullan and Pomfret, 1975: 87-91; Giacquinta, 1973: 189; Corwin, 1973: 265; Blumberg et al., 1974) suggests that whether the incentives of participation for KU will exceed the disincentives depends upon the following conditions:

- the degree to which the change project was imposed by administrators

- the manner in which the group operates, the group process skills of members, and the group's structure of authority

- prior relationships among members, including schisms and the balance of power among subgroups

- the authority of the group vis à vis administrators, on the one hand, and over the development and implementation of the innovation, on the other

- the relevance of the group's task to the members' achievement of performance goals or to other valued aspects of organizational life.

- the incentives and disincentives posed by attributes of the innovation being considered

- the degree of consensus that the group is able to achieve without coercing or alienating members of the minority

In terms of incentives/disincentives, then, features of participation that are required to foster KU would seem to be: *relevance* of the group task to perceived needs or desires, *authority* to determine tasks and roles without fear of administrative veto, *broad basis* of representation, *valued interpersonal relationships* within the decision-making group, *voluntarism* of participation, and *avoidance of overload* if not some means of reducing it.

Career Advancement

The presence or absence of opportunities for career advancement seems to be a significant factor in certain kinds of KU behavior. Since opportunities for significant advancement are very limited and visibility in the traditional role is low, any nonroutine activity that engages the attention of status judges as demonstrating a flair for professional leadership might be seen as useful for advancement. Thus, advocacy and management of highly visible innovations may be inspired by occupational ambition. Since I have already referred to the role of careerism among administrators, here I will focus on teachers.

As House (1974: 76) states: "Ambitious teachers are generally important for innovation because they see the investment in relearning as worthwhile for their future. ... Those who envision future rewards through better jobs are the ones willing to invest the extra effort." With respect to staff development projects, Mann (1976: 332) observes: "The most useful incentive seems to have been the visibility or mobility of project personnel. The more successful projects were run by people who reported changes in their career prospects while the less successful projects were run by people who were comfortably resigned to falling back to classroom teaching at the project's conclusion."

The consequence for the school of career advancement based on KU might well be that the most qualified personnel, or at least the most cosmopolitan oriented, are drained off. House (1974: 52-53) speculates that the tendency of KU advocates to be upwardly mobile accounts for "innovative waves" in schools. Unless schools are able to satisfy the career ambitions of KU advocates within their own walls, therefore, a constant process of replacement will be required and KU continuity will be difficult to maintain.

Legitimation

An incentive for KU that one would expect to arise from the insecure nature of the educational profession is the opportunity to justify or legitimize current practices or plans, including a decision *not* to implement a particular product or program. Earlier it was noted that expertise is sometimes used to justify decisions to the community, but it also seems likely that the same defensive function is served with respect to colleagues or others within the school. Because of the complex nature of the teaching task and the absence of performance feedback, one would expect personnel to look for knowledge that validated what they were doing or were thinking about doing. And in the event that a change project is opposed, specialized knowledge might be useful for forestalling change.

While the legitimative incentive for KU is often alluded to, rarely has it been measured. Hood and Blackwell (1976b) asked a group of individuals about purposes for seeking educational information that were "vital for the effective performance of your job." They found that 12 percent selected the item "support decisions already made." In a recent survey in the Virgin Islands, Sieber found that 18 percent of the teacher clients of an information service indicated "have been able to use the information to justify existing programs or practices." (Administrators checked this item only slightly more often than teachers.) This level of legitimative use is about the same as that found among officials in federal, state, and local mental health agencies according to Weiss's (1980) data. She found that 15 percent of her sample "mentioned seeking research for its credibility in documenting their arguments."

It would be interesting to know to what extent, and under what circumstances, the legitimative use of knowledge contributes to improved practice rather than to status security or some other nonperformance goal. The research is silent on this issue despite the fact that the legitimative function is fairly common.

CONCLUDING REMARKS

The foregoing discussion has served to demonstrate two reasons for studying the range of incentives/disincentives to which school personnel are susceptible: (1) to understand the customary rewards that should be heeded by change agents lest their efforts threaten to interfere with these rewards (KU disincentives); and (2) to explore ways in which KU efforts might contribute to acquisition of preferred benefits (KU incentives). With respect to the first objective, it seems that certain fundamental and customary rewards are often threatened by KU interventions, as with role efficiency, task/role autonomy, positive appraisal of pupil effects, and supportive peer relationships. At the other end of the scale, it appears that KU efforts *can* contribute to improved pupil effects, professionalized interactions, career advancement, legitimation, and enlightenment. And depending upon administrative attitudes and practices, it can also contribute to collective decision making, which is another aspect of autonomy. But the fact that a KU effort almost invariably poses disincentives, while it offers compensatory incentives only under special conditions, suggests that the social costs of KU tend to exceed the benefits.

Another general conclusion is that problem solving is a relatively weak incentive for KU. And here I note that the problem-solving approach is not an alternative to the R&D (or technological) perspective, but the local corollary of that perspective. The emphasis on problem solving has therefore overshadowed a number of more potent incentives that are unrelated to educational effectiveness, including career advancement, approval by superiors, legitimation, interpersonal rewards, and so on. And in the realm of performance-related concerns, problem solving has overshadowed the incentive of enlightenment. In particular, it has neglected the role of alternative solutions in helping to define needs, or more precisely, the important *iterative interplay* between needs and solutions.

A third conclusion is that much less is known about the sources and effects of local KU incentives than is required for effective policy making. As tiresome as the plea for "more research" is to people of practical affairs, it cannot be denied that many mistakes have been made by external change agencies because of their lack of information about the genuine incentives for KU of local educators.

But a knowledge of individual incentives in general may not be sufficient either, for schools and districts vary widely in the way they prioritize, distribute, and pursue different incentives. Thus, it is necessary to say a few words about incentive *systems,* a topic that calls for as much attention as I have allotted to *individual* incentives in the present chapter.

LOCAL INCENTIVE SYSTEMS

Space does not permit more than brief reference to some major dimensions for depicting the incentive structure of local settings. These are shown in Table 3.4.

Types of inducements refer to those listed in the taxonomy presented in Table 3.2. It should be stressed that the prevalence of threatened panalties (negative incentives) should be measured carefully to permit characterization of a setting according to emphasis on rewards versus penalties. (See Gouldner, 1954, on the "punishment centered" bureaucracy.) It is also important to distinguish between *perceived* and *actual* rewards, for there is the possibility that personnel misperceive the availability of rewards for certain actions. Thus Stephens (1974) found a good deal of "pluralistic ignorance" among school personnel with regard to norms supportive of innovation, namely: "greater perceived agreement for restrictive norms, but greater actual endorsement of supportive norms." And as Giacquinta (1975: 112) comments: "The objective risks and real losses or gains when innovations are introduced probably are not as great as the subjective or imagined estimations that may turn out to be erroneous and thus resolved more easily."

Next, one would wish to study the *distribution* of actual, perceived, and valued rewards among the parts of the organization. Are high school personnel less susceptible to certain incentives for KU than elementary

TABLE 3.4 A Taxonomy of Local Incentive Systems

Types of inducements (negative/positive, incentives/disincentives)

    Perceived and actual

    Valued and nonvalued

Structure

    Distribution among subparts of organization

        Horizontal

        Vertical—number of levels, height, peakedness

Allocation

    Congruence between different reward hierarchies

    Formalization, predictability

    Consensus among allocators

    Bases

        Performance of various kinds

        Incumbency

        Personal or social attributes

Sources of inducements

    External-internal

    Formal-informal

Scarcity/abundance of inducements

Orientations and KU predispositions of staff

    Personality patterns

    Occupational and role orientations

    Preference for KU resources

personnel, as suggested by some case studies? Are the incentives of administrators and teachers different (for example, opportunistic desire for funds versus performance effects)? And so on.

Then there is the question of how rewards are distributed vertically within groups. Many have commented on the flatness of the reward structure in education, but few have sought to determine the effect of variations in whatever "peakedness" does exist. House (1974: 97-98) notes that there are two "generic strategies to radical restructuring of the incentive and information structure of the school." One entails equalizing the power of teachers relative to administrators so that they interact as status judges, which House believes "feeds professional ambition without changing vertical ambition and substitutes intrinsic rewards for more extrinsic ones." The other way is to introduce more differentiation among teachers with graduated rewards, such as merit pay or ranks, for different levels of performance, which House thinks only increases the power of administrators. But there are probably many variations along a scale from complete and equal teacher interaction with administrators to a merito-cratic structure presided over by the latter. A primary task, then, is to measure the number of levels and the peakedness of the reward hierarchy in different schools, and to study the effect on KU.

The *allocation* system is another feature of reward structures. An important aspect of allocation is the congruence between rankings on different value scales. Thus, pay, autonomy, and prestige might or might not be *in line* for different individuals. Still other aspects of the allocation system are its predictability, the formalization and visibility of criteria, and the degree of consensus among those who do the allocating. For our purposes, however, by far the most important allocation aspect is the *basis* for rewards. As noted earlier, rewards may be rendered for role occupancy or for role performance. But then one must also distinguish between different types of role performance. A good disciplinarian is not the same as a good innovator, and, indeed, these types might be at odds on occasion. And of course there are a host of personal attributes that might determine rewards, such as sex, race, age, and so on.

Sources of rewards has also been referred to as a major dimension with respect to internal-external origins and formal-informal types of incentives/disincentives. Still another important parameter is the *abundance or scarcity* of various rewards. If certain teachers are paid more for KU behavior, for example, others may have to be paid less. Other values that are limited are power and social recognition. There seems to be only one type of reward that can be rendered for KU without reducing the pool: performance rewards. Thus, incentives that consist of greater opportunity for application of skills, value expression, enlightenment, improved perfor-mance, and so on, are almost infinitely expansible, providing that some costs for the system are not entailed. Unfortunately, the influence of such opportunities depends on certain predispositions to value these aspects of role performance, which brings us to the final major dimension of *orienta-tions* of school personnel.

The formulation of orientation types is often partly based on prefer-ences for particular benefits, and hence reflects incentive types. For example, in a factor analysis of responses to a list of reasons for becoming a teacher, Ashley et al. (1970) found three clear-cut role orientations which they labeled Worker (material benefits), Educator (idealism), and Person (pupil-centered). And Ziegler (1966) divided teachers into the sanction-prone and the sanction-fearless with respect to community pres-sures. Neither of these studies was concerned with KU, however. Further, it is possible to formulate types of orientation that affect KU but are not based on perception of benefits and costs. These types can be divided into (1) personality patterns and (2) patterns of external foci, such as cosmo-politanism versus localism, person versus task orientation, humanism ver-sus custodialism.[12]

Some Speculations

To convey some sense of the reality of a concrete incentive system, it might be helpful to speculate about a model that combines a number of features favorable to KU. Thus, the greatest disposition toward KU might be found in schools with the following features of an incentive system:

(1) a relatively flat hierarchy which is determined mainly by informal recognition by colleagues, and with formal rewards congruent with collegial standing in KU efforts;

(2) a good deal of task/role autonomy among the faculty as a group involved in KU with voluntary participation in decision making (and training in communication skills);

(3) a principal who is both a symbolic leader and a provider of organizational means for KU activity, and who has decision-making authority granted by the central administration;

(4) a cosmopolitan orientation, a grasp of the conceptual underpinnings of particular KU efforts, an opportunity to examine a range of plausible options, and role orientations founded on expectations of performance-related rewards for client-oriented behavior;

(5) visibility of performance and communication among colleagues that is both affective and task-relevant, and buttressed by an occupational community;

(6) consistency in application of criteria for allocating rewards;

(7) a perception of rewards for individual role performance stemming from both colleagues and administrators, together with a guarantee of basic system rewards for role incumbency; and

(8) compensation for unavoidable deprivation of customary sources of gratification (for example, role efficiency) imposed by a KU effort.

The combination of such features of an incentive system projects the image of a school that is socially integrated, goal-oriented, adaptive to new opportunities, and motivated to contribute to the welfare of clients and the health of the organization—in short, a school that fulfills the classical needs of professional social systems in optimal fashion.

NOTES

1. For a discussion of the full significance of this point, see the chapter by Berman in this volume.

2. This dimension will be repeated in my later taxonomy of incentive *systems* as one aspect of the source of incentives.

3. For a detailed conceptual analysis of these and other works, see Sieber (1979: 16-38).

4. My use of the term "system" does not assume a high degree of integration, functional specialization, consensus on goals, continuity, or self-corrective behavior. A social collectivity with low scores on these dimensions is nonetheless a system.

5. No doubt "common" knowledge, including role models from one's own early schooling, rules of thumb, popular psychology, and tricks of the trade, is a more

important source of guidance than systematic or expert knowledge. See Lindblom and Cohen (1979).

6. It should be noted, however, that the concept of complexity has not been well specified by educational researchers. For an analysis and critique of several definitions, see Sieber (1979: 59-61). For criticisms of the measurement and conceptualization of other innovation attributes, see Sieber (1979: 62-72).

7. This conclusion raises the perennial question of whether OD is not most successful where it is least needed.

8. For a fuller discussion of linking agents, see the chapter by Louis in this volume.

9. Personal communication from Matthew Miles.

10. There is great variation in community contexts in America, of course. For a discussion based on research of how such variation affects KU, see Sieber (1979: 138-144).

11. Paul Berman has indicated in a personal communication that about three-fourths of the projects were initiated opportunistically.

12. For a further elaboration of the domain of personal orientations, see Sieber (1979: 212-215).

4

EXTERNAL AGENTS
AND KNOWLEDGE UTILIZATION

Dimensions for Analysis and Action

Karen Seashore Louis

INTRODUCTION

The purpose of the following chapter is to explore the ways in which external actors—variously referred to as consultants, change agents, or linking agents—affect school improvement and knowledge utilization at the local level. While the chapter attempts to review the pertinent literature, the objective is not only to synthesize what is known, but also to point out the gaps and deficiencies in our current understanding of the role of external actors.

A relatively long tradition of research supports the importance of external actors in stimulating knowledge use both in schools and in other contexts. As early as the mid-1960s many educational researchers were calling for an increase in the number of consultants who could provide assistance to schools engaged in planned change programs, and even pointed to the need to establish an educational extension system, modeled after the agricultural extension model (see Carlson, 1965a, and Jung and Lippitt, 1966, for statements of the assumptions underlying these early recommendations). Among the research results that supported the need for such roles were field experiments by Glaser (1965) which showed that organizations could be made more receptive to research results through the use of external consultants and externally sponsored conferences, and the increasing attention paid to the role of "change agents" in the literature on innovation diffusion (see Rogers and Shoemaker, 1971).

Recent research in education has produced a number of studies which support the efficacy of an external helping role in increasing local school use of information. Sieber et al. (1972), for example, show that external education extension agents in the Pilot State Dissemination Project had a significant impact on the level of requests for information (receptivity). In addition, Louis and Sieber (1979) have shown that the external agents also had a significant impact on information *use* under some circumstances. Emrick et al.'s (1977) study of the National Diffusion Network produced findings which strongly support the assumption that an external agent may have a significant impact on implementation of innovations. The effects of external agents remained even when important school characteristics, such as motivation to change, local support for the project, administrator support, and sense of participation, were controlled for in regression analysis. This finding is quite critical, for these innovation support characteristics had a great deal of impact on the conclusions drawn from the Rand Corporation study of federal programs supporting educational change (Berman and McLaughlin, 1974, 1977). Evidence from the study of the R&D Utilization Program suggests that the external technical assistance provided through this program was critical in helping local schools to maintain a commitment to long-term planning and change programs, and played a particularly powerful role in increasing the magnitude of the planned change activities and the likelihood that they would be institutionalized (Louis, Rosenblum, et al., 1981). Similarly, the accumulating results of research on the outcomes of organization development (OD) programs in schools shows that externally induced programs involving strong consultive roles from third-party trainers or experts can have significant impact (see, for example, Miles, Fullan, et al., 1978a; Keys and Bartunek, 1979; Schmuck et al., 1969). Those who support the need for external agents may point with some pleasure to the apparent robustness of this set of findings, in which the impact of an external agent appears to hold in the laboratory, in field settings, and in a wide variety of different roles ranging from the nonintensive "extension agent" role (found in the Pilot State Dissemination Project or in the state facilitator role in the NDN project) to the relatively intensive and long-term arrangements found in many OD interventions.

This synthesis will address a set of questions which assume the potential value of external agents:[1] First, what is meant when we say that a strategy for change and knowledge utilization that employs external agents "works"; second, under what conditions is the agent effective; and third, what additional research is needed in order to arrive at some broader set of theories and policy decisions regarding external roles in stimulating knowledge utilization. The discussion will be grounded in the empirical literature related to external agent impacts in schools.

In order to address the above questions it is necessary to base the discussion on a clear definition of the phenomenon that we have called the "external agent." In addition, in order to further ground our discussion, a framework for looking at the knowledge utilization contexts in which external agents may be useful will be developed, and the implications of these contexts for agent roles will be briefly discussed. Once this ground-work has been laid, specific research findings related to the impact of agent roles and behaviors upon schools and individual educators will be presented, with particular emphasis on consistency of findings and areas where research is particularly impressive or thin. Finally, some implications for a research agenda on the role of external agents will be developed.

WHAT IS AN EXTERNAL AGENT?

A recent review of the literature (Glaser, 1976) pointed to over a dozen job titles that have recently been applied to the role of the external agent. Among these were: social engineer, linking agent, popularizer, change agent, research translator, learning engineer, applied behavioral scientist, and research utilization specialist. This plethora of titles suggests the wide variety of definitions which are applied to the role of the external agent. Many of these definitions suggest different ways of approaching the problem of fostering improved knowledge utilization among organizations and individuals.

Archibald (1968), for example, sees the applied social scientist as an expert who has a reformist interest, that is, one who seeks both knowledge and change. This definition assumes that the knowledge producer or at least part of the knowledge-production system is in fact a linking agent. Somewhat similarly, Rogers et al. (1976) describe the extension specialist as an individual who is a member of the knowledge production community in the university, but who is himself a synthesizer of knowledge, rather than a producer of knowledge. Rogers and Shoemaker (1971: 227) have developed a more general definition of the agent's role:

> A change agent is a professional who influences innovation decisions
> in a direction deemed desirable by a change agency.

Zaltman and Duncan (1977: 186) also view the external agent as a change agent:

> A change agent is any individual or group operating to change the
> status quo in the clients's system such that the individuals involved
> must relearn how to perform their roles.

Others, however, reject the implicit assumption that the external agent has specific objectives in mind for the targeted client organizations or individuals. Blumberg (1976: 226) severely criticizes the external imposition of change goals, and poses an alternative:

> [The term "interventionist"] implies: a) helping the client collect
> and understand valid information about his problem; b) helping the
> client develop a system of free choice; and c) helping the client
> develop internal commit to the processes authentically if that person
> is "out to change things." The use of them means that the user has
> no particular goal in mind for the organization but is willing to trust

that the people involved with valid information at hand will develop goals and problem solutions which for them best fit the situation.

Similarly, Miles and Schmuck (1971) present no explicit definition of the OD specialist or consultant but define the role of the types of organizational interventions that are acceptable within the OD framework (see Miles and Schmuck, 1971: 9; also Fullan et al., 1980). In both cases the external role is seen as a pair of hands that transmit a set of strategies or technologies for improvement in the client system. Cates's (1978: 5) recent review of educational literature related to external areas also takes a functional rather than a definitional approach, and identifies seven core functions: planning, resource utilization, communication, problem solving, process helping, implementation, and evaluation. The author implies, however, that the inventory of functions may not be useful for definitional purposes, since there is still considerable confusion and disagreement about the meaning of these functional labels (Cates, 1978: 17-18).

There is, apparently, considerably greater consensus among those who attempt to define external roles as "linking" roles. This consensus exists across as well as within disciplines. For example, Piele's (1975: 3) definition is as follows:

[Linking] agents operate at the interface between new ideas and products and current educational practice, dealing regularly with both resource and user systems for the purpose of helping the two to interact constructively.

The Social and Rehabilitation Services Agency similarly defines the role of the research utilization specialist:

[RUSs serve] as an action link between the producer and consumer of research results, bringing new and more effective findings to the attention of practitioners and administrators [and] promoting their adoption by ongoing programs [Hamilton and Muthard, 1975: 63].

Most definitions of linking agents do not explicitly refer to externally imported desirable outcomes in the target or user group. These are, however, frequently implicit, and most authors who discuss this role would agree that:

[the role of] the linker ... brings greater rationality to change oriented decisions in school systems by increasing the nature and extent of information utilized in decision-making [Nash and Culbertson, 1977: 2].

Those who do not explicitly espouse the objective of improving rationality in school systems will frequently refer to "improved problem-solving." (Crandall, 1977: 216).

Some Problems with Defining External Agents

In order to define and understand roles which external actors play in knowledge utilization processes in local schools, it is necessary to come to terms with the diversity in the definitions presented above. Given the

relative paucity of empirical studies of agents in school improvement
programs, the examination of definitions is a major means of illuminating
weaknesses or gaps in current approaches to research in this area. In the
following paragraphs, therefore, some of the problems with existing definitions of external roles will be discussed, and perspectives that will be used
in the remainder of this chapter will be articulated.

THE DEFINITIONAL DILEMMA: GENERAL VERSUS SPECIFIC

As Hood and Cates (1978: 2) point out:

> Conceptually, anyone who facilitates the transfer of educational
> knowledge could be considered the linking agent, but this simplifica-
> tion leads to a rather unacceptable situation, since virtually anyone
> in the field of education may be involved in the transfer of knowl-
> edge to someone else.

Attempts to narrow the definition, on the other hand, generally involve
specifying either the source of the information (such as research information), the technique by which information is to be transmitted (for
example, as in OD intervention strategies or "face-to-face assistance"), or
specification of outcomes (such as planned change, utilization of R&D
products, or improved organizational health). While each of these limitations has its advocates, the objective of this review is not to provide
recommendations but to define an arena for action and research. For these
purposes, greater specifications may lead to loss of conceptual generalizability.

However, Hood and Cates' dilemma should not be ignored entirely. The
study of external actors in the knowledge utilization process cannot
encompass every aspect of knowledge exchange that occurs within the
educational system. Three specifications seem appropriate. First, following
Zaltman and Duncan (1977: 187), no direct attention will be paid to the
nonpurposive stimulation of knowledge utilization and change, for example, "persons who initiate change without a particular intention to do so."
As these authors point out, the inadvertent agent may be best viewed as
part of the "bag of tricks" or strategies which the conscious external actor
can use in working with a system, a group, or set of individuals.

Second, there is the distinction made by Katter and Hull (1976)
between different orientations of external agencies involved in providing
information or knowledge to schools. The authors classify education
information service agencies (EISs) into three types:

- *Collection*-oriented agencies provide services to educators largely as a
  by-product of other activities. The primary goals and objectives of
  these agencies are to maintain, to build, and to service the collection
  of materials or information.

- *Product*-oriented agencies are concerned exclusively with dissemination of information about a specific product line of educational
  information. They are not concerned about the system the potential
  user systems need as much as about selling the product.

• *Audience*-oriented agencies seek to meet the information needs of clients. It is betterment of the client's system that drives the information exchange, rather than the organizational needs or concerns of the EIS.

The findings of a survey of EIS goals and activities presented by Katter and Hull (1976) suggest that the audience/collection/product typology may be thought of not as a set of distinctive categories, but as dimensions along which external agents and agencies may vary.[2] Using the typology in this fashion, all agencies and actors that exhibit a low audience orientation may be eliminated from consideration as external agents. This suggestion is premised on the judgment that such agencies or agents are less likely to contribute significantly to the broad objectives of school improvement. Or, if they do so, they will do so as inadvertant rather than purposive agents.

A final proposed specification is to limit our investigation to human agents. The very concept of human agents or agencies denotes an interpersonal aspect to the exchange or transmission of information. The use of written means of communication or the telephone, so long as these communication channels are personalized, are sufficient to include the agent within our definition. However, if the communication consists only of the transmission of standardized forms or information in an entirely routinized manner, it would fall out of our area of concern.[3] Presumably, such an agent or agency could be completely mechanized with appropriate technological advances.

PUBLIC ACCEPTABILITY OF EXTERNAL AGENTS

Despite evidence suggesting their importance, the role of external agents in educational improvement has not been a prominent policy issue over the last decade. One of the reasons for the lack of greater interest may be the jargon which surrounds both writing and the implementation of such roles. Another may be the lack of clarity in their role definition.

Many of the dozens of names used to refer to the external agent are either arcane or of obscure meaning to the typical educator or legislator. Thus, for example, the term "linking agent" (probably the most common term in the area of education) brings expressions of disbelief and incomprehension to the faces of policy makers who are queried regarding their interest in this area (Chabotar and Kell, 1978). Of potentially greater concern is the fact that many of these titles tend to be threatening to the practitioner or client whom the external agent seeks to serve. The title of Research Utilization Specialist, which was applied in the Social and Rehabilitation Service's experimental five-year program, elicited the following comments from those who held this job title:

> The RUSs were unanimous in the belief that the title Research Utilization Specialist detracted from their acceptance and effectiveness and was not, in fact, appropriate to the position. The word

research was a source of considerable resistance ... field staff
reacted vehemently to the perception of research as evaluative. ...
[One RUS] found that the term research created not only resistance, but also misunderstanding of the job functions. ... The title
specialist was an equal handicap. ... The RUS was sometimes perceived as a person with detailed, specific, knowledge on the subject,
at times as "the person who knows more and more about less and
less" [Hamilton and Muthard, 1975b: 78-79].

Apparently, the increasing tendency to invent new terminology to refer
not only to the external role, but also to the functions of the external role,
complicate this situation enormously. While it is certainly beyond the
objectives of this chapter to definitively determine what external agents
should be called, one may suggest that commonly understood terms, such
as consultant, or extension, or field agent, are preferable to new terms
which try to capture the novelty of the job.[4]

In addition to terminology concerns, there is a genuine problem with
the explicitness of the role. A major problem with the acceptance of OD in
school settings is that the dimensions of the innovation are difficult to
define—and may be contradictory in different settings because of the
frequency with which the term is inappropriately applied (Fullan et al.,
1978: 246; Miles, 1980). Similar problems have been observed in settings
where an educational extension agent is at work. While poorly articulated
roles may, in some cases, work to the agent's advantage (see Louis and
Sieber, 1979: 6), lack of explicitness causes many of the same problems in
diffusion and implementation of these new roles as it does in the case of
curricular or administrative innovations (see Charters and Pellegrin, 1972).
Low explicitness does not imply that immediate steps to achieve total
conceptual clarity and specification are appropriate. Some observers have
concluded that the educational extension agent is successful in large
measure because of the enormous flexibility and lack of bureaucratization
in the role (see Louis and Sieber, 1979). However, some specification is
necessary in order to present the role effectively to potential clients (see
Louis, Kell, et al., 1981; Miles, 1980).

ROLES AND GOALS

Most current approaches to specifying the roles of external agents are
based on explicit or implicit judgments about the objectives that will be
achieved through the use of such agents. In particular, there is an assumption that the external agent's major function is to import research information to facilitate the adoption of innovative programs in schools. It seems
obvious that this assumption about objectives and outcomes of using
external agents is derived from the dominant research tradition that is
associated with the study of information use, which is firmly grounded in
the agricultural extension program (see, for example, Rogers and Shoemaker, 1971). While there are other research traditions which examine

information diffusion, these have not had nearly the impact on the general consciousness of those concerned with information use as has the image of the stalwart county extension agent explaining the virtues of hybrid seed corn to a tabacco-chewing farmer.[5] In reality, as noted in some of the definitions presented above, this image of the external agent vastly oversimplifies the variety of roles which purposive actors may play.

Another major reason for this definitional bias lies in the source of concern about knowledge utilization in local schools over the last 10 years. The major funder of research on local school improvement is the federal government. The federal government is also the major supporter of research and development in both university settings and in applied R&D settings. Not surprisingly, the government is also concerned about the gap between R&D and the use of R&D by local schools (see Gideonse, 1970; Dershimer, 1976). This "technological push" perspective views schools as users of R&D rather than creators of knowledge and innovation. This viewpoint is deeply embedded in the educational literature despite attempts by some federal policy makers to make room for "craft" or practice-based knowledge (National Council for Educational Research, 1979; see also House, this volume.)

Lippitt (1969), however, takes a more complex view of this issue. Based on a number of studies conducted by the Center for Research on the Utilization of Scientific Knowledge at the University of Michigan, Lippitt distinguishes between two general patterns of research utilization. The first is the *"science consumer system,"* which imports research information from the outside. While this approach does not fully correspond to the integrated "R,D,D and U" approach first described by Havelock (1969) and elaborated on by a number of others (see Berman and McLaughlin, 1974; Louis and Sieber, 1979), it does emphasize the client system as a user. In addition, Lippitt identifies an *internal pattern of knowledge production and utilization,* whereby the system itself generates information and uses it. Lippitt argues that the internal as well as the external agent can facilitate the coordination and production of knowledge. The notion of external agent as something other than a bringer of knowledge has a long tradition in a variety of organizational intervention groups. Thus, for example, the approach used by the Tavistock Institute of Human Relations in London, England, tends to view the external agent rather as a therapist for organizations, as does the external OD role described by Schein (1970).

Concepts of Information Use and External Agent Roles

The linkage model proposed by Havelock (1969) views the information utilization cycle as involving knowledge producers and knowledge consumers with various mechanisms for connecting these two groups. Without in any way attempting to diminish a major contribution to what was at the time a field with little theoretical basis, it must be noted that this model has narrowed the conceptualization of how knowledge is used in educational organizations, for it has directed attention only to research knowledge imported from the knowledge-producing superstructure. Similarly, on the one hand, we should applaud the advances that have been made over the past few years in studying implementation of new programs as part of the school improvement process (see, for example, Gross et al., 1971; Fullan and Pomfret, 1975; Berman and McLaughlin, 1977; Rosenblum and Louis, 1978). On the other hand, however, it is important to raise again the point that information may be used in a wide variety of beneficial ways that cannot easily be classified as implementation of a new program, or an immediate change in practice—such as for staff development or long-range planning (Louis, 1975).

In examining the federal administrative agency as an information user, Sabatier (1978) draws upon two different modes for information provision to agencies. The first is the decisionistic-instrumental perspective defined by Rein and White (1977: 404). The assumption of the decisionistic-instrumental perspective is that "technical information or policy analysis is provided primarily to influence specification decisions . . . and that the information is provided only if there is some reasonable expectation that it will alter the decision outcome."

Weiss (1977), on the other hand, sees one of the main functions of providing information to administer to decision makers as a process of gradual *"enlightenment."* (This point is also made in Lindblom and Cohen, 1979). In contrast to the decisionistic-instrumental perspective, the enlightenment function emphasizes gradual learning on the part of people who make decisions. If the enlightenment function is truly in effect, improvement in a social system cannot be attributed to a particular piece of information or a single transmitter of information. Rather, improved decisions should occur over time as a consequence of small infusions of improved information, often combined with "common" knowledge.

Both the enlightenment function and the decisionistic-instrumental function assume, however, that an external organization is responsible for infusing the system. A third way of looking at change might be called the *capacity-building function.* In the capacity-building function, information is used in itself to improve the system's capacity for generating information. While the system may never become completely independent of external sources of information, it becomes more able to function autonomously and to solve its own problems without depending on an external source. The notion of capacity building involves changing the ability of the organization itself to search for and to process information.

While federal programs sponsoring improved knowledge utilization frequently aim to increase knowledge use in all of these categories, the objectives are rarely made explicit. Thus, for example, Hamilton and Muthard (1975a: 381) state that despite a major project to improve research utilization in the field of vocational rehabilitation, "no clear concept of the meaning of research utilization or of the ways in which such a process could be identified within rehabilitation has been identified."

In addition to three different modes of knowledge use, we have different types of knowledge. First of all, there is the distinction that is increasingly being made between research-based knowledge—knowledge which is generated exclusively through scientific inquiry—and craft knowledge, which is knowledge that is generated based on the experience of individuals who are engaged in practice. While again the distinctions between research knowledge and craft knowledge are not entirely clear, the source of the knowledge has considerable implications for the ways in which it may be effectively transmitted to the potential user and thus for the ways in which an external agent may function in the system.[6]

A final distinction of importance is between knowledge which is internally generated, that is, knowledge which resides in the system, and knowledge which is externally generated and must be imported. While it may seem on the face of it that there would be a high level of congruence between internally generated knowledge and craft knowledge and externally generated knowledge and research knowledge, these dimensions are in fact distinct. This may be seen in Table 4.1.

Cell I portrays the situation in which research knowledge is generated inside the group. Examples of types of activities that would fall into this setting include survey feedback activities and self-study, which can be conducted by the group. The existence of this cell may appear somewhat shocking to proponents of the linkage theory who assume that research is somehow "out there" or outside of the practitioner domain. In fact, it is very clear that many schools and school systems are happily and very productively engaged in the business of producing "research" information internally. Research-based examples of what this cell might comprise include Lyon et al.'s study of the use of evaluation information in local school districts (Lyon et al., 1979) and the types of needs-assessment activities engaged in by several of the federally funded R&D Utilization Projects. In the Pennsylvania Project, for example, a very well defined approach to the determination of specific weaknesses in basic skills was developed and implemented in more than a dozen participating schools. The approach used in this R&D utilization program emphasized external training, but staff participation in both data gathering and interpretation[7] (see also Corbett, 1980; Firestone and Donner, 1981). Evidence from research on OD in schools (OD programs frequently involve generating research-based information about the organization) suggests that the role of the external agent may be critical, particularly in the early stages where internal change agents or other members of the organization begin to acquire skills to carry out research tasks themselves. The same data indicate that overdependence on the external agent may result in noninstitutionalization of OD activities (see Miles, Fullan, et al., 1978a), a finding that is confirmed by Louis, Rosenblum, et al. (1981).

Regarding other types of research information, such as program or student evaluation, most large school districts are attempting to acquire their own experts to carry out these tasks (Lyon et al., 1979). However, internal utilization is still a problem (Alkin et al., 1979) because administrators and teachers may have trouble interpreting the action dimensions of information. Internal researchers may, therefore, need external assistance in learning how to become internal change agents, as well as

TABLE 4.1   Knowledge Utilization Contexts that Affect External
Agent Roles

	Research Knowledge	*Craft Knowledge*
	I	**II**
Knowledge internally generated	*Utilization goals:* decisionistic, enlightenment, capacity building	*Utilization goals:* decisionistic, enlightenment, capacity building
	Examples: survey feedback, school self-study or evaluation (Lippitt, 1969)	*Examples:* "temporary" systems for adapting curricula that have been previously adopted (Berman and McLaughlin, 1977)
	III	**IV**
Knowledge externally generated	*Utilization goals:* decisionistic, enlightenment, capacity building	*Utilization goals:* decisionistic, enlightenment, capacity building
	Examples: dissemination of R&D lab products for adoption by schools (Louis and Sieber, 1979)	*Examples:* League of Cooperative Schools (Goodlad, 1975), teacher center in-involving multiple dictricts

researchers. In small districts, where it is not possible to employ a broad range of researchers, there is considerable room for the expert consultant who can help the district to design and analyze information that is needed to fulfill any of the knowledge utilization functions discussed above.

Cell II involves the intersection between internally generated knowledge and craft knowledge. An example of knowledge utilization processes falling into this cell would include in-service or sharing among staff members and the development of new programs or modifications to old programs that are based on familiarity with existing curricula and methods. The findings reported by Berman and McLaughlin (1977) suggest that the process of "mutual adaptation" involves the application of locally designed improvements to adopted programs. The Concerns Based Adoption Model (CBAM) research program (Hall et al., 1975) suggests that adequate implementation will inevitably involve systematic collection of feedback and modification of practice based upon it. This does not occur as a "research" program for the adopter, but as a judgmental adjustment process. The CBAM studies indicate that an external agent may be extremely helpful in assisting individual adopters to reach this stage of thoughtful, craft-based adjustments in practice.

Cell III represents the intersection between research knowledge and externally generated knowledge, and is the cell that we most often associate with knowledge utilization in the field of education. Multiple empirical-based studies populate this cell. These include the Sieber et al. (1972) and Louis and Sieber (1979) reports about the client responses to the Pilot State Dissemination Project (1981), Emrick et al.'s (1977) study of the National Diffusion Network and the Louis et al. study of the R&D Utilization Program, as well as much of the work of the above mentioned Concerns Based Adoption Model (Hall et al., 1975). (For a comparison of several studies which fall into this cell, see Emrick and Peterson, 1978).

The functions that external agents can play under the circumstances described by this cell are also quite well documented conceptually (see below). A major issue is whether the agent operates with a *technological-push* objective (in which the goal is to persuade clients to utilize approved or "valid" research information from a preselected knowledge base), or a *demand-pull* objective (in which the client's definition of need stimulates a search for the type of research information that can best be brought to bear upon the question at hand.) A technological-push orientation almost invariably implies that the agent is intended to facilitate instrumental-decisionistic knowledge use, while a demand-pull approach can be responsive to all knowledge use types.

Cell IV, in which there is an intersection between craft knowledge and externally imported knowledge, may be typified by attempts to create networks among a variety of schools, such as the League of Cooperative Schools, and by institutions which are external to a single school and which draw upon the staffs of several schools, such as Teacher Centers. Goodlad (1975) emphasizes that the successes of the League of Cooperative Schools were attributable, in large measure, to the role of a central external agency which served as a "hub," or a clearinghouse, that facilitated the partnership between schools concerned about innovative programs and projects. Similarly, the objective of many Teacher Centers is not to improve education through the transmission of externally generated research information (see Burchinal, 1967) but through sharing a craft knowledge among teachers. Another example of a type of approach that would fall into this cell is Havelock and Mann's (1968) study of an attempt to improve the climate for research utilization within R&D labs through the use of capacity-building staff seminars. In general, this cell implies that the role of the external agent is more likely to focus on enlightenment or capacity building than upon major programmatic decisions for change. Current wisdom among educators suggests that the most well-received forms of in-service education (which focuses on capacity building at the individual level) are often of this type, or mix the use of imported and internally generated craft knowledge.[8]

Again, it should be pointed out, as does Lippitt (1969), that linking agents or generalists should be expected to be able to perform in a variety of capacities within these different cells, since the needs of clients may be quite different in each case. Thus, for example, in Cell I the client system may have the greatest need for a consultant who is able to help them with the technical aspects of a survey feedback program. In Cell IV, on the other hand, they may have the greatest need for somebody who has the strong administrative skills that are necessary to hold together a network of individuals from different organizations (Sarason and Lorentz, 1979).

Summary

To summarize, *the development of a comprehensive theory of external intervention in schools and in research plans to study the role of external agents in school improvement and knowledge utilization processes necessitates moving away from the dominant and limited mode which views external agents as individuals who bring external research knowledge for the purpose of making specific decisions and implementing new programs.*
The major problem with existing definitions of external roles and knowledge utilization is that the focus tends to be on the knowledge *producing* subsystem, which the "linker" serves, and not on the functions of information for schools, school systems and educators, and the ways in which they are likely to respond to external roles supporting knowledge use. Thus, there is an emphasis on change or implementation as the only criterion for involvement of an external agent at a time when many educators are calling for professional development and increased professional opportunities. There is a tendency to define external agents using jargon unacceptable to practitioners and to policy makers at local, state, and federal levels. There is also a tendency to define the linkage roles too narrowly so as not to encompass roles that could be brought into the dissemination and knowledge utilization system, and there is a tendency to look at knowledge so narrowly that legitimate ways of using knowledge are excluded.
Having criticized existing definitions, it is difficult to propose one that will appear at once crisp and sufficiently inclusive. Instead we must opt for a broad definition, in hopes of encompassing the field but offending few: *An external agent is an individual, group, or organization located outside of the boundaries of the client system, whose objective is to assist client(s)— individuals, groups, individual educators, groups of educators, groups of schools—to enhance the clients' functioning as educators or as an educational system.* External agents may do many things in the service of school improvement activities. In this discussion we will focus exclusively on those behaviors which are intended to directly enhance the clients' ability to locate, generate, and use information.

CURRENT DESCRIPTIONS
OF EXTERNAL AGENT ROLES

Typologies of External Roles

Typologies of the different roles that external agents can play proliferate almost as rapidly as do different titles. The most frequently cited classification schemes have been thoroughly reviewed by Hood and Cates (1978) and the following discussion relies on their presentation, which is summarized in Table 4.2.

Havelock (1969) was one of the first to lay out the wide variety of roles that external agents could play in the knowledge-transfer process, and to tie these different roles to different functions that such a role can serve. These roles include:

ROLE	FUNCTIONS
Conveyor	Transfers knowledge from producers (scientists, experts, scholars, developers, researchers, and manufacturers) to users.
Consultant	Assists users in identification of problems and resources, provides linkage to appropriate resources, assists in adaptation, serves as a process facilitator.
Trainer	Instills in the user an understanding of an entire area of knowledge or practice.
Leader	Effects linkage through power or influence in one's own group.
Innovator	Initiates diffusion in the user system (includes originator and also the first user in a social system to adopt an innovation).
Defender	Sensitizes users to the pitfalls of innovations, mobilizes public sensitivity, and public demand for adequate applications.

Most typologies proposed in the past decade are derivative of the distinctions made by Havelock, both in this formulation and in a later, more succinct set of role types (Havelock and Havelock, 1973). The major contribution of Piele (1975) and Butler and Paisley (1978) was not that of novelty, but that they flesh out the skeletal definitions provided by Havelock and tie them more firmly to the different sets of assumptions inherent in current planned change theories.

The major distinctions in these latter formulations are among change models that emphasize the *process* of innovation, those that emphasize importing universal *solutions* to generic educational problems, and those that emphasize *collaboration* and adaptation between client needs and potential resources. These three change strategies are associated with three types of agent roles: the process helper, the solution giver, and the resource linker. The Butler and Paisley (1978) formulation adds the notion that these roles are not always totally distinct, and that there is a possibility of combining the basic elements of the three in somewhat different ways (the generalist/scout, who draws minimally upon all three roles, and the "superlinker" who enacts all three simultaneously).

Crandall (1977) takes a different approach, based upon personal experience in designing and managing change programs, and focuses on the different ways that agents can relate to clients in the preimplementation ("front end") and the postimplementation ("back end") stages. However, as Hood and Cates point out, his inductive typology maps quite neatly onto the more inductive definitional efforts of Havelock, Piele, and Butler and Paisley (see Table 4.2).

These distinctions are useful in showing the complexities and alternatives that may be encompassed within the concept of the external helping role, but in general the proliferation of descriptive typologies may be judged to add relatively little to our understanding of how such agents actually function.[9] The main weakness of the effort to develop role typologies lies in their genesis. Rather than being viewed as role segments or alternative personae that an external agent may adopt under different circumstances, there is often the implicit or explicit assumption that these roles are distinctive and uniquely held by an external agent. Thus, while acknowledging that reality may be somewhat untidy, Crandall (1977) views the distinctions that he makes in linking roles as normative-imperative: They are seen as mutually exclusive, requiring different skills, different training, different support, and different types of people. The Butler and Paisley (1978) work similarly views the different types of "entitlement" of an agent to occur "modally," such that in most cases individual agents will perform a limited subset of the roles that are potentially available.[10]

The problem with this approach is that it assumes that the linker's role is controlled by the agent and his or her agency. This assumption is most striking in Hood and Cates (1978: 32), who observe that different models of change (which are presumably adopted by a sponsoring agency) imply different and distinctive external agent roles. Hutchins (1977) similarly implies that the federal government has an option to choose alternative types of external roles that will fit simply into a model of change and the change process that is preferred by policy makers. The focus on the agency definition of archetypal roles ignores both the need to tailor external agent roles to client information needs and objectives (a bottom-up approach to defining agent roles), and existing data that suggest that external agent roles cannot be defined solely by the agent or agency.

An analysis of the role-taking behavior of extension agents in the Pilot State Dissemination Program indicates that successful agents engaged in a relatively lengthy period of role negotiation and role latitude with clients and client schools (Louis and Sieber, 1979). More recently, Louis, Kell, et al. (1981) have reported that, on average, administrators in client schools have an equal or greater impact on the ways in which agents spend their time, and the activities in which they engage, than either their immediate supervisors or the directors of the projects in which they work. Similarly, Moore et al. (1977) point to mutual adaptation between the technical

TABLE 4.2 Comparison of Linking Agent Roles

Havelock (1968)	Havelock and Havelock (1973)	Piele (1975)	Butler and Paisley (1978)	Crandall (1977) "front end" roles	Crandall (1977) "back end" roles
Conveyor	Resource linker	Resource finder	Resource finder	Product finder Information linker	Product finder Information linker
Consultant leader	Process helper	Process helper	Process helper	Process enabler	Action researcher/data feedback
Trainer innovator	Solution giver	Solution giver	Solution giver	Program facilitator	Technical assister
	Catalyst		Generalist/scout		
	"Whole role"		"Superlinker"	Provocateur	Educator/capacity builder

assistant group and the local setting as being a prominent characteristic of successful change agencies. This process often involves conscious attempts to get feedback on strategies and roles, and to alter them to fit with the local school culture (Moore et al., 1977: 190-191). Agents themselves argue that one of the most important characteristics of a successful agent is the ability to make significant adaptations in one's role in order to fit school needs and capabilities (Louis, Kell, et al., 1981: 143). Finally, Rogers and Shoemaker (1971) claim that research evidence suggests that change agent success is related to a client rather than an agency orientation.

There are, of course, limitations to the ambiguity that can be maintained in a role such as the one being dealt with in this chapter. Moore et al. (1977) state, for example, that there are limits to the mutual adaptation process. Successful "technical assistance groups" clearly communicate to the client schools the values on which their assistance is based (thus, presumably, weeding out clients whose values would be so different as to cause friction and failure) and the limits to the type of assistance that would be provided. In particular, the amount of time and effort involved requires clear delineation in order to avoid disappointment (Moore et al., 1977: 102-103). Similarly, Haugerud et al. (1979) and Carlson (1981) point to the need to negotiate some boundaries to the role and service in order to avoid either role overload for the agent or client anger when the client's expectations apparently imply using the external agent as an additional "free" staff person.

In addition, overidentification with the client school may be detrimental to both the agent's job satisfaction and role performance. Louis, Kell, et al. (1981) for example, found that linking agent *marginality,* or maintaining a balance between identification with the organization sponsoring the agent and the client, was related to lower levels of job stress for the agent, and also to patterns of relationships with clients which were less manipulative. It is hypothesized that external agents who are too heavily influenced by clients may often tend to become locked in power struggles, or to become passive.

To summarize, there is a need to view the agent's role from a user perspective rather than from an agency-focused or change model perspective. This shift is necessary for two reasons. First, without this perspective, the chances are quite high of implementing yet another educational service or program that frustrates locally creative change by providing the wrong mix of resources (see Campeau et al., 1979). Second, it is essential to recognize the reality of the external helping role: External agents serve at the pleasure of the system, and must always, therefore, adjust their roles to system expectations if they are to have any impact at all. This does not mean, of course, that an agency has little or no impact in setting boundaries for the role. However, even well-defined boundaries are enacted in very different ways by different individuals faced with different school settings (Firestone and Corbett, 1979). Inappropriate role definitions proposed from higher levels of the organization will simply produce evasive behavior at lower levels, as agents attempt to deliver the services

that their schools wish to have (see especially Campeau et al., 1979; for
more discussion of the problems of imposing clear role definitions on
occupants of field agent type roles, see Louis and Sieber, 1979: ch. 3;
Louis, Kell, et al., 1981: ch. 4).

AGENT CHARACTERISTICS AND BEHAVIORS

Fortunately, there are alternative ways of examining what we know
about linking or external agent roles. The empirical literature on external
roles indicates that there are two major sets of variables that are perceived
to influence the impact of the agent upon the client. The first group
consists of *status variables* that characterize the agent and his/her context.
Irrespective of the specificity of the role, the following variables may have
a significant impact on role performance:

- homogeneity with clients;
- locus;
- organizational design—single versus team;
- personal characteristics or attributes.

In addition, there is substantial evidence to suggest that certain dimensions
of *external agent behaviors and strategies* are crucial. These include:

- initiative in outreach to clients;
- intensity of outreach activities;
- external agent expertise;
- scope of external agent activities;
- relationships with boundary personnel in client settings.

The findings and/or controversies presented in the empirical literature
on external agent status and behaviors will be discussed below. It should
be pointed out, at this juncture, that the criteria of "empirical" used in this
section are relatively loose ones. Any evidence that is apparently based
upon actual experience or study of external agents is admissible, including
secondary analyses and observations based upon "craft" knowledge, as
well as actual research.

Agent Status and Impact

According to Zaltman and Duncan (1977: 224), the case on linking
agent status is clear:

> The optimally structured change agent would be a change agent
> team consisting of an internal and external change agent who are
> homophilous [sic] with the change target system.

Indeed, based on the existing literature, there is little that one could say in
direct opposition to the above statement. There are, however, ambiguities
in a number of the terms that are used, and these deserve some discussion.

Homophyly: The need for external agents to be similar to or congruent with the intended client is, perhaps, one of the most strongly supported assertions in the change literature. In 1971, Rogers and Shoemaker reported over 40 studies supporting one or more hypotheses related to agent-client homophyly. Similarly, Corwin found that the greater the disjucture between Teacher Corps participants and those of the schools that they served, the lower the level of program innovation. Sieber et al. (1972) reported that educational extension agents tended to seek out clients in positions that were most similar to those that had been held by the agent prior to taking the extension job, while Moore et al. (1977) point out that successful technical assistance agencies make explicit their own value biases, to ensure that nonhomophyllous clients will "opt out."

On the other hand, it is useful to examine another set of literature bearing upon this point. The work of Pelz and Andrews (1966) suggests that scientists working in heterophyllous environments (such as with people in a variety of disciplines) are more creative/inventive than those working in completely homophyllous environments. An additional analysis of the data first presented in Sieber et al. (1972) revealed that, while the agent's prior status affected his/her choice of clients to some extent, it had no impact upon the amount of time spent with clients of different status: All agents, no matter whether they were former teachers or former administrators, spent considerably more time working with administrative clients (Louis and Sieber, 1979). Furthermore, agent impact, as measured by reported use of information, was not strongly related to homophyly of status between agent and client (unpublished analysis).

Perhaps more critical is research conducted on the "strength of weak ties" (Granovetter, 1973). This literature suggests that innovation is more likely to spread through individuals who are weakly connected to a network—that is, are heterophyllous on some dimensions (see Sarason et al., 1977, for a review of the literature on network and information flows). This well-supported hypothesis is significant, for it points to the weakness in the homophyly hypothesis. Most of the research that is cited in support of the need for homophyly is, in fact, of two types. The first is based on the study of agents in underdeveloped countries. In this case, heterophyly is quite extreme, and what passes for homophyly is, in fact, simply a lesser degree of heterophyly. Second, other research from contemporary cultures is largely based on findings (such as those of Corwin) which suggest that too much heterophyly is bad. These findings, which are consistent with the notion of the importance of weak ties in the information flow/change process, do not imply that total homophyly is good. Zaltman and Duncan (1977: 214), in other sections of their chapter on change agents, also point out that a degree of heterophyly may be a stimulant in the change process.

From a practical perspective, therefore, the assertion of the need for homophyly may mean nothing more weighty than the imposition of a requirement that the change agent have some set of common experiences or background that suits him/her for the job and gives the assurance that he or she provides some "source credibility" (Hovland and Weiss, 1951). In a school setting, clearly some experience with education is an advantage. However, the "craft" knowledge claims that an educational extension agent should have classroom teaching experience in order to be effective as a school-based catalyst of information use is, based on the experience of nonteacher agents, overstated.

Locus: The issue of locus is often, as in Zaltman and Duncan's work, equated with a distinction between internal and external agents. Research evidence which attempts to directly compare the value of internal and external agents is relatively rare. On the basis of a content analysis of case studies, Jones (1969) concluded that internal change agents were slightly more successful than external change agents. A laboratory experiment (Scurrah et al., 1971) concluded that external agents were more effective in introducing change, and were also perceived by the target group as more expert than internal agents occupying the same formal position. Corwin's (1973: 255) study of the Teacher Corps found that both the external agents *and* the presence of "young, flexible, supportive boundary personnel" are important in organizational adaptation. Finally, an analysis of schools in the R&D Utilization Program found that involvement of external change agents including "linkers" and trainers was generally more powerful in predicting school change, but that both internal and external agents were important (Louis, Rosenblum, et al., 1981).

Relatively little is known from the existing educational literature about the ways in which internal and external agents relate to one another, however. One systematic documentation of the existence of these two roles simultaneously, and the relative impact of each of the outcomes of an educational OD process, is found in the recent study of Miles et al. (see especially Miles, Fullan, et al., 1978a; Fullan et al., 1980). These data suggest that external agent roles are particularly critical in determining whether an OD program achieves both its anticipated objectives and unanticipated benefits. The external agent is coequal to an internal change agent and internal consultants (designed as the district coordinator) in determining whether the district will have positive attitudes about further dissemination of the OD efforts. Neither have a great impact upon institutionalization, as compared to other variables, particularly those related to scale and scope of the change activity. Thus, it seems that the role of the external agent may be stage related, and weighted toward the initiation, planning, and implementation activities that are designed primarily to affect capacity during the first years of a major change effort.

The study of the R&D Utilization Program suggests a somewhat different division of labor. External agent activities—at least those of generalist field agents—seem to be particularly critical in stimulating changes of greater *magnitude* (affecting more pupils for a greater proportion of the days) and in supporting and promoting institutionalization of new curriculum practices. Internal agent (generally principal) involvement was more important in producing enduring changes in the school's capacity to solve future problems (Louis, Rosenblum, et al., 1981).

The roles of internal agents are reviewed in detail elsewhere in this volume (see the chapter by Fullan). It suffices to state that the study of *relationships* between internal and external agents is a topic deserving of further attention.

There are a variety of contingencies which may affect the impact of locus upon success. Internal location increases the credibility of the external agent, because the client feels that the agent can be counted on. Proximity increases flexibility in responding to client or target group needs (Moore et al., 1977). An inside change agent is also better equipped to understand and deal with the local culture and resistance to change, and may be more effective at mustering internal support (Zaltman and Duncan, 1977; Berman and McLaughlin, 1977).

On the other hand, outsiders are able to choose their own settings, which helps to ensure successful change projects. In addition, outsiders are less likely to be coopted by other agendas (Moore et al., 1977). An external change agent is also more effective in dealing with the early stages of a change process, in which independence and perceived expertise authority may be critical to achieving the legitimacy of the project (Zaltman and Duncan, 1977). In addition, it is often easier for the external agent to play a variety of roles that facilitate the process of change, since he/she is not burdened by accumulated organizational perceptions of him/her as an individual.

What about the specific educational context, however? Recently, Butler and Paisley (1978: 28) have predicted that the next few years will see a major change in the locus of change or extension agents:

> In many cases, large city school districts already have the staff of specialists required for self-directed change, and there is little that an all-purpose external linking agent can offer a large district. . . . In fact, a large district is a discouraging assignment for an external linking agent.

The authors estimate that, at present, almost all "linkage" is external to the district. However, they project that by 1995 the balance will have shifted so that the expertise will reside inside the district (Butler and Paisley, 1978: 29). Similarly, Schmuck (1971) has advocated the development of corps of organizational specialists who can exist within each school district.

Without getting into an involved debate about the feasibility of such trends, it may be suggested that predictions of such a major shift *may* be both shortsighted (given the strengths of the external role discussed above) and optimistic (given rising costs, declining enrollments, and taxpayer resistance).

Even more importantly, it must be stressed that the definition of external/internal depends entirely on where one stands. From the perspective of the federal government and most writers concerned with educational policy, any organization that exists below the state level represents a blurry category known as "local." From the perspective of a school-based educator, on the other hand, a specialist situated in the district office may have no better an understanding of the problems of a particular school than an expert called in from several hundred miles away. A number of writers have noted that school systems, as organizational entities, tend to be "loosely linked" (Weick, 1976; Rosenblum and Louis, 1981; Abramowitz and Tenenbaum, 1978). The notion of loose linkages implies that there are boundaries at multiple levels within the system which distort information flows and impede systemwide activities.[11] The impact of the existence of multiple "layers" in the educational system on the role of change agents is obvious, and the gulf between school and district office in the change process is well documented among the schools involved in the R&D Utilization program. In many cases, school participants differentiated their involvement in a school-based innovation effort from most of the major change activities that had occurred previously, where orders were sent down from the district office with little or no explanation (see also Gross et al., 1971). In addition, in many cases school-based practitioners voiced extreme skepticism about the competence of district specialists, who are often seen as educators who could not "make it" in the world of teaching or administration, and, because they had tenure, were dispatched to a specialist position to defuse the damage that they might create in a line position.

Finally, it is important to point out that a role that is deliberately created "inside" in order to defuse opposition is likely to be no more effective than an outside role. Rogers et al. (1976: 69-70), in their discussion of the Research Utilization Specialist program in vocational education, comment:

> The entire RUS project illustrates the weakness and slippage inherent in a system where research priorities are set at the federal level, largely in terms of system-wide needs, and utilization is sought at the state and local level, whose priorities may be quite different. . . . The RUS represented an "outside graft" onto the state structure, rather than an organized growth out of it. . . . The traditions of federal project grants . . . reinforce a pattern in which the "federal project" is seen as an activity separate from the normal run.

Teams versus individuals: The case for a team is strongly voiced by Zaltman and Duncan (1977: 210-211), who can think of no instance in which the extra resources provided through a team do not enrich the change strategy. The strength of teams are also noted by Moore et al. (1977), for different reasons. Rather than increasing the resources available to the client, teams are seen as providing needed support to the external agent, reducing overload and improving organizational integration of dispersed members (see also Louis and Sieber, 1979). Sebring (1979) notes that teams facilitate the need for different types of expertise at different stages in the change process.

While resources and peer support may be useful functions of teams, there is a limit to the degree to which external agents should be composed of many individuals. Unpublished data from the study of the R&D Utilization program suggests that external teams consisting of more than two or three external people can provide serious system overload for the target population. In cases where the external change team consisted of a larger number of people, school-based practitioners tended to have a great deal of difficulty understanding the roles that each of the outsiders was supposed to play. In general, the locals tended to single out one or two people to relate to, and the remaining "helpers" vanished into a blur of undifferentiated meeting attendees. Furthermore, many of the client educators noted that there were major costs of collaboration, which were borne mainly by the local schools. Since meetings involving larger teams were more difficult to schedule, they were sometimes postponed or held at times that were not optimal for the locals. However, the study also provides some support for the notion that the most effective external change agent strategy is one that utilizes a division of labor between an individual playing a facilitating/generalist role and an individual or several individuals who provide more specialized training around the content area in which change is being planned (Louis, Rosenblum, et al., 1981). This division of labor does not necessarily constitute a team approach, however, since most training consists of limited episodes with little or no long-term relationship with the client.

Zaltman and Duncan, however, suggest that the team may be composed of an insider "leader" and an external agent. Evidence presented by Greenwood et al. (1975) suggests that external agents are, in fact, successful *only* when there is an internal change agent who supports their activities strongly. The single factor accounting for most of the variance in school innovativeness in Corwin's study of the Teacher Corps (1973) was the quality and innovativeness of boundary personnel located in the university and in the local school. Recently, research on OD programs in schools has suggested that OD training may effectively proceed in a two-stage process, where external agents train a small number of internal agents, who then train their peers (Keys and Bartunek, 1979; Miles, Fullan, et al., 1978a). The "turnkey" strategy of training has also been seen to work effectively in the transmission of I/D/E/A's Individually Guided Education program from a national office base to a thousand local schools that are clustered in teams led by locally based facilitators (Moore et al., 1977). In many instances, the R&D Utilization external agent strategy has been to work through a local "team" that is seen as the local change agent. In some instances team members (or a single local person) have received "change agent" training simultaneously with the external linker. In many cases, participation in a "team" has created leadership where there was apparently a leadership vacuum: Rather than simply select natural leaders, the project (or the principal) has chosen to revitalize staff participation and a sense of efficacy through participation in a decision-making group. In general, a preliminary conclusion that could be drawn from the R&D Utilization data is that the stronger the local or internal change agent/team role, the less visible the external role. However, even with a strong internal change agent, the external agent still performs vital functions in stimulating and supporting change activities (Louis, Rosenblum, et al., 1981). This conclusion is also supported by Emrick et al. (1977), who find strong correlations between the involvement of both internal and external agents and change.

Personal characteristics of agents: While there is little solid empirical work on the personal characteristics associated with effective external agents, there is agreement that certain attributes are desirable. Interviews with linking agents in the National Diffusion Network produced the following list of desirable attributes (Capla Associates, 1977, as reported in Cates, 1978):

- being candid and straightforward
- having tolerance for ambiguity
- having the ability to cope with frustrations
- being concerned and supportive
- being able to trigger enthusiasm without going overboard
- being tolerant of different viewpoints
- being flexible

The list specified by Zaltman and Duncan (1977) emphasizes the following:

- technical qualifications
- administrative ability
- interpersonal relations
- motivation and drive
- acceptance of constraints
- development of commitment
- poise and backbone
- political finesse
- poise and maturity

Almost every study that examines linking agents or other external roles makes some mention of personality characteristics. Most of these are on the level of specificity of the above two lists—they fail to distinguish characteristics that are particularly desirable in an educational consultant or extension agent from those that might be desired of anyone in a relatively important human services profession. In this instance, therefore, the only conclusion is that the avowed importance of the topic has not led to sound research.

Perhaps more importantly, observations made of turnover of linking agents in the context of the R&D Utilization program suggest that the important personality characteristics may be contingent upon the setting. In two cases of turnover that occurred after the first agent had been on the job for a year, some of the schools perceived the new, replacement agent to be an improvement, while others perceived the old agent to be preferable. In both cases there were distinct differences in the personality styles of the agents, and in their skills and experience. In addition, most agents admit that there are schools that they like working with, and others that they do not care for. The mystery of what makes one external agent effective in a school, whereas another might be ridden out on a rail, may be as difficult to solve as determining the reason why some psychotherapeutic relationships work and others do not. In both instances, craft, rather than research knowledge, may be the more valuable characteristic.

The study of the R&D Utilization Program, however, turned up one consistent finding that suggests that personality characteristics may have some effect. Agents who were, according to their self-ratings, more *innovative* in their orientation were more likely to be evaluated negatively by their clients than agents who rated themselves as more *conventional* (Louis, Kell, et al., 1981). Innovative personality characteristics are also negatively related to school improvement outcomes (Louis, Rosenblum, et al., 1981).

Research on other extrinsic status characteristics, such as educational background, age, race, or sex, is very limited—at least in educational settings. Louis, Kell, et al. (1981), however, found that older agents were more satisfied with their jobs and perceived less stress, but were also less likely to take on active boundary-spanning roles, and more likely to behave as traditional content specialists. Qualitative observations by this author of the work of more than a dozen linking agents suggests that these variables play only a limited part in explaining external agent behaviors or effectiveness. In addition, evidence from noneducational studies is mixed, except as it refers to homophyly (Rogers and Shoemaker, 1971).

Agent Behaviors:
Strategies in Support of School Improvement

A number of authors have argued for a contingency approach to understanding the relationship between change strategies and change outcomes in different contexts (see Sieber et al., 1972; Louis and Sieber, 1979; Hood and Cates, 1978). A contingency approach is only useful, however, if it has enough categories to make it reflect reality, and few enough to develop a theory that is sufficiently succinct to make it useable.

A recent attempt to generate a contingency model for choosing change tactics illustrates one half of the dilemma of choosing between the Scylla of theoretical parsimony and the Charybdis of messy reality. Zaltman et al. (1977: 92-121) have attempted to develop a matrix that would allow the potential change agent to evaluate 39 intervention tactics in terms of 16 "evaluative dimensions." The resultant *634* cell matrix cannot be used without referring extensively to the text, in which the contingencies that would impel the change agent to emphasize more heavily one "evaluative dimension" or another are laid out. While this table might be of some use to an external agent seeking to improve his/her choice or tactics, there is little basis for developing a more refined theory of interventions.

A much more limited approach has been developed by Litwak and Meyer (1966). These authors emphasize that choices of strategies should be conditioned by the *distance* between the organization and the group to be reached (which is defined very similarly to the concept of homogeneity), the *complexity* of the message to be transmitted, and the *number of people* in the target group. Strategies for outreach programs may be rated along a number of dimensions relevant to meeting these needs: *initiative,* or the amount of effort needed to reach the target population; *intensity,* or the degree to which the relationship between the external agent and the target population approximates a primary group-like relationship; *expertise,* or the technical qualifications that are required to transmit the message; and *scope,* or the number of people that can be reached at a given cost. These sets of dimensions have been used successfully to explain and analyze the outcomes of the external agent efforts in the Pilot State Dissemination Project (Louis, 1975; Louis and Sieber, 1979).

Moving back to Zaltman et al. (1977), it seems apparent that one of the reasons that the authors' discussion of change agent tactics appears more like a laundry list than a useful tool for developing researchable questions about external roles is that the underlying rationale for choice of tactics is unknown. The authors assume that the external agent will choose a set of tactics, and then determine whether they will meet the change needs:

> The change planner should be aware of how his unique array of tactics can be rated, and what this implies [Zaltman et al., 1977: 98].

This approach—planning from the tactical level up—runs counter to any model of rational planning, however. If one picks up two tools at random, it is not likely that they will be the appropriate ones with which to make a garden; if the objective is to make a garden, the appropriate tools should be determined and selected.

The recent work of Hall et al. (1979: 10-12) has attempted to develop an empirically based taxonomy of intervention levels. Five different levels of conscious interventions were identified:[12]

- *Policies:* "A policy is a rule or guideline that reflects, directs and legitimizes goals, procedures, decision and actions of the organization and individuals within the organization."[13]

- *Game Plan:* "A game plan is the overall design for the interventions that are taken to implement the innovation. The combination of all of the major components of the innovation implementation effort make up the game plan."

The change tactics identified by Zaltman et al. (1977) can, in fact, be classified as elements of a game plan. These are:

- information/linkage

- product development

- user involvement

- training/installation/support

- level

TABLE 4.3   Strategies for External Agents in Facilitating School
                   Improvement

Strategies I (adapted from Litwak and Meyer, 1966)	Strategies II (adapted from Zaltman et al. 1977)
Initiative	Activity
	Redundancy of messages
Intensity: outreach	Personal contact
	Feedback/interaction
	Follow-up
Intensity: client/involvement	Immediacy (implementation feedback, timing of)
	Time required
	User convenience
Expertise	Ease of use (for external agent)
Scope/cost	Repeatability
	Coverage
	Stability

Two of the Zaltman et al. dimensions could not be classified as strategies in this
framework. These were (1) action implications—this could be viewed more effectively
as a game plan, since it refers to the degree to which short- and long-range goals for
the system will be programmed by an external agent; and (2) imagery—this could be
better classified as a tactic, since it apparently refers to the presence or absence of
"hands-on" experience for the client group.

A complete game plan could, of course, include any combination of the
above.

- *Strategy:* "A strategy . . . is based on a set of implicit and/or explicit
  assumptions and theory about how people and organizations function in change. It translates assumptions and theory into actions."

Strategies may be best thought of as choices about the level of the
initiative, intensity, expertise, and scope as they might be applied to any
element of the game plan. In addition, the dimensions for evaluating
tactics included in Zaltman et al. can, with some regrouping, effectively be
viewed as part of the strategies level.[14] Table 4.3 presents a modification
of Litwak and Meyer's (1966) strategy dimensions and arrays the Zaltman
et al. (1977) evaluation dimensions against them.

- *Tactics:* "A tactic is an aggregation of incident interventions that in
  combination have an effect that is different from the effects of the
  individual incidents."

Hall et al. (1979: 12) note that, based on their empirical work, it is clear
that the strategies of change agents often emerge as a poorly defined

extrapolation of an accumulation of tactics. However, when this is the case "the resultant strategy may not necessarily be coherent and supportive of the change effort. All that can be predicted in advance is that there is likely to be some explicit or implicit design of interrelationship across many tactics."

- *Incidents:* "A singular occurrence of an action or event. It is the smallest intervention unit."

Zigarmi and Goldstein (1979) note that, in the change process that they studied, it was impossible to understand the higher level interventions without analyzing patterns of incidents.

The point of the above discussion is, in fact, simpler than it may appear: If one wishes to generate an effective contingency model for external helping roles, it is almost imperative to start at the strategy level, as strategies are defined by Hall et al. (1979). The level of tactics is too discrete and "messy" to serve as a basis for any applied theory, while the game plan dimension is too abstract to meet the needs of those who are engaging in external helping activities. It is to a more extensive discussion of these strategies, as they are embodied in the left-hand column of Table 4.3, that the remainder of this section will turn.

Initiative: The dimension of initiative refers to the amount of energy and effort that the external agent needs to use in order to effectively reach the client or target group. The choice of initiative level is, in part, a policy decision as well as a strategy, for certain types of choices in organizational design will either permit high initiative or impede it. Thus, for example, individual extension agents, such as those deployed by the Pilot State Dissemination Project, have the opportunities to engage in high-initiative activities, for the scope of their potential client base is not excessive (in most cases) and they are encouraged to visit schools personally by their organizational locus and position. As Rogers et al. (1976) point out, the Research Utilization Specialist program discouraged high-initiative efforts, since a single RUS was assigned to serve all vocational rehabilitation agencies in an entire state. In addition, some external agents are designed explicitly to draw potential clients in, rather than to utilize outreach tactics (see Kater and Hull, 1976; Butler-Paisley and Paisley, 1975).

However, within a given type of organizational design, there are many choices that individual agents may make. There is overwhelming evidence to suggest that, in most cases, high-initiative (face-to-face, redundant) tactics will be required to stimulate wide interest in a new service that may be offered by an external agent. The level of initiative required to stimulate potential users' interest in research is particularly high, in part because of the poor image that research has in the practitioner community (see, for example, Schmuck, 1971). Thus, for example, the original agents in the Pilot State Dissemination Program were required to engage in individual meetings with teachers and administrators at the school level before they could stimulate any interest at all in using the information retrieval system set up in this program.

Information that does not wear the Scarlet R for research may require somewhat lower initiative. While the outreach activities described by Emrick et al. (1977) are highly redundant, they do not involve the one-on-one sessions that were required to persuade the user that ERIC could be useful. Rather, high levels of interest were stimulated by group meetings (conferencing), a technique that did not work effectively in the PSDP.

Another way of interpreting the apparent differences between the amount of initiative required to involve clients in the NDN and Pilot State programs relates to the functions of knowledge use supported by the program. The PSDP implicitly served all three of the functions that have been identified in this chapter, while the NDN program supports only instrumental/decisionistic knowledge use. In the latter case client self-selection can be simpler: s/he needs only to ask whether there is any decision that needs to be made which matches the "knowledge base" offered by the NDN project. Convincing clients that information will enlighten or build their capacity for future decision making may require more persuasion.

Other data suggest that time will reduce the amount of initiative necessary to reach the typical practitioner or school. For example, I/D/E/A initially relied on intensive techniques and existing professional contacts with innovative administrators to "spread the word." As the IGE approach became more well known, and well respected in the field of education, the central office no longer felt it necessary to engage in any direct recruitment at all. Instead, they rely on a network of local facilitators to stimulate local involvement. While the approach is still intensive as, say, compared to an approach that relies on mailed brochures, legitimacy and widespread familiarity of educators have allowed for this less intensive approach (Moore et al., 1977). Similarly, Corbett (1980) states that the amount of effort required to evolve a basic skills program which is compatible with existing curricula is less than for an unfamiliar career education program.

Little or no research has been done on the amount of initiative necessary to encourage educators or educational institutions to become involved in knowledge utilization where the knowledge is internally generated. We suspect that, because the use of external experts in these roles has been relatively limited in schools, initial levels required would be high. Again, such knowledge is not seen as a precious commodity for schools at this time, because the structure of schools and the incentive systems do not typically reward knowledge production and use. (See Miles and Sieber in this volume.)

A final point is that, while the level of initiative required to stimulate clients is related to both the research/craft dimension and the dimension of time/familiarity, it will inevitably be influenced also by the characteristics of individual clients or client schools. The ever-popular S-shaped diffusion curve (Rogers and Shoemaker, 1971: 128-132) will, in all probability, never apply to the utilization of external agents for knowledge diffusion, because use of knowledge is an ongoing process, while adoption is a single-time event. Thus, some schools will initiate contact with external agents, and creatively think of all sorts of reasons to use him/her repeatedly for enlightenment or capacity-building purposes as well as to making pressing decisions. Others may come to the fountain of knowledge very late, and drink rarely. If the external agent's goals are to influence the laggards as well as the innovators, some high levels of initiative will always be required. Sieber et al. (1972) have suggested that linking agents may adjust the levels of initiative and engage in delegation of activities to internal change agents in many cases where it is apparent that face-to-face contact and redundancy are not required.

Intensity: Intensity refers to the degree to which the external agent is involved in a long-term relationship with the client, and the degree to which the relationship involves his/her time. Thus, there are two dimensions along which outreach intensity must be examined: calendar time and absolute time. Most research on intensity has focused on absolute rather than calendar time. Louis and Sieber (1979), for example, found a significant positive correlation between the amount of time that the external extension agent spent with clients and the level of use of the information. Runkel and Bell's (1976) findings suggest that, in the case of OD training, a low level of intensity is worse than no training at all: Schools actually decreased their scores on all outcomes measures with three days or less of training.[15] Louis, Rosenblum, et al. (1981) found that several types of agent intensity made independent contributions to most school improvement outcomes: time spent with the school's gatekeeper (the principal), time spent attending meetings of whatever group was responsible for planning change, and the playing of active, involved roles in the client's decision-making process.

Rogers and Shoemaker (1971: 233) also conclude that "change agent success is positively related to the extent of change agent effort." While most of the studies cited by Rogers and Shoemaker do not measure either type of time involvement, those that do measure time apparently corroborate our hypothesis.

We should not ignore, however, the existence of several critical negative findings in this area.[16] Berman and McLaughlin (1977), for example, found no strong correlation between the amount of training received and a variety of implementation measures. Preimplementation training had small positive effects on the total change perceived by the teacher, and on the continuation of project methods. In addition, quantity of follow-up training after the first year of implementation was positively related to continuation of project materials. However, while these correlations are all significant at the .10 level, they are so small and so few in number compared to other insignificant correlations between time and outcomes that we can substantially conclude that there was little impact (see Berman and McLaughlin, 1977: 107). More importantly, the presence of outside consultants (as perceived by the teachers—a measure which probably substantially underestimates consultant roles in the project) was not related to outcomes at all.[17]

Miles, Fullan, et al. (1978a), in a more exploratory study of OD in schools, present findings that contradict those of Berman and McLaughlin. These authors report, based on a survey of 76 schools using OD, that the intensity of external consultant involvement (number of days spent by external consultants) is significantly positively related to the impact of the OD program, as is the length of the OD program measured in years. Both of these factors are also strongly associated with positive attitudes toward the OD effort. *Intense* involvement by external consultants is, however, negatively related to institutionalization by the OD change programs in schools. There is, furthermore, some evidence from this study to suggest *why* external consultant intensity may facilitate knowledge use and change in some instances while in others it does not. The use of structured, prepackaged training activities was negatively related to OD impact. It is not unreasonable to conclude from these findings that consultants may fail to promote effective knowledge use and change when they are physically remote from the districts that they serve, and when they come to the district with an agenda and a method for intervention that is highly structured.[18] In addition, data presented in Emrick et al. (1977: 90) also suggest similar interpretations, as does a recent analysis of linker training in the RDU program (Spencer and Louis, 1980).

A recent study, which attempts to look at intervention intensity in a variety of different research settings represented by journal articles, found that neither type of intensity (calendar time or absolute time) was positively related to study outcomes (Porras, 1979). While the author states that the methodology of a study using secondary sources is necessarily crude, one cannot ignore the fact that one of the few significant findings indicates that less OD, rather than more, may be related to positive outcomes (Porras, 1979: 169). The author's conclusion regarding this finding is as follows:

> It may be that this outcome reflects the degree of understanding that OD practitioners have about change processes in organizations. Not enough is known about these processes and as a result only certain levels of change are achieved and any extra energy poured into the intervention is dissipated in ways that do not contribute to additional change. As a result a little and a "lot" of input yield the same outcomes [Porras, 1979: 176].

The author fails to consider, however, that client characteristics and the nature of the intended change account for this finding: Small amounts of external intervention may have large impacts in an organization that exhibits a high state of "readiness," while larger amounts may have lesser impact in one that is not ready or is more complex.[19]

In addition to the question of client characteristics as a factor mediating intensity, some data exist to support the notion that "front-end" (early stage in the information utilization process) time and "back-end" time have different consequences. The data from the Pilot State Project indicates that back-end time is more significant in determining whether information will actually be used in an immediate way (Louis and Sieber,

1979). In other words, if the objective of the KU process is *decisionistic,* back-end external assistance is clearly critical. Data from the R&D Utilization project indicate, however, that if the objective is *capacity building,* that front-end time is most critical, for it is during this period when the teachers and administrators are most open to extensive discussion of process, group dynamics, and so forth. When educators are actually faced with a new program to implement, their attention turns very strongly toward the mechanics of actual use (see Hall et al., 1975).[20] While there are no studies that examine the "enlightenment" process in any detail, it is probably most closely related to the adult socialization process, which is, according to many, most easily facilitated by a constant (but not necessarily very intense) relationship with the socializing agent in a context where there are many peers undergoing a similar learning experience (Wheeler, 1966).

Agent expertise: It is often assumed that the knowledge utilization process requires external agents who are *experts* or *specialists.* Thus, educational administrative structures at local state levels are increasingly characterized by the proliferation of specialist roles that are designed as vehicles through which information services and assistance are delivered to schools. The need for expertise is reinforced by the Agricultural Extension model, which is based on a cadre of county agents with specialized bachelor's degrees, and by the OD movement, which is dominated by individuals who have either university or National Training Laboratories backgrounds. Zaltman and Duncan (1977: 190), for example, place enormous emphasis on the need for technical expertise:

> Perhaps the single most necessary trait the change agent team leader must possess is technical competence. Dangers exist in bringing a person in from an unrelated . . . field. Alternatively, there may be dangers inherent in selecting a generalist without the in-depth expertise that may be required occasionally.

The evidence supporting the need for technical expertise is, however, mixed. First, there is an increasing tendency to discriminate between different *types* of expertise. Louis (1975), for example, distinguishes between process expertise and content expertise. The content expert is one who is a specialist in a discipline or information-based subject matter relevant to a knowledge transfer/change activity. A process expert, on the other hand, is one who is trained in specific skills related to group dynamics, institution building, and problem solving.

Scattered data indicate that different types of expertise may be most potent at different stages of the change process and affect different types of improvement outcomes. Kaplan (1978) distinguishes between client needs in the "normative stage" of a change activity, in which the emphasis is upon the human relationships in the organizational setting, and the "performance stage," in which attention is turned toward specific task-related activities. Louis, Rosenblum, et al. (1981) found, in a demonstration program that used both process generalist field agents and training by program developers and other content specialists, that there were differences in the degree to which each contributed to various types of school improvement outcomes. Generalist agents were more important in stimulating schools to address their problems more broadly and to choose curriculum innovations of greater magnitude. The amount and variety of specialized training, on the other hand, played a more significant role in determining the degree to which the designed changes actually appeared to affect pupils and the degree to which teachers reported personal growth. Both generalist support and specialized training contributed significantly to the continued use of new practices in the client schools. Sebring (1979) suggests that the most effective way to deal with this shift is to use an interdisciplinary consultant team, which combines an expert in interpersonal relations with another more expert in the arena most related to the task that is to be accomplished. The strategy of a team which focuses technical expertise on the back end (or implementation/change activity) is institutionalized quite effectively, according to Emrick, in the design of the NDN program. While neither the state facilitator nor the developer/-demonstrator are typically experts in the sense suggested by Zaltman and Duncan, the former focuses primarily on providing long-term nurturance and the latter on specific task-related training in the cases of greatest effectiveness (Emrick et al., 1977). Crandall's work (1977) implies, on the other hand, that the "front-end process" and "back-end content" distinction may be overly simplistic, and that different mixes at each stage may be more appropriate.

Some questions may be raised, however, about whether there is always a need for specialized expertise. Thus, for example, the most significant *inside* change agents identified in the Miles, Fullan, et al. (1978a) study were largely untrained and nonprofessional. Their activities contributed in significant positive ways to the success of OD programs in schools (Miles, Fullan, et al., 1978a: 50). Litwak and Meyer (1966) argue that there is a need for content expertise where the knowledge utilization involves complex technical information, but that in many cases a generalist is preferable in order to maximize homogeneity of status.

The issue of expertise is a critical one, not because the available data uniformly suggest that expertise is an important feature of the external agent strategy, but because it is a significant design issue in the development of external agent roles in educational settings. Currently, considerable effort is devoted to questions of how and what training should be provided to educational extension or change agents (see, for example, Havelock and Havelock, 1973; Butler and Paisley, 1978; Jung, 1976). Despite the concern about providing training to educational linking agents, most training in current federally funded programs does not emphasize the development of new skills and draws upon a narrow set of training approaches and resources (Spencer and Louis, 1980).

In developing a research agenda on expertise there is a need to define terms more precisely. In particular, it seems necessary to begin by distinguishing between *expertise* (that which *must* be acquired by formal training) and *skill* (that which may be either inherent in certain adult individuals or which is most effectively learned informally, by "doing"). Furthermore, in the arena of training, we should discriminate between *exten-sive training* (degree programs or courses) and the briefer *orientation-type training* (for instance, a two- or three-day National Training Laboratory course). It may be tempting, for example, to equate the external agent's ability to know when and how to intervene in a client's group decision-making process (process skill) with the ability to design, administer, and interpret survey feedback activities (process expertise). The level of training needed to support the latter is far greater, however, than for the former. Similarly, there are significant differences between the level of technical knowledge required to incorporate basic research results in the design of a new educational program (content expertise) and that which will allow the agent to locate appropriate resources and to interpret and evaluate written information in the area (content skill). To the degree that we require content or process expertise in the external agent, existing selection strategies which rely heavily on "retooling" existing populations of teachers and administrators to become facilitators or RDU linking agents are misguided and inefficient: We should be designing degree courses, or investing in specialized certificate programs. However, if skills are needed, training strategies which focus on increasing the "bag of tricks" available to the agent may be most appropriate.

Scope/Cost: Scope of agent services refers to the number of clients that can be managed at any given time by the external agent. A number of comments may be proffered as to the ways in which issues of scope are managed by existing agencies and agents. These are uniformly based on data that are primarily judgmental, however: No studies addressing the issue of the costs and benefits of different levels of scope exist, nor is much attention paid to the impact of increasing or decreasing the scope of activities of individual agents. This lack of attention is surprising, since it is the key to developing policies that are justifiable to congressional appropriations committees or other funding sources.

Louis (1975) points out that, in the context of the Pilot State Dissemination Program, scope and intensity were negatively related. Since high initiative and front-end activities were necessary to maintain high levels of clients served, increasing scope was associated with less follow-up activity (in the case of the PSDP, follow-up activities occurred after the delivery of information to a client, and usually prior to implementation of any change based on the information).

Data from the NDN study indicate that there is a negative relationship between high scope on the part of facilitators and outcome measures. High-volume outreach activities tend to generate a client response that makes follow-up activities erratic or nonexistent (Emrick et al., 1977: 61). Follow-up activities, on the other hand, are viewed as critical to successful implementation (Emrick et al., 1977: 122).

The question of "large scope" versus "small scope" is relative, however. In the Pilot State project, a high-scope linking agent may have served 10-15 new clients *per month,* not including follow-up activities on previous clients. In the R&D Utilization project, on the other hand, the number of *schools* for full-time linking agents over a *three-year period* ranged from a low of 3 to a high of 12. While the RDU program looks very low in scope compared to the PSDP, or the NDN (where a given Facilitator Project tends to serve between 3 and 25 new adoptions at the district level each year), it is high compared to a typical successful school district OD program, which may involve an external consultant (or a consultant who is hired full time as an OD consultant) for half- or full-time work over a period of several years. Other programs have different guidelines. For example, the IGE program has a rough guideline that each facilitator should expect to work with approximately 5-8 new schools each year (Moore et al., 1977: 209), while other technical assistance groups, such as the Center for New Schools and the Creative Teaching Workshop, maintain much higher ratios of staff to units served (Moore et al., 1977). Similarly, Follow-Through sponsors recommend that a single staff member devote most of his/her time to a single site (St. Pierre, 1981).

To summarize, one conclusion should be apparent: There are no clear guidelines about scope that can be extrapolated from existing practice. Each organization providing assistance tends to believe that its own preferred scope is the appropriate one—more would mean overload and poor service, less would be wasteful.

Some of the factors that might be considered in determining a research agenda to examine issues of scope are:

- The unit on which scope is measured (individual, school or district). In most cases, the unit of service is the information request or the adoption, and little attention is paid to the scope at the user level. Clearly the demands on an external agent will be greater where the client is a complex multilevel school district, as opposed to an individual teacher; however, providing considerable face-to-face service to all teachers in a school should be differentiated from consulting with one administrator.

- The importance of fidelity. Where the fidelity of a knowledge transfer process is critical, greater effort may be required for training, support, monitoring and evaluation.

- The degree to which the knowledge utilization process involves simple transfer versus the *generation* of new knowledge. Many technical assistance organizations, such as Follow-Through, or those described by Moore et al. (1977) are committed to generating improved knowledge for or by their clients, as well as providing immediate knowledge services. This commitment inevitably depresses scope.

- The presence and level of activity of formally designated internal agents. Miles, Fullan, et al. (1978a) for example, noted that most of the work in a typical school OD effort is handled by an internal agent rather than an external consultant. The formal internal agent role should, however, be differentiated from general level of effort in the client unit.

- The presence or absence of clear incentives to support increased scope versus initiative or intensity. In some instances, it is important to address the existence of powerful environmental conditions which promote quantity over quality of service.[21] In addition, choice of scope may be tied to the agency or agent emphasis upon decision-istic, enlightenment, or capacity building objectives.

AGENTS AND AGENCIES:
A BROADER VIEW

A final limitation of most definitions of external agents is that they almost invariably assume that the external agent is an individual disembodied from organizational context. The origins of this assumption are unclear, although again it should be pointed out that the common notion of the agricultural extension agent is as an educated farmer roaming the prairies in a buckboard. The notion of external agents as individuals is bolstered by much of the literature and organization development which has been generated largely by university professors who do this research as consultants in their spare time and not from a base of organizational authority. This general bias has led to a situation in which definitions of linking or change agents or other external roles tend to ignore the roles that are played by organizational entities.

Agencies as Agents

Many articles which attempt to define the external agent role make reference to the role of agencies as well as of agents (see for example, Havelock, 1969; Glaser, 1976). But the theme of change agencies is rarely well developed. This fact has hampered the development of both theories and research of intervention which involve multiple rather than single actors on the external agent team.

Several facts about change agencies can be noted. First, the number of organizations that could be thought of as educational change agencies is growing rapidly. For example, the number of intermediate education agencies, which typically exist to provide specialized information and technical assistance services to member districts, has increased during the past 15 years (Yin and Gwaltney, 1981). In addition, state departments of education have grown in size and complexity, and much of this growth is due to increased provision of services and support to districts, rather than to increased monitoring functions. In addition, many independent change agencies have sprung up, funded either by federal grants (such as Regional Laboratories, State Facilitator projects, or Title I Technical Assistance Centers) or by private sources (see Moore et al., 1977).

Second, the basic organizational features of the agencies have significant impact on the types of roles that they play as external agents of change. Moore et al. (1977) and Miles (1980), for example, document the significant effects that agency mission, staffing patterns, and preferred change strategies have upon their successful intervention with client groups, irrespective of the behaviors of individual agents who are employed to actually deliver services. Similarly, Yin and Gwaltney (1981) show that a number of organizational features of regional service agencies have a significant impact upon the ability of even the most highly regarded organizations to deliver services effectively. The features identified by the authors include:

- access to permanent or long-term sources of institutional funding, rather than reliance on fee-for-service to generate operating resources;

- a stable professional staff that engages in vigorous networking with client organizations (including recruiting clients to act as service deliverers);

- the presence of congruent mandates from superordinate governmental units (such as the federal government or state departments of education) which encourage mutual exchange and interdependence.

Not all organizations that act as change agencies derive their primary mission from these activities, however. There are few in-depth studies of the roles of universities or professional associations as significant agents in promoting systematic school improvement.

A recent paper by Lotto and Clark (1978) considers the functions of the university in the knowledge transfer system and their data suggest that universities are major contributors to outreach activities in support of knowledge utilization, particularly master's-level *public* institutions.

In many cases, university involvement is a consequence of ad hoc consulting activities developed by individual professors, and does not represent any institutional commitment. Havelock and Havelock (1973) have commented, for example, that in one state the professors at local universities presented a barrier to a systematic development of information networks. Each professor strove to establish special consulting arrangements with districts as a means of increasing salary and research opportunities. They did not look favorably upon new institutional commitments that would alter these arrangements.

In many other cases, however, universities have taken on institutional commitments to act as change agents in local schools. The Teacher Corps program is one of the most well-known examples, but our only detailed information about the success with which they have played their role dates from the early phases of program implementation (Corwin, 1972).

Conventional wisdom suggests that the image of the university as a provider of external assistance for knowledge utilization is very mixed. Many, for example, cite the "gap" between the way in which practitioners and academics view the world (Schmuck, 1971) as a factor which limits the usefulness of university-designed efforts to assist schools. It may be suggested that this tarnished image is due to the fact that many universities are well equipped to provide assistance in enlightenment functions or capacity-building functions (if there is substantial expertise in OD), but they are frequently less equipped to carry out the knowledge transfer required to support good decisions about programming or structure. This is true because the reward structure of the academic profession does not typically emphasize providing concrete technical assistance to schools. Some universities that have developed *rewarded* and differentiated TA roles are successful in overcoming popular resistance to university TA.

An examination of the ways in which organizations currently involved in KU function in schools may have *specialized* (either in a particular cell in Table 1, or in a particular KU function) seems a fruitful place to begin. In addition to taking the potential *provider* as a unit of analysis, the role of organizations as external assistants should also be examined from the comparative perspective that can only be provided by the consumer system. Case studies and/or surveys of different district experiences with external *agencies* of different types would be very useful in this regard.

One of the critical questions that deserves greater attention is posed by Moore et al. (1977): What are the characteristics that are associated with agency "success"? On the basis of six case studies of exemplary outreach technical assistance groups, Moore and his colleagues isolated a large number of factors which they felt were associated with smooth internal functioning and a reputation for client impacts. Their sample, however, was limited only to independent agencies with a "messianic" set of objectives, that is, in Katter and Hull's (1976) terminology, they were all simultaneously high on their product and audience orientation. No similar research has been conducted on the more common forms of agencies that provide direct information services to schools, or on agencies which carry a less specialized set of objectives or which may carry direct-service goals as only part of their general mission.

Agents in Agencies

At several points in this chapter, reference has been made to external agent role characteristics such as role conflict or marginality. These notions imply an organizational context for the agent that may affect what he or she does as well as the way he or she feels about the role. Sieber et al. (1972) noted that agents enter into relationships with their clients carrying all of the reputational baggage of the state and local organizations that sponsor them. In some cases this is an unanticipated hindrance in gaining access, while in other cases a propitious location greatly facilitates the legitimacy of the agent.

In addition to the impact of agency reputation and mission upon the individual agent, the organizations in which agents are located provide critical support and feedback for their work. As Louis and Sieber (1979) note, when sponsoring organizations are insensitive to the need for communication with dispersed field staff members, considerable job anxiety and dependence on clients may occur and may result in unacceptable levels of adaptation to client expectations for behavior. On the other hand, a recent analysis of field agent support systems indicates that increasing communication and influence from supervisors tends to result in higher levels of job stress (Louis, Kell, et al., 1981). Thus there is an inherent tension between the agency's desire to influence the job performance of agents, the desire to increase client orientations, and the need to minimize role conflict and job stress.

One feature of the agent's supervisory system is clear: Agents are most likely to be influenced by role partners who work closely with them and who are accessible for feedback and interaction. Thus, an agent is more likely to be influenced by a local organization (such as an intermediate service agency) in which his or her office is housed than by more distant central office or state department supervisors (Louis, Kell, et al., 1981).

Agencies which operate using branch offices, or by locating agents in dispersed field sites, should therefore pay attention to the support that their agents will receive (or not receive) at that level. (See also Miles, 1980, for a discussion of problems of coordinating agent activities across branch offices.)

SUMMARY: A RESEARCH AGENDA

The debate between supporters and opponents of external roles in facilitating knowledge utilization in schools is broader than the question of whether or not they have an impact. Those who are in favor of an external role argue that government policies which foster the proliferation of programs, studies, and knowledge, as well as technological information systems to make this knowledge accessible, are foolish in the absence of systems that will encourage the transmission of knowledge to potential users. Opponents, on the other hand, argue that the marginal returns in terms of improved schooling from the use of external agents and existing knowledge resources outweigh the investment needed to build a system that might have an impact. External technical assistance, it is argued, is too costly to implement on a large scale and it is therefore more practical to bolster a "do-it-yourself" approach to school improvement. Others point out that there is little evidence to suggest that we really know how different curricular teaching approaches and classroom organizations affect educational outcomes and that until we have such evidence, designing, implementing, and supporting an extension system to promote change is an inappropriate use of resources. Like most policy debates, this one is unlikely to be fully resolved by the incremental accumulation of sound research results. Nevertheless, it is clear that an appropriate research agenda (which would include improved conceptualizations of the problem, in addition to the collection of empirical data) could improve immeasurably the grounds upon which the debate is held.

The above discussion has pointed to many specific gaps in our knowledge about the roles of external agents in the knowledge utilization process in educational settings. These remarks have ranged from very specific hypotheses that might be addressed in future research to more general statements about the inadequacy of existing information or theory in broad areas. In the following section, the objective is to summarize the broader research issues that have been raised.

First, the overall thrust of the discussion has pointed to the serious lack of theoretical frameworks in which the study of external roles might be located. It has been proposed that one of the major gaps is the lack of attention to the functions of knowledge use for educators, and the different types of knowledge that exist to be used. This chapter has proposed a framework for identifying critical types and functions, and has attempted to show throughout how the framework (presented in Table 1) is applicable to current research and future research questions.

One of the main deficiencies of existing research is the emphasis upon a single function of knowledge use (instrumental-decisionistic) and a single type of knowledge (externally generated research information). While scattered research efforts exist in other cells, they are either outside of the mainstream of educational knowledge use research, or only marginally related to education. This situation will change quite rapidly, as current research projects at NIE have and will continue to address use of other types of knowledge. However, current research interests in the ways in which school districts use internally generated research information are, in many ways, even less well integrated with a broader frame of inquiry on knowledge use in schools. Research on district use of evaluation information also tends to ignore the role of external actors and to be unrelated to existing knowledge about the role of consultants and change agents in knowledge utilization processes.

The limited context of knowledge use research has placed equal limitations on the research about the role of external agents. Most inquiry has viewed the external agent largely within the context of the "technological-push" framework, in which schools are seen as adopters of better research products whose topics are defined by a federal agenda, rather than as participants in the process of determining what types of information would be useful. It is clear that any research agenda in this area must address this major gap.

One of the derived research gaps which was discussed earlier is the general lack of research on what schools and educators want in the way of knowledge and assistance in knowledge use (for one exception, see Hood and Blackwell, 1976a). A simple needs assessment approach would, in all probability, be an inadequate way of addressing this question: What is needed is some better synthesis of existing valued uses of external agents, coupled with a projective, exploratory inquiry into existing needs that might be filled through external assistance.

Such an inquiry would need to take into account the costs and benefits of using external versus internal agents, and the relationship between such individuals. This issue is, in general, one of the least understood in the field, and one which is perhaps the most critical to the design and planning of effective knowledge utilization systems at the local, state, and federal levels. Again, the state of knowledge seems to be so limited that a research agenda should proceed through several phases, perhaps beginning with a more systematic review of existing case studies (using techniques such as those developed by Yin et al., 1976), exploratory case analysis of ongoing change efforts, and only secondarily survey or field experimental activities.

In addition, summative questions about the relative impact of internal and external agents should be postponed until there is an improved understanding of the relationship between the two.[22]

Information on skills, skill mix, and the use of teams of agents is extremely limited, although the topic is mentioned frequently in case reports. Again, the state of the art is sufficiently primitive to indicate that the best approach is to conduct very limited reviews of existing case materials and/or limited exploratory analyses to investigate this topic.

The area of personal characteristics of linking agents associated with "success" is probably one of the most murky of all those raised. In the opinion of this author, it is also one that should receive very low priority until a better understanding of the dimensions of agent activities can be established. Existing commonsense lists of characteristics are probably sufficient to provide guidance to program planners faced with a choice among individuals for this job. Until there is evidence that psychological testing would be appropriate as a selection mechanism, however, this area of research would appear to have little policy payoff at any level.

One of the most surprising features of the existing set of research is the lack of detail about agent behaviors. The main cause of this gap appears to be the emphasis upon studies which involve multiple sites, and cross-sectional designs. The multiple site problem makes it difficult to obtain in-depth evidence about what agents actually do in any detail, particularly at the level of tactics or incidents—which Zigarmi and Goldstein (1979) report to be the most critical to understanding patterns of intervention. It may be suggested that, in addition to specific information that may be needed to complete our understanding of how different agent strategies affect client knowledge use behaviors, we need to develop better understanding of tactics. This information is particularly useful in the design of improved orientation-type training, and may also contribute to our ability to interpret accumulating knowledge about strategy impacts. Again, it should be emphasized that research on strategies and tactics must be firmly tied to a framework for understanding knowledge utilization settings in schools, and to an improved understanding of "demand-pull"-based knowledge utilization as well as "technological-push."

If we examine priorities among the different categories of strategies that were identified, it is clear that information needs are most pressing in the areas of expertise and scope/cost. In both of these cases, the conceptualization of the research problems or issues are underdeveloped, while the policy implications are very significant. Least critical is the study of initiative, with the possible exception of unique cases which pose difficult access problems (such as urban districts, which seem less likely to make effective use of external agents).

The discussion of research gaps finished with the recommendation that greater attention be paid to the ways in which organizations act as external agents. Some ways of approaching this relatively poorly researched area would be to model organizational information networks at the user level (which would begin also to identify the range and types of organizations that act as salient external agents), and to extend the preliminary work of Moore et al. (1977) to different types of agencies. In addition, particular attention should be paid to some types of agencies, particularly those that are conscious agents, those that have power relationships with school districts, and those (like universities and intermediate service agencies) which have considerable potential for becoming more self-consciously audience and information-use oriented at the institutional level.

Some additional final comments may be made about research that is not needed, either because it addresses questions that are not highly salient to school or federal policies, or because it is not likely to advance our current understanding:

- Additional literature reviews on nonempirical literature. Existing reviews, such as Hood and Cates (1978) are more than adequate; additional syntheses that are not based on empirical data and specific questions would be redundant.

- Further quasi-evaluative studies of ongoing programs that are not specifically designed to address a limited set of research questions. Two currently funded large-scale studies (the study of the R&D Utilization Program, and the study of the Office of Education Dissemination Activities) are intended to address a variety of broad exploratory issues related to external roles. The future need will be for smaller, more focused studies. We do not need any more research to arrive at the conclusion that the role of extension agents in schools is ambiguous and poorly defined.

- Large-scale action research programs that are not designed to address specific, significant policy or research questions. The current state of the art suggests that a more fruitful approach would be to engage in a period of smaller-scale, exploratory studies (for example, how best to reach urban schools) and field experiments before engaging in a major service delivery experiment.

NOTES

1. It should be pointed out that other authors are still skeptical about the importance of external agents, or even of externally developed educational knowledge. Greenwood et al. (1975) claim that externally developed innovations are less likely to be implemented than those that are internally designed, while Berman and McLaughlin (1977) found that using external consultants to provide training diminished the perceived value for local educators. Finally, there are some, like Mann (1978), who argue that a client-responsive educational system requires that "a thousand wheels be reinvented." In addition, others (like Derr, 1976) argue that schools have organizational properties that make them difficult to change and very unresponsive to outside assistance. The position of this chapter, however, is that the preponderance of evidence suggests that appropriately designed external roles are useful sources of assistance to locally initiated school improvement efforts.

2. For example, a large proportion of those agencies that were originally classified as audience-oriented were, in fact, also oriented to the delivery of a standardized set of information products. Since the authors were not looking for evidence to suggest that their typology did not "work," we may extrapolate from this that organizations may be high on more than one of these dimensions.

3. For example, an agency that conducted individualized information searches would be included. One that had a single "product line" in response to all requests would not.

4. The novelty of the titles and low role explicitness that are given to agents in demonstration projects may also be related to the difficulty of institutionalizing such individuals and their job functions when demonstration monies are gone. It should be emphasized that there are different professional subcultures that will affect the appropriateness of titles. For example, the terms "research" and "specialist" are less threatening to physicians than to educators.

5. That this image of the county extension agent as the bearer of research tidings to the innovator is far from the reality of the extension agent's actual role (see Rogers et al., 1976) is of little consequence, for the popular image dominates.

6. We must not ignore the fact that there is a rather significant type of knowledge—common knowledge—which has the greatest influence over behavior in the most rational of decision-making settings. The bulk of information about how to teach, for example, may probably be classified as common knowledge rather than as craft or research knowledge: don't scare kids, set a good example, try to be patient, use a lot of repetition. These principles of teaching are derived largely from the previous experiences of all adults with their own childhoods and with children they have known. Common knowledge, while critical to the educational function, will not be treated in this chapter because it can neither be created nor easily transferred. Rather, it is part of the general blueprint for behavior of a subculture.

7. This and other statements about the R&D Utilization Program are taken from field notes or other raw data, unless a specific report is cited.

8. In the author's experience, this is also true of other professionals, such as doctors and social workers.

9. For example, two recent attempts to generate typologies of linear roles empirically did not confirm any of the more popular typologies (see Decad et al., 1980; Louis, Kell, et al., 1981).

10. They acknowledge the possibility of a "superlinker," but express skepticism about the viability of the role.

11. The recent work of Rosenblum and Louis (1981) has shown that schools that are more "loosely linked" are, in fact, less able to implement comprehensive change projects. However, loose coupling between system parts may facilitate localized adaptation (Weick, 1976).

12. This work is based on extensive observational data collected in a single junior high school, which, as part of a Teacher Corps project, was attempting to implement a complex innovation with the assistance of an external facilitator.

13. The significance of organizational policies is that they condition all choices about interventions that are made, but cannot themselves be easily manipulated by most external or internal actors. Presumably, then, the effecting of change through policy interventions would approximate a "power model" intervention.

14. The strategies that are defined by Zaltman et al. (1977) are, in fact, general models of change processes. The authors of that volume use the terms model and strategy interchangeably, as do many others.

15. This finding points to an obvious but often overlooked policy issue in external intervention. Interventions do not have only positive or null effects; they can actually leave the system worse off than it was before (Sieber, 1981).

16. For a review of mixed and negative findings in a variety of settings, see Fullan et al. (1980).

17. It should be pointed out that the measures used in this part of the Berman and McLaughlin study are somewhat weak given our objective in this chapter. The measure of external consultant presence is obtained from teachers on a five-point scale. Given the lapsed time since the commencement of the project, this may be viewed as unreliable. In addition, while we may assume that much of the training was, at least indirectly, influenced by external consultants, we have no way of knowing for sure.

18. It should be pointed out, however, that there are some problems with interpreting the analyses presented in this study, due to the large number of variables

(20) entered into the regression equations and the small number of cases. In addition, a personal communication from Dr. Matthew Miles indicates that zero-order correlations show a positive association between the use of training materials and impacts, and that he does not, therefore, support the interpretations presented here.

19. See Rosenblum and Louis (1981) for a discussion of the impact of "readiness" on organizational change. Note that the Northwest Reading Consortium R&D Utilization Project has developed a "readiness" checklist for schools based on external agent experiences in over 30 schools. This checklist will soon be available from the NETWORK, which is compiling a sourcebook of the products produced by the seven R&D utilization projects.

20. Educators are not dissimilar to other professional groups in this regard. However, some have observed that teachers tend to have a strong preference for the "materials and curriculum" component of innovation, because they are most highly trained in analysis and using the artifacts of the educational process.

21. For example, Yin and Gwaltney (1981) show that fee-for-service funding may constrain the ability of an intermediate district to offer high quality *intensive* services, while a number of observers have commented upon the pressure within the NDN for increasing the *number* of adoptions.

22. Note that the analysis of data from the RDU project will address this relationship, and later results may shed light on the research needs. These data will not be available until mid 1981.

5

SCHOOL DISTRICT AND SCHOOL PERSONNEL IN KNOWLEDGE UTILIZATION

Michael Fullan

The purpose of this chapter is to explore what is known about the role of knowledge use and users within the school district level in order to identify a research agenda for examining knowledge use and school improvement. There are seven main sections to the chapter. The first section describes the difficulties of obtaining a clear definition and adequate data on the concept of knowledge utilization (KU). The second section provides an overview of causes of KU. The third through sixth sections examine the roles of four main groups internal to the school district— teachers, principals, district specialists/consultants, and district administrators. In the final section a research agenda is formulated arising from the analysis of the previous sections. This final section, then, synthesizes the chapter as a whole.

DEFINING KNOWLEDGE UTILIZATION

Any field which cannot define and/or obtain the necessary data on its dependent variable is in for a struggle. Such is the problem faced in the field of knowledge utilization (KU). In general, it can be said that my domain of interest concerns use of *information,* either in the form of ideas or products; information which comes from research or practice. The problem is that there are numerous dimensions and meanings of KU, not all of which are measurable. A review of this complexity will not provide any final clarity, but should help avoid the confusion which arises when KU is treated as a global or homogeneous concept. At the risk of initial confusion, I would like to identify a range of meanings and levels which can be found in the main body of work dealing with KU in education. As the reader may soon conclude, we might call this method multistrangulation. It will at least take your breath away, if not render you unconscious.

Let us begin with the seemingly simplest level—the individual knowledge user. If the use of specific information is at stake (that is, an individual seeks or receives a particular set of information on a given topic), a first approximation of defining use may take the form of Louis's (1978: 5) definition:

(1) *non-users:* persons who indicated that they had not read the information (that is, they received it, but did not look at it)

(2) *readers:* persons who indicated that they had read the information, but did not indicate that they had actually applied it in any way

(3) *planners:* persons who indicated that the information had been used for planning innovations or changes . . . but where such plans had not already been put into effect

(4) *implementers:* persons who indicated that all or part of the information had actually been used

This appears to be relatively straightforward until we add five complications. First, the specific *behavioral use* of information may not be the most frequent or even the most valuable knowledge outcome. Weiss and Bucuvalas (1980: 6) stress that decision makers often "use" knowledge for one or more of the following purposes:

to understand the background and context of program operation, stimulate review of policy, focus attention on neglected issues, provide new understanding of the causes of social problems, clarify their own thinking, reorder priorities, make sense of what they have been doing, offer ideas for future directions, reduce uncertainties, create new uncertainties and provoke rethinking of taken-for-granted assumptions, justify actions, support positions, persuade others, and provide a sense of how the world works.

In short, information could be used to *enlighten* complex issues even by showing confusion, complexity, and conflicting research findings on a particular topic (see especially Lindblom and Cohen, 1979). In this case the role of information is to stimulate thinking and to have a long-run cumulative impact on thinking and decisions. Needless to say this outcome will be extremely difficult if not impossible to measure or prove on any large scale involving numerous users (see also Larsen, 1980).

A second distinction which must be recognized, if we are to sort out what is known about KU, is that some forms of KU refer to whether a specific project or program was used, while others concern whether a general body of knowledge in a given problem area was drawn upon. Table 5.1 combines the first distinction (between specific use and diffuse or enlightenment use) and the second distinction (whether the source is a specific program or a body of knowledge in a program area). The field of career education can be used to illustrate that all four outcomes are probable. Type I occurs when a specific career education program is

TABLE 5.1   Source and Use of KU

		Source	
		Specific Program	*Program Area*
Use	Specific	I	II
	Diffuse	III	IV

adopted and used by an individual or group of individuals. Type III, which seems to involve a contradiction in terms, is in fact very likely to occur with any large body of users. Research on implementation has amply demonstrated that there are great variations in use involving any given specific program (on career education, see Farrar et al., 1979). To make matters one step more complicated, Type III would involve at least two types of use: (1) specific variations of the program in which some direct and observable form is used, and (2) general or enlightenment use (as in Weiss) which cannot possibly or feasibly be observed in the short run. Types II and IV occur when a would-be user obtains information, not on a specific career education program, but on the *field* of career education (that is, information on a whole array of alternative program possibilities). Again, in this case use could occur when a particular program was selected or developed from the array (Type II), or when the information in general stimulates thinking, questioning, and new behavior, without an observable program being selected/developed in the short run or ever (Type IV).

A third complication in all of this is that sometimes research on KU consists of examining *individualistic* users (that is, each individual is seeking or receiving information as an individual; for example, see Sieber et al., 1972), while at other times *groups of users* are involved (as when an innovative program is used in a whole school district or in multiple classrooms; see Berman and McLaughlin, 1977). Thus, the causal factors related to KU could differ in a number of respects, depending on which of these two instances are at hand. Moreover, it is extremely difficult to compare the two approaches. For example, are program-focused changes in which numbers of teachers are expected to work with the same program or information more effective than diffuse and variegated information in which individual teachers choose different things?

A fourth area of confusion occurs when different but overlapping aspects of the KU are characterized as a process. Fortunately, we can probably confine ourselves to two of these formulations—one arising from research on *dissemination,* the other from *implementation.* The Dissemination Analysis Group (1977), an OE task force of experts, agreed that four usages of dissemination could be defined:

Spread: the one-way casting out of knowledge in all its forms: information, products, ideas, and materials, "as though sowing seeds"

Exchange: the two-way or multi-way flow of information, products, ideas, and materials as to needs, problems, and potential solutions

Choice: the facilitation of rational consideration and selection among those ideas, materials, outcomes of research and development, effective educational practices, and other knowledge that can be used for the improvement of education

Implementation: the facilitation of adoption, adaptation, and installation of improvements

A different but overlapping formulation has arisen from the considerable body of research on implementation of educational programs. The most common version describes three broad phases—mobilization, implementation, and institutionalization (Berman and McLaughlin, 1977; Berman, 1980b). Both the dissemination and implementation versions are legitimate. The former is intended to describe different *types* of dissemination rather than a process, while the latter purports to describe the phases in a process of change. Taken together, the dissemination and implementation perspectives encompass several different forms of KU ranging from diffuse uses (such as spread and exchange) to particular applications (such as choice or mobilization, and implementation).

The fifth and final complication can be noted—mostly we have been assuming that KU refers to individuals or groups obtaining or receiving information for their own direct use; however, many KUs obtain information which they hope will be used by others including and sometimes not including themselves. I am not referring to formal linkers, but to any school-level personnel—the principal who obtains curricular information which he or she hopes teachers will use, the teacher who obtains or receives information which he or she intends to advocate for use by other teachers, and so on. (Hood and Blackwell, 1976b, found that 92 percent of the people in their sample of users passed on the information to others.)

Given the several variations identified above, the following implications for the study of KU can be stated.

(1) Ku itself is multidimensional and complex. Stated another way, the study of KU is itself a Type-IV problem (see Table 5.1) which may be best captured by Weiss and Bucuvalas's statement, quoted earlier. There are multiple diffuse and specific variations of KU.

(2) It is important to recognize these variations in KU in order not to be misled by research into making erroneous or superficial generalizations. For example, we have said nothing yet about factors associated with effective or ineffective KU (see the next section). Clearly, one should be aware that different causal factors and combinations of factors will operate depending on the version of KU under study. Generalizations about KU which fail to take this into account may be misleading or superficial (see Larsen, 1980).

(3) After all is said and done, we can restate in more specific terms the purpose of the rest of this chapter. We are interested in the role of human

agents within the school district in KU whether this is in the context of a specific innovation or information more generally.

(4) Since our long-term interest is in KU for school improvement, our primary interest is in KU by the teacher and the roles of other school and district personnel vis-à-vis teacher KU.

(5) Thus, the goal of the chapter is to identify what research can tell us about the role of human agents, particularly in respect to KU by teachers, for the purpose of specifying gaps and needed research to fill these gaps.

AN OVERVIEW OF CAUSES OF KU

In the next four sections, I will be examining the roles of particular groups within the school district. These groups, of course, will be considered in their roles as possible agents of KU. In this sense, they are "causes" of KU. However, before examining particular roles, it is useful to provide a general overview of the main types of factors which affect KU. This will serve as an important backdrop to the remaining sections.

My purpose here is not to carry out an exhaustive review of literature on KU. In fact, the overview will be quite general, serving mainly to provide a sense of the main types of factors associated with KU. In order to organize this task, I would like to suggest that KU is a function of three major sets of factors: (1) the nature of the *information,* (2) the *approach* used, and (3) the characteristics of the *setting* of use.

Information

Weiss and Bucuvalas (1980) examined the perceptions of 155 decision makers in mental health fields in relation to their reactions to 50 research report abstracts which they were asked to read. There are some limitations to the study because the research is based on self-reports, confined to decision makers, and (for our purposes) is in the field of mental health, not education. Nonetheless, the findings are instructive. Weiss and Bucuvalas found that five factors were related to "perceived usefulness" of the research information: (1) perceived *relevance,* (2) perceived research *quality,* (3) conformity to user's *prior expectations,* (4) *action feasibility or direction,* and (5) challenge to the *status quo.*

Weiss and Bucuvalas claim that users apply a "truth test" (factors 2 and 3—research quality and conformity to previous knowledge), and a "utility test" (factors 4 and 5—action feasibility and challenge to the status quo).[1] Weiss contends that decision makers will use research that has positive values on the five dimensions, and that use "is a much broader and more diffuse concept" than the "research for problem-solving literature" adopts.

It is very revealing to note the parallel between some of Lippitt and Gibb's work at Bethel in the late 1950s and that of Weiss and Bucuvalas.[2] Lippitt and Gibb were interested in what is needed if knowledge is to influence future behavior. They suggested three factors: (1) *clarity* about the concept, or information needed; (2) *relevance* of information—user must be able to see that the information is relevant to his or her concerns; and (3) *action images*—receiver must form some mental picture of what specific actions or interventions he or she could do in order to use the formation. The Bethel experiments tested three treatments (1, 1+2, and 1+2+3), and found progressively greater utilization of knowledge (as measured by unobtrusive behavioral measures of what was said and done with the information). In comparing the Weiss and Bucuvalas research to the Lippitt and Gibb research, two points stand out. First, there is substantial overlap—the relevance and action factors are very similar in both studies. Second, Weiss and Bucuvalas were probably not aware of the earlier research (they do not cite it), since it was not widely written up, lending credence to the likelihood that the findings were independently discovered.

Other research on implementation has also confirmed that relevant and specific information and materials are often missing, and that general or diffuse information is not helpful for stimulating KU. For example, Emrick and Peterson (1978) carried out a cross-comparison synthesis of five major change projects. One of the five findings common to the research was that "material resources at the 'how to' level are needed, particularly for utilizations involving organizational or instructional change" (Emrick and Peterson, 1978: 73).

Havelock et al. (1973: 22), in their national survey of innovations in U.S. school districts (as reported by superintendents) found that "confusion among staff about the purpose of the innovation" and "lack of precise information about the innovation" were two of the most frequently cited barriers to use (see also Hood and Blackwell, 1976b).

A directly related area of controversy concerns the question of whether the main problem is lack of good, usable "products," or whether it is the failure to use good products which are already developed and in existence. It is likely that both factors are operating (depending on the topic and situation), which contributes to the confusion when generalizations are attempted only to find contradictory data. Certainly, the lack of products in some areas of need is a major problem. Thus the R&D Utilization Program, as the title implies, was directed at stimulating use of R&D (in seven projects ranging from reading, math, and career education to in-service materials), using intensive interactive support systems to aid school districts in implementation. One of the major problems encountered concerned the lack of R&D products in some significant areas (Louis, 1980).

Hood and Blackwell (1976b: III-13) also found that only a minority of teachers and principals thought that the amount and quality of information was very adequate. This is consistent with the findings just reported, but the solution is deceptive and appears not to be simply the production of better R&D materials, although this is part of it. We know, for example, that production of intact R&D materials is not closely related to implementation (Fullan and Pomfret, 1977; Berman, 1980b). We know that adaptation and the use of a variety of materials is related to implementation (while lack of adaptation is often not: Armor et al., 1976; Berman, 1980b).[3] Recalling the more enlightenment, diffuse and developmental notion of KU, we can also surmise that working with ideas and resources to be developed at the individual and group level may have (we do not know) more pervasive effects than attempting to use a specific product. Further, some innovations such as the NEA in-service materials project (Louis, 1980) are deliberately diverse because they are directed at a variety of different needs. The way out of the dilemma may lie in the conclusion that clearer "how to" materials are needed, but that clarification is as much of *a process during implementation,* as it is intrinsic to the materials prior to implementation (see Berman, 1980b).

In considering the meaning of the above research, one gets a sense of *general* agreement that information which is relevant, clear, amenable to action images, and so on is most effective for KU. The term "general" is stressed because the research is not specifically comparable. The concepts used by different authors overlap and vary in imprecise ways, but the direction for needed research to clarify the main concepts is evident.

There is another body of research on "information systems" in education which I do not review in detail here, partly because this work is amply described in other documents, and partly because it has not yet adequately examined *utilization* (although I do draw on aspects of this research in later sections). Suffice it to say that a good deal of research is currently being conducted on the education information system, which includes knowledge base or organization of information, dissemination and linkage structures, and information seeking or receiving behavior. The most comprehensive analysis of this work is being carried out in the Educational Dissemination Support Program of the Far West Laboratory (see Hood, 1979a; Hood and Blackwell, 1976b, 1979; Paisley et al., 1979). Other large-scale information use research on which I draw later can also be found in the State Capacity Building project (Madey et al., 1979), the R&D Utilization project (Louis et al., 1979), the National Diffusion Network (Emrick et al., 1977), and so on (see also Raizen, 1979, for an overview of NIE's dissemination programs).

Approaches to Information Use

The question of what are the best strategies or approaches to facilitate effective KU is an enormous one. Again, I wish to provide a sense of the main findings rather than a thorough review. As a forewarning to the problems in answering this question, the reader is advised to reflect on the many meanings of KU which were reviewed in the first section. In somewhat oversimplified terms, the main findings are that KU (in the sense of particular uses of information) is associated with approaches that (a) provide direct *personal* forms of intervention, and (b) occur over a *period of time,* during which the user makes initial selection or adoption decisions, and receives support (in-service training, resources, psychological support) on a continuous basis during the phases of initial implementation, to eventual incorporation of the information.

Emrick and Peterson (1978) describe these two components in the following words:

> Direct personal intervention is by far the most potent technical support resource, and may be a necessary condition for many forms of utilization. . . . Continuous personal participation of the implementing staff is needed to firmly root and sustain the utilization.

One distinction within this research concerns whether the approach involves individual users or groups of users. Thus, the Pilot State Dissemination Project (Sieber et al., 1972) was based on facilitating use by *individual* teachers and others as a series of individual users, while the R&D Utilization project (Louis et al., 1979: 28) involves programs used by large *groups*. At this time, there is no way of comparing the two to learn which approach is more effective. In either case, personal contact over a period of time is needed for effective KU of a specific nature.

On the other hand, if we broaden the notion of KU to include diffuse spread and use of information, the answer to what is known about effective approaches is much more problematic. This relates to the recent and rapidly expanding area of research on linkage agents which is the subject of the chapter by Louis in this volume. Just to touch on this research, we might refer to Butler and Paisley's (1978) conceptual synthesis, and Madey's (1979) empirical follow-up. The former authors suggest that there are three main linkage roles—resource finder, process helper, and solution giver—and a more all-encompassing role of generalist. Madey (1979) attempted to verify empirically the nature of linkage roles, and discovered three main roles—resource finder, facilitator, and communicator. The first two were similar to Butler and Paisley's resource finder and process finder; solution giver became incorporated in the facilitator and communicator roles; the generalist and communicator roles were similar. Although there is a substantial amount of research currently going on, there is very little which adequately defines linkage roles and relates them to different types of KU (again, see the Louis chapter for a review of this research). We can say, however, that there is a good sense of which approaches to KU are more effective. My interest in the topic of approaches to KU is confined to the roles of personnel *internal* to the district. In other words, I will examine the approaches to KU used by what we might call internal linking agents and users of knowledge.

The Setting

The term "setting" incorporates characteristics of individuals and organizational processes which inhibit or support KU in the potential users' situation. A brief overview of those factors can be obtained by considering the roles of leadership, organizational processes (communication, climate, and so on), individual characteristics, and differences in structural conditions (specifically, elementary versus secondary schools, community characteristics, size—especially in terms of district resources and specialists and teacher unionism).

Leadership

Emrick and Peterson (1978) reviewed five large-scale projects and concluded that "administrators play a crucial role in supporting the utilization process."[4] In addition to the five major studies included in the Emrick and Peterson synthesis, all other major research indicates that administrative support from the district and school level is positively related to utilization (for example, Rosenblum and Louis, 1981, a study of the ten rural districts in the experimental schools project, and Miles et al., 1978c, study of the planning and implementation of new schools).

Organizational Processes

Similarly, virtually all of the above research indicates that peer dialogue and collegiality (frequent meetings, discussion, support) among teachers is positively related to KU. It is interesting to note that this applies to both project-related change involving groups of teachers and to individual-focused change in which teachers seek or obtain information for their own individual use (although research on the latter is much more scarce). Louis (1978) contains one of the few analyses of organization factors in relation to individual teacher use of information (as distinct from program- or project-specific use). Louis examined the extent of KU among teachers who had sought information searches (through ERIC) on topics of interest to themselves as individuals. The three strongest relationships were found for variables which were labeled *social interaction,* namely: (1) the number of different categories of people with whom the information was discussed; (2) the number of different categories to whom the information was loaned; and (3) an index of helpfulness regarding conversation with others (multiple $R = .41$). It is most interesting to observe that these correlations remained positive when the information was grouped separately for school-level and classroom-level problems. Although the correlations were smaller concerning the latter (in the .21 to .33 range), they were positive, indicating that social interaction is important even when the information is to be used solely in one's own classroom. This is not to say that individualistic and school-level or districtwide innovations operate in the same manner. Indeed, this distinction is crucial and warrants further research. It is to say that social interaction within the school and external to it (as the "approach" subsection indicated) is crucial for all types of KU. Moreover, in one of the few studies to relate teacher-to-teacher interaction and consultation to *achievement outcomes,* Armor et al. (1976: 24) found that the former was strongly related to improved reading scores for black children.

Individual Characteristics

Research on individual characteristics associated with KU remains ad hoc and inconsistent. There is some consistent evidence that level of education of teachers (master's degree or higher) is positively related to adoption and implementation. Relatively large correlations were found by Daft and Becker (1978), Corwin (1975), and Rosenblum and Louis (1981). (Yet Louis, 1978, in another study, found no relationship between education and use.) However, two aspects of the relationship are not clear. First and foremost, the research is not based on a consistent definition of KU or one which allows comparisons among different versions of KU. Second, we do not know specifically what links education to use, since there are numerous possibilities which one would have to parcel out (such as motivation to seek information, knowledge of information sources, and so on).

The roles of age and experience of teachers are also somewhat mysterious. There is some folklore that beginning teachers are too insecure to innovate (that is, they seek conformity) and very experienced teachers do not want to change their ways, or know enough not to try. The Rand research found that teacher experience was negatively related to implementation (Berman and McLaughlin, 1977). Louis (1978) reported a negative relationship between age and KU. As with education, however, the correlations are relatively small (put another way, many older teachers use KU, and many younger ones do not), and the specific function of age in interaction with other variables is unknown. Other ad hoc individual characteristics have also been found to be related to various measures of KU. The Rand change agent study found that teachers who had a high sense of efficacy or control were much more likely to implement change (Berman and McLauglin, 1977: 136), as did another Rand study of reading programs (Armor et al., 1976: 24). "Motivation to innovate" was one variable which was positively correlated with KU in the Louis (1978) analysis. In addition to their ad hoc nature, we have no idea from this research about what causes these factors in the first place.

Structural Conditions

The main factors which should be noted for future sections, and future research, concern level of schooling, type of community, size of district and associated factors, and teacher unionism.

There is no adequate body of research on comparing the KU behavior of elementary and secondary school teachers. Some studies have shown that elementary schools are more likely to adopt and implement changes (for example, Butler-Paisley and Paisley, 1975: 53; Emrick and Peterson, 1978). Havelock et al. (1973) also found that school districts were much more likely to report innovations directed at the elementary level than at the junior and senior high school levels. On the other hand, Rosenblum and Louis (1981) found a positive relationship between level of schooling and implementation, and report that secondary schools attempted more comprehensive changes. Daft and Becker (1978) examined only high schools and reported a great deal of teacher-initiated change. We need research which compares the *extent* of KU across school levels, but, more importantly, we need research which compares and describes the *nature of organizational processes* related to KU at the elementary, junior, and senior levels.

Community characteristics represent another set of potentially important factors.[5] Again, there is limited research on KU in rural versus suburban versus urban settings. House (1974: ch. 2) shows that population centers have much more access to information sources than do rural areas and that innovation does in fact spread more rapidly to these centers than to rural areas. Rosenblum and Louis (1981) did research directly on rural districts (but not comparatively) and found a variety of innovative behaviors which were explained by factors already reviewed (role of superintendent, principal, collegiality, and so on). Community supportiveness, activeness, and stability of environment are other factors which may interact with rural-urban differences in relation to KU. The size of district, including resources (such as number of district specialists) also interacts with type of community. Further specification of needed research in this area will be discussed in the final section of this chapter.

Teacher unionism and conditions of collective bargaining contracts represent another important but unknown set of factors which has come on the scene during the past five years, and which will become increasingly important.[6] Because of the recency of this phenomena, not much research has been done on it. Miles, Sullivan, et al. (1978b: 11), in the case study of one of their schools, comment about the contract: "Principals may not be able to choose teachers, but must accept ones with seniority, regardless of their interest in innovation; extra or after-school meetings are forbidden." Havelock et al. (1973) in their 1970-1971 survey, found that "disruptions" (teacher strikes, community protests, student demonstrations) were more likely to occur in large districts (over 80,000 students). They also found that these disruptions had a negative influence on innovation use (as perceived by the superintendent)—29 percent of smaller districts and 57 percent of larger districts which had experienced disruptions reported a negative influence. This research is not a commentary on teachers per se, but raises the possibility that school boards and teachers are negotiating from adversarial positions which directly (meetings being prohibited) or indirectly (polarization and bad morale) could affect KU. Collective bargaining as a factor in KU is an area of research which must be examined much more closely than it has been.

Another related contextual condition which is receiving more attention very recently, but which is not usually recognized (except by those in programs), pertains to turnover of key personnel and other individual users. In preliminary findings from the R&D Utilization project, Louis (1980) states flatly:

> Administrative turnover, more than any other single factor, accounts for changes in levels of implementation and institutionalization. Few new principals are committed to the priorities of their predecessors.

The same applies to the cumulative effect of teacher turnover. These rates vary from school to school and district to district. Obviously, turnover rates of 30 percent or 40 percent over a three or four years in a given setting could have a massive effect on the extent of KU in relation to innovation.

In summary, one major underdeveloped area of research on KU which should be tagged concerns the role of "unanticipated critical events," to use Louis's phrase. Such events—leader turnover, teacher turnover, strikes, budget cuts, and other disruptions—can be normal fare over any three- or four-year period. Their variance and impact on KU should be investigated systematically.

This section has contained a general pass through the causes of KU research. My intention has been to provide a sense of the range and types of factors at work, rather than a conclusive review of findings. The research referred to should provide a valuable context for the next four sections, which examine specific categories of people at the district level— teachers, principals, district specialists, and district administrators.

TEACHERS

Teachers are the focal point of KU for school improvement because of their direct and sustained contact with students. In order to understand the various roles of teachers in KU, I consider three different roles: (1) teachers as direct individual users of KU, (2) teachers as direct users in planned change efforts, and (3) teachers as agents of KU. The first two forms involve teachers as recipients or participants in KU, while the third form examines their initiating role in school or district innovation.

Teachers as Individual Users

Teachers can be direct users of knowledge either as individuals going about their daily, weekly, or yearly work, or as part of a planned change effort. The former is examined first.

We have very little positive evidence and some negative evidence that teachers are not heavy individual users of either research knowledge or practitioner knowledge. House (1974: ch. 4) discussed the teachers' pre- dicament in this regard. Unlike central office personnel, teachers have limited access to external sources of information. As House states, "Their heavy teaching load confines them to the classroom, which greatly restricts access to new ideas and innovations." It is also well known that R&D has limited impact on practice of teachers, partly because it is conducted in isolation from teachers, and partly because teachers do not have the time or motivation to assimilate it (see McLean, 1979, for a discussion of "the chastening of educational research").

Not only do teachers engage in limited use of external research ideas, but there also seems to be infrequent use of practitioner-generated knowl- edge. Two main reasons stand out as accounting for this situation. First, the quality and amount of technical knowledge appropriate for use is underdeveloped, whether we refer to technical knowledge from research (which is frequently too abstract, unclear, and impractical) or from practice (which is underdeveloped and unsystematized). Lortie's (1975) study of the teacher most clearly documents the lack of a language and culture among teachers to systematize their technical knowledge. The second and related reason is that teachers *do not interact* with each other on any basis which would lead to shared KU. Lortie (1975), House (1974), and Sarason (1971) all point to the segmented and isolated role of the teacher vis-à-vis other adults, and to the lack of any regular mechanisms for sharing knowledge, whether it be research- or practitioner-based. Thus, there are organizational (structure, lack of time) and cultural (professional isolation) barriers which limit the amount of KU behavior among teachers and between teachers and outsiders. There are probably many subtle, ad hoc influences that teachers have on each other, but these are rarely documented, and taken together may not meet the definition of socially validated knowledge.

Leithwood et al.'s (1978) study of curriculum decision making by teachers in three school districts in Ontario, Canada, corroborates the above findings. These authors found that the predominant pattern of teacher decision making in planning, developing, implementing, and evaluating curriculum was based on *individual* teacher preference and experience, and *individual* teacher perception of student needs and reactions. They found some influences through peer dialogue and administrative suggestions on some aspects of planning and evaluation and minimal influences by agents external to the school. In brief, their study confirms that, by and large, teachers make decisions *on their own* with limited interaction/influence from other teachers, administrators, or external resource personnel.

Additional research on teacher choice helps to explain why teachers do not seek more external information. Leithwood et al. (1978) and Lortie (1975) show that teachers are likely to judge ideas and practices in terms of how they might meet *their* students' needs and interests. Loucks and Hall's (1979) work on stages of concern of teachers indicates that personal concerns (how will the innovation affect me) are quite high at the early stages of considering a new idea, and must be addressed before impact concerns (how will it benefit students) are fully entertained. These seemingly inconsistent findings can be explained when the two issues are examined together. For example, House (1974) observes that: (a) most educational innovations have to be accepted on faith rather than demonstrable benefit, while at the same time, (b) the personal costs to teachers (time, energy, skill development, anxiety, uncertainty of benefit) of most changes are high. Thus, the conditions for individual use suffer from the double problem of low demonstrability or specificity of benefit, and high personal costs.

Having said this, I should also note that research on teachers may be missing the many and varied ways in which teacher thinking of KU is influenced. The diffuse and/or longer-term impact of educational knowledge which teachers pick up through workshops, readings, casual discussion, and so on is very difficult to identify. Teachers are certainly exposed to a great deal of information. Hood and Blackwell (1976b) asked a sample of 202 teachers how frequently they used 18 sources of information listed by the authors (a 3-point scale was used: 1 = often, 2 = sometimes, 3 = rarely). There were 4 sources listed which had means of less than 1.50, namely: textbooks (1.31), personal notes and files (1.45), face-to-face discussion within the school (1.46), and curriculum materials (1.46). Three comments are in order. First, the findings support other research which emphasizes that teachers rely on personal sources. Second, the emphasis on face-to-face discussion within the school may indicate that more KU exchanges occur than is commonly known.[7] Or, at the least, we can say that when KU does occur, fellow teachers are one of the most important sources of information, if not the most important (see the section below on teachers as agents of KU). Third, the emphasis on textbooks and curriculum materials points to another unknown area of KU. There is some evidence that textbook publishers and salespeople are major disseminators of curriculum knowledge. Boyd (1978) describes the policy-making role which publishers sometimes play. Clark and Yinger (1980: 19), in a small-scale intensive study of teacher planning, found that "the most frequently mentioned resources used in teacher planning were teacher's guides, teacher's editions of student textbooks, and student texts themselves."[8] In any case, the role of textbook publishers and personnel appears to be an extremely important but understudied aspect of teacher KU.

In fact, however, we know very little about the daily KU behavior of teachers. Clark and Yinger's (1980) work indicates that much more goes on in teacher planning than is normally known, and that further research on information sources used by teachers during planning is needed. Clark and Yinger's findings include: (1) planning is plural, important, and largely invisible to others; (2) planning is not linear or step by step; (3) teachers transform curriculum materials at their disposal during planning and instruction; (4) teachers infrequently reflect on their own planning and information use, but when they do (as when a project stimulates them to do so), they find it revealing and learn a great deal (see also Olson, 1980, for an identical finding). Thus, neither teachers nor others really know or reflect much about how they use information or make decisions[9]—another area of research in which further work would be well worthwhile (including the need to compare elementary and secondary school teachers).

Teachers as Users in Planned Change Efforts

Planned change efforts have ranged from attempting to stimulate *individual* KU (Sieber et al., 1972) to project-focused changes in which *groups* of potential users opt into or are forced into particular innovations selected for the school or district (for example, see Berman and McLaughlin, 1977; Louis et al., 1979). From the second section, we know that teacher KU does occur under the right conditions. Without repeating the details, KU among teachers occurs when: (a) the *information* is of a certain character (relevant to needs, specific in an action-implication sense, perceived to be valid/accurate); (b) the *approach* is person-intensive, interactive, and continuous in providing technical and psychological support; and (c) the *setting* (district, school) possesses characteristics of administrative support, peer interaction, and problem-solving behavior. *All three* sets of factors must be present if any widespread KU is to occur— apparently, this is something which infrequently happens.

Teachers as Agents of Change

One of the most complicated questions concerns the extent to which teachers act as initiators or advocates of change, thereby affecting policy and KU behavior in the districts or schools in which they work. Teachers as agents of reform, rather than or in addition to being individual users, is of direct interest to this review. Leaving aside for the moment the role of teachers in advocating particular changes, we have already seen that teachers are agents of KU insofar as they discuss, support, provide help, and so forth to fellow teachers. Supporting this finding is conclusive research in which teachers cite fellow teachers as the most important source of help. Typical of this research is Aoki's (1977) study of social science teachers in their use of provincewide curriculum guidelines in British Columbia. Teacher opinion of the helpfulness of various groups showed that fellow teachers were rated highest (4.03 on a 5-point scale), while district staff were rated as moderately useful (2.94), and department of education, teacher union, and university consultants were rated low (1.56 to 2.54). Kormos and Enns (1979) confirm that "other teachers" are the most preferred source of help. None of this is to say that district consultants and other external technical support are unimportant (see the section on district specialists), but it does say that teacher peers are extremely important for KU in a positive (when interaction and helpfulness is established) or negative (when isolation is the pattern) direction.

There is a great deal of other research which demonstrates that peer interaction and support among teachers is related to implementation, including Armor et al.'s (1976) finding that improved reading achievement was strongly correlated with the degree to which teachers consulted with other teachers.

In sum, without interactive support among teachers, significant KU is unlikely. Perhaps the best way of summarizing the research is to say that teachers do not frequently interact on professional instructional matters, but when they do, it can be very powerful in affecting KU.

Teachers as advocates or initiators of KU is another story. Daft and Becker (1978) examined the adoption of innovations in 13 high school districts introduced during the 1968-1972 period. They report a surprising proportion of teacher-proposed innovations summarized in Table 5.2.

Similarly, Havelock et al.'s (1973) national survey of innovations (as reported by superintendents) found that teachers (38 percent) in districts with less than 80,000 students, were the group most frequently cited as having played "a key role" in initiating or sponsoring the innovation. In

TABLE 5.2   Percentage of Innovations Proposed by Teachers

1968-1972	Percentage
All innovations	69
Innovations that benefit college-bound students	83
Innovations that benefit terminal students	55
Curriculum and teaching techniques	87
All other innovations	26

SOURCE: Daft and Becker (1978).

larger districts (more than 80,000 students) teachers were still cited in 36 percent of the cases, but other staff (district specialists), community, and other administrators were identified as frequently as teachers. Somewhat contrary findings are reported by Rosenblum and Louis, who discovered that superintendents' authority was associated with more comprehensive or districtwide change, and that teacher autonomy was negatively related to the implementation of such change. House (1974) also suggests that teachers are less likely to advocate changes.

Barrows (1980) investigated the adoption activities of 13 schools which had opted into IGE (Individually Guided Education). Remarkably, she found only 2 schools in which the teachers and principal were the initiating force (indeed, in only these 2 schools did teachers even participate in the decision to adopt after the innovation was proposed). The central district office (usually the superintendent) was the initiator of the innovation in 11 of the 13 cases, and was the *sole initiator and decision maker* in 8 of the 11 schools. Unlike Daft and Becker's (1978) study, IGE applies to elementary schools. This implies that secondary school teachers advocate innovations more frequently than elementary school teachers, but the complexities of this whole area of research are evidenced by other findings which indicate that innovation is much more frequent at the elementary level (Havelock et al., 1973; Berman and McLaughlin, 1977; Emrick and Peterson, 1978).

Thus, the KU initiation and use by elementary and secondary school teachers should be compared more directly. It is also worth noting that there is very little research on the KU activities which *lead up to* adoption or rejection of changes (that is, on what Berman, 1980b, calls the process of mobilization). Barrows (1980) is one of the few who have looked at this aspect, but she did not examine it in any depth. The process leading up to an adoption decision is not described. Similarly, Daft and Becker (1978) present conclusions on initiation of innovations, but do not indicate what their data base or indicators were, nor do they trace the activities which led up to the adoption decision.

In the meantime, the following tentative observations can be made:

(1) Teachers as a category may be responsible for and/or play key roles in many instances of KU, but this does not tell us anything about the

average KU instigation of teachers. Indeed, other evidence indicates that the average teacher is not engaged in these efforts. Nor do we know much about the average KU of individual teachers (as distinct from the initiation of KU).

(2) When teachers do push for change it is likely to involve curricular, classroom-related innovations. More comprehensive schoolwide or district changes come from other sources.

(3) The Daft and Becker (1978) and Havelock et al. (1973) research does not assess "utilization," but only initiation or adoption. Therefore, conclusions about firm KU are unwarranted. Moreover, little is known about the process of mobilization—those activities, events, and KU behavior which lead up to a decision to adopt an innovation.

(4) Teachers are important sources of support or lack of support for KU of other teachers, whether it be individual or group-based use.

(5) In sum, research is needed on: (a) the role of teachers in the processes of mobilization and decision to adopt; (b) average KU behavior of teachers; (c) elementary and secondary school differences; and (d) the different processes according to variations in rural, suburban, urban, district size, and other contextual conditions.

PRINCIPALS AS AGENTS OF KU

After twenty years of meaningless generalities that the principal is the gatekeeper of change, researchers are finally beginning to define and study exactly what the role of the principal is and might be regarding change in schools. Fortunately, there is some very good detailed research currently ongoing on the role of the principal vis-a-vis change.[10] While systematic research is not yet available, we do have some good beginnings. I review this work in three parts: (1) large-scale surveys on the role of the principal; (2) focused research findings on the role of the principal in facilitating or inhibiting change and KU of teachers; and (3) conclusions about the role of principals as KUs and as agents of KU.

Large-Scale Surveys

There have been recent national and state surveys of the role of elementary school principals (Pharis and Zakariya, 1979) and secondary school principals (Abramowitz and Tenenbaum, 1978; Byrne et al., 1978; Gorton and McIntyre, 1978) in the United States, and principals from across all levels in the province of Ontario, Canada (Eastabrook and Fullan, 1978). These studies provide a broad context for considering the role of the principal.

In the Pharis and Zakariya (1979: 28) study, the most frequent "source of ideas for recent innovation" for elementary school principals were "other principals and teachers" (23 percent named this category in a mutually exclusive rating). However, professional reading (19 percent) and local workshops (16 percent) were frequently used by substantial numbers of principals, as the percentages indicate. In rating the value of certain types of preparation for the job, 85 percent named on-the-job experience as a teacher and principal as having "much value," while only 36 percent mentioned graduate education, and 24 percent in-service programs. Since in-service programs for principals are becoming more widespread, some attention must be paid to what constitutes useful and less-than-useful in-service programs.[11] (See also Reinhard et al., 1980.)

Orlich et al. (1976) have examined the role of principals in innovation in Washington State. In a survey of 100 school principals concerning the use of social science innovation, Ruff and Orlich (1974: 390) found that textbook salesmen were listed by principals as the best source of information (53 percent), followed by the district curriculum director (40 percent); no other source was listed by more than 7 percent. In a later study of social science and science curriculum innovation, Orlich et al. (1976) found similar results. For social science, 50 percent of the principals mentioned commercial publishers as the best source, 43 percent cited district curriculum coordinators, and 33 percent mentioned books, journals, and so on. Similar results were found regarding science innovations. One further finding directly related to the purpose of the survey was that principals who had attended National Science Foundation workshops (about one-half the sample) were much more likely to list workshops as significant sources of ideas for innovation than were non-NSF principals. Thus, focused workshops can be useful, but are not frequently utilized.

In a study of the senior high school principalship, Byrne et al. (1978: 6) found that principals do report a high level of involvement in conferences and workshops—79 percent said that they attended workshops and conferences within the district, and 62 percent outside the district. The relationship to KU is unknown, but one might suspect that the effectiveness of workshops has not been great given what we know about problems of conducting effective in-service programs (again, see Reinhard et al., 1980, which is reviewed in the next section).

Senior principals were asked to rate how essential certain types of preservice courses were; it is interesting to compare the 1965 and 1977 findings summarized in Table 5.3.

For our purposes, 2 findings are worth highlighting. First, the overall amount and range of essential knowledge as seen by principals has increased dramatically (5 of the 6 categories show major increases reflecting what some principals see as the problems of role overload and the need for role clarification in the contemporary principalship). Second, curriculum development, which is closest to our concern with KU for school improvement, shows a major increase—from two-fifths of the principals who said it was essential in 1965, to three-quarters in 1977.

Even more interesting is the rank ordering of how principals "do spend time" compared to how they think they "should spend time." Program development was ranked fifth out of 9 tasks in terms of "do" and first out of 9 in terms of "should."

In a subsample of the 60 most "effective" principals (identified through reputational criteria), Gorton and McIntyre (1978) found that these so-

TABLE 5.3   Principals' Ratings

Course	Percentage Rated Essential 1977	Percentage Rated Essential 1965
School law	77	32
Curriculum and program development	76	41
School management	74	26
Supervision of instruction	71	56
Human relations	71	45
Administrative theory and practice	32	41

SOURCE: Byrne et al. (1978: 10).

called effective principals focused more on program development than the sample as a whole. In time actually spent, program development was ranked first of 9 in time spent during the previous two weeks, and third of 9 in time spent over the whole year (compared to fifth of 9 for the larger sample). However, teacher perceptions of these principals were different. Teachers indicated an actual rank order of 5, and a should rank order of 1 (we cannot compare this with the larger sample, because teachers were not sampled). Principals' roles in curriculum change varied from school to school:

> A few principals indicated that they initiate ideas, often subtly through others, but more typically the principals view themselves as catalysts, facilitators, reviewers, and resource providers [Gorton and McIntyre, 1978: 22].

Principals listed teachers, individually or by departments, as the primary initiators of curriculum changes, and themselves as the initiators or facilitators of major changes in the school. The authors of the study formulate a composite of the change strategy used by the 60 principals: (1) recognize the need and plant the seed with staff members and/or others; (2) work with people, especially those most affected—but do not impose change; (3) "provide needed resources and support" (Gorton and McIntyre, 1978: 61). The sample of exemplary principals cited "role clarification" as the number-one need, and reported that excessive paperwork and district meetings were a major drain on their time.

The exemplary principals are by definition not representative of principals as a whole. In more general surveys, the prominence of the principal on KU decisions is minimal.[12] Aoki (1977) found that principals were rarely mentioned by a large sample of social studies teachers as "sources of information." Barrows (1980) investigated the adoption decisions in 13 sites that were using Individually Guided Education. Not only were principals involved in decisions to adopt the innovation in only 2 of the 13 cases, there were only 3 cases in which principals had the "opportunity to confirm the adoption decisions" (that is, the central office made the decision in 10 of the 13 schools). Havelock et al.'s (1973) national survey of superintendents also found that principals were rarely mentioned as key factors in innovations adopted.

Generally, similar findings on time spent are reported by Eastabrook and Fullan (1978) in their Ontario sample—44 percent of the principals said that they actually spend a great deal of time on curricular tasks, while 76 percent indicated that they would ideally like to spend a great deal of time on such tasks. The percentages were reversed for administrative tasks (paperwork, meetings, and so on).

The above findings provide a general context for considering the role of the principal. Among the findings and gaps are those noted below.

(1) Principals probably are exposed to more ideas than are teachers. However, only a minority find workshops, reading, and the like valuable. Other principals and teachers are the preferred source, but this, too, is only true of the minority.

(2) Both elementary and secondary principals say that they would like to spend more time on program improvement than they do. The veracity of this statement must be examined, since this represents a socially desirable response.

(3) The overload of responsibilities in school management, administrative requirements, public relations, and so on interferes with principal involvement in KU, and makes prioritizing of activities difficult.

(4) Effective principals play a direct or facilitative role in KU and school improvement, but it is not at all clear what this means in practice (see the next section).

(5) The general findings do not indicate major differences between elementary and secondary school principals, but surely there are important differences according to size of school and level of schooling. One would expect that a principal in large secondary school would perform more of an administrative and indirect role, but the study of 60 effective senior high school principals indicated that they actively support curriculum improvement.

Research Findings on the Principal and KU

Up until 1975 there were very few empirical studies on what the principal does and does not do in relation to educational change (the number of studies is still small, although it is increasing rapidly). Wolcott's (1973) ethnography is rich in detail, but is based on a sample of one. Wolcott (1973: 178) reports that Ed's (the principal) formal preparation for the role of the principal was "simply a fact of life that he had to take courses," and that his courses were of little or no help to his work. Similarly, in-service work was done mainly to meet district requirements— "I have been involved in workshops 'up to here' " (Wolcott, 1973: 199). As to KU from research sources, Ed had a number of journals and books on his shelf, but, observes Wolcott (1973: 200) "I know of no occasion when Ed so much as glanced toward any of the materials on the shelf."

Ironically, research was cited to support certain decisions—Ed often resorted to an answer frequently employed by other principals as well: "I think you will find that studies have shown" (p. 205). Wolcott, as many others have found, adds that principals and teachers rarely interact on professional matters except to do what is minimally required for teacher evaluation. Sarason (1971) states that many principals handle the dilemma of interacting with teachers by minimizing interaction. Both sides, in effect, agree to leave each other alone.

Wolcott (1973: 307) also suggests that principals work more *to manage* change introduced from outside than *to lead* change:

> Principals talk a great deal about change. But I did not see any evidence that Ed actually contributed to this foment. The school principal is successful in his work to the extent that he is able to contain and constrain the forces of change with which he must contend as a matter of daily routine.

The principal, according to Wolcott, is interested in maintaining an *image* of change, but is more prudent in dealing with the real thing. This is reminiscent of Berman and McLaughlin's (1979) description of "the illusion of change," Argyris and Schon's (1978) distinction between espoused theory and theory-in-practice, and Miles, Sullivan, et al.'s (1978b) description of the principal at Westgate who supported open education in general, but not at a specific level.

In any case, the history of the role of the principal in educational change is not compelling. Sarason (1971: 115) states quite baldly:

> There is little in the nature of the classroom teacher, there is little in the motivation of the teacher to become a principal, there is little in the actual experience of the teacher with principals, and there is even less in the criteria by which a principal is chosen to expect that the role of the principal will be viewed as a vehicle, and in practice used, for educational change and innovation.

Recent empirical evidence confirms that the majority of principals play a limited role in educational change, but also that some principals are effective agents of KU. Crowson and Porter-Gehrie (1980) recently reported findings from an intensive observation study of 26 urban school principals. The overwhelming emphasis and pressure in their daily work was toward stability and maintenance, specifically: (1) maintaining student disciplinary control, (2) keeping outside influences under control and building external support, (3) keeping staff conflicts at bay, and (4) keeping the school supplied with adequate resources. It is revealing to note that Crowson and Porter-Gehrie's "natural" description of what principals do rarely mentions KU behavior aside from some aspects of "keeping the school supplied with adequate resources" (even the latter referred primarily to basic supplies and staff rather than KU).

In a larger-scale study directly involving innovative projects, Berman and McLaughlin (1977: 131) report that one-third of the teachers in their study thought that their principal functioned primarily as an administrator. Teachers rated these principals as ineffective and uninvolved in change. Berman and McLaughlin do not say how many of those in the other two-thirds were actively engaged in change (moreover, their sample was based on school districts which adopted innovative projects). The authors do, however, indicate what successful principals did. They found that "projects having the *active* support of the principal were the most likely to fare well (Berman and McLauglin, 1977: 124; italics in original). They claim that principals' actions serve to legitimate whether a change is to be taken seriously, and serve to support teachers. They also note that one of the best indicators of active involvement is whether principals attended workshop sessions with their teachers. Emrick and Peterson's (1978) synthesis of five major studies and the work of Hall and Loucks in Texas confirm that KU is unlikely to occur in the absence of direct administrative support, especially by principals. Cases of effective involvement by principals are cited, and indicated as in the minority. Loucks and Hall (1979: 18) describe an effective elementary school principal who was instrumental in bringing about KU of a new science program:

> In this school the teachers knew that teaching the science program was a priority, the principal makes certain that new teachers and those at new grade levels receive the necessary training to teach the new units. . . . He constantly visited classrooms, assisted with lessons, and talked about children continually.

Levels of implementation at this school were higher than in other schools where most principals gave at best a *general* endorsement of the program, and indicated that use of it was up to the teacher. In a more recent paper, Hall et al. (1980) examined nine schools more closely, using a case study methodology. In attempting to understand why teachers in some schools had more concerns about "managing" the science curriculum innovation while other teachers were concerned about the impact or achievement of students, the schools were classified according to the concerns profiles of teachers as a group. This resulted in three groups—three schools had clear management profiles, four had mixed profiles, and two were characterized by high interest in student achievement resulting from the use of the innovations. The field research concentrated on the behavior of the principals in these nine schools. In the authors' words:

> Principals in the Management Concerned schools did not get personally involved with teachers and their use of the science innovation. Rather, these principals delegated responsibility or made major decisions with little follow-up on the results. For example, in School 1, the principal assigned the administrative assistant to handle anything related to science, and in School 3, the principal assigned a teacher to handle science materials and never checked to see what happened. The principals in these schools seemed to be more concerned with general issues rather than specifics and left teachers on their own to determine how to implement the innovation. The principals in the two Impact Concerned schools, 8 and 9, were by comparison *science activists.* They were concerned about supporting and helping teachers in their use of the innovation, so on a weekly and daily basis they were monitoring what teachers were doing with

science. They set policy within the school that clearly indicated that science would be taught. They worked on teacher-specific implementation problems. They also served on the district-wide principals committee for science. In addition, these principals were described as having longer term goals and visions for their schools and teachers. There is a dynamic energy about them, a sense of commitment and direction for attaining their goals [Hall et al., 1980: 24].

Hall et al. (1980: 26) are very explicit about the implications of their results:

> For us, the single most important hypothesis emanating from these data is that *the degree of implementation of the innovation is different in different schools because of the actions and concerns of the principal.* At this time it appears that a most important factor to explain the quality and quantity of change in these schools is the concerns of the principals and what the principals did and did not do [italics in original].[13]

It seems, then, that the principal's interest in instruction is of critical importance (at least at the elementary school level). Corroborating this is Wellisch et al.'s (1978) in-depth study of 22 elementary schools in which they related "principal's leadership in instruction" to "school success in raising reading and math achievement of students." The sample was part of a national evaluation of school districts supported through the Emergency School Aid Act (ESAA). Teachers and principals were asked if the principal felt strongly about instruction, had definite ideas, and promoted a point of view (Wellisch et al., 1978: 215). They found that "schools where principals felt strongly about instruction were significantly more likely to show gains in achievement" (p. 216).[14] Owens and Steinhoff (1976: 152) describe an identical finding in which two matched urban schools were compared (matched on basic characteristics except that one school consistently outperformed the other in reading achievement tests). The only discernible difference between the two schools was "the leader behavior of the two principals" in which one principal played a direct role in instructional planning and the other did not.

Reinhard et al. (1980) provide a summary of another one of the recent field-based studies of the role of the principal in schools which were part of the Teacher Corps project. Field researchers conducted interviews with 21 principals, 16 project staff, and 42 teachers. The sample included 6 elementary, 4 middle, and 4 high schools in rural, suburban, and urban settings. Excerpts from the authors' summary best describe helpful and unhelpful behaviors of principals in successful and unsuccessful projects:

> The most successful projects we observed had principals who were intensely involved during the initial stage of the project's life. . . . It is the principal's efforts and behaviour during this stage (early stages) of the project that most surely affect later successes or failure. Behaviours observed and reported to us across projects varied from intense active involvement on the part of some principals to permitting planners and others to carry out a set of start-up activities and then blocking, resisting or ignoring the project and its mission.

[The principal's involvement in the implementation stage] was influenced most by the size and complexity of the project . . . in very small schools in our sample . . . principals were required, if the project were to proceed, to stay very much involved . . . in larger schools . . . the principal normally pulled away from the day-to-day involvement during this stage with few negative consequences. A pattern observed in successful projects was for the principal to remain interested and ready to problem-solve around obstacles that the project might encounter . . . [at the institutionalization stage] in almost every instance in which we studied a project that was near the end of its life or had ended, the principal decided what was to remain [Reinhard et al., 1980: 8-9].

In a series of other comments reflecting facilitative behavior of principals, Reinhard et al. (1980: 12-13) state:

The principal encouraged faculty participation in providing direction for the project, the principal explained to regular faculty how the project benefits them, the principal encouraged participation in in-service events, the principal facilitated staff visits to other schools, the principal selected unit leaders and helped them develop as a team. . . . The principal anticipated materials and equipment needs and had them on hand, the principal shortened the school day twice a month and used the time for planning, the principal found non-project funds for teachers to visit other schools.

Despite the appearance of many commonalities in the above studies (see also Lipham, 1980), we still know very little about the proportion of principals who may be engaged in KU efforts. Even more problematic is the lack of conceptualization and specification of *different* roles played by different principals *within the domain of change.* Stated another way, different change-directed behaviors may be more or less effective either in their own right, or under different conditions. These issues are addressed in the rest of this section.

Variations in the roles of principals have been examined by several other researchers. Hyde (1977) analyzed the problem-solving methods of 9 principals in the Documentation and Technical Assistance project. Of the 9 principals, 7 "managed" their problems in essentially an *administrative* manner (bureaucratic paperwork, announcements, and so on), 4 placed a major emphasis on *educational interaction* (curriculum, teaching, and the like), and 4 worked as *coordinating managers* (coordinating assistant principals, department chairpersons, and so on).[15] We can note for future reference that 3 of the 4 principals with educational interaction approaches were elementary school principals, and 3 of the 4 coordinating managers were at the high school level. Administrative preoccupation occurred equally at both levels.

Leithwood et al. (1978) observed and interviewed 27 principals from 3 school districts. They discovered 4 types of leaders—administrative (50 percent), facilitative (31 percent), directive (12 percent) and interpersonally oriented (8 percent). In other words, when it came to curriculum change, one-half the sample operated basically as administrators. In the words of the authors:

> The administrative leader is essentially a passive observer of the curriculum process in his school. He keeps track of what is going on and may make suggestions on an infrequent basis, he becomes directly involved only if there is a visible problem [Leithwood et al., 1978: 66].

Equally interesting is the distinction between facilitative and directive leaders, because *both* play an instructional change leadership role. The facilitative leaders were "highly involved in the curriculum decisions of teachers" (Leithwood et al., 1978: 70). They used a variety of strategies to organize and influence teachers. They established priorities, but "relied heavily upon teachers to influence other teachers" (p. 71). By contrast, the more directive leaders decided themselves on the nature of change, and attempted to get their teachers to follow their decisions. The distinction is important, because research on the principal which lumps together all principals who are involved in change may result in misleading or inconsistent findings. For example, in the Miles, Sullivan, et al. (1978b) case study of two open-space schools, one principal actively intervened in the implementation process, while the other did not. As it turned out, it was the nonactive principal who had the most influence on later implementation. This seems puzzling until we realize the key is the quality of activity and its relationship to the whole set of factors we have been discussing. Other data in the Miles, Sullivan, et al. study show that the active principal did not understand and was not committed to open education, and that he was not seen as supportive. The principal who was less active about implementation was more directly supportive of teachers (Miles, Sullivan, et al., 1978b: 204). The teachers in the latter school put in more of an effort, and reported behavior that was much more consistent with open education. A doctoral dissertation on the same project elaborated on these findings (Galanter, 1978). In the one school (the principal who did not directly intervene in implementation), Galanter found the principal's support affected the climate of "help giving" by teachers, and perceptions of "help received," with the latter being directly related to better program implementation. The principal contributed indirectly through his influence on the climate of support which teachers gave each other. In the second school, Galanter discovered that principal's support for the innovation was *negatively* related to implementation. This was the school where the principal supported the change, but did not understand it. Not understanding it, he could not give direct or indirect (for example, by obtaining resources) *specific implementation support.* Yet on the surface this principal could be classified as playing a direct instruction role.

Thus, active involvement and support of the principal is important for KU, but not in the form of direct imposition or naive endorsement of change. More generally, the complexities of the meaning of principal support for an innovation are considerable. We need more research which describes the *different* change roles played by principals because there are conflicting findings about how directive principals are or should be in change efforts and with what consequences.[16]

It is no theoretical and empirical accident, one would hope, that Thomas (1978) identified essentially the same three roles as did Leithwood et al., in her study of principals in the alternative school programs in Alum Rock, California, Minneapolis, Minnesota, Cincinnati, Ohio, and Eugene, Oregon. Thomas (1978: 12-13) describes the three roles:

> *The Director*—this principal makes the decisions in his school, both procedural and substantive. He will take a great interest in things affecting the classroom, such as curriculum, teaching techniques, and staff development and training, as well as those things affecting the school as a whole, such as scheduling and budgeting. Teachers in a school with this type of principal contribute to decisions affecting the classroom, but the principal retains final decision-making authority.

> *The Administrator*—this principal tends to separate procedural decisions from substantive decisions. He will give teachers a large measure of autonomy in their own classrooms—over what they teach and how they teach—but will tend to make the decisions in areas that affect the school as a whole. He will perceive his functions as distinct from those of his faculty, and will tend to identify with district management rather than with his staff.

> *Facilitator*—this principal perceives his role as one of support; his primary function will be to assist teachers in the performance of their duties. Unlike the administrator, however, this principal will be more concerned with process than with procedures. Principals who exhibit this type of behavior often perceive themselves as colleagues of their faculty, and are most apt to involve their teachers in the decision-making process.

We cannot entertain a detailed analysis of the 4 school districts, but the aggregate figures for the total 68 schools across the 4 districts are reported in Table 5.4.

Again, this is not a representative sample, and Thomas's definition of director is perhaps more comprehensive than Leithwood et al.'s. In any case, the percentage of administratively oriented principals (as perceived by teachers) is virtually the same in the two studies—half the sample.

The relationship between principal behavior and implementation of programs confirms what we know about administratively oriented principals, but the other two behavior types are more complex. Regarding the former, for example, in Minneapolis "the five schools where either a majority of the teachers did not follow the same classroom practices, or where the teachers were following classroom practices not consistent with their program label, were headed by principals who behaved primarily as administrators" (Thomas, 1978: 60). Conversely, the schools headed by directive and facilitative principals were consistent with their program labels and different from other schools in the system (that is, they implemented alternative programs as they had set out to do).

TABLE 5.4   Teacher Perception of Principal Roles

Perceived Principal Behavior Type	N	Percentage
Director	18	26.5
Administrator	33	48.5
Facilitator	17	25.0
Totals	68	100.0

SOURCE: Thomas (1978).

Analyzing the impact of directive and facilitative principals requires knowledge of different contextual conditions (lending support to Berman's 1980 claim that we need to know the particular combination of situationally specific variables in order to understand or plan for effective change). Thus:

> In Minneapolis, separate-site alternative program principals and some of their staff frequently received training in the program's philosophy and design before or concurrent with implementation of the program. In this context we found that principals who behaved as directors were just as effective at achieving program distinctiveness as were the "facilitator" principals who involved their teachers in decision-making [Thomas, 1978: 86].

It seemed that program leadership (a discernible leader responsible for the program's design and implementation) was essential, but this could be provided by the principal (as director) if "he is both willing to assume the responsibility and in agreement with the program's educational philosophy" or by the teacher or teachers if the principal (as facilitator) is willing to give them decision-making responsibility and active support (Thomas, 1978: 87).

In attempting to describe the nature of different change-related roles of principals, we are helped in a perverse way (the problem becomes more complex) by Blumberg and Greenfield's (1980) study of the effective principal. The authors sought out recommendations of the most effective principal, and selected eight principals to represent diversity (elementary/ secondary, rural/urban, male/female). All eight principals were very effective in their schools, but were quite different in their predominant approaches to their work. Blumberg and Greenfield describe the eight principals with eight different labels—the problem solver, the value-based juggler, the authentic helper, the broker, the humanist, the catalyst, the rationalist, and the politician. There were some common basic elements to their approaches. Blumberg and Greenfield (1980: 208) describe three— vision, initiative, and resources:

> Their individual commitment to the realization of a particular educational or organizational vision;
>
> Their propensity to assume the initiative and to take a proactive stance to the demands of their work environment;

Their ability to satisfy the routine organizational maintenance demands in a manner that permits them to spend most of their on-the-job time in activities directly related to the realization of their personal vision. They do not allow themselves to become consumed by second-order priorities.

The last comment is particularly revealing in light of the frequent finding that many principals are preoccupied with administrative details and routine.

The eight principals could not articulate conceptually what they did, but Blumberg and Greenfield (1980: 157) summarize the principals' orientation to KU:

All of them were very skilled at analyzing and determining the requirements of their school situations, and indicating alternative courses of action. This was, like their disposition to collect information as they moved through their work world, a continuous process. They were constantly sorting, sifting, categorizing, and interrelating phenomena bearing on the principalship.

A further relevant finding was the almost complete absence of interaction with fellow principals despite the desire for it (Blumberg and Greenfield, 1980: 168), and the fact that there was not a great deal of interaction with superiors. The words Blumberg and Greenfield most frequently use to describe the relationship of principals to those outside their schools are "isolation" and "loneliness."

Perhaps most significant to KU is the finding that, at the time of writing the results, seven of the eight principals had either left their positions or were planning to leave (either to promotion or alternative lines of work). Lipham (1980: 85) also found that the departure of the principal was *the* most important reason "for a school's abandoning an educational innovation"—echoes of Louis's (1980) recent findings in the R&D Utilization Project.

Conclusions about the
Role of the Principal in KU

As before, a mess of variables must be sorted out before we can understand the apparent inconsistencies and details of the KU behavior of principals. We might best summarize the research in three parts—what we know about principals as *users* of knowledge, what we know about them as *agents* of KU for teachers, and what we should identify as the most important research gaps.

PRINCIPALS AS KNOWLEDGE USERS

Principals on a per capita basis have more opportunity and access to external sources of knowledge than do teachers. The majority of principals however, do not seem to take advantage of, or the situation does not support them to investigate, these sources of information. The most effective principals (by reputation) do draw more extensively on external sources, and name curriculum or instruction as a higher priority. Blumberg and Greenfield (1980) also point to the enormous amount of information processing internal to the school environment which effective principals carry out. Needed research arising from these observations is listed below.

PRINCIPALS AS AGENTS OF KU

Research consistently found that a large percentage of principals (at least one-half) were preoccupied with *administrative* work and organizational maintenance activities. Of the other principals, the exact role in KU was somewhat ambiguous and variable. There was some evidence that *direct* leadership in instruction was strongly related to KU (see Wellisch et al., 1978), but other evidence that it may be dysfunctional (Leithwood et al., 1978). By contrast, *facilitative* leadership by principals was found to be effective (Leithwood et al., 1978).

These are not necessarily incompatible findings. There are at least three aspects of the problem which need to be clarified. First, we need more operational definitions of directive and facilitative modes. It is likely that different components and meanings are currently being included. For example, directive can range from having a clear instructional image to authoritarian imposition of poorly thought out or centrally directed programs. Facilitative can range from a laissez-faire relationship to teachers to one of active support. Second, it is possible (and there was some evidence to support this) that effective elementary school principals play a more direct instructional role and secondary school principals carry out a more indirect role. Third, returning to the multidimensional nature of KU, it may be that centrally derived programs are more effectively used by directive principals (when they agree with the program), and individualistic KU is better served by facilitative principals. Despite these variations, the research reviewed was clear that some form of *active* involvement and support by the principal was essential for KU by teachers. Furthermore, these principals had been effective at coping with (delegating, reprioritizing) administrative processes that preoccupied their colleagues.

Finally, the research was in agreement that the principal, in a positive or negative way, is critical—in fact, may be *the* most critical agent—for KU of teachers.

RESEARCH GAPS

Given that the principal is so important for KU, the research gaps in our knowledge are especially noteworthy.

(1) We need research which examines the daily KU behavior (according to our multiple definition) of principals. This research should incorporate relationships *internal* to the school vis-à-vis KU, relationships *external* to the school vis-à-vis KU, formal and informal KU, and innovation-focused and individual-focused KU.

(2) We need conceptualization and research on the meaning and main roles of principals (administrative, directive, facilitative, and so on) in relation to KU, including how some principals are able to prioritize or otherwise operate more effectively as KU agents. Research on effective forms of in-service training of principals as managers of change and KU is

especially needed (see Reinhard et al., 1980; Blumberg and Greenfield, 1980: 16).

(3) We need research which examines different conditions under which principals work and the consequences for the role of principals in KU— elementary/secondary differences, rural/urban, school size, centralized/ decentralized school districts all should be differentiated in carrying out the research referred to in items 1 and 2.

This has been a very lengthy section, partly in recognition of the central importance of the principal in KU, and partly because there is a good deal of current research which is worth reporting. The next five years promise to be even more fruitful for describing, understanding, and planning for more direct and effective KU roles of principals.

DISTRICT SPECIALISTS/CONSULTANTS

There has been a great deal of concentration on *external* linking agents in research over the past five years, but not much research on *internal* consultant/district specialists. Internal agents are probably more critical for KU than external consultants because of the necessity of continuous, personal interaction.[17] For this reason, the neglect of the role of internal district consultants is a serious problem. The lack of specific research prevents us from being able to describe the role of internal agents. The evidence we do have indicates that district consultants are *not* particularly effective, but that they can be, depending on how they are organized and how they carry out their work.

Leithwood et al. (1978) report that district resource staff ranked eighteenth on a list of factors that influence curriculum decisions of teachers (as reported by teachers). The authors also state that resource staff spend a substantial amount of time in direct verbal communication with teachers on an individual basis and in workshop groups. Leithwood rightly points out, as the in-service research literature shows (see Fullan, 1979) that little is known about the impact of these efforts. Leithwood et al. (1978: 74) did find that "utilizing peer dialogue to influence teachers' choice of objectives is an important strategy notably lacking among the resource teachers sampled in this study."

A study of school district consultants by Regan and Winter (forth-coming) in Ontario (N = 630) is one of the few large-scale surveys available about what district consultants do. Unfortunately, the study does not link consultant activity to KU by teachers, but the results are still instructive. The researchers identified 28 tasks. Of the highest ranked tasks (in terms of time spent) only 2 (in-service workshops and explaining curriculum guidelines) involved *group* activities directed at the dissemination of knowledge. Most of the high-ranked activities involved one-to-one inter-action. As the authors observe:

> When consultants deliver materials to teachers and counsel them about classroom program, the interaction is one to one with consul-

tants providing much individualized and personal assistance to the teachers involved. As a means of influencing teacher decisions, however, these tasks, by their very nature, limit the number of teachers whose needs/requests can be accommodated [Regan and Winter, forthcoming: 11-12].

The issues are complicated, however, because it is not clear whether the group work is effective. For example, we know that many in-service workshops are considered by teachers to be a waste of time. At this stage all we can do is raise the point that we need to examine more closely how district consultants spend their time and with what consequences. Of particular interest are models which combine group work and individualized follow-through (for one such example, see Pratt et al., 1980).

A second major finding of the Regan and Winter research was that district consultants "have had no other training/experience preparing them for consulting," other than basic teacher training and classroom teaching experience. Given the complexities of facilitating KU with large groups of teachers, this would appear to be an extremely fruitful area for further research, development, and assessment of possible training approaches and activities.

Kormos and Enns (1979), in a study of 500 teachers in 90 school boards in Ontario, found that "other teachers" was the most preferred source of help, and that school district curriculum consultants were also highly valued. External consultants (Department of Education staff, university consultants, and so on) were considered to be not at all helpful (Leithwood also found this to be the case).

Several other studies found that district staff was the most or second most useful source of information. Aoki (1977) carried out a provincewide study of social science teachers in British Columbia. Teacher opinion of the helpfulness of various groups showed that fellow teachers were rated highest (4.03 on a 5-point scale) and that district staff were rated as moderately useful (mean 2.94); department of education, teacher union, and university consultants were rated relatively low (means .156 to 2.54).

In their national survey of school superintendents, Havelock et al. (1973) report substantial use of internal district resources in the support of important innovations (and less use of external resources). In districts with less than 80,000 students, curriculum supervisors (32 percent) and district research and evaluation staff (32 percent) were used by one-third of the sample each (only teachers and in-service training were used more, 47 percent and 43 percent, respectively). In larger districts—above 80,000—curriculum supervisors and R&E staff were used by the majority of cases and as extensively as any other category (61 percent each for supervisor, R&E staff, and in-service, and 55 percent for teachers). It will also be recalled that Orlich et al. (1976) found that district curriculum coordinators were the second most identified group of sources for innovation for principals.

The Rand Change Agent Study provides confirmation that local resource personnel are essential for implementation and continuation of changes. McLaughlin and Marsh (1978) contend that even a carefully planned staff training program cannot anticipate the nature, timing, or individual needs of in-service assistance as they relate to classroom problems. On-line assistance by local resource personnel or consultants was necessary. They also point out that the *amount* of assistance is less important than the *quality:* "Good consultants helped by providing concrete practical advice to project teachers . . . ineffective consultants often furnished advice that was too abstract to be useful." They add that specific skill training, while necessary, is not sufficient for conceptual clarity regarding complex new ideas:

> Conceptual clarity may be fostered—but cannot be assured—by specific project goal statements or by the use of packaged materials or by lectures from outside consultants. The conceptual clarity critical to project success and continuation must be achieved during the process of implementation [McLaughlin and Marsh, 1978: 80].

The problem, however, is that internal agents (or anyone else for that matter) do not know how to set up a process of continuous interaction with teachers. Lippitt (1979: 262) sums up this aspect of the Experimental Schools (ES) project in rural districts:

> Just as the projects lack clarity in role definition for ES/Washington and its external consultants, so there is a lack of clarity in the roles of the internal agents. Staff members who were assigned to coordinate, facilitate, train or support were almost always carrying a combination of supervisory, administrative, monitoring and consultative duties. Overlapping responsibilities made it difficult to gain trust or credibility or legitimacy as a consultative helper and supporter.

Miles et al. (1978c) in investigating the planning and implementation of new schools, report two main findings pertinent to this discussion. First, district and school administrators steadfastly refused to take advantage of matching funds from the project to bring in external consultant help on the grounds that "district resource staff could provide all the help that was needed." Second, district resource staff were not in fact used to provide continuous (or in many cases any) ongoing help for teachers struggling with implementing new ideas.

Where district staff have been effective, it has been where districts set up a *deliberate, organized system* of local support. For example, the use of internal district personnel (in combination with external resources) is particularly well described and documented in the Jefferson County districtwide elementary science curriculum innovation (Pratt et al., 1980; Hall et al., 1980; Loucks and Melle, 1980).

Daft and Becker's (1978) study is one of the few which have highlighted the possible critical role of district support staff:

> The presence of a special group playing a coordinating role in the high school districts seems to make a real and positive difference to the number of innovations adopted [p. 155].

They proceed to explain why district support staff were so important:

> The coordinators arranged frequent meetings with small groups of teachers and department heads to exchange ideas and information. The coordinators also did the research work and proposal preparation for ideas the teachers wanted approved by the district superintendent and school board. Coordinators seldom proposed their own ideas for adoption. Coordinators also did extensive research work and proposal preparation for top administrators, thereby facilitating the trickle-down of administrative changes as well [p. 156].

Berman and McLaughlin (1979: 53) elaborate on the importance of school district "infrastructure for change," which they describe in one school district which reflected the most advanced state of development:

> Their [district curriculum specialists'] primary tasks are to assist teachers and principals by providing pedagogic leadership, being on call to deal with special problems, and stimulating grass roots innovation. Specialists are expected to keep abreast of the latest research and theory developments and to share these developments with Sandwood staff. The assistant superintendent for the Programs Division summed up the role of the specialists in the following way:

> "We expect them to be in tune with national developments; they're supposed to stir things up. This whole operation is geared toward destroying the status quo and the specialists are critical to this effort."

Fullan et al.'s (1978) case study of Adam's County confirms the importance of the establishment of a resource unit within the district which is integrated with ongoing program needs. External consultants are used, but mainly to train inside resource people (that is, as trainers of trainers). The resource system is clearly under the control of the district.

Organized and coordinated district efforts, however, seem to be the exception rather than the rule. Howey and Joyce (1978) in the United States and Nash and Ireland (1979) in Canada both found that there was a distinct lack of planning, coordination, job focus, and use of knowledge and principles of program planning and implementation in district inservice programs. For example, Nash and Ireland found only 3 cases out of 40 districts in which there was any relationship between stated curriculum priorities and in-service programs for curriculum implementation, and found only 2 school systems which had a planned sequence at the district and school levels to facilitate the use of a selected curriculum change. Even more revealing is Lyon et al.'s (1979) comprehensive survey of the 750 districts in the United States having 10,000 students or more. Among their findings: (1) only 43 percent of the districts have a central office for program evaluation; (2) 50 percent of the districts do not spend *any* money on consultants; (3) in those districts with evaluation units, achievement testing is the dominant topic; and (4) in those districts there are limited attempts to use evaluative data for instructional improvement.

In summary, we can draw four main conclusions about the role of district consultants:

(1) There is limited research and underestimation of the potential role of district resource staff.

(2) District staff are crucial for introducing new ideas and facilitating ongoing interaction, dialogue, help, and support.

(3) While district support staff are crucial, they are infrequently effective because (a) as individuals they often carry out their work on a one-to-one or one-to-group workshop basis, rather than on the basis of an approach geared to the management of collective change. Stated another way, district consultants themselves are not good knowledge utilizers when it comes to theories of implementation (they may be good KUs in regard to curriculum content); (b) districts have not set up organized program units as part and parcel of system planning and implementation.

(4) One of the greatest gaps in our knowledge is that we have only research on district specialists as a *category*. In reality, there are many different roles and forms of organization across districts. For example, it seems that in some cases district specialists may include administrators such as curriculum directors, while in others they may be excluded. In addition, there are a variety of staff specialists: some are general curriculum consultants, others are subject-area consultants, and still others provide special services in counseling, special education, and so on. In short, more specific research is needed to describe and examine the major line and staff roles commonly included under the general label of district specialists.

SUPERINTENDENTS

All major research on educational innovation has shown that the role of the chief executive officer at the school district is critical for major change in the system. Almost twenty years ago Brickell stated the case as follows:

New types of instructional programs are introduced by administrators. Contrary to general opinion, teachers are not change agents for instructional innovations of major scope. Implication: To disseminate new types of instructional programs, it will be necessary to convince administrators of their value.

Instructional changes which call for significant new ways of using professional talent, drawing upon instructional resources, allocating physical facilities, scheduling instructional time or altering physical space . . . depend almost exclusively upon administrative initiative.

The superintendent may not be—and frequently is not—the original source of interest in a new type of program, but unless he gives it his attention and actively promotes its use, it will not come into being [Brickell, 1961: 22-24; cited in Carlson, 1972].

However, we now know that superintendent "adoption" of new programs often bears little resemblance to "use" of these programs by teachers. When use is examined, the role of the superintendent is still critical, but it takes on a much more specific form. The research literature shows that *general* support or endorsement of a change means very little for subsequent implementation. For example, superintendents who adopt innovations for opportunistic reasons (bureaucratic, political, symbolic) do not pay attention to follow-up procedures necessary to support utilization (see Berman and McLaughlin, 1979, and the case studies by Gross et al., 1971; Smith and Keith, 1971; Wolcott, 1977). In a follow-up case study of school districts, Berman and McLaughlin (1979: 37-47) describe in concise detail how one superintendent "transformed the organization." They show a picture of active and specific involvement in changing the climate and programs in the district:

> He [the superintendent] visited every school in the district within his first year as superintendent, referred to teachers as "faculty," supported them during a teachers' strike, and invited their ideas on what needed to be changed. These activities were important as symbolic acts. Yet they would have been hollow had they not been backed by a changed administrative receptivity. The district demonstrated receptivity by creating incentives for teachers to take a chance on something new [Berman and McLaughlin, 1979: 43].

The Fullan et al. (1978) case study of Adam's County documents another example of the conceptual and interactional skills needed by a superintendent, if he or she is to be successful in bringing about change.

Deal and Nutt (1979) draw essentially the same conclusions from their review of administrators' behavior in the ten districts in the Experimental Schools Program for Rural America. Conceptual skills and specific forms of involvement are summarized in four main implications formulated by Deal and Nutt (1979: 7-8):

> First, administrators need to understand how educational organizations work.

> Second, administrators need to understand the process of change.

> Third, administrators need to be familiar with other change efforts.

> Fourth, administrators need guidelines that can be used to apply past lessons and general principles to specific change projects.

Deal and Nutt provide numerous illustrations of the pitfalls and problems of attempting change without an adequate understanding of how organizations work, and without specific behaviors which arise from this understanding. The conceptions and skills need to be as sophisticated as the complexity of the process of multiple organizational change demands, which is one way of explaining why KU does not work effectively in most cases.

One of the more interesting discussions we should consider is Rosenblum and Louis's (1981) investigation of the effect on implementation of superintendent authority on the one hand, and classroom autonomy of the teacher on the other. They found that superintendent authority (number of decision areas influenced by the superintendent) was *positively* associated with implementation, and classroom autonomy (number of classroom decisions that the teacher can make on his or her own) was *negatively* related to implementation. Rosenblum and Louis suggest that a degree of centralization is necessary for implementation of comprehensive changes (across schools) and that strong norms of classroom autonomy may actually inhibit organizational and districtwide changes—a finding somewhat similar to Daft and Becker's (1978) conclusion about adoption of college-oriented versus high-school-oriented innovations.

On the other hand, in Havelock et al.'s (1973) national survey, superintendents reported that they themselves were key participating factors in only 2 percent of the major innovations adopted in their districts.[18] Yet superintendents are making the major decisions in some districts, as Rosenblum and Louis (1981) and Barrows (1980) have found, and as several case studies cited above have shown.

One of the main problems in this whole area of research is the lack of any thorough research on the role of the superintendent. Almost no large-scale research on the superintendency and innovation has been conducted since Carlson's (1972) work, which reports on superintendency behaviour in the years 1958-1963.[19] Not only is this research outdated, but it did not, of course, benefit from subsequent research which emphasizes the necessity of doing follow-up beyond adoption to utilization.

One of the very few recent studies comes from a survey of school superintendents in New York State, which is not directly on KU (Volp and Heifetz, 1980). Part of the problem with these results is that they are based on only a 45 percent (N = 96) return rate (total N = 212), of which none of the six major metropolitan areas responded. There were some findings directly relevant to our quest. In listing the "most pressing issues locally," fiscal matters (99 percent), declining enrollment (44 percent), curriculum issues (39 percent) and student attitudes/achievement (36 percent) were the most frequently mentioned matters, stated in response to an open-ended question. The last two issues bear directly on the question of KU for school improvement and, as indicated, a little over one-third of the principals spontaneously mentioned the issues of student achievement and curriculum.

Reinforcing the importance of my earlier mention of collective bargaining, the growth of teacher unionism was the most frequently mentioned major change over the decade of 1969-1979 (mentioned by 39 percent of the sample; the next most frequently stated problem was cited by only 20 percent—the emergence of more vocal citizenry). The other findings are worth noting. There was near consensus (over 80 percent agreed) in response to three questions in which superintendents reported that (1) they cooperate willingly with researchers attempting to advance knowledge in the field; (2) they secure outside help from experts when curriculum changes are being considered; and (3) they read major journals. These results are inconsistent with some earlier findings reported (such as the Miles et al., 1978c, report that districts did not want to use outside help even when matching funds were offered). Further, in commenting on needed training elements for superintendents, the respondents mentioned personnel relations (41 percent), business and finance (19 percent), and law (14 percent) most frequently. None mentioned management of change or curriculum issues—the closest category was 11 percent who referred to general course work in administration and leadership. This is reminiscent of Reinhard et al.'s (1980) investigation of the role of the principal, in which they explicitly asked about in-service needs of the principals. They experienced mostly non-responses and conclude:

> This lack of reference to the staff development and professional growth of the administrator . . . probably mirrors the lack of thought and emphasis that has been given to what administrators need [Reinhard et al., 1980: 15].

In summary, the findings on the role of the superintendent in KU are inconsistent, ad hoc, and incomplete. A series of observations and recommendations can best describe what we know and need to know.

(1) As a generalization, it can be suggested that superintendents are important either for initiating or supporting KU efforts in school districts.

(2) This generalization does not take us very far. We really do not know what superintendents do. Under what conditions do superintendents initiate or support? What is meant by initiating, and by facilitating? How do superintendents in different size school districts vary in their roles? What is their relationship to, and what are the roles of, other central office administrators and specialists (assistant superintendent, curriculum director, district consultants, and so on)? One would expect enormous differences in urban districts of 150,000 students compared to small town and rural districts with a few thousand students—the latter of which make up the large majority of school districts.[20] Nor do we know the organizational structure, roles, and procedures as they vary across districts.

(3) In summarizing the research needs in relation to the superintendency and KU, the following points should be made:

(a) We need good, basic, demographically representative studies of the role of superintendents in KU. These should include how superintendents as individuals use knowledge in their work, and how they relate to other central staff and to schools in initiating, supporting, or facilitating KU. Variations in the nature of the role of superintendents at each of the three main phases of mobilization, implementation, and institutionalization should be examined carefully, as well as the proportion of superintendents who are involved in KU efforts at school districts. As with the principal, studies are needed of how effective superintendents manage conflicts and role overload in order to devote some attention to KU for school improvement. Size, type of school district, and geographic region would be the main bases of framing the sample.

(b) Similar research should be carried out on the immediate subordinates of the superintendent (assistant and deputy superintendents, curriculum directors). These central administrators play a more direct role in KU in many districts, and little is known about the work they do, their relationship to super-intendents, and so on. Not the least of the problem is to come to grips with the myriad of titles and organizational structures, so that one can compare practices across districts.

CONCLUSIONS: RESEARCH AGENDA

Let me first comment on the limitations of the review, and then turn to the main conclusions arising from this chapter. This review was confined to the role of individuals and groups internal to the school district. The other chapters in this volume all address issues which are related to the findings in this chapter. Even at the district level, I did not examine the role of the community. It is rare that the community is an "agent" of KU, but it does sometimes happen. More frequently the community reacts to activities of the school or school district, but sometimes it acts as an indirect cause of KU (as when it applies pressure for reform—see Berman and McLaughlin, 1979). In any case, the role of the community should be examined in its own right.

As to the issues directly addressed in this chapter, the following conclusions seem warranted. In general, the meaning and variety of KU has not been defined or examined separately in each of the sections on individual agents. Sometimes the research refers to the use of a broad-based program; other times individual use of information is the focus. More conceptualization and corresponding research is needed on the *meaning and outcomes* of different types of KU (as suggested in the first section) in relation to the major actors at the district level.

Taking each of the key groups in turn, the review identified several gaps which could form the basis of a research agenda.

Teachers

What is the average or daily KU behavior of teachers, especially in relation to possibly "hidden" forms of KU that occur during individual teacher planning and weekly interaction among teachers? Such research should examine the roles that teachers play, both in collective efforts at program change, and as individuals using information in their daily decision making. On neither count do we know very much about the mobilization phase (that is, for collective efforts, the activities which lead up to adoption of new knowledge and for individuals, the behavior associated with individual planning and decision making). Out of this research we should obtain a better sense of the extent to which teachers are engaged in new KU, and the factors which facilitate or inhibit these activities.

Certain contextual variables should be superimposed on the above research. Teachers at the elementary, junior high, and secondary schools should be examined separately, including the *organizational processes* related to KU as they may vary by school level. District type (rural, suburban, urban), school size, and the role of collective bargaining and teacher unionism should also be part of the basic set of factors investigated.

Principals

As stated earlier, we need two types of research on the role of the principal. The first type concerns the principal as *knowledge user*. To what extent and how do individual principals access and use knowledge external to the school and internal to it? The second type of research refers to the role of the principal as an *agent of KU* within the school. Better conceptualization and empirical demographics are needed on the administrative, directive, and facilitative roles discussed earlier. What are these roles and how do they vary empirically? It is particularly important that the different forms of KU be examined—for example, the role of the principal as an agent for collective program change and his or her role as an agent of individual KU by teachers. In addition to discovering the nature and distribution of these roles by principals, it will also be necessary to compare situations according to the major contextual factors named above—elementary/secondary, rural/urban/suburban, and school size. In carrying out this research, one should be alert to discovering what causes principals to behave differently across different contexts, and within identical contexts. The availability of and efficacy of different preservice and in-service professional development experiences for principals in relation to managing and facilitating KU should also be examined carefully. Finally, the rate and impact of principal turnover on KU should be directly investigated.

District Consultants/Specialists

There is such limited research on the role of district staff that almost anything would make a contribution. It would be most helpful if some basic descriptive research were to be carried out in which the different roles and organizational structures were identified across school districts of different type, size, region, and so on. In addition to identifying the various roles, research is needed on how these people go about their work, and with what consequences for KU at the principal and teacher levels. Conceptual and empirical work is needed on what characterizes these different roles (for example, the type of work started by Butler and Paisley, 1978; for external linking agents, see also Lyon et al., 1979).

In summary, the review of evidence indicated that district staff were frequently important sources of KU for teachers, but we know almost nothing about what these people do that is helpful (and what is not), nor do we know how prevalent the different behaviors are. Rate and impact of turnover and longevity of positions (some district positions are temporary or short-term) should be included in these studies.

Superintendents

Needed research on the superintendent was summarized at the end of the previous section and can be briefly restated. I observed that there have not been any large-scale investigations of what it is that superintendents do. Such research should include how the role of superintendents varies according to size and type of district; how superintendents think about and use knowledge as individuals; how they facilitate, direct, support, inhibit, or block KU by others in their districts; what barriers they experience in carrying out their roles; how they organize and relate to others in the district office, the school board, and individual schools; and what the career patterns and turnover roles are of superintendents in different settings. Similar research should be conducted on other central district administrators (assistant superintendents, curriculum directors, and the like).

The main assumption in this chapter has been that individuals and groups internal to the district are *the* most important agents for KU. This corresponds to the main findings in the implementation literature, that the characteristics of local settings dominate what happens to new ideas (see Berman and McLaughlin, 1978b). If this is the case, the review has identified some critical research gaps, since research knowledge about the KU roles of personnel internal to the district is very underdeveloped. Current emphases in the research literature on federal policies and programs (for example, Raizen, 1979; Turnbull, 1980) and external linking agents (Louis, 1980) are important, but should be counterbalanced by equally intensive research on teachers, principals, district staff, and superintendents within school districts.

NOTES

1. The remaining factor, 1–relevance, was based on a single item, and was not used by Weiss on the truth and utility tests.

2. Thanks to Matt Miles for calling this work to my attention.

3. This is not to say that specific, validated products are not effective—they frequently are (Emrick and Peterson, 1978; Louis, 1980).

4. This factor will be examined in detail in the fourth and sixth sections of this chapter. We will find that the specific supportive role of administrators is not so clearly known.

5. I do not examine the role of school communities in this review. They usually do not function as "agents" of KU, but they can put pressure on schools to "do something" about a problem. They can also be instrumental in providing support or opposition for particular innovative efforts. For excellent descriptions and analyses of the roles of individual communities in relation to change programs, see Berman and McLaughlin (1979), Armor et al. (1976), and Miles, Sullivan, et al. (1978b).

6. One indication that this area is still not recognized is that there was only one session on collective bargaining at the 1980 AERA meeting; none of the papers presented related even remotely to program change, innovation, KU, or the like.

7. The small sample and three-part rating scale using general categories (often, sometimes, and so on) do not warrant confident interpretation of the strength and meaning of the data.

8. I cite a similar finding in the fourth section of this chapter, on principals' use of textbook salespeople (Ruff and Orlich, 1974).

9. Weiss and Bucuvalas (1980) have referred to this process among policy makers as "knowledge creep and decision accretion."

10. To mention just a few of the researchers who are concentrating on the role of the principal: Gene Hall and associates, R&D Center, University of Texas; Ken Leithwood, OISE; Dan Lortie, University of Chicago; James Molitor and Karen Louis, Abt. Deal and Rallis (1980: 222) point to current commissioned research on the role of the principal and use of research in Teacher Corps projects, and to the work of Dell Hymes on ethnographic monitoring of principals.

11. The same, of course, applies to teacher in-service (Fullan, 1979).

12. This is not to say that principals are unimportant. Indeed, their lack of prominence in KU may be one of the main causes of *lack of implementation* of KU by teachers.

13. Hall et al. have recently launched a new, more systematic investigation of the role of the principal and change.

14. Successful achievement was defined in terms of student gains, according to national percentiles. On a 4-point scale of principal interest in instruction, principals in successful schools had a median of 2.9 compared to 1.0 in nonsuccessful schools.

15. The three categories were not mutually exclusive. It was possible to operate simultaneously in more than one mode as long as a major emphasis was placed on the mode (no principals showed more than two modes).

16. There are two facets to this problem. One involves obtaining a clearer distinction between directive and facilitative. The other involves identifying the conditions under which one may be more effective than the other.

17. External agents have been effective when they have worked intensively with teachers (Sieber et al., 1972; Emrick et al., 1977; Stallings, 1979; Berman and McLaughlin, 1977), but, in general, external agents are probably more instrumental for adoption than for utilization. (See Lippitt, 1979, and Rosenblum and Louis, 1981, for discussions about the limitations of external consultants in the rural experimental schools project.)

18. But they may have been key supporting or facilitating factors.

19. There are probably other studies which I have failed to locate, but I doubt if they answer the questions posed at the end of this section.

20. The Department of Health, Education, and Welfare's *Digest of Educational Statistics* shows that 26 percent of all U.S. districts have fewer than 1,000 students and only 1.2 percent have more than 25,000 students.

6

EDUCATIONAL CHANGE

An Implementation Paradigm

Paul Berman

Research on knowledge utilization and educational change is undergoing a dramatic transition. The shared understanding among researchers about how knowledge utilization and educational change should be defined and analyzed—in short, the predominant research paradigm—is different today than it was twenty years ago. Though these differences arise partly from altered political and cultural contexts, they also, and more fundamentally, reflect two decades of research findings that seriously challenge views prevalent during the fifties. This chapter contends that the accumulation of empirical studies points toward new ways of understanding, thinking about, and doing research on knowledge utilization and educational change.

It is sometimes hard to appreciate how substantial progress at the paradigmatic levels has been because the state of the art at the level of specific findings and of practical advice appears to be in disarray. The past two decades' studies have indeed produced a multitude of findings, but these findings generally are not comparable and the accumulation of specific hypotheses that have been subjected to testing has not occurred. If one naively assumes that all research is equally credible—as many reviews unfortunately do—the list of variables based on research or pseudoresearch numbers in the hundreds (see Zaltman et al., 1977; Glaser, 1976). So many variables are little better, and may be worse, than having no research results. And the prevalence of contradictory findings only heightens this confusion. What does the poor researcher—let alone the practitioner or policy maker—do when faced with some studies that "demonstrate" that, for example, staff participation helps to produce successful innovations and other studies "prove" the opposite? Researchers have little choice but to start carte blanche and find out for themselves whether participation matters and, if so, in what direction. Yet, in doing so, researchers suspect their research will not settle the question, just as preceding research had not. There are at least five reasons for this noncumulative hodge-podge.

First, studies have different objectives, ranging from generation of academic theory to evaluation of programs for government agencies to facilitation of intervention activities (such as OD work). The objectives profoundly affect research design, focus, sample, presentation of results, and so on, and thus lead to noncomparability of studies and findings. Similarly, researchers approach studies from different perspectives, as the chapter by House argues, which influence their work as well as their interpretations.

Second, the measurement and indeed conception of independent and dependent variables are seldom the same in the research reviewed here. For example, the concept of "success" has been defined so differently by researchers that one researcher might measure success where another might record failure for the same innovation. Fullan and Pomfret (1977) convincingly argue that studies can be categorized into whether they use a fidelity definition of success or an adaptation definition; such differences may be more attributable to researchers' theoretical orientations than to any objective situation. Independent variables such as participation also have discrepant meanings in different studies and often are not defined precisely (Giacquinta, 1973). With variables differing widely in both conceptualization and operationalization, the assessment of findings across studies is tenuous.[1]

Third, the unit of analysis—such as individual (teacher and so on), school, school district, local system—also differs and often renders cross-study judgments problematic. For example, "adoption of an innovation" can have different meanings if the unit of analysis is a teacher in one case and a school district in another. Moreover, the unit of observation may differ, despite similar units of analysis. For example, it is common, though usually poor methodology, for data collected from teachers to be averaged to the school level, ignoring variation across teachers within schools. The comparison of findings from such aggregated data to findings from data collected at the school level is often questionable.[2]

Fourth, many studies inadvertently confound analysis of process with analysis of variation. Mohr (1977) presents a persuasive case that process and variance analyses represent different approaches to theory development and that mixing them leads to "confusion and stagnation" of theory development.

For example, Charters and Pellegrin's (1972) case study of differentiated staffing in four high schools describes the process of a failure to implement an innovation—namely, limited initial planning, frustration during early implementation, conflict, and abandonment of the innovation. When Charters and Pellegrin conclude that successful innovation requires explicit planning, they implicitly treat one of the events, the lack of planning, as if it were a variable. But their case study data did not have variation in either the dependent variable (the projects were all abandoned) or the independent variable (the projects all had little planning). Should their inference about planning, and those of other case studies which arrive at a similar inference (for example, see Wacaster, 1975; Gross et al., 1971; Smith and Keith, 1971), be considered reliable? Despite the insight these case studies provide about the *process* of change, their *variance* type conclusions cannot be completely trusted. They dealt with failure, not success, and it is surely specious to reason about the causes or conditions of success from nonsuccess. To draw inferences about success based on evidence of failure is particularly mischievous in educational change, because we have learned a simple, if painful, lesson: There are many ways to fail, but few to succeed.

Moreover, assuming that process studies of *success* were to show that preplanning is linked to success, it would not be logically true that preplanning invariably leads to success, nor that it increases the probability of success more than marginally. Process theory has a "pull-type" causality (Mohr, 1977), in which the final effect (such as successful implementation) implies that a prior event (such as preplanning) occurred. Such information is important for theory and practice, but it should not be confused with a "push-type" causality from variance analysis in which variation in an independent variable (such as amount or type of preplanning) is used to explain variation in the dependent effect (such as successful implementation). It is thus possible for process analysis to find that a variable (that is, an event) is "important" to success in a particular case and for variance analysis to find that the same variable is not statistically "significant" over many cases. These findings would not be contradictory, just different.[3]

The point of this extended argument is that both process and variance theory are needed; they lead, however, to different types of inferences, so that those who equate results from one type to results from the other harm both.

The fifth reason for the state of confusion about educational change is ultimately most fundamental and is the one upon which this chapter focuses: The very inconsistency of research findings over the last decade may reflect educational reality, not simply inadequate methodology. Empirical studies have exposed how complex educational change is, and have consistently challenged the possibility of simple, comparable generalizations. For reasons discussed in the remainder of this chapter, research on educational change may no longer justifiably be able to test general hypotheses of a simple form—for example, the New Math or computer assisted instruction, or the Bank Street Model, or a particular curriculum revision, or the like—improve student outcomes, all other things being equal. Such hypotheses often may be essentially meaningless, not just true or false. No wonder many researchers and policy makers reared in the experimental tradition see confusion rather than progress.

But progress at the paradigmatic level is real. Significant advances have occurred in ways of thinking about educational change despite the often tedious and contradictory details of research findings. Research is at a new plateau, in which the simpler views prevalent during the fifties are being recast in more complex images of how school districts respond to pressures for change. The current confusion, inconsistency, and impracticality of research findings is symptomatic of this shift in paradigms.[4]

This chapter reviews research on educational change. The literature is too voluminous to cover exhaustively. Fortunately, several excellent reviews of specific research findings exist and will be used throughout this essay. My aim is not an inventory of results because of the contradictory and unstable nature of findings, as discussed above. Instead, this chapter describes the nature of the paradigm shift. The next section briefly identifies assumptions underlying research and policy during the fifties and sixties and suggests how research of the late sixties and early seventies challenged these assumptions; the third section proposes three meta-propositions that encapsulate a new, emergent paradigm. The chapter concludes with some reflections on future research.[5]

UNFREEZING THE
TECHNOLOGICAL-EXPERIMENTAL PARADIGM

Before proceeding to assess the current state of the art, I shall briefly identify assumptions underlying much of the research during the 1950s, 1960s, and early 1970s on knowledge utilization and educational change. These assumptions are not easy to locate because research and policy were so intertwined. Educational policy makers at local as well as federal levels looked to scientific knowledge, research and development, and systematic analysis (House, 1974), and they as well as researchers often seemed to act as if their prescriptions had a sound research basis.[6] They generally did not. Giacquinta's (1973: 178) assessment of this period is none too harsh:

> Most empirical reports reviewed were atheoretical efforts to make changes, not efforts to test theories of change. The absence of critical attention to the methodological and statistical procedures used in these studies reflects this emphasis on precipitating change rather than studying it.

Moreover, many researchers and evaluators seemed to share—or at least, by their silence, to consent to—the perspective prevalent among policy makers: a reform urgency, a faith in central direction from the federal government, a belief in the benefits of research and development strategies, and an optimism about innovation.

This chapter's task, however, is to identify the predominant research paradigm of the period, rather than to explain its policy context. The reader should nonetheless be advised that research can be more easily separated from policy now than it could then. Consequently, policy perspectives will encroach on our presentation.

A major portion of the research-policy community seemed to believe that educational change was a problem amenable to technological solutions in the following sense: Schooling—or, more precisely, dominant aspects of the teaching-learning process—was thought to encompass tasks that could be described and replicated, akin to some procedures and practices in agriculture, medicine, or manufacturing. With research knowledge as the base, developers could produce descriptions of new tasks for teachers. These descriptions, which I shall call a *technology*, could be embedded in an overall curriculum change, an innovative project, or a school improvement program. Using experimental or quasi-experimental methods, researchers and evaluators could test to determine which technologies—innovations, projects, models, educational methods, and so on—were most effective at the local level. There was a belief, in summary, that schooling could be improved if tested and replicable products (technologies) were disseminated widely to schools: Practitioners would adopt these technologies if they had information about them and resources to install them.[7]

I shall call the research paradigm implicit in the above policy-research perspective the technological-experimental (TE) paradigm. The policy belief that developers could produce replicable products had its counterpart in a corresponding research assumption that new technologies were *fixed and constant treatments,* as required by experimental design. Research conducted in the 1960s and early 1970s provided evidence that seriously challenged this assumption. The next section reviews this research, but a brief sketch of the policy-research issues may illuminate the assumption of a fixed and constant treatment.

The Head Start and Follow-Through planned variation experiments illustrate the prevailing view in the late 1960s that research and evaluation could choose superior technologies by employing experimental or quasi-experimental methods.[8] Though the actual research design was complicated, the basic methodological idea involved in the planned variation approach seemed simple enough: Select several promising educational models that address the problems of educationally disadvantaged children but vary in their programmatic content (that is, their technologies); apply the treatments in a number of school settings under experimental conditions, or as close to experimental conditions as the researchers can realize; measure student performance before and after treatments and compare results across treatment and control groups. In this way, successful educational models could be identified.

However, evaluators of Head Start and Follow-Through did not find a consistently effective model or variation. Many reasons have been advanced for this non-result, including a variety of methodological criticisms of the research design and how it and the federal experiment were executed. This chapter's concern, however, is with an explanation that has consequences beyond the programmatic issues of Head Start and Follow-Through or the administrative feasibility of federal experiments in the social arena. In the words of one of the model developers (Weikart and Banet, 1975), there was a "gap between a model-as-conceived and a model-as-implemented." The *same* model was often implemented *differently* in different classrooms, and implemented models also varied over time in the same settings.[9] This unplanned variation is surely an important explanation of why Head Start evaluators sometimes found more variation in the student outcomes from classroom to classroom nominally using the same model than they did among classrooms using different models (Lukas and Wohlleb, 1973).[10] Treatments were not fixed and constant, contrary to the assumption implicit in the TE paradigm.

This example from a planned experimental program shows how researchers and policy makers assumed new technolgies were the key to school improvements. A focus on the technology itself also characterized the vast majority of change programs that were not designed or evaluated as experiments. Stated in nonexperimental terms, many policy makers, practitioners, and researchers assumed that educational change was a *technologically dominant* process, in which the results of an innovation depended primarily on the quality of the educational method—often thought of as a replicable product—not on its user or setting.[11]

Research and policy consequently focused on how to get users to adopt "validated" innovations. It was assumed that *adoption* of successfully demonstrated projects was a sufficient as well as a necessary condition for improvement.

Federal policies of disseminating information about new practices, providing seed-money funds to stimulate adoptions, promoting demonstration projects to show off exemplary innovations, and establishing ways of "validating" practices all seemed perfectly sensible and in accord with the primacy of adoption.[12] Following traditions from technologically dominant fields such as agriculture, researchers or academics presented models for policy makers and practitioners that focused on (a) attributes of innovations that made them more likely to be adopted, and (b) characteristics of school districts that made them more likely to adopt innovations sooner.

Carlson's (1965b) work is perhaps the best example of research that studied characteristics of early or frequent adopters of innovations. This research emphasized the individual as adopter, rather than the school district organization. By so doing, it missed much of the organizational dynamics of adoption, as subsequent researchers have pointed out in no uncertain terms (Baldridge, 1975). I shall return shortly to how a shift to an organization focus radically changed the context of inquiry into educational change.

But the early adoption studies committed a more serious conceptual error. They told only part, perhaps the least important part, of a complex story. They allowed the reader to assume that adoption was tantamount to execution, so that a school district recorded as having adopted the New Math, for example, could be assumed to be using it in pretty much the way it was intended by its developers. Sarason's (1971) insightful reflections on his experience with the New Math and other change efforts showed that they were hardly implemented at all. Smith and Keith's (1971) in-depth case study of an organizational change effort in an

elementary school showed that considerable general agreement existed at
the time of adoption, but nonetheless the innovation was abandoned.
Gross et al. (1971) document a similar failure of implementation after
adoption, as do a number of other case studies (see Charters and Pellegrin,
1972; Wacaster, 1975; Bredo and Bredo, 1975). The next section cites
further evidence that shows that the mere adoption of an innovation
should not be counted as a successful innovation.

Where does this leave more recent studies of adoption? The works of
Baldridge (1975), Corwin (1975), and Daft and Becker (1978) explicitly
acknowledge that they are studying innovativeness—the propensity to
adopt innovations—and not equating such studies with successful
innovation. They do, in fact, attempt to relate broader organizational and
contextual variables to innovativeness. For example, Baldridge (1975) used
aggregate data from Illinois and from a Stanford Center study of schools in
the San Francisco Bay Area to argue that organizational and environmental variables matter. Corwin (1975) found that teacher characteristics
within schools (including the number of teachers having graduate degrees)
explained 12 percent of the variance in innovativeness at 131 schools. Daft
and Becker's (1978) thoughtful study of 13 innovative high schools also
suggested that professionalism of the staff is related to innovativeness.
They further indicate that other organizational and environmental variables affect innovativeness, but they went considerably further than Baldridge and Corwin in examining the adoption process and in conceptualizing it in empirically based terms.

In conclusion, studying innovativeness per se enables researchers to
compare similar studies in other fields.[13] Findings about innovativeness
can be misleading, however, because in the context of educational change
they represent partial analysis of an integral process. Until they are
embedded in the full process of educational change, the "findings" must
be treated cautiously.

Finally, this brief review of the technological-experimental paradigm—
and its slow unfreezing—would be incomplete if I ignored the peculiar use
of various models of educational change—such as Research, Development,
and Diffusion; Problem Solving; Linkage, and so on.[14] The formulations
typical of this genre were presumably descriptive, though description was
seldom based on research findings and the line between description and
prescription was never clearly drawn (as Sieber, 1974, observes). For
present purposes—identifying research beliefs rather than policy perspectives—the distinctive feature of these models was their rationalization of
school district behavior vis-à-vis the change process. That is, the following
types of assumptions were made by different writers at different times: (1)
school officials adopt innovations to pursue educational goals; (2) they are
motivated by a "performance gap," which is a discrepancy between
district needs and accomplishments (Zaltman et al., 1977); (3) they
actively search for alternative innovations to fill this gap; (4) they discard
innovations that are not effective; (5) the school district organization acts
as coherent system; and (6) the process of educational change is a linear

sequence of stages. The evidence reviewed in the next section clearly disputes the law-like status of these assumptions, as we shall see.

More pointedly, despite their shaky research foundations, these models shared a common faith with many experimental and correlational studies: They accepted the possibility and necessity of empirical generalizations, *a la* propositions in the physical sciences, that could be formed into predictive models or general explanatory theories of school district behavior. This belief was consistent with the predilection of federal and state policy toward uniform incentives, rules, and guidelines for school districts. Once again, the evidence presented in the next section questions whether the search for nomothetic propositions and the research strategy of testing for simple hypotheses are likely to be fruitful.

In summary, the TE paradigm assumed that educational innovations were like technologies that could be replicated faithfully by school districts: that innovations could be evaluated as if they were fixed and constant treatments; that the process of educational change was technologically dominant and could be described rationalistically; that adoption— often conceived of in individual instead of organizational terms—was a sufficient condition for change; and that general models composed of law-like propositions could be developed to describe school district behavior in response to change efforts.

Federal and state policies that accepted these assumptions have often been ineffective, and empirical research has found these premises to be questionable. The conditions thus seem ripe for an unfreezing of the old paradigm and the emergence of a new, more realistic understanding of the process of educational change. The next section explores this prospect.

META-PROPOSITIONS OF A NEW PARADIGM

The focus of research studies in the last five or perhaps ten years has shifted dramatically. Research has changed emphasis from analysis of replicable products to studies of process; from fixed and constant treatments to broad evaluations; from the primacy of adoption to consideration of the whole change process; from a quest for superior technologies to an exploration of organizational and contextual explanations of change; from the formulation of general rationalistic models of school district behavior to empirical, albeit often particularistic, findings.

These changes have challenged the validity of the technological-experimental paradigm, but articulation of a new paradigm has proceeded haltingly. Researchers, and surely policy makers, are understandably reluctant to abandon the comforts of coherent principles—as in the TE paradigm—for complex and amorphous statements that promise merely more understanding. The case for a new paradigm is pressing, however, because the more research we do, the more confused we seem to be at the level of specific findings, as the introduction noted. If we continue to design research and interpret findings using technological-experimental lenses, I fear more contradictions and less credible results.[15]

This section offers elements of a paradigm that reflects current research assumptions and tendencies, as well as cumulative findings. It is less complete than desirable, but I hope it provides material for others to build on.

The constituents of a research paradigm are shared understandings among researchers about how problems in their field of study (in this case, educational change) should be defined and approached. It thus includes conceptualizations, frameworks for analysis, partial theories, identification of key variables and events, and so on. The new paradigm will be characterized by three meta-propositions. They are called propositions to denote their empirical foundation. The prefix "meta" serves to warn the reader that these statements refer to ways of thinking about educational change, not specific hypotheses.

Implementation-Dominance

Meta-Proposition 1:   *Educational change typically involves an implementation-dominant process.*

As defined earlier, a technologically dominant process is a fairly predictable change process, the outcomes of which are determined primarily by the characteristics of the adopted technology (educational treatment, innovation, school improvement effort, change policy, and so on). A new type of seed in agriculture, a birth control pill in health care, or a new dye-stamping machine in a factory illustrate common situations of technological-dominance, for when the seed is planted, the pill swallowed, or the machine introduced, effects follow automatically. In these cases, the interaction between a technology and its setting—which defines implementation—is reasonably certain, or at least predictable within probability estimates.[16]

The contrasting ideal type is an implementation-dominant process in which events occurring after the adoption of a technology determine outcomes to a large extent, and these events cannot be accurately forecast from the content of the technology itself.

Many promising educational technologies are themselves uncertain, or, as Glennan et al. (1978) put it, they are not "well in hand." Open education, differentiated staffing, alternative schools, and team teaching, for instance, are intrinsically indeterminate technologies for two reasons: One, they require significant change in individual behavior, organizational roles, or school standard operating procedures; and two, the development of the new behavior, roles, and procedures imply considerable discretion on the part of users and, hence, cannot be fully specified in advance. The outcomes of change efforts in these cases would be uncertain regardless of the organizational setting within which they are implemented.

In contrast, some adopted technologies can be highly certain. This chapter calls a technology certain insofar as it can be divided and subdivided into tasks that can be replicated faithfully by users regardless of their idiosyncrasies. Minor alterations in curriculum or school procedure often fit this definition, as do such "innovative projects" as field visits to the zoo (funded by the former Title III of the Elementary and Secondary Education Act) or career education innovations consisting of placement tests and reading materials (funded by the Vocational Education Act, Part D, Exemplary Programs). Major federal programs also can have components whose change requirements are determinate. For example, Title I's monitoring and accounting procedures, which are assigned to insure the required disbursement of funds to schools with economically disadvantaged students, consists of predetermined rules that do not imply significant role or organizational change on the part of teachers or administrators. The certainty of these types of change efforts notwithstanding, their implementation can be rocky. Procedures for the use of Title I funds illustrate the point. The program initially experienced overt resistance and symbolic compliance from school districts, despite the ease with which these procedures could be specified and replicated (see Murphy, 1971, for an account of Title I's early years). But school districts by and large have now accepted the requirements; implementation is routine after thirteen years of federal persistence (Kirst and Jung, 1980).

In short, the interaction between an educational technology and its setting can be uncertain because of the technology's characteristics or how it is used. Whatever the cause of uncertainty, this chapter calls the resulting process an implementation-dominant process.

Cumulative empirical findings from the last decade's research, as discussed in this section, strongly support an implementation-dominant view of educational change (excluding change efforts that are essentially minor or mechanical alterations in curriculum, school procedures, or administrative rules). The best research and evaluation, whether qualitative or quantitative, suggest that how an innovation is implemented may be as important to outcomes as its initial technology. The innovation's substance surely constrains what happens after adoption—thus, adopted reading programs usually wind up being about reading, and bilingual education programs turn out to involve bilingual instruction. Wide variation nonetheless can occur within the constraints implied by the initial content of an adopted innovation. Let us review evidence for these assertions as they have evolved over the past decade or so of research.

A variety of carefully documented case studies identified implementation problems, rather than content, as reasons for failures of innovations (Smith and Keith, 1971; Sarason, 1971; Gross et al., 1971; Charters and Pellegrin, 1972; Wacaster, 1975; Bentzen, 1974; Bredo and Bredo, 1975). The general findings from these process studies are supported by variance studies. Thus, Goodlad et al.'s (1970) study involving 158 classrooms of 67 schools in 26 districts provides quantitative evidence of the importance of implementation: In almost 60 percent of the classrooms there was no implementation of the innovations involved, and in only 5 classrooms was the innovation implemented to a high degree. More reliable and direct quantitative evidence comes from several large-scale evaluation studies. If the technology (or treatment or innovation) were dominant, one would expect evaluations to show that the same innovation produces similar results regardless of the site in which it is installed. Such was not the case in the Head Start or in the Follow-Through programs discussed earlier (Lukas and Wohlleb, 1973; Lukas, 1975; Weikart and Banet, 1975; Elmore, 1978).

An evaluation of OE's Project Information Packages (PIPs) presents further compelling evidence about implementation because it examined innovations that were specified to a greater extent than most of the educational models in the planned variation experiments (Stearns and Norwood, 1977). The PIPs program initially involved (a) the selection of locally developed projects that had been successful in their originating sites and "validated" as exemplary by the Education Division's Joint Dissemination Review Panel, and (b) the development of these innovations into six packages that could be disseminated to new sites. The evaluation by SRI was of a two-year field test of PIPs at nineteen sites. Although at least five of the six packages were highly specified as to procedure, management, and materials, the evaluation found results that differed from site to site for the same package and did not replicate the highly successful results in the originating site. The very specificity of the PIPs treatment (unlike the more diffuse treatments examined in the case study work) provided an acid test of whether educational innovations that had been successful elsewhere led to a fairly predictable, successful outcome: they did not.

Still other evidence comes from the Rand evaluation of 293 innovations in over 1000 schools in a nationwide sample. Because of the large sample size and the wide range of innovations included in the study, there was an opportunity to determine how much project outcomes were affected by the content of the innovations, which were funded by four federal programs providing school districts with "seed money" for innovations. The researchers found that the content of the innovations had, at best, minor effects on outcomes (Berman and Pauly, 1975).

All the studies cited above, as well as others, suggest that outcomes of a change effort depend critically on how it is carried out. The dynamics of the process can be further expressed by the following corollary: *The interaction of an educational innovation with its setting (that is, its implementation) generally results in changes in the initially conceived innovation.* The empirical evidence for this phenomenon, which has been called the *mutation* phenomenon (Berman and M.Laughlin, 1974), is quite strong. The Head Start planned variation evaluation examined 12 educational models or technologies installed in 31 sites that included 100 classrooms and found that the *same* model was implemented *differently* by teachers within the same site (Lukas and Wohlleb, 1973). The Follow-Through evaluation found similar results (Elmore, 1978), much to the dismay of federal sponsors. It could be argued that these changes or adaptations of the innovation during implementation are the result of the vague or unspecific quality of the innovation. Thus, it may not be surprising that Shipman's (1974) report on the highly unspecific innovative process for curriculum revision in 38 mostly secondary schools in Great Britain indicated wide variation from school to school. Nor is it surprising that the Rand study of a Los Angeles Unified School District reading program, in which schools were given a general mandate with broad guidelines about developing individualized instruction, resulted in wide variation from school to school and class to class (Armor et al., 1976). But, as discussed above, the Stearns and Norwood (1977) evaluation of the PIPs field test also found considerable mutation, despite the highly specific nature of the packaged innovations.

Accepting educational change as an implementation-dominant process that intrinsically involves adaptation of the innovation to its setting implies a need to rethink many aspects of research as well as policy and practice. It is beyond the scope of this essay to do more than briefly mention one implication of particular importance for the conduct of research.

Researchers should not expect a faithful replication of innovations. Variation, not replication, is to be expected (House, 1976). Consequently, the notion of what constitutes a "successful" innovation requires—and is undergoing—drastic revision. It makes sense in a technologically dominant process—that is, a process in which the replication of a technology would produce a desirable result with a high degree of certainty—to consider the innovation to be successful if the installed innovation replicates the originally conceived innovation with a high degree of fidelity.[17] The same logic does not apply for an implementation-dominant process. In this situation, the attempt to obtain high fidelity may *create* implementation problems, not overcome them (Berman, 1980a). Instead of measuring success in terms of fidelity per se, alternative definitions based on the expectation that adaptation will—and ought to—take place are appropriate. (See Fullan and Pomfret, 1977, for an extended discussion of a fidelity versus an adaptation perspective).

At the present time, there are no commonly accepted measures of successful innovation based on an adaptation perspective. The adaptation perspective may imply that different definitions of success are necessary under different circumstances, a point discussed subsequently. Though the empirical studies cited throughout this review generally do not use common conceptualizations—let alone similar measurements—of success, they all employ: (1) multiple measures of the effects of change efforts, including measures of outcomes not intended or anticipated in the original goals; and (2) measures of the process per se, in addition to—often in place of—impact measures.[18]

Loosely Coupled Process

Meta-Proposition 2:   *The educational change process consists of three complex organizational subprocesses—mobilization, implementation and institutionalization—that are loosely, not linearly, coupled.*

This proposition constitutes a broad framework for the analysis of change processes in educational as well as in other organizations (Hage and Aiken, 1970; Zaltman et al., 1973). The terms "subprocess," "organizational," and "loosely coupled" were chosen to symbolize a shift away from linear models prevalent under the technological-experimental paradigm. The meaning of these terms will be discussed first, followed by a synthesis of evolving views about each subprocess.[19]

The term "subprocess" is used rather than the more common "stage" for several reasons. First, "stage" often connotes a rational planning process, as suggested in the earlier works on planned organizational change (Bennis, 1966; Bennis et al., 1969; Havelock, 1969; Clark and Guba, 1965). Whether school districts in fact follow a rational sequence of stages requires an empirical answer. The evidence suggests they generally do not, as shall be detailed shortly. Dropping the term "stage" may help rid the language of research of an implicit rational bias.

Second, "stage" implies a linear metaphor: that the process of change steps from discrete stage to discrete stage. The process attendant to a change effort is, of course, a continuous—that is, linear—time-ordered flow of events involving many people and many interactions. However, researchers do and must impose a theoretical structure on these events. Research statements or propositions about the process of change are, therefore, theoretical constructs and should be judged on their value to the scientific undertaking. The notions of stages and a sequence of linearly connected stages as descriptive of the process of change are thus theoretical constructs, not actual events. This linear construct may have been useful in reference to problems of diffusion of technology to individual users (Rogers and Shoemaker, 1971).[20] It is less germane when the "users" are complex organizations, like school districts, and the technology is uncertain (House, 1971).

For example, Daft and Becker's (1978) analysis of innovative high schools found that the adoption decision generally served to legitimize choices made during proposal generation, and proposal generation itself consisted of interactions among staff and administrators. In other words, the significant part of the subprocess here called mobilization resided, for Daft and Baker's sample, in a complex iterative process, not a linear one, the fruition of which was signaled by a formal decision to adopt an innovation. Miles et al.'s (1978) case studies of new schools show that planning, considered here a part of mobilization, continued throughout the innovative process and was inextricably related to implementation. Finally, to cite an example that encompasses all three subprocesses, Berman and McLaughlin (1977) examined case study and interview material about the fate of over 200 innovations several years after the close of federal funds. They found that those projects that were being institutionalized went through a process of remobilization, and, moreover, steps toward institutionalization had been taken from the projects' outset. In short, though neither these nor other studies provide a convincing theory of the subprocesses or of the overall change process, the linear stage model no longer seems adequate.

Finally, the term subprocesses is chosen because it connotes a flow of events punctuated by choice opportunities. This image is a more realistic view of organizational change than the usual decision-making or problem-solving metaphors in which decisions cause or are caused by other decisions. For example, some commentators discuss the decision to search for an innovation, leading to a decision to adopt, followed by a series of implementation decisions, resulting in a decision to continue or discontinue a project. This perspective suggests more or less rational decisions, usually by key officials, and thus introduces a top-down bias (as opposed to a user view) of change. The example cited earlier of the Daft and Becker description of proposal generation indicates that adoption decisions in their innovative high schools were almost a formality set in motion by other forces that cannot be easily described in decision-making terms. Similarly, Berman and McLaughlin's discussion of institutionalization leaves little doubt that a decision to continue or not continue an innovation is often not made—innovations just fade away—and, when a decision is made, it may have little to do with the resulting reality. The term process or subprocess may, in short, help avoid an overly simplistic decision-making view.

If the process of educational change is not usefully described as a linearly related sequence of stages based on discrete decisions, how should it be characterized, and should it be divided into subprocesses?

Educational change can be conceptualized as a process within the school district considered as an organizational system.[21] The state of an organization (such as a school district) at any time can be described by the routine behaviors of its members. From this system's perspective, organizational change is a change in state of the system—that is, it is a change in routine behaviors. The process of change consists of the events and activities as the system moves from one state to another. Empirical observation suggests the division into three subprocesses—research indicates that different actors engage in different activities during the three subprocesses, and that these activities serve different functions for the organizational system undergoing change. The three subprocesses can be defined in system terms as follows.

Mobilization is the process whereby the system prepares for a change in state. Mobilization includes the decision to adopt a change effort or innovation, but it neither begins nor ends with this decision. Mobilization activities occur intermittently—before, during, and after activities associated with implementation and institutionalization. This chapter uses the label "mobilization," instead of such terms as adoption or initiation, to connote (a) a nonsequential, organizational process, not an individual decision; (b) an assumption that the school district is an ongoing system that selects and uses an innovation, rather than the technological assumption in which an innovation is seen as causing the system to change; and (c) a highly political and conflictual process, not the cold, rational image unintentionally conveyed by the technology paradigm.

Implementation is the process whereby the system attempts a change in state—that is, it comprises the activities of users attempting to use an innovative idea. Institutionalization is the process whereby the system stabilizes a change in state. Because a state change consists of alteration in routine behavior, institutionalization involves activities relevant to establishing new routines. In a widely cited article, Weick (1976) suggests that school districts are loosely coupled organizations in the sense that teachers work more or less autonomously from other teachers and administrators and that schools work more or less autonomously from each other and from school district administration. As a consequence of loose coupling, implementation can occur in different parts of the system (for example, in a teacher, a grade level, or a school) at different times. Institutionalization can therefore be interspersed with implementation, as research cited later shows.

Now that the mobilization, implementation, and institutionalization have been defined, research relevant to each subprocess will be discussed in turn.

Mobilization. Mobilization encompasses an innovation's "beginnings" in a school district. Some innovations have straightforward beginnings, easily traced from problem to innovative idea for solution to adoption. For many, perhaps most innovations, however, no simple or single decision flow can be found. Moreover, the process seems to vary for different types of innovations and different contexts. Consequently, different authors identify and emphasize various pieces of what is coming to be regarded as an exceedingly complex phenomenon.

For example, Daft and Becker's (1978) study of innovation adoption in 13 suburban high schools adds a prior stage to "adoption"—namely, "proposal generation." Rosenblum and Louis's (1981) study of 10 rural school districts includes a stage called "readiness," which they postulate to be prior to "initiation." Emrick et al.'s (1977) study of the National Diffusion Network divides the beginning into initial awareness, secondary awareness, and preimplementation training. Miles et al.'s (1978) study of 5 new schools within existing school districts refers to planning, which includes much of what is often included in initiation or in the subprocess here called mobilization. These theoretical and semantic distinctions make sense in the context of each study cited, which, unfortunately, creates confusion for developing a common paradigm. The Daft and Becker study deals with highly innovative high schools in which staff in fact generated proposals; the Rosenblum and Louis analysis was part of an evaluation of a federal program that provided money to selected rural districts so that they would introduce change, and the readiness issue was implicit in the program design; the Emrick distinctions follow the steps in the National Diffusion Network's strategy; and Miles et al.'s investigation of the creation of new schools naturally focuses on the extensive planning involved in such activities. In short, these discrepant conceptualizations reflect different realities that frustrate generalization.

Nonetheless, these studies describe a similar phenomenon in terms of the functioning of a school district as a system attempting change. The various activities described above comprise different organizational aspects of the system in preparation for change in the routine behavior of its members, which is the meaning of mobilization as defined earlier. A broad review of the literature suggests that the activities that constitute mobilization can be grouped into four functions: (1) policy image development, (2) planning, (3) internal support generation, and (4) external support generation. Except for planning, the names of these functions may seem strange. They are used to purge research language of its overly rationalistic bias.

The first-mentioned function, policy image development, is not necessarily first chronologically. It involves a series of activities that the literature tends to describe in rational terms—such as awareness of a problem, perception of performance gap, needs assessment, search for solution, idea generation, proposal generation, and so on (Rogers, 1962; Rogers and Shoemaker, 1971; Zaltman et al., 1973; Zaltman et al., 1977). Yet the few studies that have actually described how and why school districts attempt innovation reveal a far more complicated, more disorderly, and more varied picture.

For example, Berman and McLaughlin (1975a) found little evidence of search behavior in the adoption of innovations supported by four federal seed money programs. On the contrary, most projects in their sample were started opportunistically in order to benefit from federal largesse, not to solve pressing educational problems. Several studies have shown that political and bureaucratic considerations play a bigger role in the selection of proposals to innovate, or in the acceptance of projects from outside the district, than do educational considerations (House, 1974; Kent, in Herriott and Gross, 1979; Cohen and Farrar, 1977).

Moreover, the often unchallenged assumption that perceived problems—economic, political, bureaucratic, or educational—generate solutions in the form of the adoption of innovations is open to serious question. Cohen et al.'s (1972) investigation of higher education lead them to postulate that organizations such as universities are "organized anarchies" characterized by problematic preferences, unclear technology, and fluid participation of key actors in decision processes. These characteristics are similar to those described for elementary and secondary education (Miles, 1967; Hawley, 1975; Elboim-Dror, 1973; Berman and McLaughlin, 1979). In an organized anarchy, problems and solutions (that is, innovative ideas) are not neatly linked: Problems may not elicit search for solutions, and indeed, innovative ideas may "search" for problems to justify their adoption. Daft and Becker (1978) argue that this organized anarchy model provides a useful interpretation of how innovations were proposed and accepted in their sample of high schools.

The evidence seems clear that the old perception of how innovations are adopted is inaccurate both in its rational bias and in its assumption that only one kind of process exists. Solutions lead to problems in some cases—for example, in the internally generated proposals for innovations described by Daft and Becker, and in the sometimes serious, often opportunistic proposals to obtain federal funds studied by Berman and McLaughlin—whereas problems, particularly those derived from externally imposed conditions (Stiles and Robinson, 1973) can also stimulate solutions, though less frequently than imagined. Moreover, numerous examples in the literature of direct federal or state involvement, as in the Alum

Rock Voucher experiment (Levinson, 1978), the Rural Experimental Schools Program (Herriott and Gross, 1979), the National Diffusion Network (Emrick et al., 1977), Project Information Packages (Stearns and Norwood, 1977), and the Pilot State Dissemination Program (Sieber et al., 1972), suggest complex processes in which solutions define problems and problems mold, if not actively seek, solutions.

The organizational literature outside of education supports this view of a complex process involving much rationalization and less rationality than usually postulated (Weick, 1969). One of the few empirical studies of such decisions concludes that the "process is characterized by novelty, complexity, and openendedness, by the fact that the organization usually begins with little understanding of the decision situation it faces or the route to its solution, and only a vague idea of what the solution might be" (Mintzberg et al., 1976).

Stepping back from the details of this process, it appears that a major function of these activities is the formation of a policy image of a future state of affairs that organizational researchers would like to see realized (House, 1978). In other words, the decision to adopt an innovation, to seek funds to innovate, and all associated activities define what a school district intends to do and communicates these intentions to various audiences, both external and internal to the district. Policy image formation is not necessarily a self-conscious effort, and the emergent image is often understood only in retrospect (Weick, 1969). Moreover, the policy image evolves and develops over time, sometimes throughout the life of a specific project (Rogers and Eveland, 1977). For example, Smith and Keith's (1971) research illustrates that organizational members can hold different images of the meaning, intent, and substance of an innovation, and that the continuing lack of a common image can lead to frustration, conflict, and failure. Moore et al.'s (1977) in-depth study of six successful technical assistance groups and Miles et al.'s (1978) study of five new schools [22] suggest that successful innovations develop a policy image that becomes commonly held by project participants.

A second activity during mobilization is planning. Though planning represents the seemingly "rational" aspect of mobilization—proposal writing, assignment of personnel, allocation of resources, setting of objectives, and the like—it once again does not proceed in an orderly, linear fashion (Sarason, 1972). Miles et al.'s study of new schools is one of the few studies that systematically investigates planning, and their reflection on the case study material speaks for itself: "Many important decisions seemed to flash by in seconds . . . 'rationality' turned out to include many non-rational features . . . political motives were implicit in much planner/ implementer behavior" (Miles et al., 1978). Moreover, Miles et al. observed that planning continued throughout the project's life and plans themselves constantly evolved. Indeed, they suggest that "meta-planning"—that is, designing the planning process—also develops and evolves in more effective projects. Little can be concluded of a propositional nature from the empirical work accomplished thus far about planning, except that virtually every writer believes that school district planning is extremely difficult to do well and is inadequate as currently practiced.

The remaining activities of mobilization concern the generation of external and internal support for an innovation. Though relatively little research has been devoted to understanding how support is generated from local and larger communities, there is a consensus that such support, the lack of it, or indeed active opposition has profound effects on the change process. For example, despite the mandate for parent involvement in many federal and state programs, the evidence is overwhelming that parents and community members are seldom involved in innovative efforts (see Cohen and Farrar, 1977; Paul, 1977). Nonetheless, when community opposition is aroused, innovations can be seriously affected (Paul, 1977). And when community support is actively engaged the prospects for implementation are enhanced (Herriott and Hodgkins, 1969; Moore et al. 1977). More broadly speaking, the prevalence and importance of political interactions between school districts and outside sources of support clearly emerges in a wide variety of case study analyses (Smith and Keith, 1971; Gideonse in Herriott and Gross, 1979; Miles et al., 1978; Moore et al., 1977).

The generation of internal support—that is, support of board members, district officials, teachers, and administrators—for an innovation is complex for two reasons. First of all, individuals hold different views about an innovation's educational value and its impact on themselves. These differences in perceived value and personal consequences are often cited as reasons for "resistance to change" (Gross et al., 1971; Zaltman et al., 1977; Gross, in Herriott and Gross, 1979). Secondly, generating support for a project is complex because school districts are loosely coupled organizations, as Weick (1976) observes. Thus, Berman and McLaughlin (1977) argue that innovations can be supported by central district administrators independently of support from school staff, and vice versa. They suggest that high levels of support from both the district level and the actual users of an innovation are necessary to successful innovations. Fullan (1974), Fullan and Pomfret (1977), and Paul (1977) review evidence from various studies supporting part or all of this proposition.[23]

Though the four activities which make up mobilization—policy image development, planning, external support generation, and internal support generation—have been discussed separately, they occur or fail to occur together. Research on mobilization has been quite limited, and much more needs to be done to understand how this subprocess works under different conditions.

Implementation. Unlike mobilization, the subprocess of implementation has been studied extensively during the past decade.[24] Stepping back from the details and richness of these studies, it is apparent that no single generic process encompasses the implementation experiences described in the literature. Cases that trace successful implementation do not present mirror images of cases that document unsuccessful processes. Successful processes do not seem robust, but rather consist of fragile concatenations of events, people, and ideas at the right times in the right places. A single missing, misplaced, or mistimed element seems likely to collapse the delicate "assembly" leading to success (Bardach, 1977). Consequently, there are many ways to fail and few ways to succeed.

Though a single theory of implementation is thus unlikely, some significant characterizations of this subprocess have been advanced that help interpret the disparate details described by case materials.

There are three models of implementation representing the ways researchers currently view the process. The *managerial* model sees implementation as a process whereby administrators attempt to overcome resistance to change (engendered before, during, or after mobilization) and take actions that enable implementors to do their job (such as gathering resources, buffering teachers from community forces or from state and federal officials, or providing training). The managerial perspective is evident, for example, in the writings of Gross (Gross et al., 1971; Gross, in Herriott and Gross, 1979) and Zaltman (Zaltman et al., 1977), as well as in the literature on educational administration. The *learning* model views implementation as a process whereby individuals, generally teachers, attempt to learn new behavior and the organization, generally schools and districts, tries to learn how to change its coordination, control, and information systems. Some of the work of Miles (1964), Sarason (1971), Goodlad (1975), Shipman (1974), Elliott and Adelman (1974), and Moore et al. (1977), take the learning perspective at either the individual, the organizational, or both levels. The *bargaining* model views implementation as a conflictual process in which the bargaining among various stakeholders defines what is done and how. Though the bargaining perspective is most often employed to describe relationships between school district administration and "external" forces (such as community, school board members, federal and state officials; as in Wirt and Kirst, 1972; Iannocone and Lutz, 1970; House, 1974), it has also been used to describe or interpret decisions made during implementation (for example, see Baldridge, 1975; Levinson, 1976; Cohen and Farrar, 1977).

The managerial, learning, and bargaining models direct research attention to different aspects of implementation. Consequently, the findings from studies taking these perspectives can be incompatible, as are their measures of effective implementation. Despite these difficulties, it seems unlikely that only one model can capture the multiplicity of events and activities characteristic of implementation.

Regardless of the model used, two activities—adaptation and clarification—are frequently identified as fundamental attributes of implementation.

The importance of adaptation was recognized early in studies of educational change (for example, Miles, 1964), but its full significance for understanding implementation was not identified until empirical studies began to reveal the mutation phenomeonon discussed previously. Berman and McLaughlin (1974, 1975a, 1978b) argue that adaptation is so pervasive that implementation processes can be classified in terms of adaptation at the user's level. They propose that the initial innovation can be adapted to classroom, school, and district, and that routine organizational behavior of teachers, principals, and officials can be adapted to the innovation. If only the innovation is changed significantly, but not individual and institutional behavior, they call the process cooptation. If neither the innovation nor the organization adapts significantly, the process is one of two kinds—a symbolic implementation where everything remains essentially the same (Charter and Jones, 1973), or a breakdown in operations of the type described by such case studies as Smith and Keith (1971) Gross et al. (1971), Wacaster (1975), and Bredo and Bredo (1975). If both innovation and organization adapt, the process is called *mutual adaptation.* Berman and McLaughlin propose that effectively implemented innovations are characterized by mutual adaptation.

What is the current status of the mutual adaptation hypothesis and of adaptation more generally? Berman and McLaughlin did not define these theoretical concepts in precise operational terms and the measurements they employed were weak. Subsequent research has explored the concepts in more depth and attempted to unravel the research—and policy—conundrums they imply. Stearns and Norwood (1977), Emrick et al. (1977), and Moore et al. (1977) are among the major studies that both confirm and give richer and more differentiated meaning to mutual adaptation. In particular, the Moore et al. study of technical assistance groups documents how mutual adaptation occurs. They also raise important issues about whether mutual adaptation can occur without negating the "core" ideas defining an innovation. Other researchers have tackled the difficult operational problems of measuring adaptation and mutual adaptation. For example, Rogers et al. (1977), working on innovations in nonschool public organizations, developed a measurement of the degree of "re-invention"— which is synonymous to adaptation—for a computer processing information system. The measurement consists of determining how much the applied system deviates from a "main line," or core description, of the innovative idea. Rogers et al. do not measure mutual adaptation, however, and consequently their work still focuses on the innovation, and deviations from it, as the issues to be examined. Moreover, their attempts to use similar methods of analysis on the Dial-a-Ride system were not as fruitful (Rogers, 1978). Hall and Loucks's (1977) efforts to measure the "levels of use" of an innovation are directed toward a fidelity notion of effective implementation. Nonetheless, their measurements can be reinterpreted as indicating how much adaptation occurs in actual practice as an innovation is implemented; they do not directly measure mutual adaptation. Despite these and other serious operational difficulties, the concepts of adaptation and mutual adaptation seem established as aspects of implementation.

Clarification, the second concept that characterizes activities during implementation, is less firmly established than adaptation. Many researchers have suggested that users need to be clear about the change effort if it is to be effectively implemented (for example, Gross et al., 1971). Earlier research took the position that roles, tasks, and plans should be specified ahead of time, before implementation. However, recent research has taken a different and more sophisticated turn on this issue.

For example, Berman and McLaughlin (1977) analyzed responses of 1072 teachers to survey questions about innovations and found specificity of goals was correlated with effective implementation of the innovations. However, they found that "specificity" was not invariably achieved *prior to* implementation. On the contrary, highly structured innovations involv-

ing only a small amount of change (such as computer-assisted instruction)
required specificity before implementation, but less structured innovations
(such as open education) achieved specificity during implementation. For
the latter type of innovation, prespecification could be damaging.[25]
Moreover, Berman and McLaughlin's case study analysis of unstructured
innovations suggested that achieving specificity involved learn-by-doing
activities in which individuals became clearer about the project's philosophy as well as its operational objectives. In other words, clarification is a
process whereby each user develops his or her understanding of—and belief
in—the innovation as it evolves *during* implementation. Insofar as staff
become clear in their own terms, specification can occur almost as a post
hoc codification of shared understanding among participants. The Moore
et al. (1977) analysis showed how clarification can proceed from initial
vague ideas to specific tasks and roles with the help of outside assistance.
Rogers et al.'s (1977) research on an information-processing technique
offers an explicit conceptual formulation of clarification activities, which
they call specification. They trace decisions about the technology's operational definition and its use and find that "the tendency is to move toward
greater specification of innovation, but this process is by no means simple
and linear" (Rogers et al., 1977: 14).[26]

In summary, implementation consists of the adaptation of an innovative idea to its institutional setting. Effective user implementation seems to
be characterized by mutual adaptation at the user level and by the staff's
clarification of the innovation's goals and required role behaviors. The
managerial model of implementation views adaptation and clarification as
tasks that project and administrative leadership must handle, channel, and
control; the learning model sees them as necessary aspects of individual
growth and organizational development; the bargaining model assumes
that these activities are a by-product of conflict resolution. No single
theory of implementation will probably be able to capture these multiple
realities.

Institutionalization. This subprocess has received scant research attention in either educational or broader organizational research. The notion
that institutionalization—that is, stabilizing change within an organization—is fundamental to the full process of change is an old concept in
sociology (Janowitz, 1971). Lewin's (1958) work in social psychology of
individuals and small groups specified a refreezing stage after unfreezing of
old patterns and learning of new ones. However, Hage and Aiken's (1970)
analysis of routinization—following initiation and implementation—updated the concept and placed it squarely in an organizational context.

As for empirical studies, the Ford Foundation's (1972) report on their
experience with "lighthouse" projects showed few lasting effects after the
foundation's grants had terminated. Berman and Pauly (1975) and Berman
and McLaughlin (1977) studied the institutionalization of about 300
innovations funded by federal "seed money" and found that most innovations, even successfully implemented ones, did not last long after the end
of federal funding or were so emasculated that their impact on the school

district and students were minimal. Yin et al. (1978) examined hard technologies installed in a variety of public organizations and came to a more optimistic assessment of the routinization of innovations in his sample. Rosenblum and Louis (1981) analyzed 10 rural school district participants in the Rural Experimental School Program to determine the degree of routinization of changes associated with the program. Miles et al. (1978) studied the stabilization of new schools and found stabilization to be a complex and fragile process, as did Rogers et al.'s (1977) study of 53 adoptions of a computer information processing system installed in public organizations.[27]

Though this literature does little more than scratch the surface of an important research and policy problem, it does suggest several concepts that future inquiries might pursue. Berman and McLaughlin (1977) contend that loose coupling within school districts implies that institutionalization involves different processes at the user and district levels. Teachers and school staff need to *assimilate* what they have learned during implementation; districts need to *incorporate* new routines engendered by the innovative process into decision making about budget, personnel, support services, and instruction. Berman and McLaughlin argue that change developed during implementation is unstable, isolated, or merely symbolic unless *both* assimilation and incorporation occur to a high degree.

Whereas Berman and McLaughlin's measurements of incorporation are weak, Yin et al.'s (1978) analysis of hard technologies offers the possibility of powerful operational measurements of this aspect of institutionalization. He proposes that routinization (that is, incorporation) can be measured by the number of organizational passages (which are discrete decisions marking the transition of an innovation from one status to another with the organization) and cycles (such as budget reviews) that a new practice survives.

The subprocess of institutionalization, like mobilization and implementation, cannot be described in simple rational terms. The district's loose coupling requires complex conceptualizations and measurements. Moreover, case study materials in Berman and McLaughlin (1977) and in Herriott and Gross (1979) describe incorporation as a highly political process, involving bargaining within and outside of the district, in which the innovation's educational success plays a distinctly secondary role.

The Conditional Nature of Explanation and Prediction

Meta-Proposition 3: *Outcomes of educational change efforts tend to be context-dependent and time-dependent.*

The preceding meta-propositions concern the educational change process qua process, whereas Meta-Proposition 3 refers to how researchers are beginning to—or should—think about explaining variation in outcomes. The process statements are related to the variance statement above, for Meta-Propositions 1 and 2 imply Meta-Proposition 3, as this section explicates in detail.

Meta-Proposition 3 requires considerable discussion. Before entering into this discussion, however, an alternative formulation might clarify the statement. Research traditionally aims to identify factors affecting outcomes of educational change efforts, to determine the direction of their effects, and to estimate how much each factor influences outcomes. The usual form of a hypothesis is: a standard variation in factor X produces b variation independent variable Y, *all other things being equal.*

However, in research on educational change, hypotheses of this simple type have seldom been confirmed by successive studies. This section contends that one among several reasons for such inconsistency is that the *ceteris paribus* is too far reaching; rather, statements of the following form seem better suited to the complexity of educational change: a standard variation in factor X produces b variation in dependent variable Y, *under certain specified conditions of time and place.*[28] In plain English, Meta-Proposition 3 says that findings may be better stated conditionally so that results are known to apply to particular situations and in particular organizational settings.

This section contends that the past decade's research convincingly points to the necessity for such conditional explanations of variation in educational outcomes. The small number of research findings and studies cast in conditional terms will be reviewed, and a categorization for sorting factors into a conditional format will be advanced.

Inconsistencies and the Anatomy of Conditions. Averch et al.'s (1974) comprehensive review of the literature found no consistent relationship between educational treatment and outcomes. That is, some studies showed that a treatment had positive effects, whereas other studies did not. This lack of consistency is in fact a finding, a significant—indeed consistent—finding of two decades of research. Similarly, Cronbach (1975) reviewed studies involving aptitude-treatment interactions and found widely inconsistent results. He attributes this instability to the extreme variation of interaction effects from school setting to school setting and from time to time.[29] Inconsistency of findings is not limited to relationships between "treatments" and student outcomes: It also is found for the effects of organizational variables (such as participation) on a broad range of measurements of success of innovative efforts in both educational settings and other organizational contexts (Downs and Mohr, 1976; Berman, 1978a, 1978b).

Though inconsistency is commonplace, its causes could be many, including weak measurements and ambiguous conceptualizations. Aside from these problems, which are not this chapter's focus, context dependency can lead to inconsistent results in several ways.

First, if the context matters, does *not* vary *within* the sample of sites for each of two studies, and does vary *between* the two studies, then findings from the two studies can disagree. For example, the Rand study of 293 educational innovations found active involvement of principals and teacher participation in project decisions to enhance implementation, whereas the Rosenblum and Louis (1981) study of districts involved in the

Rural Experimental Schools program found various measures of participation to have no significant or a somewhat negative effect on implementation. Ignoring, for the sake of this illustration, differences of conceptualization and measurement between the studies,[30] the opposite conclusions may be attributable to different contexts: The latter study dealt with rural schools, and the former examined a national sample containing few rural schools.

It would have been appropriate for Rosenblum and Louis to have stated their finding in conditional terms of the form: *In rural districts,* participation of teachers and involvement of principals does not affect success. The Rand researchers also could have examined whether participation affected success differently in the few rural districts in their sample compared to nonrural districts. If they had, they might have found that participation did not matter in rural and did matter in nonrural areas, thereby resolving the discrepancy between the studies and adding to the validity of each. (Of course, they might have found that participation was important in both rural and non-rural districts.)

Second, if the context matters, varies within the sample of a particular study, and the variation is not taken into account, the study may produce spurious results. In other words, the study is making the error of not specifying the context as a variable. Such "specification errors" can, among other possibilities, wash out the effects of a variable. For example, if participation has a positive effect in nonrural areas and a negative effect in rural areas, if the proportion of rural and nonrural sites in a sample is about the same, and if the researcher ignores the rural variable, then a "finding" of no effect for participation might result despite a contrary reality. This simplified illustration is only one of many specification errors that can produce inconsistency. At the risk of offering pious advice, I suggest that better theoretical understanding of the process is the best way to reduce specification difficulties. In many cases, this understanding may allow a researcher to identify a context variable that should be considered in interaction with other factors, not simply ignored or controlled away. Such context variables will be called *conditions* in this chapter.

Aside from aptitude-treatment research, few organizational analyses of educational change systematically examine interactions.[31] Daft and Becker (1978) study a number of interactions in their analysis of innovative high schools. For example, they consider the type of innovation adopted to interact with (that is, is contingent or conditional on) the level of professionalism of the school (which is an example of what is here called a condition). Professionalism showed little if any relationship to the number of innovations adopted (which is the dependent variable); however, schools having a higher level of professionalism adopted more innovations of a curriculum or educational nature, whereas schools having a lower level of professionalism adopted more innovations of a purely administrative nature (which is an independent variable).

Berman and Pauly (1975) used elementary versus secondary schools as a condition and found, for example, that many implementation strategies, such as training, that were effective in elementary schools were not effective in high schools, and vice versa. Berman and McLaughlin (1977) used the type of innovative project as a condition. They found that support from the principal positively and strongly affected how well the project was implemented for relatively unstructured classroom-organization-type innovations, but not for structured individualization-type projects. On the other hand, they found that effective project directors were important to the implementation of structured individualization projects, not classroom organization innovations.

Rosenblum and Louis (1981) conducted an extensive interaction analysis and their results strongly indicate context dependency. For example, they found that, for their sample of rural schools, "tension in a school may either facilitate or impede planned change, depending on the size of the school. Small schools characterized by high levels of tension between role partners are significantly less likely than other schools to be high implementors, while large schools with high levels of tension are significantly more likely to be high implementors." Using the terminology proposed earlier in this chapter, school size is the condition, tension is an independent variable, and degree of implementation is the dependent variable for this interaction analysis.[32]

A third source of inconsistency concerns the context indirectly. It was argued earlier that the same innovative idea is implemented differently in different sites (or contexts). More specifically, some characteristics of innovations do not vary from context to context; one example is cost in dollars. But many so-called attributes of innovations are not invariant: Their value depends on the context and thus changes from site to site for the "same" innovative idea. For example, one item on Rogers and Shoemaker's (1971) list of attributes of innovations (important to adoption) is compatibility—that is, how compatible the innovation is with the adopting organization. However, compatibility is not an intrinsic property of innovation, but rather depends on the match between the innovation and the organizational context.[33] Moreover, the innovative idea changes over time. It becomes adapted and clarified, during implementation, so that the same innovative idea in the same site varies over time. Consequently, how compatible it is with the existing context also varies. Such variables are thus context- and time-dependent; they will be called *endogenous* variables.

Inconsistent results can arise when researchers treat endogenous variables as if they were given and fixed inputs (which could be called exogenous variables). A study that examines the success of an innovation in one site might come to the opposite conclusion of a study of the "same" innovation installed in a different site, because the substance of the innovation changes—indeed is defined—over time in each site and thus can be expected to diverge during implementation.

Several techniques can ease problems of inconsistency caused by endogenous variables. Endogenous variables should not be treated as if they were factors defined independently of the context. The substance of an innovation, for example, often should be defined in terms of the perceptions and practices of the users. Moreover, the unit of analysis for studying educational change should "no longer be the organization but the organization with respect to a particular innovation, no longer the innovation, but the innovation with respect to the particular organization" (Downs and Mohr, 1976: 706). Specifically, the unit of analysis should be the lowest organizational unit for which the substance does not change; in many cases this unit is the teacher in a classroom, because empirical studies have shown that the same innovation in a particular district and particular school often has different substance from classroom to classroom (Berman and Pauly, 1975; Pauly's analysis in Armor et al., 1976).[3][4] Finally, measurements of endogenous variables should be made at different times during the process. For example, the substance of a project during early periods of mobilization can be quite different from what is implemented, and both can be quite different from the institutionalized innovation.

A final source of inconsistency is that the same factor could have different effects at different times or on different phases of the change process (Hage and Aiken, 1970; Zaltman et al., 1977). Some writers argue, for example, that broad-based participation is deleterious at early stages of project development, but is helpful during implementation (Corwin, 1973; Yin et al., 1978). Among the few empirical studies of differential effects over time is Rosenblum and Louis (1981), who examined the effects of a number of factors (including participation) on *both* initiation and implementation. Berman and McLaughlin (1977) analyzed the effects of factors on both implementation and institutionalization. Both studies also analyzed how various measures of implementation influenced institutionalization. These studies thus attacked the problem of time dependency by using outcomes that measured interim process results (and they also considered some outcome measures or dependent variables to be endogenous.).[3][5]

In summary, findings from research are often inconsistent because outcomes of the educational change process are context- and time-dependent.

CATEGORIZATION OF
EXPLANATORY VARIABLES

The preceding section's intention should not be misconstrued. Though several ways were suggested to sort out inconsistencies across studies, I did not mean to imply that casting analysis in conditional forms (for example, interactions and simultaneous equations) would "solve" the problem: It might help reduce the prevalence of contradictory findings, but at the cost of limiting our ability to generalize.

The crux of the matter is this: The number of significant interactions among variables may be too numerous and too complex to develop and test powerful generalizations or unified theory. In the extreme, so many conditions about the context may have to be stated (to insure a reasonable

TABLE 6.1　Categorization of Factors Affecting the Educational Change
Process

I.	Local contextual conditions
II.	Primary attributes of change efforts
III.	Local policy choices
IV.	Endogenous variables
V.	External factors (outside variables subject to change during implementation)

level of push-type causal explanation and prediction) that "findings"
would hold only for individual districts—or, indeed, individual schools.

I am not convinced, however, that the case for this nominalistic
extreme has yet been demonstrated. The past decade's progress on understanding educational change processes suggests a more optimistic assessment. I expect we will be able to develop limited, time-bound generalizations and partial theories within broad classes of contextual conditions.

For example, it may be that educational change occurs so differently in
elementary schools as compared to secondary schools (particularly in
urban areas) that essentially different theories are needed. Similarly,
schools in rural areas may have distinctively unique dynamics as compared
to schools in nonrural areas.[36] These two gross conditions are, of course,
obvious, and several other potentially major conditions could easily be
mentioned—such as community, demographic, and student characteristics—without even introducing less obvious but perhaps more powerful
organizational characteristics. The number of such conditions, together
with other plausible variables, quickly becomes too large to encompass
within a single feasible sample (particularly if higher-level interactions are
considered). The alternative is to draw samples and conduct research
within a selected contextual category—for example, rural elementary
schools in stable environments—and to limit generalization to that category. Insofar as consistent results accumulate within a category, findings
and limited theories could be compared across categories.

Let me state the argument succinctly. Given the inherent complexity of
educational change, the long road to more useful variance findings requires
several steps: (1) the categorization of variables into types that reflect
their status in the educational change process; (2) the development of a
taxonomy of contextual conditions; (3) the deliberate selection of samples
to do research within contextual categories; (4) analysis within categories
that take into account such issues as interactive, endogenous, and simultaneous relations; and (5) comparison of findings across categories.

In part, the last section suggests how to think about the first step, the
categorization of different types of variables so as to clarify their context
and time dependency. Table 6.1 classifies variables that could affect the
educational change process into five broad groups; Table 6.2 provides
illustrations of these categories.

TABLE 6.2   Factors Affecting the Educational Change Process—
Illustrative Variables Suggested by the Literature

Factor		Variables
I.	Local contextual conditions	District characteristics (such as school board traits, leadership of administration, organizational structure, level of professionalism, organizational health, size, financial status, priorities)
		Characteristics of implementing subsystem (such as elementary or secondary, size, leadership traits, staff attributes, organizational climate)
		Student characteristics
		Community characteristics
II.	Primary attributes of change effort	Core substance of technology
		Certainty of technology
		Complexity of change effort
		Scope of change effort
		Centrality of change effort
		Cost
III.	Local policy choices	Participation strategies
		Staff development activities
		Coordination, control, communication procedures
IV.	Endogenous variables	Attitude of users over time
		Attitude of key actors over time (for example, administrators, board members)
		Evolution of policy image
		Support for change effort
		Extent and quality of planning
		Degree of conflict over change effort
		Community involvement
		Clarity about innovation
		Change in user behavior, organizational arrangements, and technology
V.	External variables subject to change during implementation	Stability of funding
		Federal and state regulations
		Episodic changes in context (such as new superintendent, new principal, teacher strike, Proposition 13)

The first category, local contextual conditions, represents variables that are relatively fixed for each school district—for example, over a three- to five-year period—but differ across school districts. These conditions are constraints inherent in the context of school districts. Table 6.2, which enumerates factors that the literature suggests are important to the outcomes of educational change policies, divides these contextual conditions into regular or stable characteristics of (a) the district's organization, (b) the subsystem implementing a change effort (for example, one or more elementary schools along with support staff), (c) the relevant student population, and (d) the affected local community. A taxonomy of contextual conditions for the purpose of doing comparative research could be drawn from these categories.

The other condition listed in the table is the class of variables associated with an innovation itself. Many critical aspects of change efforts are adapted and clarified during the process of change, as discussed earlier, and are, therefore, endogenous variables listed under category III. But some aspects do not change over time. This invariant core, or group of primary characteristics, constrains how much adaptation occurs. For example, projects that begin as reading programs generally wind up as reading, not math, programs; open education innovations are unlikely to become highly structured pull-out projects; low-funded innovations are unlikely to evolve into massive change operations with high expenditures. Researchers do not yet know how to isolate the core from those aspects subject to adaptation and clarification. Nonetheless, it seems obvious that the process and outcomes of educational change are conditioned by constraints inherent in the technology that school districts choose to implement (Majone and Wildavsky, 1978).

The third class of variables is called local policy variables, which refers to choices that school districts and their members make. Research has conclusively shown that such strategic choices matter to the course and result of change policies (Fullan and Pomfret, 1977). The items listed in the table represent choices often mentioned in the literature as significant. Yet, it is hard to take any one of these strategies and find consistent evidence that they work all the time under all conditions.[37] The problem for researchers, then, is to state which strategies work under what contextual conditions (category I) and for which attributes of change efforts (category II).

For example, Berman (1978b, 1980) proposes that broad-based participation is appropriate under the conditions of relatively unstructured innovations characterized by high uncertainty and complexity (such as differentiated staffing or open education), but may be inefficient and harmful for highly structured innovations.[38] Moreover, he suggests that the choice to use participative strategies should depend on the extent of agreement over the change policy among members in the local setting and on the nature of the district's administrative system. Fullan (1980c) makes a parallel argument referring to educational innovations, as do Britain (1978) and Delbecq and Gill (1979) discussing evaluation issues in other social policy arenas. Interaction analysis of the type discussed earlier would be appropriate to explore those conditional hypotheses.

The point, of course, is not to test all possible interactions—an infeasible and fruitless undertaking. Rather, interactions should be selected that relate directly to practice. The examination of local policy choices conditioned on (that is, interacted with) contextual constraints and primary attributes of innovations may lead to partial theories that are relevant to officials who make choices within their own realities.

The remaining two categories, endogenous and external variables, were discussed earlier, and no more than a brief mention needs be made of them. The main consideration is that research should move toward taking into account process variables that necessarily change over time. For instance, the least researchers could do is distinguish between the initial change effort (which comprises the original policy, planned organizational arrangements, and adopted technology) and the state of the change effort at later times during or after implementation (that is, the evolved policy, the actual change in organizational arrangements, and the implemented technology). Similarly, the evidence clearly indicates that participants' understanding of and attitudes toward a change effort alter during implementation (Smith and Keith, 1971; Gross, in Herriott and Gross, 1979). The apparent importance of such time-dependent variables argues for longitudinal research that can both observe the change process and make measurements necessary to more sophisticated variance analysis.

The comparative approach outlined above offers no guarantee of the eventual emergence of a unified theory of educational change. Instead, it accepts lowered expectations for research findings. By limiting generalizations, making sensible distinctions among different types of variables, experimenting with time-dependent measurements and longitudinal research designs, and structuring analysis in conditional forms, researchers might be able to reduce inconsistency across studies and produce results relevant to policy and practice.

NOTES

1. Glass (1976, 1979) uses systematic coding and statistical analysis of findings to integrate research literatures and cull out specific findings exhibiting a high level of agreement across studies.

2. The subject of the appropriate choice of a unit of analysis is complex. For discussion, see Light (1979).

3. They might, however, lead to contrary policy actions. For example, school district officials might want to follow the conclusion from process analysis because they want their particular project to work. Federal or state officials might place their bets according to a variance analysis that suggests how much weight each independent variable has in influencing successful implementation because they aim to obtain as many successes as possible.

4. I believe this shift is part of a much larger movement unfolding in the social sciences as they separate from their physical-sciences ancestry. In line with Kuhn's (1970) observation about paradigm shifts, various writers have noted the incompatibility of research findings with the usual (physical) scientific paradigm (for example, in psychology see Cronbach, 1975). Some writers suggest this shift is toward a "systems" theory (Churchman, 1979) or a "holistic" paradigm (see Walker, 1979, for a provacative discussion of mechanistic versus holistic paradigms and their relation-

ship to theories of implementation); others see a trend toward a phenomenological formulation (Schutz, 1967). It is beyond the scope of this chapter to trace these developments or to place the change in research on knowledge utilization and educational change into the broader context of the potential "revolution" of social science.

5. This chapter does not draw inferences about policy or practice so as to present a clear message about the state of the art in research on educational change. Moreover, it does not review the methodological literature on evaluation nor suggest direct implications for conducting evaluations.

6. This trust in science, technology, and rational analysis during the fifties and sixties was by no means limited to education, as Nelson (1974) observes.

7. For an explicit statement of this research, development, and diffusion strategy set in the policy context of central direction from federal agencies, see Clark and Guba (1965). Also see Brickell (1961) for a view from the state perspective. Guba and Clark (1974) later presented a view of educational change that is more consistent with the paradigm discussed within the next section.

8. For a discussion of the research design and the policy context of Head Start and Follow-Through, see Elmore (1976), House (1974) and Williams and Evans (1969). Rivlin (1971) offers an explicit rationale for the experimental approach, which she later reconsidered in Rivlin and Timpane (1975); also see Riecken and Boruch (1974).

9. Weikart and Banet (1975) indicate that implemented models not only changed over time, but different models tended to converge over time, a finding similar to the convergence of the mini-schools in the so-called voucher experiment (Weiler, 1981).

10. Similarly, in different programs, Evans and Sheffler (1974) found as much difference in instructional procedures among teachers using Individually Prescribed Instruction (IPI) as between IPI and non-IPI teachers.

11. The most extreme statement of technological dominance was a call for the development of "teacher proof" practices. In this view held by some developers, the individual teacher was the culprit, being either inadequate or out of date, and the solution was to produce procedures that would compensate for and guard against user deficiencies. When evidence cited in the next section began to accumulate, revealing ineffectiveness of many R&D products and packages, far too many researchers and public officials drew the conclusion that school staff were unable or unwilling to use the technologies in their intended way—the user "problem" again, in a different guise. In this view, resistant practitioners failed to use superior technologies properly, an interpretation that unfortunately lingers on. See Fullan (1974) for a review and sensitive discussion of the limited attention paid to users during the 1950s and 1960s.

12. Federal policy makers were not the only believers in devising schemes for adoption. The Ford Foundation (1972), for example, also had faith in a "lighthouse" demonstration approach, but their experience failed to support their faith.

13. It is possible that the more school districts innovate, the less they change. For example, Berman and Pauly (1975) found that innovativeness of a district was not highly correlated with the continuation of innovations after the end of federal funding for 293 innovations sponsored by 4 federal "seed money" programs. Zaltman et al. (1973) suggest that organizations which concentrate on adoption may be less able to implement innovations effectively. Berman and McLaughlin (1979) present case study evidence of how organizational dynamics within school districts can operate to use innovations for maintaining the existing system, rather than changing it.

14. See Havelock (1969) for a widely cited discussion of models. See Paul (1977) for an update on the formulation of models.

15. Research on leadership exhibits symptoms parallel to research on knowledge utilization and educational change—inconsistent, confusing, and impractical findings. Thus, Stogdill (1974: vii) observes that "four decades of research on leadership have produced a bewildering mass of findings. . . . It is difficult to know what, if anything,

has been convincingly demonstrated by replicated research." The current malaise in the field of leadership research may provide a prophetic image of our future. Some writers diagnose the problem of leadership research as a need for a new papadigm that reflects, rather than ignores, research contradictions (McCall and Lombarde, 1978).

16. These illustrations are too simply stated, for they all refer to "hard" technologies. Thus, it might appear that technology-dominant processes involve only "hard" technologies, whereas implementation-dominant processes involve "soft" technologies. Put more precisely, if the interaction between a technology and its setting is uncertain, then it is an implementation-dominant process (see Berman, 1978b). Such uncertainty can occur in the implementation of hard technologies (for example, computer-assisted instruction) as well as in soft technologies (such as open education).

17. Gene Hall and associates have gone far in developing fidelity measurement instruments (Hall et al., 1975; Hall and Loucks, 1977).

18. Writers on the methodology of evaluation make a strong case for both of the above points. For example, see Scriven (1967) on point 1 and or Deutscher (1976) on point 2. This chapter offers no definition of "successful" innovations for the reasons cited above, though the term will be used when necessary. In these instances, the definition used by the cited research study will be accepted without comment.

19. The three subprocesses named here assume many aliases in the literature, and some researchers expand their number to five or six. The various names of and divisions within mobilization, implementation, and institutionalization will be discussed as each subprocess is explained. Despite the usefulness of finer distinctions for particular purposes, the case for expanding the number of subprocesses beyond three does not seem justifiable in terms of advancing a general paradigm.

20. Recent literature on technological diffusion has moved away from, though not renounced, the linear sequence model. See Kelly and Kranzberg (1978).

21. The use of systems terminology has become more widespread in educational research during the last decade. See the chapter by Miles in this volume.

22. Miles et al. use the term "vision development" in a way that closely resembles this chapter's policy image development. Rogers and Eveland (1977) label this function agenda setting, matching, and redefining.

23. This proposition about support generation should be distinguished from the issue of participation, which will be discussed subsequently. Many writers contend that participation leads to support, but this hypothesis has been seriously challenged as inaccurate, imprecise, or both (Giacquinta, 1975; Rosenblum and Louis, 1981). Support can be generated by strategies other than participation—for example, persuasion, information, or change in incentives. This article therefore considers participative strategies as a factor and deals only with the generic function of internal support generation in this section.

24. The term "implementation" has two meanings in this chapter, as it has in the literature. Earlier, implementation referred broadly to the interaction of an innovation with its setting. The above or subprocess meaning has a narrower connotation—namely, the activities of users (for example, teachers) actually attempting to use an innovation. The broader definition is particularly appropriate for viewing the process from afar—outside of a school district or of many districts—as a federal or state policy official might; it thus might be thought of as macro-implementation in contrast to the narrower definition that focuses on micro-implementation by users. From a macro perspective, mobilization—or at least that part which follows adoption—and institutionalization are aspects of implementation. See Berman (1978a) for a fuller discussion of macro- and micro-implementation. For reviews of the literature on implementation outside of education, see Hargrove (1975), Elmore (1978), and Bardach (1977).

25. The work of Stearns and Norwood (1977) on the evaluation of Project Information Packages tends to support this generalization. The one innovation that was relatively unstructured (a gaming simulation) seemed to fail in part because of its prespecification.

26. Rogers and Eveland (1977: 7) measure specificity as "the amount of agreement between two or more people about some characteristic. When people agree, specificity is high." In contrast, Berman and McLaughlin define both specificity and clarity in individual terms, not necessarily as agreement among staff. This difference illustrates only one of the many hurdles to overcome in developing operational concepts.

27. Institutionalization goes under different names in the literature. The authors mentioned here use the following labels: Lewin, refreezing; Hage and Aiken, routinization; Berman and McLaughlin (1974) accept Giacquinta's (1973) incorporation, but later (1977) use institutionalization; Yin, routinization; Rosenblum and Louis, routinization; Miles, stabilization; Rogers, interconnecting.

28. This form of conditional statement is perhaps the simplest form. More complex forms, including interactive and simultaneous formulations, will be discussed subsequently.

29. Cronbach concludes that empirical social science laws of the usual type cannot be determined because of the vast number of interactions and their instability. Cronbach had earlier called for complex experimental designs that could test aptitude-treatment interactions (see Bracht, 1970), but he believed in 1976 that the interactions were too many, too complex, and too unstable.

30. For a review on participation, see Giacquinta (1973) and Dachler and Wilpert (1978).

31. Outside of education, an active literature under the name of contingency theory pursues topics similar to the ones discussed above. For reviews and applications, see Mohr (1969), Downs and Mohr (1978), Downs (1978), and Berman (1980). Fiedler's work on leadership effectiveness (Fiedler, 1964, 1972; Bons and Fiedler, 1976; Fiedler et al., 1976) uses contingency theory for practical purposes, namely, training leaders. Lawrence and Lorsch (1967) and Lorsch (1976) provide examples of contingency theory applied to broader issues of organizational response and design.

32. Rosenblum and Louis ran many interesting interactions, though not of the form suggested above. For example, they interact school size and percentage male, which are, in our terminology, both conditions—that is, characteristics that are not subject to change by short-run policy decisions. This chapter distinguishes between policy decisions and constraints, with the latter referred to as a condition.

33. Downs and Mohr (1976) refer to an invariant characteristic as a primary attribute and a characteristic that depends on the perceptions of members of the adopting organization—and thus varies with the context—as a secondary attribute.

34. Downs and Mohr (1976) argue that if 10 innovations are studied in 100 organizations, the sample ought to be 1,000. Given that users adapt innovations to their own context during implementation, Downs and Mohr's argument is not quite accurate. If 10 innovations are being studied in 100 school districts having an average of 100 teachers each, the sample ought to be 10 X 100 X 100, or 100,000.

35. More precisely, many studies cited earlier use measures of process, not simply input-output measures such as student achievement. For example, measures of the effectiveness of implementation and of change in teacher behavior attempt to assess interim effects. Such measures are really cause and effect of both factors and outcome, but the literature seldom attempts to treat them in this simultaneous manner. Berman and Pauly (1975) and Berman and McLaughlin (1977) offer a simultaneous approach, which is described in the latter work as follows:

> Because a project is likely to mutate during the implementation, its effectiveness after four or five years depends not only on its initial design but also on its evolution. In turn, its evolution depends on characteristics of the innovation and its institutional setting. In other words, the implemented project should be treated as both an independent and a dependent variable in a system of relationships. Consequently, the effectiveness of implementation will be analyzed, on the one hand, as a function of the factors identified earlier, and on the other hand, as a factor affecting teacher change, continuation of method and materials, and student improvement. . . . Moreover, teachers may

learn from and adapt to the project during implementation in ways the original designers may or may not have intended. Such changes in teaching style or behavior constitute an outcome of the project as it was implemented. Furthermore, improved student performance and continuation of project methods or materials depend on the teacher's style and behavior as they were both before and as a result of the project. Therefore, the change in the teacher's behavior can be classed as both cause and effect in the system of relationships determining what happens to an innovation [Berman and McLaughlin, 1977: 45-46].

36. Even this illustration is far from simple in operational terms because the organizational characteristics of rural school districts (and the regional cooperatives that assume administrative functions for many of them) are in flux. Moreover, the definition of rural itself raises serious questions (Bass and Berman, 1979).

37. The factors listed are, of course, not operational concepts, but simply suggestive and directionless categories. It is assumed that operational measurements could be made from these abstract factors.

38. Specifically, Berman argues that unstructured innovations require an *adaptive* implementation strategy, of which broad-based participation would be an essential element. Structured innovations could be handled, in contrast, by a *programmed* strategy, provided that contextual conditions were suitable.

BIBLIOGRAPHY

ABBOTT, M. G. (1969) "The school as social system: indicators for change." Socio-Economic Planning Services 2: 167-174.

ABRAMOWITZ, S. and E. TENENBAUM (1978) High School '77: A Survey of Public Secondary School Principals. Washington, DC: National Institute of Education.

ALKIN, M., R. DAILLAK, and P. WHITE (1979) Using Evaluations: Does Evaluation Make a Difference? Beverly Hills, CA: Sage.

ALLAN, G. S. and W. C. WOLF, Jr. (1978) "Relationships between perceived attributes of innovations and their subsequent adoption." Peabody Journal of Education LV, 4: 332-336.

ALLISON, G. (1971) Essence of Decision. Boston: Little, Brown.

AOKI, T. T. (1977) British Columbia Social Studies Assessment: Volumes 1-3. Victoria, British Columbia: British Columbia Ministry of Education.

ARCHIBALD, K. (1968) "The utilization of social research and policy analysis." Ph.D. dissertation, Washington University.

ARGYRIS, C. and D. SCHON (1978) Theory into Practice. San Francisco: Jossey-Bass.

ARMOR, D. et al. (1976) Analysis of the School-Preferred Reading Program in Selected Los Angeles Minority Schools. Santa Monica, CA: Rand Corporation.

ASHLEY, B., H. COHEN, D. McINTYRE, and R. SLATTER (1970) "A sociological analysis of students' reasons for becoming teachers." Sociological Review 18, 1: 53-69.

AVERCH, H. A. et al. (1974) How Effective Is Schooling? Englewood Cliffs, NJ: Educational Technology Publications.

––– (1972) How Effective Is Schooling? A Critical Review and Synthesis of Research Findings. Santa Monica, CA: Rand Corporation.

BALDRIDGE, J. V. (1975) "Organizational innovation: individual, structural, and environmental impacts," in J. V. Baldridge and T. E. Deal (eds.) Managing Change in Educational Organizations: Sociological Perspectives, Strategies, and Case Studies. Berkeley, CA: McCutchan.

––– and R. A. BURNHAM (1975) "Organizational innovation: individual, organizational, and environmental impacts." Administrative Science Quarterly 20: 165-176.

BALDRIDGE, J. V. and T. E. DEAL (1975) Managing Change in Educational Organizations: Sociological Perspectives, Strategies, and Case Studies. Berkeley, CA: McCutchan.

BALDRIDGE, J. V. et al. (1974) "The relationship of R&D efforts to field users: problems, myths, and stereotypes." Phi Delta Kappan LV, 10: 701-706.

BALE, R. L. (1977) "A model of organizational innovation in American elementary schools." Presented at the annual meeting of the American Educational Research Association. ED 137 939.

BANK, A., N. SNIDMAN, and M. PITTS (1979) "Evaluation, dissemination, and educational improvement: how do they interact?" Presented at the annual meeting of the American Educational Research Association.

BARDACH, E. (1977) The Implementation Game: What Happens After a Bill Becomes a Law. Cambridge, MA: MIT Press.

BARNARD, C. I. (1938) The Functions of the Executive. Cambridge, MA: Harvard University Press.

BARROWS, L. (1980) "Findings and implications of the thirteen schools study." Presented at the annual meeting of the American Educational Research Association.

BASS, G. V. (1978) A Study of Alternatives in American Education, Volume I: District Policies and the Implementation of Change. Santa Monica, CA: Rand Corporation. R-2170/1-NIE.

––– and P. BERMAN (1979) Federal Aid to Rural Schools: Current Patterns and Urgent Needs. Santa Monica, CA: Rand Corporation.

BENNIS, W. G. (1966) Changing Organizations. New York: McGraw-Hill.

––– (1959) "Leadership theory and administrative behavior: the problem of authority." Administrative Science Quarterly.

––– K. D. BENNE, and R. CHIN (1969) The Planning of Change. New York: Holt, Rinehart & Winston.

BENTZEN, M. M. (1974) Changing Schools: The Magic Feather Principle. New York: McGraw-Hill.

BERGER, P. L. (1974) Pyramids of Sacrifice. New York: Basic Books.

BERMAN, P. (1980a) "Thinking about programmed and adaptive implementation: matching strategies to situations," in H. Ingram and D. Mann (eds.) Why Policies Succeed or Fail. Beverly Hills, CA: Sage.

––– (1980b) "Toward an implementation paradigm." Prepared for the Program on Research and Practice, National Institute of Education.

––– (1978a) "The study of macro- and micro-implementation." Public Policy 26, 2: 157-184.

––– (1978b) Designing Implementation to Match Policy Situations: A Contingency Analysis of Programmed and Adaptive Implementation. Santa Monica, CA: Rand Corporation.

––– and M. W. McLAUGHLIN (1979) An Exploratory Study of School District Adaptation. Santa Monica, CA: Rand Corporation. R-2010-NIE.

––– (1978a) Rethinking the Federal Role in Education. Santa Monica, CA: Rand Corporation.

––– (1978b) Federal Programs Supporting Educational Change, Volume VIII: Implementing and Sustaining Innovations. Santa Monica, CA: Rand Corporation. R-1589/8-HEW.

––– (1977) Federal Programs Supporting Educational Change, Volume VII: Factors Affecting Implementation and Continuation. Santa Monica, CA: Rand Corporation.

––– (1975a) Federal Programs Supporting Educational Change, Volume IV: The Findings in Review. Santa Monica, CA: Rand Corporation.

––– (1975b) Federal Programs Supporting Educational Change, Volume III: The Process of Change. Appendix B: Innovations in Reading. Santa Monica, CA: Rand Corporation.

––– (1974) Federal Programs Supporting Educational Change, Volume I: A Model of Educational Change. Santa Monica, CA: Rand Corporation. R-1589/1-HEW.

BERMAN, P. and E. W. PAULY (1975) Federal Programs Supporting Educational Change, Volume II: Factors Affecting Change Agent Projects. Santa Monica, CA: Rand Corporation.

BERNSTEIN, R. S. (1978) The Restructuring of Social and Political Theory. Philadelphia: University of Pennsylvania Press.

BIDWELL, C. (1965) "The school as a formal organization," in J. G. March (ed.) Handbook of Organizations. Skokie, IL: Rand McNally.

BLACK, H. (1967) The American Schoolbook. New York: William Morrow.

BLAU, P. M. and R. W. SCOTT (1962) Formal Organizations: A Comparative Approach. New York: ITT.

BLAUNER, R. (1960) "Work satisfaction and industrial trends in modern society," pp. 336-354 in W. Galenson and S. M. Lipset (eds.) Labor and Trade Unionism. New York: John Wiley.

BLOCK, A. and T. van GEEL (1975) "State of Arizona curriculum law," in T. van Geel with A. Block (eds.) Authority to Control the School Curriculum: An Assessment of Rights in Conflict. Washington, DC: National Institute of Education. ED 125 070.

BLUMBERG, A. (1980) "School organizations: a case of generic resistance to change," pp. 15-29 in M. M. Milstein (ed.) Schools, Conflict and Change. New York: Teachers College Press.

——— (1976) "OD's future in schools—or is there one?" Education and Urban Society 8: 213-227.

——— and W. GREENFIELD (1980) The Effective Principal. Boston: Allyn & Bacon.

BLUMBERG, A., J. MAY, and R. PERRY (1974) "An inner-city school that changed—and continued to change." Education and Urban Society 6, 2.

BONS, P. and F. FIEDLER (1976) "Changes in organizational leadership and the behavior of relationship and task motivated leaders." Administrative Science Quarterly 21: 453-473.

BOURDIEU, P. and J.-C. PASSERON (1977) Reproduction in Education, Society, and Culture. London: Sage.

BOYD, W. L. (1979a) "The politics of curriculum change and stability." Educational Researcher 8, 2: 12-18.

——— (1979b) "Retrenchment in American education: the politics of efficiency." Presented at the annual meeting of the American Educational Research Association.

——— (1979c) "The changing politics of curriculum policy-making for American schools," in J. Schaffarzick and G. Sykes (eds.) Curriculum Issues: Lessons from Research and Experience. Berkeley, CA: McCutchan.

——— (1978) "The changing politics of curriculum policy making for American schools." Review of Educational Research 48, 4: 577-628.

BRACHT, F. (1970) "Experimental factors related to aptitude-treatment interactions." Review of Educational Research 40: 627-649.

BREDO, A. E. and E. R. BREDO (1975) "Effects of environment and structure on the process of innovation," pp. 449-468 in J. V. Baldridge and T. E. Deal (eds.) Managing Change in Educational Organizations: Sociological Perspectives, Strategies, and Case Studies. Berkeley, CA: McCutchan.

BRICKELL, H. M. (1964) "State organization for educational change: study and a proposal," pp. 493-532 in M. B. Miles (ed.) Innovation in Education. New York: Teachers College Press.

——— (1961) Organizing New York State for Educational Change. Albany, NY: State Department of Education.

BRITAIN, G. M. (1978) "Experimental and contextual models of program evaluation." Evaluation and Program Planning 1: 29-234.

BURCHAM, D. W. and C. A. COHN (1979) "California educational policy making by initiative: the specter of unintended outcomes." Politics of Education Bulletin 9, 1: 8-10.

BURCHINAL, L. (1967) "Needed: local, one-step information centers." Educational Researcher, Special Supplement: 8-9.

BURLINGAME, M. (1978) "The impact of policy decisions in schools," in L. S. Shulman (ed.) Review of Research in Education, Volume 5. Itasca, IL: Peacock.

BURNS, T. and G. M. STALKER (1961) The Management of Innovation. London: Tavistock.

BUTLER, M. and W. PAISLEY (1978) Factors Determining Roles and Functions of Educational Linking Agents. San Francisco: Far West Laboratory for Educational Research and Development.

BUTLER-PAISLEY, M. and W. PAISLEY (1975) Communication for Change in Education: Linkage Programs for the '70s. Stanford, CA: Institute for Communication Research, Stanford University.

BYRNE, D., S. HYNES, and L. McCLEARY (1978) The Senior High School Principalship. Reston, VA: National Association of Secondary School Principals.

CAMPBELL, D. T. (1975a) "Assessing the impact of planned social change," in G. M. Lyonds (ed.) Social Research and Public Policies. Dartmouth, NH: Public Affairs Center, Dartmouth College.

——— (1975b) "Degrees of freedom and the case study." Comparative Political Studies 8, 2: 178-193.

——— (1973) "The social scientist as methodological servant of the experimenting society." Policy Studies Journal 2.

——— (1972) "Reforms as experiments," in C. H. Weiss (ed.) Evaluating Action Programs: Readings in Social Action and Education. Boston: Allyn & Bacon.

CAMPEAU, P., J. BINKLEY, P. TREADWAY, J. APPLEBY, and B. BESSEY (1979) Final Report: Evaluation of Project Information Package Dissemination and Implementation. Palo Alto, CA: American Institutes for Research.

Capla Associates (1977) National Diffusion Network Skills Taxonomy. Rochelle Park, NJ: Author.

CAPLAN, N. (1979) "The two-communities theory of knowledge utilization." American Behavioral Scientist 22, 3: 459-470.

——— and R. F. RICH (1976) Policy Uses of Social Science Knowledge and Perspectives: Means-Ends Matching Versus Understanding. Ann Arbor: Center for Research on Utilization of Scientific Knowledge, University of Michigan.

CARLSON, R. O. (1981) "Negotiating and learning the agent role," in K. S. Louis et al. (eds.) The Human Factor in Knowledge Use: Field Agent Roles in Education. Cambridge, MA: Abt Associates.

——— (1972) School Superintendents: Careers and Performance. Columbus, OH: Charles Merrill.

——— (1965a) "Barriers to change in public schools," in R. O. Carlson et al. (eds.) Change Processes in the Public Schools. Eugene: Center for Advanced Study of Educational Administration, University of Oregon.

——— (1965b) Adoption of Educational Innovations. Eugene: Center for the Advanced Study of Educational Administration, University of Oregon.

——— (1964) "Environmental constraints and organizational consequences: the public school and its clients," pp. 262-276 in D. E. Griffiths (ed.) Behavioral Science and Educational Administration. Chicago: University of Chicago Press.

CATES, C. (1978) A Preliminary Inventory of Educational Linking Agent Functions with Brief Explanations. San Francisco: Far West Laboratory for Educational Research and Development.

——— M. MALKAS, B. SULKIS, and P. HOOD [eds.] (1979) The State of the States: Report of Discussions at the 1978 Dissemination Forum. San Francisco: Far West Laboratory for Educational Research and Development.

Center for New Schools (1975) A Multi-Method Study of the Development and Effects of an Alternative School Learning Environment, Volumes I-IV. Chicago, IL: Author.

CHABOTAR, K. and D. KELL (1978) Linking R&D to Local Schools: A Program and Its Policy Context. Cambridge, MA: Abt Associates.

CHARTERS, W. W., Jr., and J. E. JONES (1975) "On neglect of the independent variable in program evaluation," in J. V. Baldridge and T. E. Deal (eds.) Managing Change in Educational Organizations. Berkeley, CA: McCutchan.

——— (1973) "On the risk of appraising nonevents in program evaluation." Educational Researcher 2, 11.

CHARTERS, W. W., Jr., and J. S. PACKARD (1979) Task Interdependence, Collegial Governance, and Teacher Attitudes in the Multiunit Elementary School. Eugene: Center for Educational Policy and Management, University of Oregon.

CHARTERS, W. W., Jr., and R. PELLEGRIN (1972) "Barriers to the innovation process: four case studies of differential staffing." Educational Administration Quarterly 9, 1: 3-14.

CHARTERS, W. W., Jr., et al. (1973) Contrasts in the Process of Planned Change of the School's Instructional Organization. Eugene: Center for the Advanced Study of Educational Administration, University of Oregon.

CHESLER, M., R. A. SCHMUCK, and R. LIPPITT (1963) "The principal's role in facilitating innovation." Theory into Practice 2: 269-277.

CHIN, R. and K. BENNE (1961) "General strategies for effecting changes in human systems," pp. 32-59 in W. Bennis et al. (eds.) The Planning of Change. New York: Holt, Rinehart & Winston.

CHURCHMAN, C. W. (1979) The Systems Approach and Its Enemies. New York: Basic Books.

CLARK, C. and R. YINGER (1980) "The hidden world of teaching." Presented at the annual meeting of the American Educational Research Association.

CLARK, D. L. and E. GUBA (1965) "An examination of potential change roles in education." Presented at a seminar on Innovation in Planning School Curriculum, October.

CLARK, P. B. and J. Q. WILSON (1961) "Inventive systems: a theory of organizations." Administrative Science Quarterly 6, 2: 129-166.

COCH, L. and J.R.P. FRENCH (1948) "Overcoming resistance to change." Human Relations 1: 512-532.

COHEN, D. K. (1977) "Ideas and action: social science and craft in educational practice." Harvard University. (unpublished)

——— (1975) "Reforming school politics." Harvard Educational Review 48, 4.

——— and E. FARRAR (1977) "Power to the parents?" Public Interest 48: 72-97.

COHEN, D. K. and M. S. GARET (1975) "Reforming educational policy with applied research." Harvard Educational Review 45, 1.

COHEN, E. G. (1973) "Open-space schools: the opportunity to become ambitious." Sociology of Education 46: 143-161.

——— J. W. MEYER, W. R. SCOTT, and T. E. DEAL (1979) "Technology and teaming in the elementary school." Sociology of Education 52, 1: 20-33.

COHEN, M. D., J. G. MARCH, and J. P. OLSEN (1972) "A garbage can model of organizational choice." Administrative Science Quarterly 17: 1-25.

COLE, H. (1971) Implementation of a Process Curriculum by the Campus Team Strategy. Syracuse, NY: Eastern Regional Institute for Education.

COLLINS, B. E. and H. GUETZKOW (1964) A Social Psychology of Group Processes for Decision-Making. New York: John Wiley.

COOK, T. D. and C. L. GRUDES (1978) "Metaevaluation research." Evaluation Quarterly 2: 5-52.

CORBETT, D. (1980) The Field Agent in School Improvement: Client Contributions to the Role. Philadelphia: Research for Better Schools.

CORWIN, R. G. (1975) "Innovation in organizations: the case of schools." Sociology of Education 48: 1-37.

——— (1973) Reform and Organizational Survival—The Teacher Corps as an Instrument of Educational Change. New York: John Wiley.

——— (1972) "Strategies for organizational innovation: an empirical comparison." American Sociological Review 37.

——— (1971) "The school as a formal organization," in L. C. Deighton (ed.) Encyclopaedia of Education, Volume 8. New York: Macmillan.

——— (1967) "Education and the sociology of complex organizations," in D. A. Hansen and J. E. Gerstl (eds.) On Education: Sociological Perspectives. New York: John Wiley.

——— (1965) "Professional persons in public organizations." Educational Administration Quarterly 1: 1-22.

——— and R. A. EDELFELT (1978) "The limits of local control over education," pp. 3-36 in R. G. Corwin et al. (eds.) Perspectives on Organizations: Schools in the Larger Social Environment. Washington, DC: American Association of Colleges for Teacher Education.

CRANDALL, D. P. (1980) "The study of dissemination efforts supporting school improvement: an overview." Presented at pre-session of the annual meeting of the American Educational Research Association.

――― (1977) "Training and supporting linking agents," in N. Nash and J. Culbertson (eds.) Linking Processes in Educational Improvement. Columbus, OH: University Council for Educational Administration.

――― and R. C. HARRIS (1978) "Views on the Utilization of Information by Practitioners." NTS Research Corporation. (unpublished)

CRONBACH, L. J. (1975) "Beyond the two disciplines of scientific psychology." American Psychologist 30, 2: 116-121.

CROWSON, R. and C. PORTER-GEHRIE (1980) "The school principalship: an organizational stability role." Presented at the annual meeting of the American Educational Research Association.

CUSICK, P. A. (1973) Inside High School. New York: Holt, Rinehart & Winston.

CYERT, R. M. and J. G. MARCH (1963) A Behavioral Theory of the Firm. Englewood Cliffs, NJ: Prentice-Hall.

DACHLER, H. P. and B. WILPERT (1978) "Conceptual dimensions and boundaries of participation in organizations: a critical evaluation." Administrative Science Quarterly 23: 1-39.

DAFT, R. L. and S. W. BECKER (1978) The Innovative Organization: Innovation Adoption in School Organizations. New York: Elsevier North-Holland.

DALIN, P. and V. RUST (1979) Can Schools Learn? Oslo: IMTEC.

DEAL, T. E. (1979) "Linkage and information use in educational organizations." Presented at the annual meeting of the American Educational Research Association.

――― and L. D. CELOTTI (1977) "Loose Coupling" and the School Administrator: Some Recent Research Findings. Stanford, CA: School of Education, Stanford University.

DEAL, T. E. and S. NUTT (1979) Promoting, Guiding—and Surviving—Change in Small School Districts. Cambridge, MA: Abt Associates.

DEAL, T. E. and S. RALLIS (1980) "Promoting interaction among producers and users of educational knowledge," pp. 193-228 in Interorganizational Arrangements for Collaborative Efforts: Commissioned Papers. Portland, OR: Northwest Regional Educational Laboratory.

DEAL, T. E., J. W. Meyer, and W. R. SCOTT (1975) "Organizational influences on educational technology," in J. V. Baldridge and T. E. Deal (eds.) Managing Change in Educational Organizations: Sociological Perspectives, Strategies, and Case Studies. Berkeley, CA: McCutchan.

DEAL, T. E. et al. (1975) A Survey Feedback Approach to Developing Self-Renewing School Organizations: Research and Development Memorandum No. 131. Stanford, CA: Stanford Center for Research and Development on Teaching ED 099 389.

DeARMAN, J. W. (1975) Investigation of the Abandonment Rate and Causes of Abandonment of Innovative Practices in Secondary Schools. Columbia: University of Missouri. ED 133 872.

DECAD, J., D. MADEY, E. ROYSTER, and F. BACKER (1980) A Special Study of Linker Roles and Activities, Volume III: Building Capacity for Improvement of Educational Practice. Durham, NC: NTS Research Corporation.

DELBECQ, A. L. and S. L. GILL (1979) "Political decision-making and program development," in R. F. Rich (ed.) Translating Evaluation into Policy. Beverly Hills, CA: Sage.

DENTON, T. (1976) "Unmeasurable programs or unacceptable goals: the dilemma of goal formulation in social policy." Human Organization 34: 398-399.

DERR, C. B. (1976) "OD won't work in schools." Education and Urban Society 8, 2: 227-241.

DERSHIMER, R. (1976) The Federal Government and Educational R&D. Lexington, MA: D. C. Heath.

DeTURK, P. H. (n.d.) P.S. 2001: The Story of the Pasadena Alternative School. Bloomington, IN: Phi Delta Kappa and National Alternative School Project.

DEUTSCH, C. P. (1979) "Presidential message." SPSSI Newsletter (Society for the Psychological Study of Social Issues): 151.

DEUTSCHER, I. (1976) "Toward avoiding the goal trap in evaluation research," in C. C. Abt (ed.) The Evaluation of Social Programs. Beverly Hills, CA: Sage.

Dissemination Analysis Group (1977) Dissemination in Relation to Elementary and Secondary Education. Washington, DC: Office of the Assistant Secretary of Education.

DOLLAR, B. (n.d.) "Federal attempts to change the schools." Proceedings of the National Academy of Political Science 33.

DOWNS, A. (1966) Inside Bureaucracy. Boston: Little, Brown.

DOWNS, G. W., Jr. (1979) Bureaucracy, Innovation, and Public Policy. Lexington, MA: D. C. Heath.

——— (1978) Complexity and Innovation Research: Discussion Paper No. 122. Ann Arbor: Institute of Public Policy Studies, University of Michigan.

——— and L. B. MOHR (1978) Toward a Theory of Innovation: Discussion Paper No. 92. Ann Arbor: Institute of Public Policy Studies, University of Michigan.

——— (1976) "Conceptual issues in the study of innovation." Administrative Science Quarterly 21: 700-714.

DOYLE, W. and G. A. PONDER (1977-1978) "The practicality ethic in teacher decision-making." Interchange 8, 3: 1-12.

DUNN, W. F. and F. S. SWIERZIEK (1977) "Planned organizational change: towards a grounded theory." Journal of Applied Behavioral Science 13, 2: 135-158.

DUNN, W. W. (1980) "The two-communities metaphor and models of knowledge use: an exploratory case study." Knowledge: Creation, Diffusion, Utilization 1, 4: 515-536.

EASTABROOK, G. and M. FULLAN (1978) School and Community: Principals and Community Schools in Ontario. Toronto: Ministry of Education, OISE Press.

ELBOIM-DROR, R. (1973) "Organizational characteristics of the educational system." Journal of Educational Administration 9 (May).

——— (1970) "Some characteristics of the education policy formation system." Policy Sciences 1: 231-253.

ELLIOTT, J. and C. ADELMAN (1974) Inovation in Teaching and Action Research: An Interim Report on the Ford Teaching Project. England: University of East Anglia.

ELLUL, J. (1964) The Technological Society. New York: Knopf.

ELMORE, R. F. (1978) "Organizational models of social program implementation." Public Policy 26, 2: 185-228.

——— (1976) "Follow-through planned variation," in W. Williams and R. F. Elmore (eds.) Social Program Implementation. New York: Academic.

EMERY, F. E. and E. L. TRIST (1965) "The causal texture of organizational environments." Human Relations 18: 21-32.

EMRICK, J. A. and S. M. PETERSON (1978) A Synthesis of Findings Across Five Recent Studies in Educational Dissemination and Change. San Francisco: Far West Laboratory for Educational Research and Development.

——— and R. AGARWOLA-ROGERS (1977) Evaluation of the National Diffusion Network. Menlo Park, CA: Stanford Research Institute.

ERICKSON, K. A. and R. L. ROSE (1976) "Inservice education," in S. E. Goodman (ed.) Handbook on Contemporary Education. New York: Bowker.

ETZIONI, A. (1961) A Comparative Analysis of Complex Organizations. New York: Macmillan.

EVANS, W. J. and J. W. SHEFFLER (1974) "Degree of implementation: a first approximation." Presented at the annual meeting of the American Educational Research Association.

EVELAND, J. D., E. M. ROGERS, and C. KEPPER (1977) The Innovation Process in Public Organizations. Ann Arbor: Department of Journalism, University of Michigan.

FARRAR, E., J. E. deSANCTIS, and D. K. COHEN (1980) "Views from below: implementation research in education." Teachers College Record 82, 1: 77-100.

——— (1979) Views from Below: Implementation Research in Education. Cambridge, MA: Huron Institute.

FELLER, I. (1979) "Three coigns on diffusion research." Knowledge: Creation, Diffusion, Utilization 1, 2: 293-312.

FIEDLER, F. E. (1972) "The effect of leadership training and experience: a contingency model and interpretation." Administrative Science Quarterly 17: 453-470.

––– M. M. CHEMERS, and L. MAHAR (1976) "Fiedler's contingency theory: a summary." Administrative Science Quarterly 21: 496-505.

FIRESTONE, W. A. (1980) "Images of schools and patterns of change." American Journal of Education 88, 4: 459-487.

––– and D. CORBETT (1979) Rationality and Cooperation in External Assistance for School Improvement. Philadelphia: Research for Better Schools.

FIRESTONE, W. A. and W. W. DONNER (1981) Knowledge Use in Educational Development: Tales from a Two-Way Street. Philadelphia: Research for Better Schools.

FIRESTONE, W. A. and R. A. HERRIOTT (1980) Images of the School: An Exploration of the Social Organization of Elementary, Junior High, and High Schools. Philadelphia: Research for Better Schools.

FISCHER, J. [ed.] (1970) The Social Sciences and the Comparative Study of Educational Settings. Scranton, PA: International Textbooks.

Ford Foundation (1972) A Foundation Goes to School: The Ford Foundation Comprehensive School Improvement Program. New York: Author.

FRASER, G. (1969) "Organizational properties and teacher reactions." Presented at the annual meeting of the American Educational Research Association.

FREEMAN, J. (1979) "Going to the well: school district administrative intensity and environmental constraint." Administrative Science Quarterly 24: 119-133.

––– and M. T. HANNAN (1975) "Growth and Decline processes in organizations." American Sociological Review 40: 215-228.

FRIEDMAN, J. (1973) Retracking America: A Theory of Transactive Planning. Garden City, NY: Doubleday.

––– (1969) "Notes on societal action." Journal of the American Institute of Planners 35: 311-318.

FULLAN, M. (forthcoming) The Meaning of Educational Change. Toronto: Ontario Institute for Studies in Education.

––– (1980a) "An R&D prospectus for educational reform," pp. 27-48 in Interorganizational Arrangements for Collaborative Efforts: Commissioned Papers. Portland, OR: Northwest Regional Educational Laboratory.

––– (1980b) "Research on the implementation of educational change," in R. Corwin (ed.) Research on Organizational Issues in Education. Greenwich, CT: Jai.

––– (1980c) "The relationship between evaluation and implementation in curriculum," in A. Levy (ed.) Evaluation Roles.

––– (1979) School-Focused In-Service Education in Canada. Prepared for Centre for Educational Research and Innovation, OECD Project on In-Service Education for Teachers.

––– (1974) "Overview of the innovation process and the user." Interchange 3, 2-3: 1-46.

––– and A. POMFRET (1977) "Research on curriculum and instruction implementation." Review of Educational Research 47, 1: 335-397.

––– (1975) Review of Research on Curriculum Implementation. Toronto: Ontario Institute for Studies in Education.

FULLAN, M., M. B. MILES, and G. TAYLOR (1980) "Organizational development in schools: the state of the art." Review of Educational Research 50, 1: 121-183.

––– (1978) OD in Schools: The State of the Art, Volume IV: Case Studies. Toronto: Ontario Institute for Studies in Education.

FULLER, F. F. (1969) "Concerns of teachers: a developmental conceptualization." American Educational Research Journal 6, 2: 207-226.

GALANTER, W. (1978) "Elementary school staff support system effects on program implementation and job satisfaction." Ph.D. dissertation. Fordham University.

GALLAHER, A. (1965) "Directed change in formal organizations: the school system," in R. O. Carlson (ed.) Change Processes in Public Schools. Eugene: Center for Advanced Study of Educational Administration, University of Oregon.

GARDNER, J. W. (1963) Self-Renewal. New York: Harper & Row.

GAYNOR, A. K. (1979) "Toward a structural theory of innovation in public schools." Presented at the annual meeting of the American Educational Research Association.

––– (1977) "The study of change in educational organizations: a review of the literature," pp. 234-260 in L. Cunningham et al. (eds.) Educational Administration: The Developing Decades. Berkeley, CA: McCutchan.

GIACQUINTA, J. B. (1978) "Educational innovation in schools: some distressing conclusions about implementation." Presented at the annual meeting of the American Educational Research Association.

––– (1975) "Status risk-taking: a central issue in the initiation and implementation of public school innovations." Journal of Research and Development in Education 9, 1: 102-114.

––– (1973) "The process of organizational change in schools," pp. 178-208 in F. B. Kerlinger (ed.) Review of Research in Education. Itasca, IL: Peacock.

––– and C. KAZLOW (1979) "The growth and decline of public school innovations: an analysis of the open classroom." Presented at the annual meeting of the American Educational Research Asociation.

GIDEONSE, H. (1970) Educational Research and Development in the United States. Washington, DC: Government Printing Office.

GITTELL, M. with B. HOFFACKER, E. ROLLINS, and S. FOSTER (1979) Citizen Organizations: Citizen Participation in Educational Decisionmaking. Boston: Institute for Responsive Education.

GLASER, E. (1976) Putting Knowledge to Use: A Distillation of the Literature Regarding Transfer and Change. Los Angeles: Human Interaction Research Institute.

––– (1965) "Utilization of applicable research and demonstration results." Journal of Counseling Psychology 12, 2: 201-205.

––– and H. ROSS (1971) Increasing Utilization of Applied Research Results. Los Angeles: Human Interaction Research Institute.

GLASER, R. (1978) "The contributions of B. F. Skinner to education and issue counterinfluences," in P. Suppes (ed.) Impact of Research on Education. Washington, DC: National Academy of Sciences.

GLASS, G. V. (1979) "Policy for the unpredictable (uncertainty research and policy)." Educational Researcher (October): 12-14.

––– (1976) "Primary, secondary, and meta-analysis of research." Educational Researcher 5: 3-8.

––– and M. L. SMITH (1979) "Meta-analysis of research on class size and achievement." Educational Evaluation and Policy Analysis 1, 1: 2-16.

GLENNAN, T. K., Jr., W. F. HEDERMAN, Jr., L. L. JOHNSON, and R. A. RETTIG (1978) The Role of Demonstrations in Federal R&D Policy. Santa Monica, CA: Rand Corporation. R-22088-OTA.

GOFFMAN, E. (1961) Asylums. Chicago: Aldine.

GOLD, B. A. and M. B. MILES (1978) "Change and conflict: educational innovation in community context," in M. B. Miles et al. Designing and Starting Innovative Schools: A Field Study of Social Architecture in Education, Part III. New York: Center for Policy Research.

GOODENOUGH, W. H. (1978) "Multiculturalism as the normal human experience," in E. M. Eddy and W. L. Partridge (eds.) Applied Anthropology in America. New York: Columbia University Press.

GOODLAD, J. I. (1975) The Dynamics of Educational Change: Towards Responsive Schools. New York: McGraw-Hill.

––– M. F. KLEIN, and Associates (1970) Behind the Classroom Door. Worthington, OH: Charles A. Jones.

GORTON, R. and K. McINTYRE (1978) The Senior High School Principalship, Volume II: The Effective Principal. Reston, VA: National Association of Secondary School Principals.

GOULDNER, A. W. (1954) Wildcat Strike. Yellow Springs, OH: Antioch.

GRANOVETTER, M. (1973) "The strength of weak ties." American Journal of Sociology 78: 1360-1380.

GREENWOOD, P. W., D. MANN, and M. W. McLAUGHLIN (1975) Federal Programs Supporting Educational Change, Volume III: The Process of Change. Santa Monica, CA: Rand Corporation.

GROSS, N. (1978) "Basic issues in the management of educational change efforts," in R. E. Herriott and N. Gross (eds.) The Dynamics of Planned Educational Change. Berkeley, CA: McCutchan.

——— J. B. GIACQUINTA, and M. BERNSTEIN (1971) Implementing Organizational Innovations: A Sociological Analysis of Planned Educational Change. New York: Basic Books.

GUBA, E. and D. C. CLARK (1976) Research on Institutions of Teacher Education, Volume III: An Institutional Self-Report on Knowledge Production and Utilization Activities in Schools, Colleges and Departments of Education. Bloomington, IN: RITE Project.

——— (1974) The Configurational Perspective: A Challenge to the Systems View of Educational Knowledge Production and Utilization. Washington, DC: Council for Educational Development and Research.

HAGE, J. (1965) "An axiomatic theory of organizations." Administrative Science Quarterly 10.

——— and M. AIKEN (1970) Social Change in Complex Organizations. New York: Random House.

——— (1969) "Routine technology, social structure, and organizational goals." Administrative Science Quarterly 14, 3: 366-377.

——— (1967) "Program change and organizational properties: a comparative analysis." American Journal of Sociology 72: 503-519.

HALL, G. (1974) A Concerns-Based Model: A Developmental Conceptualization. Austin, TX: Research and Development Center for Teacher Education.

——— and S. F. LOUCKS (1977) "A developmental model for determining whether the treatment is actually implemented." American Educational Research Journal 14, 3: 263-276.

——— (1976) A Developmental Model for Determining Whether or Not the Treatment is Really Implemented. Austin: Research and Development Center for Teacher Education, University of Texas.

HALL, G. and W. L. RUTHERFORD (1976) "Concerns about implementing team teaching." Educational Leadership (December).

HALL, G., S. HORD, and T. GRIFFIN (1980) "Implementation at the school building level: the development and analysis of nine mini-case studies." Presented at the annual meeting of the American Educational Research Asociation.

HALL, G., P. ZIGARMI, and S. HORD (1979) "A taxonomy of interventions: the prototype and initial testing." Presented at the annual meeting of the American Educational Research Association.

HALL, G., S. LOUCKS, W. RUTHERFORD, and B. NEWLOVE (1975) "Levels of use of the innovation: a framework for analyzing innovation adoption." Journal of Teacher Education 26, 1: 52-56.

HALPERIN, S. (1980) "The educational arena." Educational Evaluation and Policy Analysis 2, 1: 27-36.

HALPERN, R. (1978) Treeline Case Study, Project CEDISS. Cambridge, MA: Abt Associates.

HAMILTON, L. S. and J. E. MUTHARD (1975a) "Research utilization specialists in vocational rehabilitation: five years of experience." Rehabilitation Counseling Bulletin 2: 377-386.

––– (1975b) Research Utilization Specialists in Vocational Rehabilitation. Gainesville: Rehabilitation Research Institute, University of Florida.

HANCOCK, G. K. (1974) "The resource colleague experiment," pp. 262-281 in D. E. Edgar (ed.) The Competent Teacher. London: Angus and Robertson.

HANSON, E. M. (1978) "Organizational control in educational systems: a case study of governance in schools." Presented at the annual meeting of the American Educational Research Association. ED 150 723.

––– (1975) "The modern educational bureaucracy and the process of change." Educational Administration Quarterly 11, 3: 21-36.

HANUSHEK, E. A. (1978) "A reader's guide to educational production functions." Prepared for the NIE National Invitational Conference on School Organization and Effects, San Diego, California, January 27-29.

HARGROVE, E. (1975) The Missing Link: The Study of Implementation of Social Policy. Washington, DC: Urban Institute.

HAUGERUD, A., J. GORMAN, A. MURPHY, W. BEECROFT, L. ROKOVITZ, and D. CAMPBELL (1979) School Improvement Efforts via Linkers and Linkage Systems. Olympia: Northwest Reading Consortium, Washington State Department of Education.

HAVELOCK, R. G. (1969) Planning for Innovation. Ann Arbor: Center for Research on Utilization of Scientific Knowledge, University of Michigan.

––– (1968) "Dissemination and translation roles," in T. L. Eidell and J. M. Kitchell (eds.) Knowledge Production and Utilization in Educational Administration. Eugene: Center for Advanced Study of Educational Administration, University of Oregon.

––– and M. C. HAVELOCK (1973) Training for Change Agents. Ann Arbor: Center for Research on Utilization of Scientific Knowledge, University of Michigan.

HAVELOCK, R. G. and A. M. HUBERMAN (1978) Solving Educational Problems: The Theory and Reality of Innovation in Developing Countries. New York: Praeger.

HAVELOCK, R. G. and F. C. MANN (1968) Research and Development Laboratory Management Knowledge Utilization Study. Ann Arbor: Center for Research on Utilization of Scientific Knowledge, University of Michigan.

HAVELOCK, R. G. and M. C. HAVELOCK, with E. A. MARKOWITZ (1973) Educational Innovation in the United States, Volume I: The National Survey: The Substance and the Process. Ann Arbor: Center for Research on Utilization of Scientific Knowledge, University of Michigan.

HAWLEY, W. D. (1976) "Horses before carts: developing adaptive schools and the limits of innovation," in S. Gove and F. M. Wirt (eds.) Political Science and School Politics. Lexington, MA: D. C. Heath.

––– (1975) "Dealing with organizational rigidity in public schools: a theoretical perspective," in F. M. Wirt (ed.) The Polity and the School: Political Perspectives in Education. Lexington, MA: D. C. Heath.

HEIGHTON, R. H., Jr., and C. HEIGHTON (1978) "Applying the anthropological perspective to social policy," in E. M. Eddy and W. L. Partridge (eds.) Aplied Anthropology in America. New York: Columbia University Press.

HENRY, J. (1963) Culture Against Man. New York: Random House.

HENSLEY, S. E. and C. NELSON (1979) "Information about users and usages: a literature review." Prepared for Program on Dissemination and Improvement of Practice, National Institute of Education, Washington, D.C. (unpublished)

HERRIOTT, R. E. (1979) Federal Initiatives and Rural School Improvement. Cambridge, MA: Abt Associates.

––– and N. GROSS [eds.] (1979) The Dynamics of Planned Educational Change: An Analysis of the Rural Experimental Schools Program. Berkeley, CA: McCutchan.

HERRIOTT, R. E. and B. J. HODGKINS (1973) The Environment of Schooling. Englewood Cliffs, NJ: Prentice-Hall.

––– (1969) "Social context and the school." Rural Sociology 34: 149-166.

HERSKOVITZ, M. J. (1963) Cultural Anthropology. New York: Knopf.

HILL-BURNETT, J. (1978) "Developing anthropological knowledge through applications," in E. M. Eddy and W. L. Partridge (eds.) Applied Anthropology in America. New York: Columbia University Press.

HOLZNER, B. (1974) "Uses of sociological theory—an essay on theory, action and practice." Presented at the Symposium on Knowledge Utilization, Greystone Conference Center, Riverdale, New York.

HOOD, P. (1979a) Indicators of Educational Knowledge Production, Dissemination, and Utilization: A Conceptual Framework. San Francisco: Far West Laboratory for Educational Research and Development.

——— [ed.] (1979b) New Perspectives on Planning, Management and Evaluation in School Improvement: A report on the 1979 Far West Laboratory Summer Workshop on Educational Dissemination and School Improvement. San Francisco: Far West Laboratory for Educational Research and Development.

——— and L. BLACKWELL (1979) Indicators of Educational Knowledge Production, Dissemination, and Utilization: An Exploratory Data Analysis. San Francisco: Far West Laboratory for Educational Research and Development.

——— (1976a) Study of Innovation Requirements in Education, Volume I: Key Educational Information Users and Their Styles of Information Use. Santa Monica, CA: Systems Development Corporation.

——— (1976b) The Educational Information Market Study, Volumes I and II. San Francisco: Far West Laboratory for Educational Research and Development.

HOOD, P. and C. S. CATES (1978) Alternative Approaches to Analyzing Dissemination and Linkage Roles and Functions. San Francisco: Far West Laboratory for Educational Research and Development.

HOOD, P., C. MICK, and R. V. KATTER (1976) Study of Information Requirements in Education, Volume II: A Mail Survey of User Information Requirements. Santa Monica, CA: Systems Development Corporation.

HOTVEDT, M. O. (1973) Communication Patterns Within the Gifted Program. Urbana-Champaign: Center for Instructional Research and Curriculum Evaluation, University of Illinois.

HOUSE, E. R. (1980) "Three perspectives on innovation: the technological, the political, and the cultural." Prepared for the Program on Research and Educational Practice, National Institute of Education.

——— (1979a) "The objectivity, fairness, and justice of federal evaluation policy as reflected in the Follow Through evaluation." Educational Evaluation and Policy Analysis 1, 1: 28-42.

——— (1979b) "Technology versus craft: a ten year perspective on innovation." Journal of Curriculum Studies 11, 1: 1-15.

——— (1978) "The relevance of evaluation," in R. Rippey (ed.) Studies in Transactional Evaluation.

——— (1976) Transferability and Equity in Innovation Policy. Urbana-Champaign: Center for Instructional Research and Curriculum Evaluation, University of Illinois.

——— (1974) The Politics of Educational Innovation. Berkeley, CA: McCutchan.

——— (1971) "A critique of linear change models in education." Educational Technology 11, 10.

——— T. KERINS, and J. M. STEELE (1972) "A test of the research and development model of change." Educational Administration Quarterly 8 (Winter).

HOVLAND, C. I. and W. WEISS (1951) "The influence of source credibility on communication effectiveness." Public Opinion Quarterly 15: 635-650.

HOWEY, K. and B. JOYCE (1978) "A data base for future directions in in-service education." Theory Into Practice 27, 3.

HUBERMAN, M. (1981) "Finding and using recipes for busy kitchens: a situational analysis of knowledge use in schools." Prepared for the Program on Research and Educational Practice, National Institute of Education.

HUGUENIN, K., R. ZERCHYKOV, and D. DAVIES (1979) Narrowing the Gap Between Intent and Practice: A Report to Policymakers on Community Organizations and School Decisionmaking. Boston: Institute for Responsive Education.

HUTCHINS, C. L. (1977) "Options paper on an NIE extension agent initiative." National Institute of Education, Washington, D.C (unpublished)

HYDE, A. (1977) Capacities for Problem Solving: Problems and Problem Solving Methods for School Principals. Chicago: Center for New Schools.

IANNACONE, L. and F. LUTZ (1970) Politics, Power, and Policy: The Governing of a School District. Columbus, OH: Charles E. Merrill.

INTILI, J. K. and T. E. DEAL (1977) The Labyrinths of Diagnostic-Prescriptive Instruction. Stanford, CA: School of Education, Stanford University.

JACKSON, P. (1968) Life in Classrooms. New York: Holt, Rinehart & Winston.

JACQUES, E. (1951) The Changing Culture of a Factory. London: Tavistock.

JANOWITZ, M. (1971) Institution Building in Urban Education. Chicago: University of Chicago Press.

JONES, G. (1969) Planned Organizational Change: A Study in Change Dynamics. New York: Praeger.

JUNG, C. (1976) "Training materials and training for OD in education." Education and Urban Society 8: 145-158.

––– and R. LIPPITT (1966) "The study of change as a concept." Theory Into Practice 5, 1.

JURKOVICH, R. (1974) "A core typology of organization environments." Administrative Science Quarterly 19, 3: 380-394.

KAPLAN, R. (1978) "Stages in developing a consulting relation: a case study of a long beginning." Journal of Aplied Behavioral Science 14: 43-60.

KATTER, R. and C. HULL (1976) Survey of Educational Information Service Sites. Santa Monica, CA: Systems Development Corporation.

KATZ, D. and R. KAHN (1966) The Social Psychology of Organizations. New York: John Wiley.

KATZ, M. B. (1975) Class, Bureaucracy and Schools: The Illusion of Educational Change in America. New York: Praeger.

KELLY, D. G. (1977) "The effects of curriculum organizational structure on curriculum innovation." Presented at the annual meeting of the American Educational Research Asociation.

KELLY, P. and M. I. KRANZBERG [eds.] (1978) Technological Innovation: A Critical Review of Current Knowledge. San Francisco: San Francisco Press.

KERR, N. D. (1964) "The school board as an agency of legitimation." Sociology of Education 38: 34-59.

KESTER, R. J. and W. L. HULL (1973) Identification of Empirical Dimensions of the Diffusion Process: Interim Report. Columbus, OH: Center for Vocational Education.

KEYS, C. and J. BARTUNEK (1979) "Organization development in schools: goal agreement, process skills, and diffusion of change." Journal of Applied Behavioral Science 15: 61-78.

KING, E. J. (1979) Other Schools and Ours: A Comparative Study for Today. New York: Holt, Rinehart & Winston.

KIRST, M. W. (1980) "Interview." Educational Evaluation and Policy Analysis 2, 1: 77-83.

––– (1978) "Strengthening federal-local relationships supporting educational change," pp. 274-279 in R. E. Herriot and N. Gross (eds.) The Dynamics of Planned Educational Change. Berkeley, CA: McCutchan.

––– and R. JUNG (1980) "The utility of a longitudinal approach in assessing implementation: a thirteen year view of Title I, ESEA." Presented at the annual meeting of the Science Association, San Francisco, March 30.

KNOTT, J. and A. WILDAVSKY (1980) "If dissemination is the solution, what is the problem?" Knowledge: Creation, Diffusion, Utilization 1, 4: 537-578.

KOHL, J. W. (1973) "The viability of the development council: a voluntary educational change agency." Presented at the annual meeting of the American Educational Research Association.

KORMOS, J. M. and R. J. ENNS (1979) Professional Development Through Curriculum Development. Toronto: Ontario Teachers' Federation.

KOUZES, J. M. and P. R. MICO (1979) "Domain theory: an introduction to organizational behavior in human service organizations." Journal of Applied Behavioral Science 15, 4: 449-469.

KUHN, T. S. (1970) The Structure of Scientific Revolutions. Chicago: University of Chicago Press.

LARSEN, J. (1980) "Knowledge utilization: what is it?" Knowledge: Creation, Diffusion, Utilization 1: 421-442.

LAU, L. J. (1978) "Educational production functions: a summary." Prepared for the National Institute of Education Conference.

LAWRENCE, P. R. and J. W. LORSCH (1967) Organization and Environment. Cambridge, MA: Harvard Business School.

LEITHWOOD, K., J. CLIPSHAM, F. MAYNES, and R. BAXTER (1976) Planning Curriculum Change: A Model and Case Study. Toronto: Ontario Institute for Studies in Education.

LEITHWOOD, K. J. et al. (1978) An Empirical Investigation of Teachers' Curriculum Decision-Making Processes and Strategies Used by Curriculum Decision Managers to Influence Such Decision Making. Toronto: Ontario Institute for Studies in Education.

LEVINSON, E. (1976) The Alum Rock Voucher Demonstration: Three Years of Implementation. Santa Monica, CA: Rand Corporation.

LEWIN, K. (1958) "Group decision and social change," pp. 197-211 in E. E. MacCoby et al. (eds.) Readings in Social Psychology. New York: Holt, Rinehart & Winston.

LIEBERMAN, A. (1977) "Political and economic stress and the social reality of schools." Teachers College Record 79, 2: 259-267.

——— and L. MILLER (1979) "The social realities of teaching," pp. 54-68 in A. Lieberman and L. Miller (eds.) Staff Development: New Demands, New Realities, New Perspectives. New York: Teachers College Press.

LIGHT, R. J. (1979) "Capitalizing on variation: how conflicting research findings can be helpful." Educational Researcher (October): 7-11.

——— and P. V. SMITH (1971) "Accumulating evidence: procedures for resolving contradictions among different studies." Harvard Educational Review 41: 419-471.

LIGHTHALL, F. F. (1973) "Multiple realities and organizational nonsolutions: an eassay on anatomy of educational innovation." School Review (February): 255-287.

LIN, N. et al. (1966) The Diffusion of an Innovation in Three Michigan High Schools: Institution Building Through Change. East Lansing: Michigan State University.

LINDBLOM, C. and D. K. COHEN (1979) Usable Knowledge. New Haven, CT: Yale University Press.

LIPHAM, J. (1980) "Change agentry and school improvement: the principal's role," pp. 61-96 in Interorganizational Arrangements for Collaborative Efforts: Commissioned Papers. Portland, OR: Northwest Regional Educational Laboratory.

LIPPITT, R. (1979) "Consultation: traps and potentialities," in R. E. Herriott and N. Gross (eds.) The Dynamics of Planned Educational Change. Berkeley, CA: McCutchan.

——— (1969) "The process of utilization of social research to improve social practice," in W. G. Bennis et al. (eds.) The Planning of Change. New York: Holt, Rinehart & Winston.

LITWAK, E. and H. MEYER (1966) "A balance theory of coordination between organizations and community primary groups." Administrative Science Quarterly 11: 31-58.

LORSCH, J. W. (1976) "Contingency theory and organization design," pp. 141-165 in R. H. Kilmann et al. (eds.) The Management of Organization Design, Volume I. New York: Elsevier North-Holland.

LORSEN, J. K. and R. AGARWOLA-ROGERS (1977) "Re-invention of innovative ideas: Modified? Adopted? None of the above?" Evaluation 4: 136-140.

LORTIE, D. C. (1977a) An Exploration of Urban School Structure and Teacher Professionalism. Chicago: Center for New Schools.

——— (1977b) "Two anomalies and three perspectives: some observations on school organization," pp. 20-38 in R. G. Corwin et al. (eds.) Perspectives on Organizations: The School as a Social Organization. Washington, DC: American Association of Colleges for Teacher Education.

——— (1975) Schoolteacher: A Sociological Study. Chicago: University of Chicago Press.

LOTTO, L. S. and D. L. CLARK (1978) Education Knowledge Production and Utilization: An Assessment of Current and Potential Capabilities of Schools of Education, with Recommendations for Federal Support Strategies. San Francisco: Far West Laboratory for Educational Research and Development.

LOUCKS, S. and G. HALL (1979) "Implementing innovations in schools: a concerns-based approach." Presented at the annual meeting of the American Educational Research Association.

LOUCKS, S. and M. MELLE (1980) "Implementation of a district-wide curriculum: the effects of a three year study." Presented at the annual meeting of the American Educational Research Association.

LOUIS, K. S. (1980) "Meet the project: a study of the R&D Utilization Program." Presented at the annual meeting of the American Educational Research Association.

——— (1978) "Using information in an organizational context." Presented at the annual meeting of the American Educational Research Association.

——— (1975) "The development of linking organizations in an educational context." Ph.D. dissertation, Columbia University.

——— and S. D. SIEBER (1979) Bureaucracy and the Dispersed Organization—The Educational Extension Agent Experiment. Norwood, NJ: Ablex.

LOUIS, K. S., D. KELL, and A. YOUNG (1981) The Human Factor in Knowledge Use: Field Agent Roles in Education. Cambridge, MA: Abt Associates.

LOUIS, K. S., S. ROSENBLUM, and J. MOLITOR (1981) Linking R&D Outcomes with Local Schools, Volume II: The Process and Outcomes of Knowledge Utilization. Cambridge, MA: Abt Associates.

LOUIS, K. S., J. MOLITOR, G. SPENCER, and R. YIN (1979) Linking R&D with Local Schools: An Interim Report. Cambridge, MA: Abt Associates.

LUKAS, C. (1975) "Issues of implementation in Head Start planned variation," in A. Rivlin and M. Timpane (eds.) Planned Variation in Education: Should We Give Up or Try Harder? Washington, DC: Brookings.

——— and C. WOHLLEB (1973) Implementation of Head Start Planned Variation: 1970-71, Parts 1 and 2. Cambridge, MA: Huron Institute.

LYON, C., L. DOSCHER, P. McGRANAHAN, and R. WILLIAMS (1979) Evaluation and School Districts. Los Angeles: Center for the Study of Evaluation, UCLA.

McCALL, M. W., Jr., and M. M. LOMBARDO [eds.] (1978) Leadership: Where Else Can We Go? Durham, NC: Duke University Press.

MacDONALD, B. and R. WALKER (1976) Changing the Curriculum. London: Open Books.

McGREGOR, D. M. (1960) The Human Side of Enterprise. New York: McGraw-Hill.

MACHLUP, F. (1979) "Uses, value, and benefits of knowledge." Knowledge: Creation, Diffusion, Utilization 1, 1.

McLAUGHLIN, M. W. and D. MARSH (1978) "Staff development and school change." Teachers College Record 80, 1.

McLEAN, L. D. (1979) "The chastening of educational research." Ontario Institute for Studies in Education, Toronto. (unpublished)

McPHERSON, G. (1973) "The teacher and the class: an investigation of the process and functions of identification," in S. D. Sieber and D. E. Wilder (eds.) The School in Society. New York: Macmillan.

MADEY, D. L. (1979) "A study of the relationships among educational linker roles and selected linker functions." Ph.D. dissertation, Duke University.

――― E. C. ROYSTER, J. K. DECAD, R. F. BAKER, and E. W. STRANG (1979) Building Capacity for Improvement of Educational Practice: An Evaluation of NIE's State Dissemination Grants Program. Durham, NC: NTS Research Corporation.

MAHAN, J. M. (1972) "Frank observations on innovation in elementary schools." Interchange 3, 2-3: 144-160.

MAJONE, G. and A. WILDAVSKY (1978) "Implementation as evolution," in H. E. Freeman (ed.) Policy Studies Review Annual: Volume II. Beverly Hills, CA: Sage.

MANN, D. [ed.] (1978) Making Change Happen. New York: Teachers College Press.

――― (1976) "The politics of training teachers in schools." Teachers College Record 77, 3: 323-338.

MARCH, J. G. and J. P. OLSEN (1976) Ambiguity and Choice in Organizations. Bergen, Norway: Universitetsforlaget.

――― (1975) "The uncertainty of the past: organizational learning under ambiguity." European Journal of Political Research 3: 147-171.

MARCH, J. G. and H. SIMON (1958) Organizations. New York: John Wiley.

MEYER, J. W. and E. COHEN (1971) The Impact of the Open-Space School upon Teacher Influence and Autonomy: The Effects of an Organizational Innovation. Technical Report 21. Stanford, CA: Stanford Center for Research and Development in Teaching.

MEYER, J. W. and B. ROWAN (1978) "The structure of educational organizations," pp. 78-107 in M. W. Meyer et al. (eds.) Environments and Organizations. San Francisco: Jossey-Bass.

――― (1977) "Institutionalized organizations: formal structure as myth and ceremony." American Journal of Sociology 83, 2: 340-363.

MEYER, J. W., W. R. SCOTT, S. COLE, and J. K. INTILI (1978) "Instructional dissensus and institutional consensus in schools," pp. 233-263 in M. W. Meyer et al. (eds.) Environments and Organizations. San Francisco: Jossey-Bass.

MICHAELSON, J. R. (1977) "Revision, bureaucracy, and school reform: a critique of Katz. School Review 85, 2: 229-245.

MILES, M. B. (1980) Linkage in a New Key: The DTA Experience. New York: Center for Policy Research.

――― (1978) On Networking. Washington, DC: National Institute of Education.

――― (1976) "Diffusing OD in the schools: the prospects." Education and Urban Society 8: 242-254.

――― (1975) "The teacher centre: educational change through teacher development. Reflections and commentary on the Syracuse Conference on the Teacher Centre," in A. E. Adams (ed.) In-Service Education and Teacher Centres. Oxford: Pergamon.

――― (1974) "A matter of linkage: how can innovation research and innovation practice influence each other?" pp. 199-216 in S. V. Tempin and M. V. Brown (eds.) What do Research Findings Say About Getting Innovations into Schools: A Symposium. Philadelphia: Research for Better Schools.

――― (1967) "Some properties of schools as social systems," in G. Watson (ed.) Change in School Systems. Washington, DC: National Training Laboratories, NEA.

――― (1965) "Planned change and organizational health: figure and ground," pp. 11-36 in R. O. Carlson et al. (eds.) Change Processes in the Public Schools. Eugene: Center for Advanced Study of Educational Administration, University of Oregon.

――― (1964) Innovation in Education. New York: Teachers College Press.

――― and R. A. SCHMUCK (1971) "Improving schools through organization development: an overview," pp. 1-27 in R. A. Schmuck and M. B. Miles (eds.) Organization Development in Schools. La Jolla, CA: University Associates.

MILES, M. B., M. FULLAN, and G. TAYLOR (1978a) Organizational Development in Schools: The State of the Art, Volume III: OD Consultants/OD Programs in School Districts. New York: Center for Policy Research.

——— (1978b) Organizational Development in Schools: The State of the Art, Volume V: Implications for Policy, Research and Practice. New York: Center for Policy Research.

MILES, M. B., P. H. CALDER, H. A. HORNSTEIN, D. M. CALLAHAN, and R. S. SCHIAVO (1969) "Data feedback and organizational change in a school system," pp. 457-467 in W. G. Bennis et al. (eds.) The Planning of Change. New York: Holt, Rinehart & Winston.

MILES, M. B., E. W. SULLIVAN, B. A. GOLD, B. L. TAYLOR, S. D. SIEBER, and D. E. WILDER (1978a) Project on Social Architecture in Education, Volume I: Planning and Implementing New Schools. New York: Center for Policy Research.

——— (1978b) Project on Social Architecture in Education, Volume III: Westgate Schools: A Case Study of Two Open-Space Elementary Schools. New York: Center for Policy Research.

——— (1978c) Project on Social Architecture in Education, Volume IV: Conclusions—Reflections on the Case Studies and Implications. New York: Center for Policy Research.

MINTZBERG, H., D. RAISINGHAIN, and A. THORET (1976) "The structure of 'unstructured' decision processes." Administrative Science Quarterly 21: 246-275.

MISKEL, C. (1979) "Demographic characteristics, faculty attributes and school structure." Presented at the annual meeting of the American Educational Research Association.

MOHR, L. B. (1977) Process Theory and Variance Theory in Innovation Research. Discussion Paper No. 115. Ann Arbor: Institute of Public Policy Studies, University of Michigan.

——— (1969) "Determinants of innovation in organizations." American Political Science Review 63, 1: 111-126.

MOORE, D. E., M. SCHEPERS, M. HOLMES, K. BLAIR, et al. (1977) Assistance Strategies of Six Groups that Facilitate Educational Change at the School Community Level. Chicago: Center for New Schools.

MORRISH, I. (1976) Aspects of Educational Change. New York: John Wiley.

MOWLANA, H. and A. E. ROBINSON (1976) "Ethnic mobilization and communication theory," in A. A. Said and L. R. Simmons (eds.) Ethnicity in an International Context. New Brunswick, NJ: Transaction.

MURPHY, J. T. (1971) "Title I of ESEA: the politics of implementing federal education reform." Harvard Educational Review 41, 1: 35-62.

NASH, C. and D. IRELAND (1979) "In-service education: cornerstone of curriculum development or stumbling block?" Presented at the annual meeting of the Canadian Society for the Study of Education.

NASH, N. and J. CULBERTSON (1977) "Introduction," pp. 1-5 in N. Nash and J. Culbertson (eds.) Linking Processes in Educational Improvement. Columbus, OH: University Council for Educational Administration.

National Council for Educational Research (1979) Statement of Policy on Dissemination for the National Institute of Education. Washington, DC: National Institute of Education.

National Institute of Education (1976) Current Issues, Problems, and Concerns in Curriculum Development. Washington, DC: Author.

NAUMANN-ETIENNE, M. (1974) "Bringing about open education: strategies for innovation." Ph.D. dissertation, University of Michigan, Ann Arbor.

NEAL, M. A. (1965) Values and Interests in Social Change. Englewood Cliffs, NJ: Prentice-Hall.

NELSON, M. (1975) The Adoption of Innovations in Urban Schools. New York: Bureau of Applied Social Research.

––– and S. D. SIEBER (1976) "Innovations in urban secondary schools." School Review 84: 213-231.

NELSON, R. K. (1974) "Intellectualizing about the moon-ghetto metaphor: a study of the current malaise of rational analysis of social problems." Policy Sciences 5: 375-414.

––– and S. C. WINTER (1977) "In search of useful theory of innovation." Research Policy 6: 36-76.

NIEDERMEYER, F. C. (1979) "A model for the implementation of outcomes-based instructional products." Presented at the annual meeting of the American Educational Research Association.

NOAH, H. J. and M. A. ECKSTEIN (1969) Toward a Science of Comparative Education. New York: Macmillan.

NTE Research Corporation (1979) The State Dissemination Grants Program: 1978 State Abstracts, with an Analysis Across the States. Durham, NC: Author.

OLSON, J. (1980) "Teacher constructs and curriculum change: innovative doctrines and practical dilemmas." Presented at the annual meeting of the American Educational Research Association.

ORLICH, D., T. RUFF, and E. M. HANSON (1976) "Stalking curriculum: or where do principals learn about new programs?" Educational Leadership 33: 614-621.

OWENS, R. and C. STEINHOFF (1976) Administering Change in Schools. Englewood Cliffs, NJ: Prentice-Hall.

PACKARD, J. S. (1977) Schools as Work Organizations. Eugene: Center for Educational Policy and Management, University of Oregon.

––– W. W. CHARTERS, Jr., and K. E. DUCKWORTH, with T. D. JOVICK (1978) Management Implications of Team Teaching: Final Report. Eugene: Center for Educational Policy and Management, University of Oregon.

PAISLEY, W., M. CIRKSENA, and M. BUTLER (1979) Conceptualization of Information Equity Issues in Education. San Francisco: Far West Laboratory for Educational Research and Development.

PARSONS, T. (1965) "An outline of the social system," pp. 30-79 in T. Parsons (ed.) Theories of Society. New York: Macmillan.

PAUL, D. A. (1977) "Change processes at the elementary, secondary and post-secondary levels of education," in N. Nash and J. Culbertson (eds.) Linking Processes in Educational Improvement. Columbus, OH: University Council for Educational Administration.

PAULSTON, R. G. (1976) Conflicting Theories of Social and Political Change. Pittsburgh, PA: Center for International Studies, University of Pittsburgh.

PAULY, E. (1978) "The decision to innovate: career pursuit as an incentive for educational change," pp. 261-284 in D. Mann (ed.) Making Change Happen. New York: Teachers College Press.

PELLEGRIN, R. J. (1978) "Sociology and policy-oriented research on innovation," in M. Radnor et al. (eds.) The Diffusion of Innovations: An Assessment. Evanston, IL: Center for Interdisciplinary Study of Science and Technology, Northwestern University.

––– (1976) "Schools as work settings," in R. Dubin (ed.) Handbook of Work, Organization, and Society. Skokie, IL: Rand McNally.

PELZ, D. and F. ANDREWS (1966) Scientists in Organizations. New York: John Wiley.

PERROW, C. (1972) Complex Organizations: A Critical Essay. Glenview, IL: Scott, Foresman.

PHARIS, W. and S. ZAKARIYA (1979) The Elementary School Principalship in 1978: A Research Study. Arlington, VA: National Association of Elementary School Principals.

PIELE, P. K. (1975) Review and Analysis of the Role, Activities and Training of Education Linking Agents. Eugene: University of Oregon.

PINCUS, J. (1974) "Incentives for innovation in the public schools." Review of Educational Research 44, 1: 113-144.

PORRAS, J. I. (1979) "The comparative impact of different OD techniques and intervention intensities." Journal of Applied Behavioral Science 15: 156-178.

PRATT, H., M. MELLE, and J. METSDORF (1980) "The design and utilization of a concerns-based staff development program for implementing a revised science curriculum." Presented at the annual meeting of the American Educational Research Association.

RADNOR, M., I. FELLER, and E. ROGERS [eds.] (1978) The Diffusion of Innovations: An Assessment. Evanston, IL: Center for Interdisciplinary Study of Science and Technology, Northwestern University.

RAIZEN, S. (1979) "Dissemination programs at the National Institute of Education, 1974 to 1979." Knowledge: Creation, Diffusion, Utilization 1: 259-292.

RASPBERRY, W. (1978) "For ailing schools home remedies are best." Washington Post (February 13).

REGAN, E. and C. WINTER (forthcoming) "Tasks performed by consultants to influence the curriculum decisions of teachers," in K. Keithwood (ed.) Studies of Curriculum Decision-Making.

REIN, M. and S. WHITE (1977) "Policy research: belief and doubt." Policy Analysis 3: 239-271.

REINHARD, D. et al. (1980) "Great expectations: the principal's role and in-service needs in supporting change projects." Presented at the annual meeting of the American Educational Research Association.

RICH, R. F. (1979) "The pursuit of knowledge." Knowledge: Creation, Diffusion, Utilization 1, 1.

RIECKEN, H. W. and R. F. BORUCH (1974) Social Experimentation. New York: Academic.

RIECKEN, H. W. and G. C. HOMANS (1954) "Psychological aspects of social structure," pp. 786-829 in G. Lindzey (ed.) Handbook of Social Psychology. Cambridge, MA: Addison-Wesley.

RIVLIN, A. (1971) Systematic Thinking for Social Action. Washington, DC: Brookings.

——— and M. TIMPANE [eds.] (1975) Planned Variation in Education: Should We Give Up or Try Harder? Washington, DC: Brookings.

ROGERS, E. M. (1978) "Re-invention during the innovation process," in M. Radnor et al. (eds.) The Diffusion of Innovations: An Assessment. Evanston, IL: Center for the Interdisciplinary Study of Science and Technology, Northwestern University.

——— (1962) Diffusion of Innovations. New York: Macmillan.

——— and J. D. EVELAND (1977) The Innovation Process in Public Organizations: Some Elements of a Preliminary Model. Ann Arbor: University of Michigan.

ROGERS, E. M. and F. SHOEMAKER (1971) Communication of Innovations. New York: Macmillan.

ROGERS, E. M., J. D. EVELAND, and A. BEAN (1976) Extending the Agricultural Extension Model. Stanford, CA: Institute for Communication Research, Stanford University.

ROSENBLUM, S. and K. S. LOUIS (1981) Stability and Change: Innovation in an Educational Context. New York: Plenum.

——— (1978) A Measure of Change: The Process and Outcomes of Planned Change in Ten Rural Districts. Cambridge, MA: Abt Associates.

ROSS, D. [ed.] (1958) Administration for Adaptability. New York: Metropolitan School Study Council.

RUBIN, L. (1971) The In-Service Education of Teachers. Boston: Allyn & Bacon.

RUDDUCK, J. (1977) "Dissemination as encounter of cultures." Research Intelligence 3: 3-5.

RUFF, T. and D. ORLICH (1974) "How do elementary school principals learn about curriculum innovations?" Elementary School Journal: 389-392.

RUNKEL, P. J. and W. E. BELL (1976) "Some conditions affecting a school's readiness to profit from OD training." Education and Urban Society 8: 127-144.

RUTTER, M., B. MAUGHAM, P. MORTIMER, J. OUSTON, with A. SMITH (1979) Fifteen Thousand Hours: Secondary Schools and Their Effects on Children. Cambridge, MA: Harvard University Press.

SABATIER, P. (1978) "The acquisition and utilization of technical information by administrative agencies." Administrative Science Quarterly 23: 396-417.

SAID, A. A. and L. R. SIMMONS (1976) "The ethnic factor in world politics," in A. A. Said and L. R. Simmons (eds.) Ethnicity in an International Context. New Brunswick, NJ: Transaction.

St. PIERRE, R. (1981) Three Ways of Learning More from Follow Through. Cambridge, MA: Abt Associates.

SAPOLSKY, H. (1967) "Organizational structure and innovation." Journal of Business 40, 4:497-510.

SARASON, S. B. (1972) The Creation of Settings and the Future Societies. San Francisco: Jossey-Bass.

――― (1971) The Culture of the School and the Problem of Change. Boston: Allyn & Bacon.

――― and E. LORENTZ (1979) The Challenge of the Resource Exchange Network. San Francisco: Jossey-Bass.

SARASON, S. B., C. CARROLL, K. MATON, S. COHEN, and E. LORENTZ (1977) Human Services and Resource Networks. San Francisco: Jossey-Bass.

SCHAFFARZICK, J. (1975) "The consideration of curriculum change at the local level." Ph.D. dissertation, Stanford University.

SCHEIN, E. H. (1970) Organizational Psychology. Englewood Cliffs, NJ: Prentice-Hall.

SCHMUCK, R. (1971) "Developing teams of organizational specialists," in R. Schmuck and M. B. Miles (eds.) Organization Development in Schools. Palo Alto, CA: National.

――― and M. B. MILES [eds.] (1971) Organization Development in Schools. Palo Alto, CA: National.

SCHMUCK, R., P. RUNKEL, J. M. ARENDS, and R. I. ARENDS (1977) The Second Handbook of OD in Schools. Palo Alto, CA: Mayfield.

SCHON, D. (1979) "Generative metaphor: a perspective on problem setting in social policy," in A. Ortony (ed.) Metaphor in Thought. Cambridge, England: Cambridge University Press.

SCHULTZ, C. (1969) "The role of incentives, penalties, and rewards in attaining effective policy," in U.S. Congress, Joint Economic Committee, Economic Analysis and the Efficiency of Government, Part 3: Hearings of the Subcommittee on Economy in Government, September and October. Washington, DC: Government Printing Office.

SCHUTZ, A. (1967) The Phenomenology of the Social World. Evanston, IL: Northwestern University Press.

SCRIVEN, M. (1976) "Maximizing the power of causal investigations: a modus operandi method," in G. V Glass (ed.) Evaluation Studies Review Annual, Volume 1. Beverly Hills, CA: Sage.

――― (1967) "The methodology of evaluation," in R. E. Stake et al. (eds.) Perspectives on Curriculum Evaluation: AERA Monograph Series on Curriculum Evaluation, 1. Skokie, IL: Rand McNally.

SCURRAH, M., M. SHANI, and C. ZIPFELD (1971) "Influence of internal and external change agents in a simulated educational organization." Administrative Science Quarterly 16: 113-120.

SEBRING, R. (1979) "Knowledge utilization in organizational development." Journal of Applied Behavioral Science 15: 194-197.

SHARP, L., A. BIDERMAN, and J. FRANKEL (1978) Performers of Research and Research-Related Activities in the Field of Education. Washington, DC: Bureau of Social Science Research.

SHEPARD, H. (1967) "Innovation-resisting and innovation-producing organizations." Journal of Business 40, 9: 470-477.

SHIPMAN, M. (1974) Inside a Curriculum Project. London: Metheun.

SIEBER, S. D. (1981) Fatal Remedies: The Ironies of Social Intervention. New York: Plenum.

——— (1979) "Incentives and disincentives for knowledge utilization in education—a synthesis of research." Available through ERIC. (unpublished)

——— (1978) Presentation at the Abt Associates workshop for case study writers. Abt Associates, Cambridge, Massachusetts.

——— (1977) "Innovation and educational finance." Educational Technology (January): 34-38.

——— (1974) "Trends in diffusion research: knowledge utilization." Viewpoints, Bulletin of the School of Education, Indiana University 50, 3: 61-81.

——— (1972) "Images of the practitioner and strategies of educational change." Sociology of Education 45: 362-385.

——— (1968) "Organizational influences on innovative roles," pp. 120-142 in T. L. Eidell and J. M. Kitchel (eds.) Knowledge Production and Utilization in Educational Administration. Eugene: Center for the Advanced Study of Educational Administration, University of Oregon.

——— and P. F. LAZARSFELD (1966) The Organization of Educational Research in the United States. New York: Bureau of Applied Social Research.

SIEBER, S. D., K. S. LOUIS, and L. METZGER (1972) The Use of Educational Knowledge: Evaluation of the Pilot State Dissemination Program, Volumes I and II. New York: Bureau of Applied Social Research.

SILBERMAN, C. (1970) Crisis in the Classroom. New York: Vintage.

SILVER, C. B. (1973) Black Teachers in Urban Schools. New York: Praeger.

SILVERMAN, D. (1971) The Theory of Organizations. New York: Basic Books.

SIMON, H. A. (1978) "Rational decision-making in business organizations." Nobel Prize Lecture, Stockholm, November 24.

SMITH, A. G. and A. C. GRANVILLE (1978) Bayfield Case Study, Project CEDISS. Cambridge, MA: Abt Associates.

SMITH, L. M. and W. GEOFFREY (1968) The Complexities of an Urban Classroom. New York: Holt, Rinehart & Winston.

SMITH, L. M. and P. M. KEITH (1971) Anatomy of Educational Innovations: An Organizational Analysis of an Elementary School. New York: John Wiley.

SMITH, R. B. (1979) "Cumulative social science: paradigms, social research theory and development," in R. B. Smith and P. K. Manning (eds.) Handbook of Social Science Methods, Volume I: Qualitative Social Research. New York: Irvington.

SPADY, W. G. (1974) "Authority and empathy in the classroom," pp. 87-125 in D. W. O'Shea (ed.) Sociology of the School and Schooling. Washington, DC: National Institute of Education.

SPENCE, L. D., Y. TAKEI, and F. M. SIM (1978) "Conceptualizing loose coupling: believing is seeing or the garbage can as myth and ceremony." Presented at the annual meeting of the American Sociological Association.

SPENCER, G. and K. S. LOUIS (1980) Training and Support of Educational Linking Agents. Cambridge, MA: Abt Associates.

SPUCK, D. W. (1974) "Reward structures in the public high school." Educational Administration Quarterly 10, 1: 18-34.

STALLINGS, J. A. (1979) "Follow Through: a model for in-service teacher training." Curriculum Inquiry 9, 2: 163-181.

STEARNS, M. S. and C. L. NORWOOD (1977) Evaluation of the Field Test of Project Information Packages. Menlo Park, CA: Stanford Research Institute.

STEPHENS, J. M. (1967) The Process of Schooling. New York: Holt, Rinehart & Winston.

STEPHENS, R. (1979) Education Service Agencies: Status and Trends. Burtonsville, MD: Stephens Associates.

STEPHENS, T. (1974) "Innovative teaching practices: their relation to system norms and rewards." Educational Administration Quarterly 10, 1: 35-43.

STEWARD, J. H. (1955) Theory of Culture Change: The Methodology of Multilinear Evolution. Urbana: University of Illinois Press.

STILES, L. J. and B. ROBINSON (1973) "Change in education," in G. ZALTMAN et al. (eds.) Processes and Phenomena of Social Change. New York: John Wiley.
STOGDILL, R. (1974) Handbook of Leadership. New York: Macmillan.
SULLIVAN, E. W. and E. W. KIRONDE (1976) "Circumvention and cooptation in the planning of new schools." Presented at the annual meeting of the American Educational Research Association.
Teacher Education Reports (1979) "Teachers back public schools but favor changes in programs." Teacher Education Reports 1, 15.
THOMAS, M. A. (1978) A Study of Alternatives in American Education, Volume II: The Role of the Principal. Santa Monica, CA: Rand Corporation.
THOMAS, W. I. (1918) The Polish Peasant in Europe and America. Chicago: University of Chicago Press.
THOMPSON, J. D. (1967) Organizations in Action. New York: McGraw-Hill.
TRIST, E. (1976) "Action research and adaptive planning," in A. W. Clark (ed.) Experimenting with Organizations' Life. New York: Plenum.
TUMIN, M. (1977) "Schools as social organizations," pp. 39-57 in R. G. Corwin et al. (eds.) Perspectives on Organizations: The School as a Social Organization. Washington, DC: American Association of Colleges for Teacher Education.
TURNBULL, B. J. (1980) "The proliferation of federal systems promoting knowledge-based school improvement." Presented at the annual meeting of the American Educational Research Association.
——— L. I. THORN, and C. L. HUTCHINS (1975) Promoting Change in Schools: A Diffusion Casebook. San Francisco: Far West Laboratory for Educational Research and Development.
TYLER, R. W. and S. H. WHITE [chairmen] (1979) Testing, Teaching and Learning: Report of a Conference on Research on Testing. Washington, DC: National Institute of Education.
van GEEL, T. (1979) "The new low of the school curriculum," in J. Schaffarzick and G. Sykes (eds.) Curriculum Issues: Lessons from Research and Experience. Berkeley, CA: McCutchan.
VOLP, F. and L. HEIFETZ (1980) "School superintendents in New York State: role perceptions and issues orientations." Presented at the annual meeting of the American Educational Research Association.
WACASTER, C. T. (1975) "The life and death of differentiated staffing at Columbia High School," pp. 467-481 in J. V. Baldridge and T. E. Deal (eds.) Managing Change in Educational Organizations: Sociological Perspectives, Strategies, and Case Studies. Berkeley, CA: McCutchan.
WALKER, E. B. (1979) "Doing-by-learning: adaptive implementation and transactional evaluation in social action programs." School of Public Policy, University of California, Berkeley. (unpublished)
WALKER, W. E. and J. M. CHAIKEN (1981) "The effects of fiscal contraction on innovation in the public sector." Prepared for the Program on Research and Educational Practice, National Institute of Education.
WALLER, W. (1932) The Sociology of Teaching. New York: John Wiley.
WAYLAND, S. (1964) "Structural features of American education as basic factors in innovation," in M. B. Miles (ed.) Innovation in Education. New York: Teachers College Press.
WEBER, M. (1964) The Theory of Social and Economic Organization. New York: Macmillan.
——— (1925) Wirtschaft und Gesellschaft. Tubingen: J.C.B. Mohr (Paul Siebeck).
WEICK, K. E. (1980) "Loosely coupled systems: relaxed meanings and thick interpretations." Presented at the annual meeting of the American Educational Research Association.
——— (1976) "Educational organizations as loosely coupled systems." Administrative Science Quarterly 21: 1-19.
——— (1969) The Social Psychology of Organizations. Reading, MA: Addison-Wesley.

WEIKART, D. and B. BANET (1975) "Planned variation from the perspective of a model sponsor." Policy Analysis 1, 3.

WEILER, D. M. (1981) A Study of Alternatives in American Education: Summary and Policy Implications. Santa Monica, CA: Rand Corporation.

WEISBORD, M. (1978) "Input- versus output-focused organizations: notes on a contingency theory of practice," pp. 13-26 in W. W. Burke (ed.) The Cutting Edge: Current Theory and Practice in Organization Development. La Jolla, CA: University Associates.

WEISS, C. (1980) "Knowledge creep and decision accretion." Knowledge: Creation, Diffusion, Utilization 1, 3: 381-404.

——— (1979) "The many meanings of research utilization." Public Administration Review (September/October): 426-431.

——— (1977) "Research for policy's sake: the enlightenment function of social research." Policy Analysis 3: 531-545.

——— and A. BUCUVALAS (1980) "Truth tests and utility tests: decision-makers' frames of refernce for social science research." American Sociological Review 45, 2: 302-312.

WEISS, J. A. (1979) "Access to influence: some effects of policy sector on the use of social science." American Behavioral Scientist 22, 3: 437-458.

WELLISCH, W., A. MacQUEEN, R. CARRIERE, and G. DUCK (1978) "School management and organization in successful schools." Sociology of Education 51: 211-226.

WHEELER, S. (1966) "The structure of formally organized socialization settings," pp. 53-116 in O. G. Brim and S. Wheeler, Socialization After Childhood: Two Essays. New York: John Wiley.

WHYTE, W. F. (1978) "Organizational behavior research—where do we go from here?" in E. M. Eddy and W. L. Partridge (eds.) Applied Anthropology in America. New York: Columbia University Press.

WILLIAMS, W. and J. W. EVANS (1969) "The politics of evaluation: the case of Head Start." Annals of the American Academy of Political and Social Science 385: 112-132.

WILLOWER, D. J. (forthcoming) "Some issues in research on school organizations," in G. L. Immegart and W. L. Boyd (eds.) Currents in Administrative Research: Problem Finding in Education. Lexington, MA: D. C. Heath.

——— (1979) "Ideology and science in organization theory." Presented at the annual meeting of the American Educational Research Association.

——— (1971) "Social control in schools," in L. C. Deighton (ed.) Encyclopedia of Education, Volume 8. New York: Macmillan.

——— (1970) "Educational change and functional equivalents." Education and Urban Society 2 (August).

WILSON, J. Q. (1966) "Innovation in organization: notes toward a theory," in J. D. Thompson (ed.) Approaches to Organizational Design. Pittsburgh, PA: University of Pittsburgh Press.

WIRT, F. M. and M. W. KIRST (1972) The Political Web of American Schools. Boston: Little, Brown.

WISE, A. E. (1977) "The hyper-rationalization of American education." New York University Education Quarterly 8, 4: 2-6.

WOLCOTT, H. F. (1977) Teachers vs. Technocrats. Eugene: Center for Educational Policy and Management, University of Oregon.

——— (1973) The Man in the Principal's Office: An Ethnography. New York: Holt, Rinehart & Winston.

WOLF, R. L. (1973) A Case Study of Change in the Illinois Gifted Program. Urbana-Champaign: Center for Instructional Research and Curriculum Evaluation, University of Illinois.

WOODWARD, J. (1958) Management and Technology. London: Her Majesty's Stationery Office.

YIN, R. K. and M. GWALTNEY (1981) Organizations Collaborating to Improve Educational Practice. Cambridge, MA: Abt Associates.

YIN, R. K., S. K. QUICK, P. M. BATEMAN, and E. L. MARKS (1978) Changing Urban Bureaucracies: How New Practices Become Routinized. Santa Monica, CA: Rand Corporation.

YIN, R. K., K. A. HEALD, M. E. VOGEL, P. D. FLEISHAUER, and B. C. VLADECK (1976) A Review of Case Studies of Technological Innovation in State and Local Services. Santa Monica, CA: Rand Corporation.

ZALD, M. and D. JACOBS (1978) "Compliance/incentive classifications of organizations—underlying dimensions." Administration and Society 9, 4: 403-424.

ZALTMAN, G. and R. DUNCAN (1977) Strategies for Planned Change. New York: John Wiley.

——— and J. HOLBEK (1973) Innovation and Organizations. New York: John Wiley.

ZALTMAN, G., D. FLORIO, and L. SIKORSKI (1977) Dynamic Educational Change. New York: Macmillan.

ZAND, D. E. and R. E. SORENSEN (1975) "Theory of change and the effective use of management science." Administrative Science Quarterly 20, 4: 532-545.

ZIEGLER, H. (1966) The Political World of the High School Teacher. Eugene: Center for Advanced Study of Educational Administration, University of Oregon.

ZIGARMI, P. and M. GOLDSTEIN (1979) "A mapping technique for the analysis of ethnographic data." Presented at the annual meeting of the American Educational Research Association.

ABOUT THE AUTHORS

PAUL BERMAN received his Ph.D. in political science from the Massachusetts Institute of Technology and taught in this field at Yale University. He currently teaches at the Graduate School of Public Policy at the University of California, Berkeley. He has published numerous articles and reports on public policy and on education. He directed and was the principal author of the Rand Change Agent Study in Education, and is now the Senior Vice-President and chief scientist of Manifest International, Berkeley. The chapter presented in this volume is drawn from a forthcoming book, *Some Things Work Sometimes: Learning to Do Social Policy,* a project funded by NIE.

MICHAEL FULLAN is the Assistant Director of the Ontario Institute for Studies in Education, Toronto. He has published and consulted widely in Canada, the United States, and Europe on problems of implementing educational programs, evaluation, dissemination, and policy making in education. His most recent publication is *The Meaning of Change,* Teachers College Press.

ERNEST R. HOUSE is Professor of Administration, Higher, and Continuing Education in the Center for Instructional Research and Curriculum Evaluation (CIRCE) at the University of Illinois in Urbana. He received a bachelor's degree from Washington University in 1959 (graduating Phi Beta Kappa), taught high school, received a master's degree from Southern Illinois University in 1964, and a doctor's degree from the University of Illinois in 1968. His first project was a large-scale evaluation of the Illinois Gifted Program. Since that time he has been evaluating educational and other social programs. In recent years he has been evaluating evaluations. His publications include *School Evaluation: The Politics and Process* (1973), *The Politics of Educational Innovation* (1974), and *Survival in the Classroom* (with S. Lapan, 1978). He has served as consultant to many organizations in the United States and other countries. In 1976 he was chairperson of the annual meeting of the American Educational Research Association, and he is currently on the editorial board of *Educational Evaluation and Policy Analysis.*

MICHAEL KANE is an Assistant Director at the National Institute of Education, where he heads the Research and Educational Practice Unit of NIE's Dissemination and Improvement of Practice Program. He is responsible for a program of evaluation studies, exploratory research, and research syntheses designed to increase understanding of what constitutes effective dissemination and use of knowledge to improve educational practice and enhance educational equity. He holds a doctorate in educational administration and organizational analysis from Columbia University. Immediately prior to joining NIE, he spent six years at Abt Associates, Inc., where he conducted and managed educational policy research. He had previously been involved in both research and practice in schools, universities, the federal government, and private civil rights agencies.

ROLF LEHMING is a Senior Associate at the National Institute of Education, where he heads the Knowledge Use Studies Team in NIE's Research and Educational Practice Unit. The team explores how knowledge resources—new ideas, programs, practices, materials, and technologies—become incorporated into the operating routines of elementary and secondary schools, and what changes these organizations undergo in the process. He received his training as a sociologist at the University of Chicago. His professional interests include organizational change and adaptation, the development of science and its role in social and political life, and the diffusion of innovations. He had previously analyzed aspects of the research and development enterprise in education and other fields.

KAREN SEASHORE LOUIS is a Senior Analyst at Abt Associates, Inc., Cambridge, Massachusetts. She received her Ph.D. in sociology from Columbia University after completing a dissertation based on the study of one of the first educational dissemination programs to employ field agents. Her research interests focus on organizational behavior and knowledge utilization (which she has examined in both educational and medical contexts) and educational policy. Her books include *The Dispersed Organization,* with Sam D. Sieber, and *Stability and Change: Innovation in an Educational Context,* with Sheila Rosenblum. She is currently completing a study concerning the use of R&D-based materials in local schools, and is working on a book dealing with issues in integrating qualitative and quantitative methods in large-scale policy research.

MATTHEW B. MILES, Senior Research Associate at the Center for Policy Research, is a social psychologist with long-term interest in the study of planned change efforts at the small group and organizational levels. His research and writing have covered areas from group training methods to educational innovation, organization development, educational R&D systems, and knowledge dissemination and utilization. His current research focuses on methodological problems in the analysis of qualitative data using ethnographic information on the implementation of innovations in schools.

SAM D. SIEBER received his Ph.D. from Columbia University in 1963. He specialized in educational research and evaluation at the Bureau of Applied Social Research, Columbia University, for ten years, and became a free-lance research analyst and consultant in 1973. He has published articles and books on education, labor management relations, role theory, research methods, knowledge utilization, government policy formation, and law. He currently resides in the U.S. Virgin Islands.